REVIEWING THE
NUCLEAR NONPROLIFERATION TREATY

Henry Sokolski
Editor

May 2010

Published by Books Express Publishing
Books Express, 2011
ISBN 978-1-780395-18-0

Books Express publications are available from all good retail and online booksellers. For
publishing proposals and direct ordering please contact us at: info@books-express.com

CONTENTS

FOREWORD

The following volume consists of research that the Nonproliferation Policy Education Center (NPEC) previously commissioned along with previously published essays. Funding for this project came from the Carnegie Corporation of New York and the Ploughshares Foundation. The key project managers of these foundations, Stephen Del Rosso, Carl Robichaud, and Paul Carroll were generous with their time and their support. NPEC's intern, Kristen Gehringer, did much of the initial heavy lifting in preparing the book manuscript; along with NPEC's project coordinator, Tamara Mitchell, NPEC's research associate, Daniel Arnaudo; and the staff of the Strategic Studies Institute (SSI). Without their help, and that of Dr. James Pierce, the Strategic Studies Institute's Director of Publications, this book would not have been possible.

HENRY SOKOLSKI
Executive Director
The Nonproliferation
    Policy Education Center

PART I

INTRODUCTION AND OVERVIEW

CHAPTER 1

THE NUCLEAR NONPROLIFERATION TREATY'S UNTAPPED POTENTIAL TO PREVENT PROLIFERATION

Henry Sokolski

As currently interpreted, it is difficult to see why the Nuclear Nonproliferation Treaty (NPT) warrants much support as a nonproliferation convention. Most foreign ministries, including that of Iran and the United States, insist that Article IV of the NPT recognizes all states' "inalienable right" to develop "peaceful nuclear energy."[1] This includes money-losing activities, such as nuclear fuel reprocessing, which can bring countries to the very brink of acquiring nuclear weapons. If the NPT is intended to ensure that states share peaceful "benefits" of nuclear energy and prevent the spread of nuclear bomb making technologies, it is difficult to see how it can accomplish either if the interpretation above is correct.

Some argue, however, that the NPT clearly proscribes proliferation by requiring international nuclear safeguards against military diversions of fissile material. Unfortunately, these procedures, which are required of all non-nuclear weapons state members of the NPT under Article III, are rickety at best. The International Atomic Energy Agency (IAEA) nuclear inspections, which are intended to detect illicit nuclear activities and materials, certainly have a mixed record. Not only has the IAEA failed to find existing covert reactors and fuel-making plants, which are critical to bomb making, the agency still cannot assure the continuity of inspections for spent and fresh reactor fuels that could be processed into bomb usable materials at roughly two-thirds of the sites that it currently inspects. What is easily as worrisome is that even at declared nuclear fuel-making sites, the IAEA routinely loses count of many bombs' worth of production each year.

Finally, in the practical world, the NPT hardly admits of modification and is far too easy for violating states to withdraw from. Under Article X, treaty members are free to leave the NPT with no more than 3 months notice merely by filing a statement of the "extraordinary events [relating to the subject matter of the treaty] it regards as having jeopardized its supreme interests." As North Korea demonstrated with its withdrawal from the NPT, these slight requirements are all too easy to meet.

As for amending the treaty, it is nearly impossible. Not only must a majority of NPT members ratify any proposed amendments, but every member of the IAEA government board and every NPT nuclear weapons state member must ratify the proposal as well, and this is only to get amendments for consideration by those states that have not yet ratified the NPT. Ultimately, any state that chooses not to so ratify is free to ignore the amendment, and the treaty is functionally unamendable.

For all of these reasons, the NPT is not just seen as being weak against violators and difficult to improve, but it is seen effectively as a legal instrument that *enables* nations to acquire nuclear weapons technology. Former President George W. Bush highlighted this in a February 2004 nuclear nonproliferation speech in which he argued that the NPT had created a "loophole" in promoting all aspects of civilian nuclear technology including nuclear fuel making. This allowed proliferating states to "cynically manipulate" the treaty to develop and acquire nearly all the technology and materials they needed to make nuclear weapons. President Bush attempted to shore up the NPT by calling on the world's nonweapons states that have not yet developed nuclear fuel making to foreswear such activities and to allow more intrusive civilian nuclear inspections in exchange for their assured access to nuclear fuel from those states now producing enriched uranium.

Bush's appeal, however, was hardly successful: Australia, Canada, South Africa, Jordan, Iran, and Argentina, among other states, were unwilling to give up their "right" to make nuclear fuel. Then, in September 2007, Israel bombed a covert Syrian nuclear reactor that was under construction. This act of violence, which followed months of intelligence consultations with the United States, was a clear vote of no confidence in the IAEA nuclear inspections system.

Compounding these setbacks, in 2005 the U.S. Government proceeded to negotiate a civilian nuclear cooperation agreement with India — a nonweapons state under the NPT that had already violated its pledges not to misuse previous U.S. and Canadian civilian nuclear energy aid and that had tested nuclear weapons in 1974 and 1998. Implementation of this agreement prompted Pakistan, Israel, and North Korea to call for similar treatment. Finally, as early 2010, Washington and its allies had still not seriously penalized, much less reversed, the nuclear misbehavior of Iran and North Korea, two states that the IAEA found to be in clear breach of their NPT safeguards obligations.

Each of these developments has undermined the NPT's nonproliferation credibility and led to a chorus of pleas from policy analysts for members of the NPT to take any number of steps to strengthen the treaty. Some of these measures would require nonweapons states to adopt more intrusive nuclear inspection procedures. Others would increase IAEA safeguards funding and establish automatic penalties for safeguard agreement violations.

The most prominent of these proposals, however, have to do with implementation of the NPT's famous disarmament Article VI. Under this article,

> Each of the Parties to the Treaty undertakes to pursue negotiations in good faith on effective measures relating to cessation of the nuclear arms race at an early date and to nuclear disarmament, and on a treaty on general and complete disarmament under strict and effective international control.

As to what Article VI might entail, the NPT's preamble is quite explicit: the NPT member states should support a global ban on nuclear testing, cease producing nuclear weapons and their means of delivery, and pursue nuclear and general disarmament.

Nonweapons states point out that none of these objectives has yet been met. For all of the reductions that have been made in U.S., allied, and Russian nuclear weapons deployments (down from over 75,000 nuclear weapons to fewer than 10,000), both the United States and Russia, they note, still retain thousands of nuclear weapons in storage. Also, the five original NPT nuclear weapons states have yet to bring the Comprehensive Nuclear Test Ban Treaty (CTBT) into force and have yet to reach any agreement to cease nuclear weapons production.

When one digs deeper, though, this indictment of the NPT weapons states become a bit more complicated. After all, most of the declared nuclear weapons states have reduced their weapons deployments and have announced moratoriums on the further production of uranium or plutonium for weapons purposes and on the further testing of nuclear weapons. Also, the states most opposed to concluding formal international agreements on nuclear testing and production are not the NPT nuclear weapons states, but rather states outside of the NPT, such as India, North Korea, and Pakistan, or states such as Egypt, which refuses to ratify the CTBT until Israel signs the NPT and eliminates its nuclear weapons assets.

Combine these complications with the ones already reviewed and the NPT Review Conference scheduled for May 2010, which allows all NPT members to share their views on what needs fixing in the treaty's implementation, and you have the makings for everything but consensus. This is so although President Barack Obama succeeded in getting the United Nations Security Council (UNSC) to adopt an ambitious resolution last fall detailing a number of worthy NPT Review Conference goals.

How, then, will the NPT be viewed after the May conference is held? One strong possibility is that the NPT will become more and more of a diplomatic talking point—a nuclear version of the Biological Weapons Convention, a set of agreed international goals rather than an international understanding with concrete, operational consequences. What this risks is letting the NPT become a dead letter like the Kellogg-Briand Pact, which vainly tried in 1929 to ban war—i.e., a solemn, albeit ineffective legal attempt to prohibit the worst of what is certain to occur.

All of this is likely, but only so long as the NPT is viewed as it is now—as a set of nuclear bargains at war with one another. True, most nuclear nonproliferation experts insist that any reading of the treaty that might alter or curtail NPT members' nuclear rights as they are currently viewed is simply a nonstarter. Such a view, however, is unnecessarily fatalistic. In fact, the NPT is open to interpretation and has already been significantly altered as a result.

Here, the clearest demonstration is the way that the NPT's Article V promise to share the possible benefits of peaceful nuclear explosives has played itself out. When this article was first proposed in the 1960s, most nations, including the United States and Russia, believed that nuclear explosives could be employed as "ploughshares" to create canals and to complete other civil engineering tasks, including mining and excavation. To assure nonweapons states the possible benefits of such nuclear applications, the NPT allowed nuclear weapons states to share such benefits by supplying nuclear explosive services to nonweapons states on a turnkey basis.

To date, no state, though, has applied for such assistance nor has any state offered it—for two unanticipated reasons. First, the possible benefits of peaceful nuclear explosives turned out to be negative: Given the costs of cleaning up the radioactive debris that the use of peaceful nuclear explosives would produce, it became clear that it would be far cheaper to use conventional explosives for any proposed civil engineering applications. In short, it turned out that there were no benefits to share.

Second, and closely related, the few states that insisted on conducting their own "peaceful nuclear test explosions"—India and Russia—were strongly suspected of cynically using Article V as a cover for nuclear weapons testing. Certainly, the United States and most nuclear supplying states sanctioned India for its 1974 test of a "peaceful" nuclear device by depriving it of access to most controlled civilian nuclear supplies. In time, any nuclear explosion, peaceful or not, was seen as a violation of an implied norm against any form of nuclear testing.

This example of Article V's reinterpretation, although not well known or understood, speaks directly to several of the NPT's current difficulties. As already noted, the common, current view of an inalienable right to peaceful nuclear energy recognized by the NPT is that this right automatically allows states to participate in any nuclear activity, no matter how uneconomical or dangerous, so long as it has some conceivable civilian application and the materials or activities in question are occasionally inspected by IAEA inspectors or their equivalent. This is Japan's view, and that of the Netherlands, Germany, South Africa, Brazil, Iran, and also the United States.

Yet, the recasting of Article V suggests that there is another more sensible way to read Article IV. This view recognizes the explicit qualifications made in the NPT with regard to exercising the inalienable right to peaceful nuclear energy. This right, the NPT notes in Article IV, must be implemented "in conformity" with the treaty's clear strictures in Articles I and II. These two articles, in turn, deny nuclear weapons states the right "in any way to assist, encourage, or induce any non-nuclear-weapon State to manufacture or otherwise acquire nuclear weapons or other nuclear explosive devices," and the articles ban nonweapons states from seeking or receiving "any assistance in the manufacture of nuclear weapons."

Properly understood, being in conformity with Articles I and II implies also being in conformity with Article III, setting forth the NPT requirement that all nonweapons states accept the imposition of international nuclear safeguards on all of their civilian nuclear activities and materials to prevent their military diversion to making bombs. Certainly, a nonweapons state refusing such safeguards would be in implicit violation of Article II. Thus, the final statement of the 2000 NPT Review Conference refers to the need for nonweapons state members to exercise their Article IV activities in conformity with Articles I, II *and* III.

Technically, this safeguard condition is not easily met. Not all nuclear activities and materials can in fact be safeguarded to prevent their diversion to make bombs. Some activities, e.g., nuclear fuel making and operating large nuclear programs in hostile, noncooperative states (e.g., North Korea or Iran), cannot be inspected in a fashion that can reliably assure detection of a possible military diversion early enough to provide sufficient time to intervene to prevent the production of a bomb. Similarly, some nuclear materials are so weapons adaptable (e.g., highly enriched uranium, separated plutonium, or plutonium based fuels) that reliable and timely detection of their diversion to make bombs is simply not possible.

This, then, raises a question: If a nuclear activity or material is so close to bomb making that it cannot be safeguarded against military diversion, is it protected as being "peaceful" under the NPT? In the 1970s, it was hoped that nuclear fuel making in Japan, Brazil, South Africa, the Netherlands, and Germany could be safeguarded. Yet, recent discoveries of nuclear weapons usable materials unaccounted for (MUF) in Japan and the United Kingdom (UK) raise serious questions as to whether or not these assumptions were ever sound. We also know from experience in Iraq, Libya, Iran, Syria, and North Korea that the IAEA inspections system cannot be relied upon to find covert nuclear weapon-related activities in states that refuse to cooperate fully with IAEA inspectors.

How, then, should one proceed? Should we continue to allow new states to make nuclear fuel even though we now know that these activities cannot be effectively safeguarded against military diversion? What of states that we have reason to believe may cheat, e.g., Egypt, Algeria, Syria, or Saudi Arabia — states that have all hidden their acquisition of nuclear technologies or nuclear capable delivery systems? Should we nonetheless allow them to develop large nuclear energy programs in the vain hope that IAEA safeguards somehow will work?

Many less developed states would answer that the NPT's preamble explicitly stipulates that all of peaceful nuclear energy's benefits, including "any technological by products which may be derived from the development of nuclear explosives," should be available for civilian purposes to all states. This would suggest that the NPT recognizes and protects an intrinsic right of all states to get to the very brink of making bombs.

Yet, if the NPT is dedicated to sharing the benefits of peaceful nuclear energy, these benefits presumably must be measurably beneficial *and* be distant enough from bomb making or the risk of being easily diverted to that purpose such that inspections could reliably detect their military conversion in a timely fashion (i.e., well before any bombs might be made). At the very least, what is protected ought not to be dangerous and clearly unprofitable. That, after all, is why the NPT bans the transfer of civilian nuclear explosives, why it allowed the sharing of civilian nuclear explosive services only on a turnkey basis, and why ultimately this offer was never acted upon.

By this set of standards, what currently is defended as being "peaceful nuclear energy" and protected by the NPT, ought to be questioned. Are nuclear fuel making and large nuclear programs economically competitive, i.e., "beneficial" in places like the Middle East when compared to making power with readily available natural gas or buying nuclear fuel from other producers? How economically competitive are such programs against safer alternatives in any region? Can nuclear fuel making be surveilled anywhere with rigor sufficient to reliably detect military diversions in a timely fashion? Are not such activities a threat in any nonweapons state? Should these activities be allowed to be expanded in nonweapons states and to new locales?

This set of questions, then, brings us back to the current prevailing reinterpretation of Article V. If the benefits of a nuclear activity are negative as compared to nonnuclear alternatives, and if the nuclear activity or material is dangerously close to producing a nuclear weapon, is there any reason to believe that it is a peaceful benefit protected by the NPT? These questions deserve answers. More important, the answers must be allowed to affect how the NPT is read and what states view as NPT protected activities.

The same is true regarding the NPT's withdrawal clause under Article X. The problem with Article X is that it has been read to give states like North Korea the freedom to violate the treaty and then withdraw with little or no adverse consequence. Yet, the Vienna Convention on Treaties points out that states that violate an agreement should and can be held accountable for their transgressions whether they choose to withdraw from the agreement or not. France and the United States now insist that this is the appropriate way to read the NPT.

Reading Article X this way would mean that violating states inclined to leave the NPT, such as North Korea and Iran, would have far greater difficulty doing so with impunity. It is unclear whether this view, which the UNSC supported last September with the adoption of UNSC Resolution 1887, will prevail. Yet, creating as many useful interpretative challenges of this sort as possible will be critical if the NPT is to remain effective against further proliferation.

Certainly, such a goal informs the present volume's design. Each chapter, dedicated to clarifying the NPT's key ambiguities, is roughly structured to trace the NPT's text article by article. The analysis set forth here was mostly written or commissioned by the Nonproliferation Policy Education Center.

Much more, of course, could have been included in this book. But rather than seeking to be comprehensive, the aim throughout is to provide a guide for both policymakers and security analysts. This guide should assist in navigating the most important debates over how best to read and implement the NPT and, in the process, spotlighting alternative views of the NPT that are sound and supportable.

ENDNOTES - CHAPTER 1

1. NPT, Chapter 2 of this volume, p. 21.

PART II

THE NUCLEAR NONPROLIFERATION TREATY
AND ITS HISTORY

CHAPTER 2

THE TREATY ON THE NONPROLIFERATION
OF NUCLEAR WEAPONS

The States concluding this Treaty, hereinafter referred to as the Parties to the Treaty,

Considering the devastation that would be visited upon all mankind by a nuclear war and the consequent need to make every effort to avert the danger of such a war and to take measures to safeguard the security of peoples,

Believing that the proliferation of nuclear weapons would seriously enhance the danger of nuclear war,

In conformity with resolutions of the United Nations General Assembly calling for the conclusion of an agreement on the prevention of wider dissemination of nuclear weapons,

Undertaking to co-operate in facilitating the application of International Atomic Energy Agency safeguards on peaceful nuclear activities,

Expressing their support for research, development and other efforts to further the application, within the framework of the International Atomic Energy Agency safeguards system, of the principle of safeguarding effectively the flow of source and special fissionable materials by use of instruments and other techniques at certain strategic points,

Affirming the principle that the benefits of peaceful applications of nuclear technology, including any technological by-products which may be derived by nuclear-weapon States from the development of nuclear explosive devices, should be available for peaceful purposes to all Parties to the Treaty, whether nuclear-weapon or non-nuclear-weapon States,

Convinced that, in furtherance of this principle, all Parties to the Treaty are entitled to participate in the fullest possible exchange of scientific information for, and to contribute alone or in co-operation with other States to, the further development of the applications of atomic energy for peaceful purposes,

Declaring their intention to achieve at the earliest possible date the cessation of the nuclear arms race and to undertake effective measures in the direction of nuclear disarmament,

Urging the co-operation of all States in the attainment of this objective,

Recalling the determination expressed by the Parties to the 1963 Treaty banning nuclear weapons tests in the atmosphere, in outer space and under water in its Preamble to seek to achieve the discontinuance of all test explosions of nuclear weapons for all time and to continue negotiations to this end,

Desiring to further the easing of international tension and the strengthening of trust between States in order to facilitate the cessation of the manufacture of nuclear weapons, the liquidation of all their existing stockpiles, and the elimination from national arsenals of nuclear weapons and the means of their delivery pursuant to a Treaty on general and complete disarmament under strict and effective international control,

Recalling that, in accordance with the Charter of the United Nations, States must refrain in their international relations from the threat or use of force against the territorial integrity or political independence of any State, or in any other manner inconsistent with the Purposes of the United Nations, and that the establishment and maintenance of international peace and security are to be promoted with the least diversion for armaments of the world's human and economic resources,

Have agreed as follows:

ARTICLE I

Each nuclear-weapon State Party to the Treaty undertakes not to transfer to any recipient whatsoever nuclear weapons or other nuclear explosive devices or control over such weapons or explosive devices directly, or indirectly; and not in any way to assist, encourage, or induce any non-nuclear-weapon State to manufacture or otherwise acquire nuclear weapons or other nuclear explosive devices, or control over such weapons or explosive devices.

ARTICLE II

Each non-nuclear-weapon State Party to the Treaty undertakes not to receive the transfer from any transferor whatsoever of nuclear weapons or other nuclear explosive devices or of control over such weapons or explosive devices directly, or indirectly; not to manufacture or otherwise acquire nuclear weapons or other nuclear explosive devices; and not to seek or receive any assistance in the manufacture of nuclear weapons or other nuclear explosive devices.

ARTICLE III

1. Each non-nuclear-weapon State Party to the Treaty undertakes to accept safeguards, as set forth in an agreement to be negotiated and concluded with the International Atomic Energy Agency in accordance with the Statute of the International Atomic Energy Agency and the Agency's safeguards system, for the exclusive purpose of verification of the fulfilment of its obligations assumed under this Treaty with a view to preventing diversion of nuclear energy from peaceful uses to nuclear weapons or other nuclear explosive devices. Procedures for the safeguards required by this Article shall be followed with respect to source or special fissionable material whether it is being produced, processed or used in any principal nuclear facility or is outside any such facility. The safeguards required by this Article shall be applied on all source or special fissionable material in all peaceful nuclear activities within the territory of such State, under its jurisdiction, or carried out under its control anywhere.

2. Each State Party to the Treaty undertakes not to provide: (a) source or special fissionable material, or (b) equipment or material especially designed or prepared for the processing, use or production of special fissionable material, to any non-nuclear-weapon State for peaceful purposes, unless the source or special fissionable material shall be subject to the safeguards required by this Article.

3. The safeguards required by this Article shall be implemented in a manner designed to comply

with Article IV of this Treaty, and to avoid hampering the economic or technological development of the Parties or international co-operation in the field of peaceful nuclear activities, including the international exchange of nuclear material and equipment for the processing, use or production of nuclear material for peaceful purposes in accordance with the provisions of this Article and the principle of safeguarding set forth in the Preamble of the Treaty.

4. Non-nuclear-weapon States Party to the Treaty shall conclude agreements with the International Atomic Energy Agency to meet the requirements of this Article either individually or together with other States in accordance with the Statute of the International Atomic Energy Agency. Negotiation of such agreements shall commence within 180 days from the original entry into force of this Treaty. For States depositing their instruments of ratification or accession after the 180-day period, negotiation of such agreements shall commence not later than the date of such deposit. Such agreements shall enter into force not later than eighteen months after the date of initiation of negotiations.

ARTICLE IV

1. Nothing in this Treaty shall be interpreted as affecting the inalienable right of all the Parties to the Treaty to develop research, production and use of nuclear energy for peaceful purposes without discrimination and in conformity with Articles I and II of this Treaty.

2. All the Parties to the Treaty undertake to facilitate, and have the right to participate in, the fullest possible exchange of equipment, materials and sci-

entific and technological information for the peaceful uses of nuclear energy. Parties to the Treaty in a position to do so shall also co-operate in contributing alone or together with other States or international organizations to the further development of the applications of nuclear energy for peaceful purposes, especially in the territories of non-nuclear-weapon States Party to the Treaty, with due consideration for the needs of the developing areas of the world.

ARTICLE V

Each Party to the Treaty undertakes to take appropriate measures to ensure that, in accordance with this Treaty, under appropriate international observation and through appropriate international procedures, potential benefits from any peaceful applications of nuclear explosions will be made available to non-nuclear-weapon States Party to the Treaty on a non-discriminatory basis and that the charge to such Parties for the explosive devices used will be as low as possible and exclude any charge for research and development. Non-nuclear-weapon States Party to the Treaty shall be able to obtain such benefits, pursuant to a special international agreement or agreements, through an appropriate international body with adequate representation of non-nuclear-weapon States. Negotiations on this subject shall commence as soon as possible after the Treaty enters into force. Non-nuclear-weapon States Party to the Treaty so desiring may also obtain such benefits pursuant to bilateral agreements.

ARTICLE VI

Each of the Parties to the Treaty undertakes to pursue negotiations in good faith on effective measures relating to cessation of the nuclear arms race at an early date and to nuclear disarmament, and on a treaty on general and complete disarmament under strict and effective international control.

ARTICLE VII

Nothing in this Treaty affects the right of any group of States to conclude regional treaties in order to assure the total absence of nuclear weapons in their respective territories.

ARTICLE VIII

1. Any Party to the Treaty may propose amendments to this Treaty. The text of any proposed amendment shall be submitted to the Depositary Governments which shall circulate it to all Parties to the Treaty. Thereupon, if requested to do so by one-third or more of the Parties to the Treaty, the Depositary Governments shall convene a conference, to which they shall invite all the Parties to the Treaty, to consider such an amendment.
2. Any amendment to this Treaty must be approved by a majority of the votes of all the Parties to the Treaty, including the votes of all nuclear-weapon States Party to the Treaty and all other Parties which, on the date the amendment is circulated, are members of the Board of Governors of the International Atomic Energy Agency. The amendment shall enter into force for each Party that deposits its instrument

of ratification of the amendment upon the deposit of such instruments of ratification by a majority of all the Parties, including the instruments of ratification of all nuclear-weapon States Party to the Treaty and all other Parties which, on the date the amendment is circulated, are members of the Board of Governors of the International Atomic Energy Agency. Thereafter, it shall enter into force for any other Party upon the deposit of its instrument of ratification of the amendment.

3. Five years after the entry into force of this Treaty, a conference of Parties to the Treaty shall be held in Geneva, Switzerland, in order to review the operation of this Treaty with a view to assuring that the purposes of the Preamble and the provisions of the Treaty are being realised. At intervals of five years thereafter, a majority of the Parties to the Treaty may obtain, by submitting a proposal to this effect to the Depositary Governments, the convening of further conferences with the same objective of reviewing the operation of the Treaty.

ARTICLE IX

1. This Treaty shall be open to all States for signature. Any State which does not sign the Treaty before its entry into force in accordance with paragraph 3 of this Article may accede to it at any time.

2. This Treaty shall be subject to ratification by signatory States. Instruments of ratification and instruments of accession shall be deposited with the Governments of the United Kingdom of Great Britain and Northern Ireland, the Union of Soviet Socialist Republics and the United States of America, which are hereby designated the Depositary Governments.

3. This Treaty shall enter into force after its ratification by the States, the Governments of which are designated Depositaries of the Treaty, and forty other States signatory to this Treaty and the deposit of their instruments of ratification. For the purposes of this Treaty, a nuclear-weapon State is one which has manufactured and exploded a nuclear weapon or other nuclear explosive device prior to 1 January 1967.

4. For States whose instruments of ratification or accession are deposited subsequent to the entry into force of this Treaty, it shall enter into force on the date of the deposit of their instruments of ratification or accession.

5. The Depositary Governments shall promptly inform all signatory and acceding States of the date of each signature, the date of deposit of each instrument of ratification or of accession, the date of the entry into force of this Treaty, and the date of receipt of any requests for convening a conference or other notices.

6. This Treaty shall be registered by the Depositary Governments pursuant to Article 102 of the Charter of the United Nations.

ARTICLE X

1. Each Party shall in exercising its national sovereignty have the right to withdraw from the Treaty if it decides that extraordinary events, related to the subject matter of this Treaty, have jeopardized the supreme interests of its country. It shall give notice of such withdrawal to all other Parties to the Treaty and to the United Nations Security Council three months in advance. Such notice shall include a statement of the extraordinary events it regards as having jeopardized its supreme interests.

2. Twenty-five years after the entry into force of the Treaty, a conference shall be convened to decide whether the Treaty shall continue in force indefinitely, or shall be extended for an additional fixed period or periods. This decision shall be taken by a majority of the Parties to the Treaty.

ARTICLE XI

This Treaty, the English, Russian, French, Spanish and Chinese texts of which are equally authentic, shall be deposited in the archives of the Depositary Governments. Duly certified copies of this Treaty shall be transmitted by the Depositary Governments to the Governments of the signatory and acceding States.

IN WITNESS WHEREOF the undersigned, duly authorized, have signed this Treaty.

DONE in triplicate, at the cities of London, Moscow and Washington, the first day of July, one thousand nine hundred and sixty-eight.

Entered into force March 5, 1970

In accordance with Article X, paragraph 2, the Review and Extension Conference of the Parties to the Treaty on the Non-Proliferation of Nuclear Weapons decided that the Treaty should continue in force indefinitely on May 11, 1995.

CHAPTER 3
WHAT DOES THE HISTORY
OF THE NUCLEAR NONPROLIFERATION
TREATY TELL US ABOUT ITS FUTURE?[1]

Henry Sokolski

When experts discuss the prospects of the Nuclear Non-proliferation Treaty (NPT), they naturally focus on impending events. Will nonaligned nations tie their continued adherence to reaching a comprehensive test ban? Will North Korea, Algeria, Iraq, and Iran live up to their NPT obligations? Will NPT's inspectorate, the International Atomic Energy Agency (IAEA), strengthen its inspection procedures?

The answers to these questions—like the future itself, however—are necessarily speculative. In contrast, the NPT's history is known. More importantly, it is arguably the most relevant factor in gauging the treaty's chances for future success. To understand the NPT's past, after all, is not only to understand what the treaty's original intentions were but to consider how practical and relevant these aims are today and how viable they are likely to be.

In general, of course, we already know what the NPT is supposed to do: limit the spread of nuclear weapons. What we are less clear on, however, is exactly how the NPT is supposed to achieve this end. Was the goal of curbing the transfer of nuclear weapons technology to be subordinated to the NPT's stated aim of ending the arms race between Washington and Moscow? Did smaller nations, in fact, have a right—as the NPT's Article 10 suggests—to withdraw from the treaty if, in their estimation, neither Washington nor Moscow had taken effective measures to end the nuclear arms race or if a neighboring adversary acquired nuclear weapons of its own? Did the NPT, in fact, reflect the view that nuclear proliferation was less of an evil than either of these two outcomes?

And what of nuclear safeguards? Were nuclear activities and materials that were quite close to bomb making or nuclear weapons themselves to be allowed if they were claimed to be for peaceful purposes and were acquired or transferred under international inspections? Did the drafters of the NPT's provisions for safeguards consciously limit the intrusiveness of inspections in order to protect any and all transfers of civilian nuclear energy?

Certainly, if the answer to these historical questions is yes, the NPT's future as an effective nonproliferation agreement would be in doubt. At a minimum, it would suggest that the prospects for strengthening the International Atomic Energy Agency (IAEA) and NPT and for getting near-nuclear or undeclared-nuclear nations to join were distant.

The NPT's history, though, is not that clear. It is true that the NPT's framers finally opposed intrusive IAEA inspections, encouraged the sharing of peaceful nuclear energy, described the greatest proliferation threat as being the superpowers' continued buildup of nuclear arms, and even claimed that nations had the right to acquire nuclear weapons under extraordinary events. Yet, each of these propositions was debated and arguably balanced by the NPT's first two articles prohibiting the transfer or acquisition of nuclear weapons "directly or indirectly." These articles, first suggested by the Irish in 1958 as an intermediate step toward superpower nuclear arms control, presumed that the further spread of nuclear weapons threatened accidental and catalytic nuclear war and instability, both for states with and those without nuclear weapons.

These "Irish" articles are important, then, if only because they seem at odds with the NPT's other provisions. These include language – backed by a substantial negotiating record – that provides for NPT members' rights under Articles 3, 4, and 10 to (1) withdraw from the treaty (and, thus, legally acquire nuclear weapons), (2) engage in the "fullest possible exchange" of nuclear technology, and (3) keep nuclear inspections under the NPT from "hampering [NPT members'] economic or technological development."

Critics of the NPT argue that Articles 1 and 2 should rule over the interpretation and implementation of the rest of the treaty.[2] However, this is neither the way the NPT is popularly understood nor the way most of the NPT's framers saw the treaty when they finalized it in 1968. Then, as now, the predominant nuclear threat in the eyes of the treaty's supporters was not accidental or catalytic war, but the possibility that nuclear competition between major nations might get out of hand, start a war, or – short of this – encourage nonweapons states to go nuclear. As the NPT's framers saw it, the best way to prevent this would be to agree to total nuclear disarmament, while mutual nuclear deterrence at very low levels of nuclear armament among nations would be second best. Indeed, smaller nations might prefer to acquire their own nuclear forces rather than allow an ever-escalating and threatening nuclear arms race between the major nuclear states go unchallenged or have to depend on unreliable superpower guarantees of nuclear security.

From this perspective, asking states without nuclear weapons to forgo acquiring them is asking them to forgo exercising a right that could be in their national security interest. As such, forswearing nuclear weapons required a quid pro quo — i.e., a requirement for the superpowers to take effective measures to end the nuclear arms race and facilitate the fullest possible transfer of civilian nuclear technology (which the nuclear powers gained by developing weapons) from the nuclear haves to the nuclear have-nots.

Such deal making, however, is unnecessary if one focuses on the security concerns highlighted in the Irish's original United Nations (UN) resolution of 1958. Curbing the threat of accidental and catalytic nuclear war would be a good that states with and without nuclear weapons would benefit from — a good of such high value that subordinating all other aspects of the NPT to achieve it would be worthwhile.

This, then, is the challenge facing today's supporters of the NPT. They must recognize that there are two different ways to interpret the treaty: through the lens of the Irish resolutions (i.e., Articles 1, 2, and — arguably — 3) or through the subsequent articles. For the policymaker, making this choice is critical to determining just how viable the NPT is likely to be and what, if anything, remains to be done.

To choose wisely requires an understanding of what sort of proliferation threat the NPT was originally intended to address; how and why this original concern was largely displaced by the new concerns noted above; how much of a tension between these views remained at the time of the NPT's signing in 1968; and which of these views makes more sense today. In short, we must go back to NPT's origins.

1958-65: THE IRISH RESOLUTION AND PREVENTING CATALYTIC NUCLEAR WAR AND THE FURTHER SPREAD OF NUCLEAR WEAPONS

Although the proliferation of nuclear weapons is now synonymous with the spread of know-how, nuclear materials, and specialized equipment to rogue states such as Iran, this was not the central worry animating those who first suggested the need for an international nonproliferation agreement in the late 1950s. Instead, their concern was the actual and proposed American transfers of nuclear weapons to Germany and the North Atlantic Treaty Organization (NATO).

Starting with the Eisenhower administration in 1953, the United States began to deploy nuclear artillery in Europe for use by NATO forces under a dual key control arrangement. The United States had custody of the nuclear-artillery warheads, while U.S. and NATO armies had nuclear-capable artillery tubes integrated into their ground forces. If an occasion arose when the U.S. President deemed use of the nuclear artillery necessary, he could order the release of the nuclear warheads to the NATO commander, and the commander of the NATO ally would give authority to release use of the nuclear-capable artillery tubes. Following this model, the United States was able to deploy nuclear weapons not only to NATO ground forces, but to U.S. and Allied air forces in Europe without losing control of the weapons themselves.

Unfortunately, Warsaw Pact members and the world's neutral powers believed that U.S. authority over these weapons was less than complete. In 1956-57, the Soviet Union was so concerned about the U.S. stationing of nuclear weapons in Germany that it proposed a ban on the employment of nuclear weapons of

31

any sort in Central Europe.[3] The United States, meanwhile, submitted a draft disarmament plan before the UN Disarmament Commission in which transfer of control of U.S. nuclear weapons to NATO allies was permitted if their use was necessary to fend off an armed attack.[4]

In 1958 concern with controls over such nuclear transfers was heightened further when the U.S. Congress passed an amendment to the U.S. Atomic Energy Act that permitted the transfer of weapons materials, design information, and parts to nations that had "made substantial progress in the development of nuclear weapons."[5] Also, with the continued transfer of nuclear weapons to NATO, U.S. control arrangements became less rigid: one congressional investigation discovered German aircraft that were fueled, ready to take off at a moment's notice, and loaded with U.S. nuclear weapons.[6]

This trend toward laxer U.S. restraints on authority for the transfer of nuclear weapons came at the same time as progress toward disarmament negotiations in the UN had reached an impasse. The United States and the Soviet Union had agreed to a voluntary moratorium on nuclear testing in the fall of 1958, but the United States and its allies tied their continued adherence to this test ban to progress toward disarmament and a general easing of tensions. Last, but hardly least, the United States had threatened or considered using nuclear weapons on at least six separate occasions since Eisenhower had assumed the presidency in 1953.[7]

Against this backdrop, the Irish offered their draft resolution concerning the "Further Dissemination of Nuclear Weapons" before the First Committee of the General Assembly of the UN on October 17, 1958. This resolution was quite modest, merely addressing the possibility that "an increase in the number of states possessing nuclear weapons may occur, aggravating international tensions" and making disarmament "more difficult." It went on to recommend that the General Assembly establish an ad hoc committee to study the dangers inherent in the further dissemination of nuclear weapons.[8]

The Irish offered to amend the resolution so as to urge parties to the UN's disarmament talks not to furnish nuclear weapons to any other nation while the negotiations were under way and to encourage other states to refrain from trying to manufacture nuclear weapons, but Western support for the amendment was thin. On October 31, 1958, the Irish withdrew the resolution when it became clear that no NATO nation was yet ready to endorse the initiative.[9]

The Irish, however, pursued the idea. The following year, their foreign minister resubmitted yet another version of the resolution to the General Assembly and made it clear that the proposal was a minimal proposition which all parties ought to accept. It was "hardly realistic," he argued, to expect any "early agreement on the abolition of nuclear weapons." But "what we can do," he argued, "is to reduce the risks which the spread of these weapons involves for this generation, and not to hand on to our children a problem even more difficult to solve than that with which we are now confronted." Indeed, the Irish foreign minister argued that "if no such agreement is made, they [the nuclear powers] may well be forced by mutual fear and the pressure of their allies, to distribute these weapons, and so increase geometrically the danger of nuclear war."[10]

Why was such nuclear proliferation so dangerous

and likely? First, without an international nonproliferation agreement, "a sort of atomic *sauve-qui-peut*" — every man for himself — was likely in which states, "de-
spairing of safety through collective action," would
seek safety for themselves by getting nuclear weapons
of their own.[11] This trend was likely to get worse, the
Irish argued, since there was "no conceivable addition" to the list of countries possessing nuclear weapons which would not cause a change in the pattern
of regional and world politics. Such a change could
be "great enough to destroy the balance of destructive
weapons . . . which has given the world the uneasy
peace of the last few years."[12] As the Irish foreign minister later explained,

> the sudden appearance of nuclear weapons and their
> almost instantaneous long-range delivery systems in a
> previous nonnuclear state may be tantamount, in the
> circumstances of the world today, to be pushing a gun
> through a neighbor's window. . . . It may even be re-
> garded as an act of war by neighboring countries who
> have not the second strike nuclear capacity possessed
> by great nuclear powers [who] may be able to elimi-
> nate the threat by taking limited measures.[13]

The second reason that nuclear proliferation posed
a great danger was that nations without nuclear weapons would try to acquire them from their nuclear-
armed allies, who, out of a misguided sense of political convenience, were likely to be cooperative. All this
would do, however, was give these smaller nations
"the power to start a nuclear war, or to engage in nuclear blackmail — conceivably against a former ally."
In short, without an international agreement against
further transfers of nuclear weapons, accidental and
catalytic wars would become more likely, and nations
would drift into "a nightmare region in which man's

powers of destruction are constantly increasing and his control over these powers is constantly diminishing."[14]

The third and final reason was that nuclear weapons technology itself was becoming more available. As the Irish foreign minister explained, weapons-usable plutonium was a direct by-product of nuclear electrical-power reactors, and these generators were being built in states without nuclear weapons. It would become increasingly difficult, he believed, for the governments of these countries to "resist domestic pressure to take the further step of producing nuclear weapons [on the] grounds of economy and security, if not for considerations of prestige."[15]

These considerations were all factored into the original bargain inherent in the Irish resolution: The states with nuclear weapons would forgo relinquishing control of their weapons to their allies, and states without nuclear weapons would refrain from manufacturing or acquiring them and accept inspection of their reactors and territories to ensure that they were living up to their undertakings. This was the full extent of the bargain. All states — with or without nuclear weapons — would be better off because the possibility of accidental or catalytic war would be reduced. Beyond this, nonweapons states would be spared the expense of having to develop strategic weapons, and the weapons states would have less reason to advance the qualitative development of their own strategic systems.

The Irish insisted on no direct linkage with progress on capping or reversing the arms rivalry between Moscow and Washington. Nor was there any notion that the nuclear nations should offer peaceful nuclear technology to the nonweapons states to get them to open their territories to inspection. In fact, as the

35

Irish foreign minister later made clear, nonweapons nations ought to welcome having their nuclear facilities inspected or, at least, not object since they might later serve as arms control test beds. Nor, he argued, should the inequity of nonweapons states opening their nuclear facilities to inspections (from which nuclear states would be exempt) be seen as involving any loss of prestige. After all, several nonweapons states had already endorsed the idea of regional disarmament and European nuclear-weapons-free zones that required asymmetrical inspections. Nonproliferation inspections were only an extension of the same idea.[16]

The United States and other states with nuclear weapons, however, initially had misgivings about the Irish resolutions. As has already been noted, most NATO nations abstained when the Irish resolution was first put to a vote in 1958. In 1959, though, the Soviet Union also opposed the resolution, complaining that it was too permissive: it would allow the United States to transfer nuclear weapons to European soil so long as the United States retained control of the weapons. Meanwhile, France abstained, arguing that the transfer of fissionable materials and nuclear weapons was difficult to control, and that the real problem was ending manufacture of these items. At the time, France was itself getting ready to test its first nuclear weapon and was assisting the Israelis in their nuclear weapons efforts.[17]

As for the United States, it supported the 1959 Irish resolution after abstaining in 1958, arguing that it permitted serious study of critical issues. Yet, when the resolution was modified in 1960 to call upon the weapons states to declare at once their intention to "refrain from relinquishing control of such weapons to any nation not possessing them and from transmit-

ting to it the information necessary for their manufacture," the United States again objected.[18] Although the
Soviets decided to reverse themselves and support the
draft, the United States at the time was pushing the
idea of giving NATO nuclear armed submarines for a
multilateral force (MLF). Mindful of that idea, the U.S.
representative to the UN complained that the Irish
resolution failed to recognize the critical responsibility of the nations with nuclear weapons. The U.S. representative went on to ask how the Irish could expect
other nations to forgo nuclear weapons if the weapons
states refused to end their own nuclear buildup. Besides, he argued, a commitment of indefinite duration
of the sort the resolution called for was unverifiable.[19]

The United States objected again in 1961 when the
Swedes resubmitted a similar resolution recommending that an inquiry be made into the conditions under which countries not possessing nuclear weapons
might be willing to enter into specific undertakings
to refrain from manufacturing or otherwise acquiring
such weapons and to refuse to receive, in the future,
nuclear weapons on their territories on behalf of any
other country.[20]

The resolution's new language worried the United
States. The resolution was no longer focused on re-
straining weapons nations from relinquishing control
of nuclear weapons but on getting nonweapons nations to refuse receiving nuclear weapons on their territories. In short, it appealed to all of NATO to stop
hosting U.S. nuclear weapons. This point was hardly
lost on the Soviets, who immediately incorporated
the Swedish language (i.e., "refrain from transferring
control [and] refuse to admit the nuclear weapons of
any other states into their territories") into their own
draft treaty for general and complete disarmament in

1962.[21]

The United States objected to the Swedish resolution, complaining that it effectively called "into question the right of free nations to join together in collective self-defense, including the right of self-defense with nuclear weapons if need be."[22] Yet, the U.S. representative was equally insistent that the United States supported the goal of nonproliferation. His proof was that the U.S. draft program for general and complete disarmament—like the Irish resolution—required states with nuclear weapons to "refrain from relinquishing control" of nuclear weapons to nonweapons states.[23]

1965–68: BARGAINING TO KEEP STATES FROM EXERCISING THEIR RIGHT TO ACQUIRE NUCLEAR WEAPONS

For the next 4 years, the United States continued to insist that it was interested in promoting nuclear nonproliferation.[24] However, it opposed a variety of nonproliferation resolutions backed by the Soviets, Swedes, and others, which, if accepted, would have jeopardized existing nuclear-sharing arrangements with NATO or the possibility of creating a multilateral nuclear force for a "United States of Europe." Ultimately, the United States focused on reaching an international nuclear nonproliferation agreement only when it became clear that Germany and other NATO nations were not keen on reaching an MLF agreement. With the MLF disposed of and the Soviets willing to accept language that would allow the United States to deploy nuclear weapons in NATO—assuming they were kept under U.S. control—the United States was ready to negotiate a nonproliferation agreement.[25]

By early 1966, however, the terms of UN debate over proliferation had changed. Whereas in 1958, nonproliferation was seen as a good in itself — equally beneficial to states with and without weapons — by the early 1960s, smaller nations perceived nuclear nonproliferation as a potential obstacle to assuring their national security, while the United States and Soviet Union continued to refine and expand their own nuclear arsenals.

Another key difference in the debate was how nations viewed superpower nuclear deterrence. In 1959 the Irish downplayed the threat presented by nuclear superpower rivalry: "That situation, fraught with danger as it is, is nonetheless one with which we have managed to live for a number of years. Techniques have been evolved to deal with it." The key concern was not with this set of dangers but with those "likely to flow with the wider dissemination of nuclear weapons."[26]

By the mid-1960s, however, faith in the stability of the superpower nuclear balance and concerns about the threat of accidental and catalytic war had begun to wane. In their place, worries about the superpower arms races and the threat of the superpowers' nuclear imperialism over nonnuclear nations gained traction. As India's UN representative explained in 1966,

> [the] dangers of dissemination and independent manufacture [of nuclear weapons] pale into the background when one views the calamitous dangers of the arms race which is developing today as a result of the proliferation of nuclear weapons by the nuclear weapon powers themselves, large and small. For many years now, the super powers have possessed an over-kill or multiple-destruction capacity and even their second-strike capabilities are sufficient to destroy the entire world. They have hundreds of missiles of varying ranges which are capable of devastating the

surface of the earth. They are continuing to test underground, miniaturizing warheads, improving pen-
etration capabilities and sophisticating their weapons
and missiles. The other nuclear weapons powers are
also following the same menacing path, conducting
atmospheric weapons tests, proceeding from manned-
bomber delivery systems to missile systems and
submarines. Only 4 days ago, the People's Republic
of China conducted yet another weapons test, firing
an intermediate-range guided missile with a nuclear
warhead. When we talk of the dangers of the arms
race, therefore, we face the dangers of the most titanic
proportions. It is here that the proliferation of nuclear
weapons has its most catastrophic consequences.[27]

Egypt's representative to the UN disarmament talks
made the same point somewhat differently:

The nonnuclear countries will in law renounce their
right to nuclear weapons, but nuclear stockpiles and
the threat of a nuclear confrontation will in fact continue to exist indefinitely. . . . This de facto situation
could always constitute an incitement to manufacture
or acquire nuclear weapons. To diminish this risk still
further it will be necessary, pending the complete
elimination by radical measures of nuclear stockpiles
and the nuclear threat, to include in the treaty a formal
and definite indication of what the nuclear Powers
propose to do with the existing nuclear armament.[28]

Why did this shift occur? First, nonnuclear nations
who were eager for a nonproliferation treaty in the
very early 1960s but frustrated by the impasse created
by the Soviet Union, the United States, and NATO nations over the issue decided to work without the superpowers' cooperation. As has already been noted,
in 1961 the Swedes submitted a resolution before the
UN General Assembly calling for an inquiry as to the
conditions under which nonweapons states might be

willing to refrain from acquiring nuclear weapons. The idea here was to force the nuclear states' hand by demonstrating the popularity of nuclear nonproliferation and threatening to promote it without the superpowers. However, the very premise of the inquiry — that nonweapons nations would naturally acquire nuclear weapons unless certain conditions were met — was at odds with the idea that nonproliferation was equally a security imperative for both weapons and nonweapons states.

Second, beginning in the late 1950s, an intellectual shift occurred in the way nuclear arms and deterrence were viewed. During this period, a new nuclear theory — finite deterrence — emerged. According to this view, smaller nations could keep larger nuclear powers from threatening them militarily by acquiring a small number of nuclear weapons of their own. With their limited nuclear arsenal, the smaller nations might not be able to prevail in war against a larger power but could effectively "tear an arm off" by targeting the larger nation's key cities, and thus deter such nations from ever attacking.[29] Closely related to this point was a critique of the superpowers' constant quantitative and qualitative improvement of their strategic forces. This buildup was considered unnecessary and provocative because a nation needed only a small nuclear arsenal to threaten to knock out an opponent's major cities.[30]

In 1962, this view was reflected in replies to the UN secretary-general's inquiry about the conditions under which nonweapons states "might be willing to enter into specific undertakings to refrain" from acquiring weapons.[31] Sixty-two nations replied, most of them wanting specific neighbors or all the states within their region to foreswear acquiring nuclear weapons as a condition for their doing likewise. Other nations, such as Italy, wanted the nuclear powers to halt their nuclear buildup.[32] Meanwhile, the three nuclear powers that answered the inquiry indicated that general and complete disarmament was the best solution.[33]

For the next 2 years, the debate over the merits of establishing a European MLF made it impossible for the Soviet Union, the United States, and most NATO nations to reach any agreement over nuclear nonproliferation.[34] At the very least, no progress in nonproliferation seemed likely until moves toward disarmament made progress. The world's nonaligned nonweapons states, on the other hand, were eager to secure a separate nonproliferation treaty and called on the UN to convene an international conference to negotiate such an agreement.[35] In June 1965, India and Sweden suggested a new approach to the UN Disarmament Commission: a nonproliferation agreement combined with measures that would begin to cap the arms race between the superpowers. Italy also suggested imposing a time limit on the nonnuclear nations' agreement to refrain from acquiring nuclear weapons. Advocates of this limit—a threat of coercive leverage—argued that it would serve as an inducement to the superpowers to disarm. With support from the world's nonaligned nations, the resolution passed overwhelmingly.[36]

From this point on, the debate over reaching a nuclear nonproliferation agreement presumed that nonweapons nations had a right to acquire nuclear weapons, and that the only question was what they should get in exchange for not exercising it. Each nation expressed this right in a different fashion. For China, it was essential that nonnuclear nations not be "deprived of their freedom to develop nuclear weapons to resist US-Soviet nuclear threats."[37]

For Brazil, the prerogative of nonnuclear nations to go nuclear was nothing less than their right to self-defense. As Brazil's representative explained,

> if a country renounces the procurement or production by its own national means of effective deterrents against nuclear attack or the threat thereof, it must be assured that renunciation—a step taken because of higher considerations of the interests of mankind—will not entail irreparable danger to its own people. The public could never be made to understand why a government, in forswearing its defense capability, had not at the same time provided reasonable and lasting assurances that the nation would not be, directly or indirectly, the object of total destruction or of nuclear blackmail.[38]

For Brazilians, this meant that any nuclear nonproliferation agreement had to include guarantees that states with nuclear weapons would not use or threaten to use them against states without such weapons.

Other states, however, thought that nothing less than nuclear disarmament was necessary. Tunisia, like Brazil, was "not happy about renouncing [its] right to acquire nuclear weapons" but thought that it was too poor ever to try to acquire them and thus could be truly secure only in a disarmed world.[39] Sweden, which was still developing a nuclear weapons option of its own,[40] shared Tunisia's views but saw giving up "the most powerful weaponry that has ever been produced by man" as something it—as one of the "smaller and more defenseless nations"—could do only if the superpowers disarmed.[41]

India, which was also developing a nuclear weapons option,[42] was the most outspoken in defending its right to unrestricted development of nuclear energy. This stance, in part, was simply a reflection of India's established opposition to international safeguards, which—it had argued since the early 1950s—would interfere with its economy's development and its "inalienable right [to] produce and hold the fissionable material required for [its] peaceful power programs."[43] After China exploded its first nuclear device in May 1964, though, protecting this right became even more imperative. As the Indian minister of external affairs explained in 1967,

> most of the countries represented at the disarmament committee appreciated India's peculiar position with regard to the nonproliferation treaty. . . . China would be a nuclear state which would not be called upon to undertake any obligations. India could have become a nuclear country if it had exploded the bomb as China did. But because India had shown restraint, a desire for peace, and opposition to the spread of nuclear armaments, under this treaty it would find itself in a much worse position than China. . . . The result of our restraint is that we are a nonnuclear power which will have to suffer all the disadvantages. On the other hand, China, which has shown no restraint, will not suffer from any disadvantage even if it signs the treaty, as it is already a nuclear power.[44]

What were the Indians talking about? The minister of external affairs left little doubt that they were referring to every nuclear advantage the weapons nations enjoyed—including nuclear testing. After all, he noted, the draft nonproliferation treaty would "seriously hamper and impede" peaceful nuclear research since it would prevent nonnuclear countries from undertaking underground explosions for the purpose of carrying out nuclear research while imposing no such obligation on states with nuclear weapons.[45] The ability to produce weapons-usable materials free from intrusive and discriminatory international safeguards and the freedom to develop all aspects of nuclear energy — including nuclear explosives, the minister continued — was critical to secure India's "sovereign right of unrestricted development" of nuclear energy.[46]

If it were just India making these arguments, they might be dismissed as being peculiar to a nation "exposed to nuclear blackmail."[47] Yet, Brazil's representative shared India's views, arguing that:

> nuclear energy plays a decisive role in [the] mobilization of resources. We must develop and utilize it in every form, including the explosives that make possible not only great civil engineering projects but also an ever-increasing variety of applications that may prove essential to speed up the progress of our peoples. To accept the self-limitation requested from us in order to secure the monopoly of the present nuclear-weapon powers would amount to renouncing in advance boundless prospects in the field of peaceful activities.[48]

At the time, Brazil was developing a nuclear weapons option of its own.[49]

It would be wrong, however, to dismiss Brazil's and India's interest in peaceful nuclear explosives (PNE) and sensitive nuclear activities as a cynical move. The United States, after all, had been touting the possible advantages of PNEs since the early 1960s as the reason for its opposition to reaching a comprehensive nuclear test ban with the Soviets. The United States also was enthusiastic about the need to develop fast-breeder reactors that would use reprocessed plutonium fuels.[50] Thus, Nigeria, Mexico, and Ethiopia, which had no nuclear programs, were every bit as insistent as India and Brazil that any treaty on nonproliferation not place them "in a position of perpetual inferiority in any field of knowledge."[51] Nigeria's recommendation to solve this problem was that non-nuclear weapons powers would not only have nuclear explosives, through an international organization, for their peaceful projects but also have opportunities for their scientists to develop to the full their intellectual capabilities in all fields, including that of nuclear-explosive technology.[52]

These nations were just as adamant that whatever international safeguards the NPT required not interfere with their development of new power reactors and fuels. In this, they were joined by Japan and Germany, who feared that the United States and Soviet Union would use the NPT's safeguard provisions to steal industrial nuclear secrets from their civil nuclear programs. As Germany's foreign minister explained in 1967,

> The unhindered civilian utilization of the atom is a vital interest of the Federal Republic. . . . It is known that German scientists are working with the prospect of success on the development of the second generation of reactors, the so-called fast breeders. . . . We go on the assumption that the placing into effect of controls does not interfere with the economic operations of factories, does not lead to the loss of production secrets, but counters the dangers of misuse. For this purpose it is adequate to control the end-product points, and to have a control which possibly could be exercised by automated instruments.[53]

Germany's foreign minister argued that nations like his own were already apprehensive of states with nuclear weapons trying to monopolize the civilian nuclear field by dint of their commanding lead in military nuclear technology.[54] At least as great a worry, he argued, was the extent to which inspections under the proposed NPT might compromise the pace and commercial confidentiality of civil nuclear developments by nonweapons states.

In the end, the NPT's preamble and Article 3 stipulated that nations like Germany could meet their safeguards obligations through somewhat less threatening but equivalent procedures under Western Europe's nuclear safeguarding organization, EURATOM, that inspections would be restricted to monitoring the flows of source and fissionable materials at "certain strategic points," and that they would be designed "to avoid hampering the economic or technological development of the Parties."

The NPT also emphasized in Articles 4 and 5 that nothing in the treaty should be "interpreted as affecting the inalienable right of all the Parties to the Treaty to develop research, production and use of nuclear energy for peaceful purposes without discrimination." Indeed, the treaty called on all parties to "undertake to facilitate [the] fullest possible exchange of equipment, materials and technological information for the peaceful uses of nuclear energy." The treaty established procedures for sharing the benefits of peaceful nuclear explosives, although it prohibited the direct transfer of explosive devices to or development by nonweapons states.

Finally, in Article 6 the treaty called on the weapons states to "pursue negotiations in good faith on effective measures relating to the cessation of the nuclear arms race at an early date and to nuclear disarmament." Even the Italians' suggestion to leverage the superpower nuclear reductions (i.e., 6 months before the end of a fixed period, nations could give notice of their intent to withdraw from the treaty) was retained after a fashion in Article 10. The 6-month option was rejected along with Nigerian demands that the NPT explicitly empower members to withdraw if the treaty's disarmament aims were "being frustrated."[55] But it was agreed that the treaty would not be of indefinite duration. Instead, it would last 25 years and be reviewed as to whether or not it should be extended and, if so, how. As the Swiss noted, it was "preferable" that the treaty be "concluded for a definite period" so as to avoid "tying" the hands of non-weapons states who could not be expected to wait indefinitely on the weapons states to disarm.[56] Thus, any party to the treaty, under Article 10, retained the right to withdraw if it "decides that extraordinary events, related to the subject matter of this treaty, have jeopardized the supreme interests of its country."[57]

WHICH PAST AS PROLOGUE?

Reading the NPT today, one can easily forget that the original bargain of the Irish resolutions of the late 1950s and early 1960s is present in the final version of NPT. Indeed, Articles 1 and 2, which prohibit the direct or indirect transfer and receipt of nuclear weapons, nuclear explosives, or control over such devices, read very much like the original Irish resolutions themselves. In Article 3, the treaty also calls on parties to accept and negotiate a system of safeguards that would prevent "diversion of nuclear energy from peaceful uses to nuclear weapons or other nuclear explosive devices." Finally, the treaty makes it clear in Article 4 that parties to the NPT could exercise their right to develop peaceful nuclear energy only "in conformity with Articles I and II."

Nor did the NPT's framers abandon their original concerns about the threat of catalytic or accidental nuclear war. The Germans in 1967, for example, defended the NPT aims "because it is frightening to think what would happen if possession of nuclear weapons were spread chaotically through the world, if some adventurous state were one day irresponsibly to use such a weapon." Echoing this view, Germany's foreign minister argued that "even only one additional nuclear power would start a chain reaction that would be hard to control."[58] The Canadians made essentially the same point, arguing that some discrimination against nonweapons states was "the only alternative to allowing the continued spread of nuclear weapons . . . and such a process in the end would have no other result than nuclear war . . . on the greatest scale."[59] The British representative to the General Assembly was just as emphatic:

> We are concerned not only that new possessors of nuclear weapons may employ them against each other, or against a non-nuclear state; we see an even greater danger in the possibility that the use of nuclear weapons by a third country could precipitate a war which would end in a nuclear exchange between the two so-called Superpowers. In our view, and I would think in that of the Soviet Union as well, each additional nuclear power increases the possibility of nuclear war, by design, by miscalculation, or even by accident.[60]

Arrayed against these concerns, however, was the view expressed by the Indian delegation that:

> further proliferation is only the consequence of past and present proliferation and that unless we halt the actual and current proliferation of nuclear weapons, it will not be possible to deal effectively with the problematic danger of further proliferation among additional countries.[61]

This alternative view, along with the idea that non-

nuclear nations had inalienable rights to develop civilian nuclear energy and to withdraw from the NPT
(and thus acquire nuclear weapons legally) if the superpowers did not disarm (or their security interests
were at serious risk), became the NPT consensus view
and was captured in Articles 4, 5, 6, and 10 as well as
most of the NPT's preamble.

Articles 1 and 2, in contrast, reflected the original
bargain of the Irish resolutions, which were concerned
about the threat of accidental and catalytic nuclear
war, whereas the NPT's other articles (with the possible exception of Article 3) generally reflected the finite deterrence theorizing of the time.

The problem is that these two views, both propounded in the NPT, are at odds. Certainly, it is difficult to argue that the further spread of even small
numbers of nuclear weapons to other nations will
significantly increase the risk of accidental or catalytic
nuclear war, while at the same time recommending
that nonweapons states limit the nuclear arsenals of
weapons states by threatening to acquire such weapons themselves. Yet, this is precisely the tension present in the negotiations leading up to the NPT and reflected in the treaty's text (i.e., Articles 1, 2, 6, and 10).

More important, this tension continues to be reflected in the debate over what constitutes "peaceful"
nuclear development under Article 4 in conformity
with Articles 1 and 2. Nations that subscribed to the
notion that the superpower arms race was a key cause
of horizontal proliferation believed that nonweapons
states deserved access to any and all civilian nuclear
energy transfers to compensate them for their restraint
and to assure them equal access to technology that the
states with nuclear weapons already had.

For most of these nations, any civilian nuclear

transfer made under safeguards was automatically "in conformity with Articles I and II." Indeed, for the Dutch, Belgians, and Luxembourgians—and, at times, even the Americans—the line between safeguarded and unsafeguarded activities under the NPT was, as one nonproliferation expert recently noted, "quite bright."[62] In May 1968, the representative of the Netherlands government, for example, urged the superpowers to live up to their disarmament obligations under Article 6, explaining that the obligation of nonweapons states to forgo the acquisition of nuclear weapons should "in no way" restrict their access to civil nuclear technology:

> My delegation interprets Article I of the draft treaty to mean that assistance by supplying knowledge, materials and equipment cannot be denied to a non-nuclear-weapon State until it is clearly established that such assistance will be used for the manufacture of nuclear weapons or other nuclear devices. In other words, in all cases where the recipient parties to the treaty have conformed with the provisions of Article III, there should be a clear presumption that the assistance rendered will not be used for the manufacture of nuclear weapons and other explosive devices.[63]

The Americans were just as insistent that "peaceful applications of energy derived from controlled and sustained nuclear reactions—that is, reactions stopping far short of explosion, [had] nothing to do with nuclear weapons" and, thus, development of such applications would not be affected by the NPT's prohibitions.[64]

Yet, other evidence indicates that the NPT's framers felt uncomfortable about obligating the nuclear powers to provide any and all forms of nuclear-energy technology or materials, save nuclear explosives themselves. In the final debates over the NPT, Spanish and Mexican attempts to create a duty on the part of the nuclear haves to provide nuclear-energy aid to the nuclear have-nots and to reference "the entire technology of reactors and fuels" in the NPT's text, were rejected.[65] This rejection, it has been argued, suggests that the NPT's framers understood that some forms of civil nuclear energy (e.g., weapons-usable nuclear fuels and their related production facilities) were so close to bomb making that sharing them might not be in "conformity" with Articles 1 and 2.

More important, safeguarding such dangerous activities and materials was probably impossible. Certainly, if inspections lived up to Article 3's requirement to "avoid hampering" nations' "technological development" and remained heedful of the NPT's concern—registered in its preamble—for focusing on the "flow" of source and special fissionable materials at "certain strategic points," they would have difficulty accounting for significant quantities of weapons-usable materials at enrichment and reprocessing facilities, at reactors that used weapons-usable fuels, and at their respective fuel-fabrication plants. Nor would timely warning of diversions be likely. Such "safeguarding," as we see above would only mask the probable transfer or acquisition of nuclear weapons and thus violate the NPT's prohibitions in Articles 1 and 2 and Article 3's stricture that safeguards serve the purpose of verifying member nations' fulfillment of their NPT obligations.[66]

It would be reassuring if the NPT's negotiating record could settle such disputes. Unfortunately, it only raises them. Indeed, tension between the first three articles and those that follow in the NPT still exists today. Unaligned nations such as Indonesia and Mexico still argue that weapons states must go much further in reducing their nuclear arsenals and in sharing the benefits of peaceful nuclear energy to keep nonweapons states from abandoning the NPT. And the issue of just what constitutes effective safeguards under the treaty for problematic nations such as North Korea, Libya, Iran, Algeria, and Iraq, and for dangerous nuclear activities such as reprocessing in Japan, is as much a concern as ever.

A number of things, however, have changed since 1968. With the demise of the Soviet Union, the former rivalry is now largely muted. Rather than an ever-escalating nuclear arms race, the United States and former Soviet republics are cooperating in reducing the number of nuclear weapons.

As for the promised benefits of peaceful nuclear power, these too seem less compelling. Certainly, few — if any — nations now believe that PNEs promise any economic benefits. The United States, India, and Russia — the only nations to experiment with such devices — no longer use them, and even Brazil and Argentina, who initially rejected the NPT because it would not allow them to acquire such devices, have renounced their development. Economically viable nuclear electricity, meanwhile, has been limited to uranium-fueled thermal reactors operating only in the most advanced economies of North America, Europe, and East Asia. The economical use of weapons-usable plutonium or mixed-oxide fuels in thermal or fast reactors is, at best, still many decades away.[67]

Meanwhile, the security dangers of certain types of civilian nuclear power and of reactor development in some regions have become all too apparent. Iraq, Iran, North Korea, and Algeria all have nuclear energy programs that are monitored by the IAEA. Yet, all harbor a desire to develop nuclear weapons and have attempted to evade IAEA inspections and proper import procedures. It is unclear whether even special IAEA inspections could provide sufficient warning of dangerous activities in these politically turbulent nations.[68] IAEA monitoring of plutonium fabrication and reprocessing activities in such stable nations as Japan has also been criticized as dangerously deficient. In fact, the quantity of weapons-usable materials produced by such plants threatens to exceed the amount of fissile material present in the arsenals of weapon states.[69]

Finally, there is a newfound awareness that finite deterrence — based on a circumscribed though nonetheless painful response as opposed to all-out nuclear retaliation — and the supposed stability that might come from threatening to attack a few of an opponent's cities, are nowhere near as sound as once supposed — either in theory or practice. The release of new information on the Cold War suggests that nuclear deterrence even between the superpowers was anything but automatic or guaranteed. Indeed, a nuclear incident in Cuba and/or possible war over intermediate-range nuclear force (INF) deployments in Europe was far more likely than many people imagined.[70]

Nor has finite deterrence proved to be as cheap or easy as originally promised. In the case of the French — the original innovators of finite deterrence — developing and maintaining a *force de frappe* have required spending billions of dollars annually to field several generations of strategic forces that have never seemed quite credible (or survivable enough) to other members of NATO — even against a limited Soviet attack. Smaller nations aiming to deter their weapons-state neighbors or nuclear-imminent neighbors are likely to face similar challenges that proportionally will be at least as stressful.

These developments, of course, do not change the NPT's negotiating history. But they do suggest the relative risks of emphasizing the NPT framers' concerns of the late 1960s over those they originally had in 1958. More important, by focusing on the NPT's original concerns, we are more likely to correct for its current deficiencies, which are themselves rooted in views that were all too popular at the time of its signing. Indeed, how well we focus on these concerns today will determine what worth the NPT will have in the decade ahead.

ENDNOTES – CHAPTER 3

1. Previously published in Henry Sokolski, ed., *Fighting Proliferation: New Concerns for the Nineties*, Maxwell Air Force Base, AL: Air University Press, 1996, pp. 3-29.

2. See, for example, Frank Barnaby and Shaun Burnie, *The Nonproliferation Treaty: A Critical Assessment*, Amsterdam, the Netherlands: Greenpeace International, January 17, 1994.

3. See "Soviet Proposal Introduced in the Disarmament Subcommittee: Reduction of Armaments and Armed Forces and the Prohibition of Atomic and Hydrogen Weapons, May 18, 1957," U.S. Department of State, *Documents on Disarmament, 1945-1959*, Washington, DC: U.S. Government Printing Office, 1960, pp. 756–57.

4. *Ibid.* See "Western Working Paper Submitted to the Disarmament Subcommittee: Proposals for Partial Measures of Disarmament, August 29, 1957," *Documents on Disarmament, 1945–1959*, p. 870.

5. The Atomic Energy Act of 1954, U.S. Code secs. 54, 64, 82, 91(c), 92, as amended, 1954.

6. See George Bunn, *Arms Control by Committee: Managing Negotiations with the Russians*, Stanford, CA.: Stanford University Press, 1992, p. 62.

7. The Eisenhower administration had threatened to use or considered using nuclear weapons to end the Korean War in 1953, to save the French in Vietnam in 1954, to save the Republic of China in 1954, 1955, and 1958, and to prevent any invasion of Kuwait in 1958. Atomic howitzers also were deployed by U.S. forces landing in Lebanon in 1958. The Russians, meanwhile, threatened the use of nuclear weapons to end the Suez crisis in 1956. See Peter Lyon, *Eisenhower: Portrait of the Hero*, Boston: Little, Brown and Company, 1969, pp. 534, 541, 583, 606, 610, 624, 639–40, 719, 775–76, 784.

8. The resolution initially passed with 37 affirmative votes, but 44 nations — including the United States, UK, Italy, Japan, France, Greece, Belgium, Turkey, and the Netherlands — abstained. See "Irish Draft Resolution Introduced in the First Committee of the General Assembly: Further Dissemination of Nuclear Weapons, October 17, 1958," in *Documents on Disarmament, 1945–1959*, pp. 1185–1186.

9. *Ibid.*

10. *Ibid.*, pp. 1474–1478. See "Address by the Irish Foreign Minister [Aiken] to the General Assembly, September 23, 1959 [extract],"

11. *Ibid.*

12. *Ibid.*, pp. 1520–1526. See "Statement by the Irish Foreign Minister [Aiken] to the First Committee of the General Assembly, November 13, 1959."

13. See "Statement of Irish Foreign Minister [Aiken] to the First Committee of the General Assembly, November 6, 1962," U.S. Arms Control and Disarmament Agency, *Documents on Disarmament, 1962*, Washington, DC: U.S. Government Printing Office, 1963, pp. 1025–1028.

14. See "Statement by the Irish Foreign Minister, November

13, 1959," *Documents on Disarmament, 1945–1959*, pp. 1520–1526. In this speech, Foreign Minister Aiken attributes these views to Howard Simons, "World-Wide Capabilities for Production and Control of Nuclear Weapons," *Daedalus*, Vol. 88, No. 3, Summer 1959, pp. 385–409, which was a summary of "The Nth Country Problem: A World-Wide Survey of Nuclear Weapons Capabilities," a study by the American Academy of Arts and Sciences, which would be published by the National Planning Association in 1959.

15. "Statement by the Irish Foreign Minister, November 13, 1959," in *Documents on Disarmament, 1945–1959*, pp. 1520–1526.

16. See "Statement of Irish Foreign Minister . . . November 6, 1962," in *Documents on Disarmament, 1962*, pp. 1025–1028.

17. See Lawrence Scheinman, *Atomic Energy Policy in France under the Fourth Republic*, Princeton, NJ: Princeton University Press, 1965, pp. 183ff.; and Avner Cohen, "Stumbling into Opacity: The United States, Israel, and the Atom, 1960–63," *Security Studies*, Vol. 4, No. 2, Winter 1994, pp. 199–200.

18. See United Nations Department of Political and Security Council Affairs, *The United Nations and Disarmament, 1945–1970*, New York: United Nations Publications, 1971, pp. 260–261.

19. *Ibid.*

20. *Ibid.*, pp. 265. The Swedes submitted this resolution, 1664 (16), December 4, 1961.

21. *Ibid.*

22. See "Statement by the United States Representative [Yost] to the First Committee of the General Assembly: Spread of Nuclear Weapons, November 30, 1961," in US Arms Control and Disarmament Agency, *Documents on Disarmament, 1961*, Washington, DC: U.S. Government Printing Office, 1962, pp. 691–692.

23. *Ibid.*

24. See, for example, "Statement by ACDA Director Foster

to the Eighteen Nation Disarmament Committee: Non-dissem-ination of Nuclear Weapons, February 6, 1964," in U.S. Arms Control and Disarmament Agency, *Documents on Disarmament, 1964*, Washington, DC: U.S. Government Printing Office, 1965, pp. 32–33, in which restraint in international nuclear nonprolif-eration was urged since without it there "would be no rest for anyone . . . no stability, no real security and no chance of effective disarmament." It was also argued that because the acquisition of nuclear weapons by smaller countries would "increase the like-lihood of the great Powers becoming involved in what would otherwise remain local conflicts," both the security of weapons and nonweapons states in U.S. eyes was at stake.

25. See Bunn, pp. 66–75.

26. See "Statement by the Irish Foreign Minister, November 13, 1959," *Documents on Disarmament, 1945–1959*, pp. 1520–1526.

27. See "Statement by the Indian Representative [Trivedi] to the First Committee of the General Assembly: Nonproliferation of Nuclear Weapons, October 31, 1966," U.S. Arms Control and Disarmament Agency, *Documents on Disarmament, 1966*, Wash-ington, DC: U.S. Government Printing Office, 1967, p. 679.

28. *Ibid.*, pp. 156–157. See "Statement of the Egyptian Repre-sentative [Khallaf] to the Eighteen Nation Committee on Disar-mament, March 3, 1966."

29. One of the earliest expressions of this idea can be found in Jacob Viner, "The Implications of the Atomic Bomb for Inter-national Relations," *International Economics: Studies by Jacob Viner*, Glenco, IL: Free Press, 1951, pp. 300–309. For the earliest popu-lar presentation of finite deterrence theory, see Pierre M. Gallios, "Nuclear Aggression and National Suicide," *The Reporter*, Vol. 18 November 1958, pp. 22–26.

30. See, for example, P. H. Backus, "Finite Deterrence, Con-trolled Retaliation," *U.S. Naval Institute Proceedings*, March 1959, pp. 23–29; and George W. Rathjens, Jr., "Deterrence and Defense," *Bulletin of the Atomic Scientists*, September 1958, pp. 225–228.

31. United Nations Department of Political and Security

Council Affairs, *The United Nations and Disarmament*, pp: 260-261.

32. In fact, it was in a NATO gathering held in February 1962 that Italy first voiced reservations about agreeing not to acquire nuclear weapons unless the nuclear weapons nations promised to disarm. Later that year, however, it acquiesced and supported a U.S. draft resolution that would allow the use of U.S. weapons by a multilateral NATO naval force. For details, see George Bunn, Roland M. Timerbaev, and James F. Leonard, "Nuclear Disarmament: How Much Have the Five Nuclear Powers Promised in the Non-Proliferation Treaty?" John B. Rhinelander and Adam M. Scheinman, eds., *At the Nuclear Crossroads: Choices about Nuclear Weapons and Extension of the Non-Proliferation Treaty*, Lanham, MD: University Press of America, Inc., 1995, p. 15.

33. See *The United Nations and Disarmament, 1945–1970*, p. 266.

34. See, for example, the exchange between the Soviet and U.S. representatives to the Eighteen Nation Disarmament Committee, July 2, 1964, in *Documents on Disarmament, 1964*, pp. 241–56.

35. *Ibid.*, pp. 485–490. For a review of the nonaligned nations' actions along these lines, see "Statement by the U.A.R. Representative [Fahmy] to the First Committee of the General Assembly: Nonproliferation of Nuclear Weapons, October 22, 1965."

36. See *The United Nations and Disarmament, 1945–1970*, p. 269. Italy and others continued to promote this idea through 1967. See, for example, "Statement by the Burmese Representative [Maung Maung] to the Eighteen Nation Disarmament Committee: Nonproliferation of Nuclear Weapons, October 10, 1967"; and "Statement by the Italian Representative [Caracciolo] to the Eighteen Nation Disarmament Committee: Draft Nonproliferation Treaty, October 24, 1967," in U.S. Arms Control and Disarmament Agency, *Documents on Disarmament, 1967*, Washington, DC: U.S. Government Printing Office, 1968, pp. 463, 529.

37. See, for example, "Chinese Communist Comment on Draft Nonproliferation Treaty, September 3, 1967," in *Documents on Disarmament, 1967*, pp. 381.

38. *Ibid.*, p. 370. See "Statement by the Brazilian Representative [Azeredo da Silveira] to the Eighteen Nation Disarmament Committee: Draft Nonproliferation Treaty, August 31, 1967."

39. *Ibid.*, p. 429. See "Address by President Bourguiba of Tunisia to the General Assembly, September 27, 1967 [extract]."

40. See Steve Coll, "Neutral Sweden Quietly Keeps Nuclear Option Open," *The Washington Post*, November 25, 1994, p. A1.

41. See "Statement by the Swedish Representative [Alva Myrdal] to the Eighteen Nation Disarmament Committee: Nonproliferation of Nuclear Weapons, October 3, 1967," in *Documents on Disarmament, 1967*, p. 444.

42. For a brief history of India's nuclear weapons program, see Leonard S. Spector, *Nuclear Proliferation Today*, New York: Vintage Books, 1984, pp. 23ff.

43. See Roberta Wohlstetter, "The Buddha Smiles: Absent-minded Peaceful Aid and the Indian Bomb," *Energy Research and Development Administration*, Monograph 3, contract no. (49-1)-3747, Marina del Rey, CA: Pan Heuristics, April 30, 1977, pp. 30–75.

44. See "Extract from News Conference Remarks by the Indian External Affairs Minister [Chagla], April 27, 1967," in *Documents on Disarmament*, 1967, pp. 204–205.

45. *Ibid.*

46. *Ibid.*, p. 235. See "Statement by the Indian Representative [Trivedi] to the Eighteen Nation Disarmament Committee: Nonproliferation of Nuclear Weapons, May 23, 1967."

47. *Ibid.*

48. *Ibid.*; and "Statement by the Brazilian Representative [Correa da Costa] to the Eighteen Nation Disarmament Committee: Peaceful Uses of Nuclear Energy, May 18,1967," p. 226.

49. For a description of Brazil's attempt to secure a safeguard-

ed military production reactor during this period, see Spector, pp. 236–238.

50. See Albert Wohlstetter *et al.*, *Swords from Plowshares: The Military Potential of Civilian Nuclear Energy*, Chicago, IL: University of Chicago Press, 1979, pp. 85–86; and Albert Wohlstetter *et al.*, *Can We Make Nuclear Power Compatible with Limiting the Spread of Nuclear Weapons?* Vol. 1-l, "The Spread of Nuclear Bombs: Predictions, Premises, Policies," ERDA contract no. E(49-1)-3747, Los Angeles, CA: Pan Heuristics, November 15, 1976, pp. 9– 32, 89–108.

51. See, for example, "Statement by the Ethiopian Representative [Zelleke] to the Eighteen Nation Disarmament Committee: Nonproliferation of Nuclear Weapons, October 5, 1967"; and "Statement by the Mexican Representative [Castaneda] to the Eighteen Nation Disarmament Committee: Latin American Nuclear-Free Zone, May 18, 1967," *Documents on Disarmament, 1967*, pp. 228, 449–450.

52. *Ibid.*, p. 377. See "Statement by the Nigerian Representative [Sule Kolo] to the Eighteen Nation Disarmament Committee: Draft Nonproliferation Treaty, August 31, 1967." The Germans also shared this view; "Statement by Foreign Minister Brandt to the Bundestag: Nonproliferation of Nuclear Weapons, February 1, 1967 [extracts]."

53. *Ibid.*, pp. 211–212. See "Statement by Foreign Minister Brandt to the Bundestag on Proposed Nonproliferation Treaty, April 27, 1967."

54. *Ibid.*, p. 53. See, for example, "Statement by Foreign Minister Brandt to the Bundestag: Nonproliferation of Nuclear Weapons, February 1, 1967 [extracts]."

55. *Ibid.*, pp. 557–558. See "Statement by the Nigerian Representative [Sule Kolo] to the Eighteen Nation Disarmament Committee: Draft Nonproliferation Treaty, November 2, 1967 [extract]."

56. *Ibid.*, p. 573. See "Swiss Aide Memoire to the Co-Chairmen of the Eighteen Nation Disarmament Committee: Draft Nonpro-

liferation Treaty, November 17, 1967."

57. On the point that this language meant that nonweapons nations might be compelled to withdraw if the weapons states did not live up to their pledge to disarm, see, for example, "Statement by the Swedish Representative [Alva Myrdal] to the Eighteen Nation Disarmament Committee: Nonproliferation of Nuclear Weapons, February 8, 1968"; "Statement by the Ethiopian Representative [Makonnen] to the First Committee of the General Assembly: Nonproliferation of Nuclear Weapons, May 6, 1968"; and "Statement by the Indian Representative [Husain] to the Eighteen Nation Disarmament Committee: Nonproliferation of Nuclear Weapons, February 27, 1968," U.S. Arms Control and Disarmament Agency, *Documents on Disarmament, 1968*, Washington, DC: U.S. Government Printing Office, 1969, pp. 45, 293–294, and 116.

58. See "Television Interview with Chancellor Kiesinger: Nonproliferation Negotiations, February 17, 1967 [extract]"; and "Statement by Foreign Minister Brandt to the Bundestag on Proposed Nonproliferation Treaty, April 27, 1967," *Documents on Disarmament, 1967*, pp. 91, 215.

59. *Ibid.*, p. 315. See "Statement by the Canadian Representative [Burns] to the Eighteen Nation Disarmament Committee: Nonproliferation of Nuclear Weapons, August 3, 1967."

60. *Ibid.*, p. 458. "Statement by the British Representative [Hope] to the First Committee of the General Assembly, December 14, 1967."

61. *Ibid.*, p. 432. See "Statement by the Indian Representative [Trivedi] to the Eighteen Nation Disarmament Committee: Nonproliferation of Nuclear Weapons, September 28, 1967."

62. See, for example, Eldon V. C. Greenberg, *The NPT and Plutonium: Application of NPT Prohibitions to "Civilian" Nuclear Equipment, Technology and Materials Associated with Reprocessing and Plutonium Use*, Washington, DC: Nuclear Control Institute, 1993, pp. 18–19.

63. See "Statement by the Dutch Representative [Eschauzier]

to the First Committee of the General Assembly: Nonproliferation of Nuclear Weapons, May 6, 1968 [extract]," *Documents on Disarmament, 1968,* pp. 295–296.

64. *Ibid.,* p. 721. See "Statement by ACDA Director Foster to the First Committee of the General Assembly: Nonproliferation of Nuclear Weapons, November 9, 1966."

65. *Ibid.,* p. 40. See "Spanish Memorandum to the Co-Chairmen of the Eighteen Nation Disarmament Committee, February 8, 1968"; and "Mexican Working Paper Submitted to the Eighteen Nation Disarmament Committee: Suggested Additions to Draft Nonproliferation Treaty, September 19,1967," *Documents on Disarmament, 1967,* pp. 394–395.

66. For this interpretation, see Greenberg; and Arthur Steiner, "Article IV and the 'Straightforward Bargain'," PAN Paper 78-832-08, Wohlstetter *et al., Towards a New Consensus on Nuclear Technology,* Vol. 2, Supporting Papers, ACDA Report no. PH-78-04-832-33, Marina del Rey, CA: Pan Heuristics, 1977.

67. For the latest economic forecast as to when such fuels might make economic sense, see, for example, Brian G. Chow and Kenneth A. Solomon, *Limiting the Spread of Weapon-Usable Fissile Materials,* Santa Monica, CA: RAND, October 1993, pp. 25–54.

68. See David Kay, "Detection and Denial: Iraq and Beyond," Washington, DC: Consortia for the Study of Intelligence, June 1994.

69. See, for example, Chow and Solomon, pp. xiv–xv; and Paul Leventhal, *IAEA's Safeguards Shortcomings – A Critique,* Washington, DC: Nuclear Control Institute, September 12, 1994.

70. See, for example, William T. Lee, "The Nuclear Brink That Wasn't – and the One That Was," *The Washington Times,* February 7, 1995, p. A19.

PART III:

THE NPT AND NUCLEAR WEAPONS–
ARTICLES I, II, AND VI

CHAPTER 4

HOW WILL THE NUCLEAR WEAPONS
STORY END?*

Victor Gilinsky

Most know the story of nuclear weapons. The United States developed them to protect against a possible German program; then the Soviet Union built them to match America, then Britain, France and China, then Israel, South Africa, India, and Pakistan, and, most recently, North Korea.[1] A competitive spiral keeps nuclear countries locked in and attracts new members to the nuclear club, slowly perhaps, but nevertheless continually. Where this will end, none of us knows. It is a subject to which we should pay more attention.

CAN WE KEEP THE BOMBS ON THE SHELF INDEFINITELY?

We sometimes contemplate the possibility of a worldwide nuclear breakdown, but I think we do so only on an intellectual level. We do not really believe it can happen. If we did, we would behave differently. Meanwhile, there is no sign that any of the current nuclear countries are ready to give up their arsenal, and the number of nuclear bombs in the world is still in the tens of thousands.[2]

---

*Remarks of Victor Gilinsky prepared for The 10th PIIC Beijing Seminar on International Security, Xiamen, China, September 24-29, 2006, available from *www.npec-web.org/Presentations/20060924-Gilinsky-BeijingRemarks.pdf.* Adapted slightly for publication.

The subtitle of this seminar is "Harmony Makes the World Stable and Secure." In a world of so many nuclear weapons, can we count on harmony to restrain use *indefinitely*? Can we rely on so-called rational behavior (so-called because it is not always clear what "rational" means)? And, in any case, people often do not behave in their best interests, at least not in their collective best interests, and sometimes humanity displays a self-destructive streak. Did it make sense, for example, to build more than 100,000 nuclear weapons during the Cold War?

A pressing reason to look ahead more seriously than we do is that once one country breaks the taboo on nuclear weapons use, it is likely that restraints against further use will weaken. At that point, the organizing principles of the world will have to change. Our cities, our economic systems, and our civil societies, will all become anachronisms. Of course, the number of warheads and the dangers of a worldwide catastrophe are now reduced from what they were during the Cold War. A great deal of writing is devoted to explaining how to maintain nuclear stability in a world of many nuclear weapons. Optimists argue that, since even at the most dangerous time of the Cold War the antagonists did not use nuclear bombs, the nuclear future is "manageable."

But to me, the Cold War experience suggests a different conclusion—that the nonuse of nuclear weapons since 1945 had less to do with these theories and more to do with simple human awe that made everyone hesitate to open Pandora's Box, an awe that will not last forever. (If you remember the story, Pandora could not resist opening the Box and unleashed human misery.)

We were also just plain lucky, especially in the

early years of the Cold War. Up to the mid-1950s, there were many bombs that one person had the ability to detonate, and some of them were small enough for one person to carry. Fortunately, none got into the wrong hands.

We were lucky in other ways. To protect against a Soviet surprise attack, the U.S. Air Force took to keeping some bombers fully loaded with nuclear weapons in the air at all time. Some of these planes suffered accidents and dropped their bombs. Altogether, about a dozen dropped thermonuclear bombs were never found. Fortunately, none detonated. I am sure other countries had similar accidents.

THE CUBAN MISSILE CRISIS

The great nuclear crisis of the Cold War was, of course, the 1962 Cuban missile crisis. At that time, we experienced some scenes that could have come straight out of the movie, *Dr. Strangelove* (1964). We discovered since then that the situation during the crisis was even more dangerous than it seemed at the time. I do not think we should flatter ourselves to think that we are much smarter today and that we could not get into a similar dangerous situation. Basic human nature hasn't changed much in the last half century. One thing that surely has not changed is the cult of toughness in high-level decisionmaking. It is always safer to be thought "hard" than "soft." This is a problem that has been with mankind since ancient times.

One of the experiences along these lines that affected me greatly was a talk after the Cuban crisis given by a Strategic Air Command (SAC) major general who had led U.S. bombers during the crisis on what he believed at the time was an attack on the Soviet Union.

The general, a kind and thoughtful man, told us how difficult it was to say goodbye to his wife before his mission. He described in detail the extensive planning, the long training, and the tremendous discipline required. During the initial stages of the flight, he had time to reflect on his orders. The crews understood perfectly that each plane carried many megatons of nuclear explosives whose use would have awful consequences. When the bombers reached a certain point over the Arctic, they were to continue to their targets if they got a coded "Go" signal, and to return home if they did not.

The expected signal did not come, and at the last moment the general gave the order for the planes to turn around. (What a relief, I thought.) The general drew himself up, paused, looked out across the audience, and told us that having to give the order to turn around was the most disappointing(!) moment of his entire life.

It did not change my opinion of him as a good person. It did, however, give me new insight into human nature. The point I want to make is that no one, no matter how decent, can spend a lifetime training for something and not have some part of them want to apply their training, no matter how awful the consequences.

I do not want to leave you with the impression that this is a comment on the United States or the U.S. Air Force. It is a comment on human nature. It sometimes pulls us in the wrong direction.

WHAT ABOUT THE SCIENTISTS?

Just like the military want to apply their training, scientists like to see their ideas work in the real world.

When the Los Alamos, New Mexico, scientists heard of the Hiroshima, Japan, atomic bomb detonation, many cheered. In retrospect, of course, that was a dreadfully inappropriate reaction. But it was only human nature. They were not cheering the deaths; they were cheering the first successful uranium explosion.

The lesson we need to remember is that most people cannot work on something with all their heart, not even an awful bomb, and not want to see it work. But as we know, that tendency can have unfortunate consequences.

Herb York, a former director of the Livermore Laboratory, wrote in his 1970 book, *Race to Oblivion*, that the problem of controlling nuclear weapons activities was made more difficult because those devoted to pursuing them were mostly sincere persons acting in good faith. They really believe in what they are doing. At the same time, he writes, the real motives for this work are not necessarily what they are represented to be.[3]

The line between genuine concern for the defense of one's country and unchecked personal ambition is often unclear. The real driving force is often the sense of importance, and sometimes real prominence, that comes from working on powerful weapons.

The U.S. and Soviet weapons scientists became powerful figures. The same is certainly true in other weapons states. Last month, for example, the Indian Prime Minister had to publicly mollify the top scientists in the Indian weapons establishment to get support for his nuclear deal with the United States. Or consider the privileged status in Pakistan of A. Q. Khan, despite such misdeeds as divulging nuclear weapons secrets to North Korea.

THERMONUCLEAR WEAPONS

Sometimes the irresistible attraction of the weapons is scientific. Physicists, especially, are enthralled with the idea that their scribbles on the blackboard can change the world, whether it is for better or for the worse.

Robert Oppenheimer, who initially opposed the U.S. development of the thermonuclear bomb, was ultimately won over by the Teller-Ulam idea that made it work. Oppenheimer called the idea "technically sweet."[4] The phrase betrays the seduction of interesting scientific problems, even if they are associated with weapons for mass killing. The same pull operated among physicists in other countries, perhaps even more strongly.

I should say that not all were seduced by temptation nor anxious at all costs to maintain their status with the powerful. Of the famous scientists who took part in the American debate over thermonuclear weapons in 1950, I am most impressed with Enrico Fermi and I. I. Rabi. When the question of building the thermonuclear bomb first arose, they took a firmer stance than Oppenheimer. They said, "The fact that no limit exists to the destructiveness of this weapon makes its very existence and the knowledge of its construction a danger to humanity as a whole."[5] Their advice was ignored, and we now live with that danger.

By 1952, the United States detonated a many-megaton thermonuclear device, the so-called Mike shot, on an island in the Pacific Ocean. Eventually the scientists learned to make small thermonuclear devices, too. But the main thing was the possibility of powerful warheads. The military liked big bombs for use in massive attacks because in those days bombers and missiles were highly inaccurate. You had to have high yield in order to have a high probability of destroying a target a continent away. Years later, when the accuracy of weapons was increased by orders of magnitude, there was no corresponding reduction in weapons yields. Warhead yields remain outrageously high in all countries.

SOVIET BIG BOMB

The Soviets, too, launched a crash program to develop thermonuclear weapons, and eventually overtook the United States in numbers. When Nikita Khrushchev wanted a huge bomb with which to intimidate the West, a Soviet team led by Andrei Sakharov produced a 100-megaton bomb — the largest bomb ever designed or used. The Soviets detonated it in 1961 with an intentionally reduced yield of 50 megatons, because anything higher would have destroyed the plane that dropped it. Sakharov received a "Hero of Socialist Labor" award for it.

I mention this because we associate Sakharov's name with human rights, not mass destruction. Of course, his role as a heroic opponent of the Soviet government came later. But the interesting thing is that when he wrote his *Memoirs* in 1990, he was still proud of designing the Big Bomb, just as Robert Oppenheimer, for all his later reflections, remained proud of having built the first fusion bomb.

I saw a copy of the Big Bomb in the bomb museum at Russia's Chelyabinsk 70 weapons laboratory. An Italian woman in our group asked the old laboratory director, "How could you build such a horrible bomb?" He smiled and said, "When the orders come down from the Kremlin, for some funny reason, you do it."[6]

What I am saying is that the state's drive for big weapons is only part of the story, whether in the Soviet Union or anywhere else. From my own observation, it is more often the scientists and the weapons laboratories that entice the powerful in government with new ideas for bombs, rather than the other way around.

WHAT SHOULD ONE DO?

What about individual scientists? How is a scientist to act? Let me say a word especially to those whose careers are ahead of them. We have to think of our country's defense because if we do not, who will beyond the military establishment itself? But — to paraphrase the ancient Jewish sage and teacher, known simply as Hillel — if we think *only* of our own country, what are we? There are ethical/moral lines we should not cross, even for our motherland.

Each person has ultimately to wrestle with himself as to what is legitimate defense and what crosses the line. The important thing, it seems to me, is to bring to your work your sense of what is right, and to ask yourself: What if everyone around the world did as I do? Is that acceptable behavior? And you need to ask this *during* your professional career, when your decisions matter, not to wait until they are merely of academic interest.

HOW LONG CAN WE TICKLE THE DRAGON'S TAIL?

I bring all this up because the importance of nuclear weapons seems again to be on the increase. The stated reasons for developing them or upgrading nuclear forces have supposedly to do with national defense, but I think the factors I have mentioned – the importance it gives to the participating individuals and weapons laboratories – also plays an important role in urging governments in this direction. The governments seem to hold to the optimistic notion that they can brandish the weapons and gain psychological and political advantage without risking that the weapons will actually be used. We assume we can do nuclear shadow boxing so carefully that no one gets hurt.

This reminds me of an experiment Los Alamos scientists conducted during World War II that was called "tickling the dragon's tail." The aim was to determine the critical masses of nuclear explosives by tapping two subcritical masses toward each other with a screwdriver, all the while measuring the neutron count. The idea was to control the dangers by tapping slowly and carefully so as to cause only very tiny movements. One day the experimenter's screwdriver slipped and the two pieces got knocked too close together, and before the physicist could knock the pieces apart, he got a lethal dose and died a horrible death.[7]

We may be underestimating the worldwide dangers in the same way.

ENDNOTES – CHAPTER 4

1. South Africa built bombs but dismantled them and became a Nonproliferation Treaty signer.

2. The United States and Russia have reduced their stockpiles significantly and apparently will reduce them further, one should note, something for which they should get more credit than they do. But they both intend to hang on to a pile of these weapons indefinitely.

3. See Herbert York, *Race to Olivion: A Participant's View of the*

Arms Race, New York: Clarion Press, 1970, pp. 224-239, available from *www.learnworld.com/ZNW/LWText.York.Race Access.html*.

4. See *A History of National Security: Mike Shot*, Los Alamos, NM: Los Alamos National Laboratory, April 6, 2010, available from *www.lanl.gov/history/postwar/mikeshot.shtml*.

5. See Enrico Fermi and I. I. Rabi, "An Opinion on the Development of the 'Super'," in *The General Advisor Committee to the Atomic Energy Commission Majority and Minority Reports on Building the H-Bomb*, Washington, DC: The U.S. Atomic Energy Commission, October 30, 1949, available from *www.atomicarchive.Com/ Docs?Hydrogen?GACReport.shtml*.

6. Recollection of events by the author of this chapter.

7. See Bryan Hubbard, "A Critical Accident 'Tickling the Dragon's Tail'," *Military.com*, April 7, 2010, available from *www. Military.Com/Content/More Content1/?file=cw_nuclear_slotin*.

CHAPTER 5

MOVING TOWARD ZERO AND ARMAGEDDON?*

Henry Sokolski

Assuming current nuclear trends continue, the next 2 decades will test America's security and that of its closest allies as they never have been tested before. Before 2020, the United Kingdom will find its nuclear forces eclipsed not only by those of Pakistan, but of Israel and of India. Soon thereafter, France will share the same fate. China, which has already enough separated plutonium and highly enriched uranium to triple its current stockpile of roughly 300 nuclear warheads, could expand its nuclear arsenal too. Meanwhile, Japan will have ready access to thousands of bombs worth of separated plutonium. U.S. and Russian nuclear weapons-usable material stocks—still large enough to be converted back to many tens of thousands of weapons—will decline only marginally while similar nuclear weapons-usable stores in Japan and other nuclear weapons states could easily double.[1]

Compounding these developments, even more nuclear weapons-ready states are likely: As of 2009, at least 25 states have announced their desire to build large reactors—historically, bomb starter kits—before 2030. None of this will foster the abolition of nuclear weapons. Certainly, the current battery of U.S.-backed arms control measures, including the ratification of

---

*A version of this chapter was published in the April 2010 edition of the *Armed Forces Journal*.

major arms reductions treaties with Russia, a Comprehensive Test Ban, a cut-off treaty banning further military nuclear fissile production, and enhanced inspections of civilian nuclear programs—are unlikely to be enough to head off the troubling trends described. What is worse, the expected arms control measures, if executed too hastily, could easily make matters worse.

Thus, congressional critics of strategic arms reductions with Moscow argue that if the United States and Russia cut their strategic nuclear deployments too deeply and too quickly, it might undermine the credibility of our nuclear security alliances with states like Japan and Turkey who, in turn, might be tempted to go nuclear themselves. As for pushing ratification of a Comprehensive Test Ban Treaty, this too could backfire: India, whose last nuclear test series was followed by a Pakistani nuclear test, recently debated whether to resume nuclear testing to beat what some in India fear is an approaching nuclear test ban deadline. Meanwhile, American test ban treaty opponents have urged the U.S. Senate to tie the treaty's test limits to what other states, like Russia, say the treaty might allow. Pegging the treaty to this limit, however, could conceivably actually encourage some forms of low-yield nuclear testing.

As for securing a nondiscriminatory, global ban against the "military" production of separated plutonium and enriched uranium for nuclear weapons, this also could inflict unintended harm. Here, the danger is that the treaty bans the production only of fissile material for military purposes and, as such, could encourage increased production for civilian purposes. The odds of inspectors catching military diversions from such "peaceful" plants are quite low. Finally, with the growing popularity of "peaceful" nuclear energy, nuclear supplier states are claiming that exporting new power reactors will strengthen nonproliferation since it will come with the application of enhanced nuclear inspections. Unfortunately, in most of the truly worrisome cases, even enhanced inspections may not be reliable enough to safeguard against significant military diversions. As it is, international nuclear inspections are failing to maintain continuity of inspections over most of the world's spent or fresh fuel that can be enriched and reprocessed to make weapons-usable fuels. These nuclear fuel-making plants, moreover, can be hidden from inspectors and, even when declared, be used to make weapons-usable materials without necessarily being detected in a timely fashion.[2]

Several of these points are beginning to receive attention in the United States. The debate over these matters, however, needs to be broadened. Why? Because even if Washington's favorite nuclear control initiatives are well-executed and avoid running the risks noted above, the United States and its allies will still face a series of additional nuclear proliferation dangers of major proportions.

A PACKED NUCLEAR ARMED CROWD?

The first of these is that as the United States and Russia reduce their nuclear weapons deployments, China, India, Pakistan, and Israel are likely to increase theirs. Currently, the United States is proposing to reduce U.S. and Russian strategic weapons deployments to as low as 1,000 warheads each. As a result, it is conceivable that in 10 years' time the nuclear numbers separating the United States and Russia from the other nuclear weapons states might be measured in the hundreds rather than the thousands of weapons (see Figure 1). In such a world, relatively small changes in any state's nuclear weapons capabilities will have a much larger impact than it might on the world's international security today.

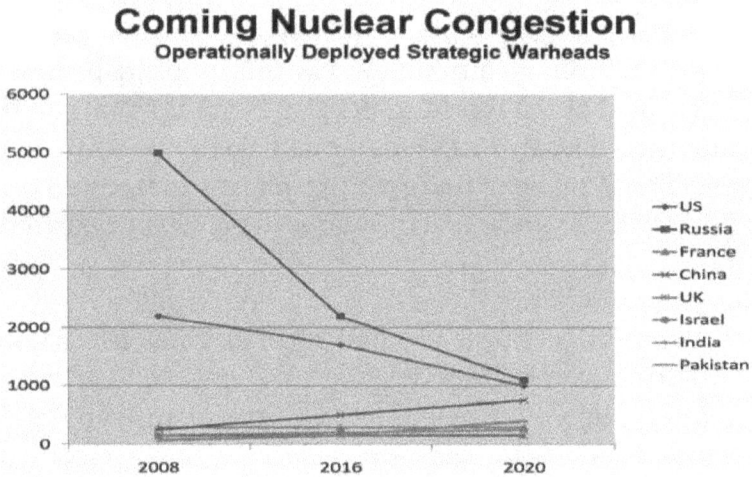

Coming Nuclear Congestion
Operationally Deployed Strategic Warheads

Figure 1. Coming Nuclear Congestion.[3]

Compounding the international volatility that this set of trends is likely to induce are the large and growing stockpiles of nuclear weapons-usable materials (i.e., of separated plutonium and highly enriched uranium) in several states. These already exceed tens of thousands crude bombs' worth of material in the United States and Russia and are projected to grow in Pakistan, India, China, and Israel (not to mention Japan, which currently has no nuclear weapons). This will enable these four states to increase their current nuclear deployments much more quickly and dramatically than ever was possible previously. (See Figures 2 and 3 for these states' current holdings of nuclear weapons fuel waiting in the wings).

Metric tons [MT]

Stockpile available for weapons
Naval (fresh)
Naval (irradiated)
Civilian Material
Excess (mostly for blenddown)
Eliminated

Data for Russia
highly uncertain
± 300 MT

137 MT

*Estimate

165 MT

—30 MT*
50 MT*
590 MT*

96 MT
137 MT
—30 MT
100 MT

250 MT

6.4 MT

1.5 MT
4.5 MT

China	France	India	Israel	Pakistan	Russia	U.K.	United States	NNW States
20 MT*	30 MT*	0.6 MT*	0.1 MT*	2.0 MT*		16.4 MT		10 MT

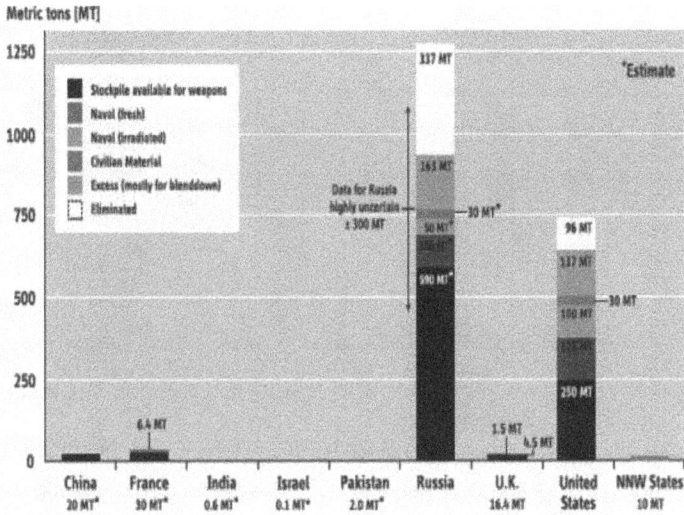

Civilian stocks are for January 2007 and based on the latest national INFCIRC/549 declarations to the IAEA (with the exception of Germany). Civilian stocks are listed by ownership, not be current location. Weapon stocks are based on nongovernmental estimates except for the UK and the United States, whose governments have made declarations. India's plutonium separated from unsafeguarded spent PHWR fuel is categorized as an additional strategic stockpile.

Figure 2. National Stocks of Highly Enriched Uranium as of Mid-2008.[4]

Metric tons [MT]

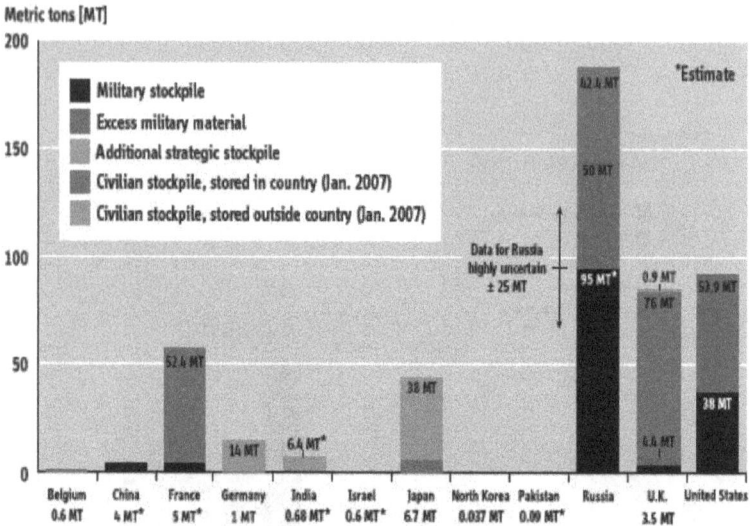

The numbers for the UK and the United States are based on official information. Numbers with asterisk are nongovernmental-estimates, often with large uncertainties. Numbers for Russian and U.S. excess HEU are for June 2008. HEU in non-nuclear weapon (NNW) states is under IAEA safeguards.

Figure 3. National Stocks of Separated Plutonium.[5]

Moreover, 20 years out, there could be more nuclear weapons-ready states — countries that could acquire nuclear weapons in a matter of months, like Japan and Iran. As already noted, more than 25 states have announced plans to launch large civilian nuclear programs. If they all realize their dreams of bringing their first power reactors on line by 2030, it would constitute a near doubling of the 31 states that currently have such programs, most of which are in Europe (see Figures 4 and 5).

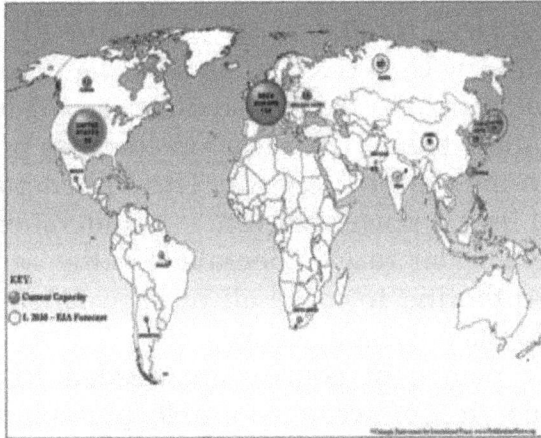

Figure 4. Today Number of States or Regions
with Power Reactors Is Limited.[6]

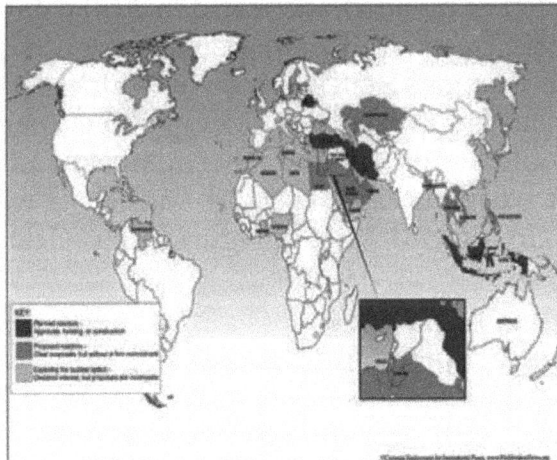

Figure 5. Planned for 2030.[7]

Such a nuclear expansion could have major military implications. Every current weapons state first brought a large reactor on line prior to acquiring its first bomb. The United Kingdom (UK), France, Russia, India, Pakistan, and the United States all made many of their initial bombs from reactors that also provided power to their electrical grids. The United States, in fact, still uses a power reactor, a "proliferation resistant" light water reactor operated by the Tennessee Valley Authority, to make all of its weapons grade tritium for its nuclear arsenal.

Other plants, of course, are needed to chemically separate out weapons-usable plutonium from the spent reactor fuel or to enrich the uranium used to power such machines. Yet, as the recent cases of Iran and North Korea demonstrate, such plants can be built and operated in ways that make it difficult to detect diversions in a timely fashion. Certainly, if all of the announced civilian nuclear programs are completed as planned, the world in 2030 would be far less stable. Instead of there being several confirmed nuclear weapons states — most of which the United States can claim are either allies or strategic partners — there could be an unmanageable number of additional nuclear weapons capable-states — armed or weapons-ready — to contend with, as Figures 6 and 7 depict.

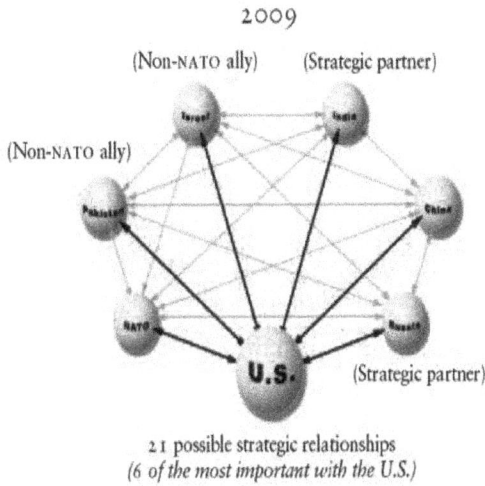

2009

(Non-NATO ally)   (Strategic partner)

(Non-NATO ally)

(Strategic partner)

21 possible strategic relationships
(6 of the most important with the U.S.)

Figure 6. Current proliferation seems manageable,
but DPRK and Iran are problematic.

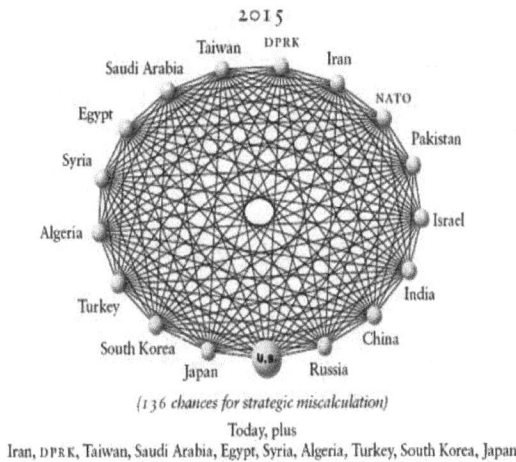

2015

Taiwan   DPRK

Saudi Arabia   Iran

                              NATO

Egypt

                              Pakistan

Syria

Algeria   Israel

                              India

Turkey

South Korea   China

Japan   U.S.   Russia

(136 chances for strategic miscalculation)

Today, plus
Iran, DPRK, Taiwan, Saudi Arabia, Egypt, Syria, Algeria, Turkey, South Korea, Japan

Figure 7. With more nuclear-ready states will we
ramp up to a nuclear World War I?

In such a world, the United States might know who its friends and potential adversaries might be, but Washington would have difficulty knowing what such states might do in a crisis—close ranks with the United States, go their own way developing weapons options, or follow the lead of some other nuclear-capable nation. As for America's possible adversaries, Washington would have difficulty determining just how lethal these adversaries' military forces might be.

All of this would only heighten the prospects for nuclear terrorism. Not only would there be more opportunities to seize nuclear weapons or nuclear weapons materials, there would be more military and civilian nuclear facilities to sabotage. Finally, the potential for miscalculation and nuclear war could rise to a point where even non-nuclear acts of terror could ignite larger conflicts that could turn nuclear.

Taken together, then, these trends could easily duplicate or exceed the kind of volatility that preceded World Wars I and II—periods in which overly ambitious arms control objectives were pursued while states completed major covert and overt military preparations that heightened tensions and subsequently were employed in total wars.

MAKING THE MOST OF ZERO

All of this raises the question of whether we can avoid such a future. The short answer is yes, but only if we attend more closely to four basic principles. Let us discuss them in turn. First, as nuclear weapons deployments decline, more care must be taken to ensure that military reductions or additions actually work to decrease the chances for war. If our security guarantees are to continue to neutralize the nuclear weapons yearnings of our allies, it is critical that we avoid doing anything to undermine the favorable correlation of forces the United States enjoys against its key nuclear competitors. In addition to making roughly equal nuclear reductions with Russia, then, the United States will have to keep other nuclear-armed states, such as China and India, from trying to catch up with U.S. nuclear weapons deployment levels and — as in the case of India and China, Pakistan and India, and Japan and China — from trying to catch up with each other. This means that additional nuclear restraints, either in the form of nuclear weapons reductions or further limits on the production or stockpiling of weapons-usable fuel, will need to be reached with Russia, of course, but also with China, India, and Pakistan. As a practical matter, this also means that other nuclear weapons-ready or virtual weapons states (e.g., Japan) will have to be persuaded to curtail or end their production of nuclear weapons-usable materials or to dispose of some portion of what they currently have.

To date, the United States has not publicly grappled with how best to do this. President Barack Obama has called for the negotiation of a fissile material cut-off treaty. But this agreement allows civilian nuclear fuel production, which is virtually identical to military fuel production. Also, after decades of fruitless negotiations in Geneva, it is unclear whether any such agreement could ever be brought into force. Some officials, including those advising Secretary of State Hillary Clinton, have suggested a complementary approach to these negotiations known as the Fissile Material Control Initiative. Instead of a binding treaty, both NPT weapons states *and* nonweapons states would simply identify what portion of their separated plutonium and highly enriched uranium stocks was in excess of either their military *or* civilian requirements and secure or dispose of them.[8]

Yet another practical idea, which would have direct bearing on India's nuclear weapons activities, would be to ensure that implementation of the U.S. civilian nuclear cooperative agreement with New Delhi does nothing to help India make more nuclear weapons-usable fuels than it was producing when the deal was finalized late in 2008. Under the NPT, the states that had nuclear weapons in 1967 — the United States, Russia, France, the UK, and China — swore not to help any other state outside of these five ever to acquire them directly or indirectly. Meanwhile, under the Hyde Act, which authorized the civilian U.S.-Indian nuclear deal, the White House is routinely required to report to Congress on just how much uranium fuel India is importing, how much it is using to run its civilian reactors, how much uranium it is producing domestically, and the extent to which the operation of its unsafeguarded reactors is expanding its stockpiles of unsafeguarded plutonium with either the direct or indirect help of NPT weapons states.[9]

India's unsafeguarded plutonium stockpiles might grow faster per year than was the case prior to the nuclear cooperative agreement's finalization in 2008 because Indian uranium imports from one or more of the NPT weapons states could allow India to use more of its domestically produced uranium in its unsafeguarded reactors to make bomb usable plutonium. If this ever happened, the exporting nuclear weapons states would be implicated in violating the NPT. To prevent such a violation or, at least, limit the harm it might do, the United States should urge all other nuclear-supplying states to suspend civilian nuclear assistance until India's unsafeguarded nuclear weapons-usable material production declines. The logical venue at which to make this request would be the Nuclear Suppliers Group. Such vigilance should also be matched with efforts to keep Pakistan from expanding its nuclear weapons capabilities as well.

As for trying to maintain the relative parity of competing nuclear-armed state forces through nonnuclear military assistance or buildups, the trick will be to substitute conventional arms for nuclear ones in a manner that avoids increasing one or both side's interest in acquiring more nuclear weapons. Unfortunately, deploying more advanced non-nuclear systems to compensate for forgone nuclear systems will not necessarily assure this. Consider long-range precision strike and advanced command control and intelligence systems in the case of India and Pakistan. Pakistan believes it must threaten to use its nuclear weapons first to deter India's superior conventional forces. Precision strike systems, however, could conceivably target Pakistan's nuclear weapons. As a result, one could imagine that arming India with such weapons would only put Pakistan even more on nuclear alert and encourage Islamabad to acquire even more nuclear weapons. Building up the wrong kinds of advanced nonnuclear weapons systems in India or helping it to build them in disproportionate numbers could adversely affect any restraint Pakistan might be inclined to show in its nuclear weapons plans.

Ballistic missile defenses could also be tricky. Under the right circumstances, having such defenses could provide a nonnuclear form of deterrence that might facilitate reducing the numbers of deployed nuclear weapons. Instead of neutralizing a possible opponent's missiles by targeting them with nuclear or non-nuclear offensive weapons, active missile defenses might be used to counter them after launch. They also could be useful as a form of insurance against cheating on any future nuclear-capable ballistic missile reduction agreements. To secure these benefits, though, it is important to deploy missile defenses correctly.

Again, consider the Indian and Pakistani case. While Pakistan insists it must use its nuclear weapons first in any major war against India, New Delhi is hoping to use its conventional forces to capture enough of Pakistan from a cold start to induce Islamabad to quickly sue for peace. Under these circumstances, sharing equal amounts of missile defenses with India and Pakistan would only give India yet another nonnuclear military edge against Islamabad. This, in turn, risks encouraging Pakistan to beef up its offensive nuclear missile forces even more. The only way to counter this eventuality and help secure the benefits of missile defense for both countries would be to address the underlying conventional asymmetry between them. One idea regional security experts have long favored is creating, low, medium, and high conventional deployment zones on both sides of the Indo-Pakistani border to equalize each side's ability to launch quick conventional attacks against one another. Such schemes might also attenuate the perceived stability risks of deploying more advanced, discriminate nonnuclear military systems.[10]

Elsewhere other measures might be required. As China increases its nuclear and nonnuclear missile superiority over Taiwan and its capability to target U.S. carrier battle groups with conventional ballistic missiles, the United States and its Pacific allies must worry that Beijing may be able to overwhelm the missile defenses the United States is now working on. China, meanwhile, is considering developing ballistic missile defenses of its own to counter possible missile attacks. Thus, reaching an agreement limiting ballistic missile might make sense for both sides.

Several precedents exist. START, which limits U.S. and Russian strategic ballistic missile delivery systems, is one. The Intermediate Nuclear Forces (INF) Treaty, which covers Russian and NATO missiles with ranges between 500 and 5,500 kilometers, is another. The Missile Technology Control Regime (MTCR), which limits commerce in missiles with 300 kilometer range and 500 kilogram payload capabilities, is another still. The trick in reaching additional ballistic missile limits is to make sure they are robust enough to address the ballistic missiles that matter without creating new categories of permissible missiles. It certainly would make little sense to eliminate ballistic missiles above 500 kilometers range only to end up legitimizing slightly lower range missile systems that are above the limits restricted by the MTCR.

The second basic principle is that, in reducing existing nuclear weapons and nuclear-capable delivery systems, we include steps for preventing their further spread. Currently, the connection between reducing nuclear arms and preventing their spread is mostly symbolic. As the United States and Russia reduce their nuclear deployments, other nuclear-armed states, it is argued, should follow the U.S-Russian example so as to persuade nonweapons states to submit to much more intrusive inspections of their civilian nuclear activities. Putting aside the hard cases of Iran and North Korea, this line of reasoning ignores several key technical developments and turns on several questionable political assumptions.

Certainly, after failing to detect the covert nuclear programs in Iraq, Iran, Syria, and North Korea, it is an open question whether even enhanced international nuclear inspections will be able to reliably detect future illicit nuclear activities. This is especially so if, as some believe, large civilian nuclear programs spread in regions like the Middle East.

Not only the United States but Israel, Japan, NATO, Russia, and China are planning to deploy ballistic missile defense systems. Yet, the approach of the United States and its allies to controlling nuclear strategic threats is practically silent as to whether these defense programs should be promoted or restricted, and how. Nor, outside of strategic reduction talks with Russia, is there much discussion as to whether or how other states' development of ballistic missiles (both nuclear and nonnuclear) should be approached.

Then there are the political questions. How likely is it that Russia will agree to further nuclear cuts beyond the current START negotiations? Will there be yet another START agreement to lower numbers to 1,000 strategic deployed warheads? Will Russia agree to limit its nonstrategic nuclear weapons? What demands will Moscow make for such reductions? Will Russia demand that the United States and NATO cripple their conventional and missile defense plans? Finally, when, if ever, might such agreements be reached? The success of the White House's arms control and nonproliferation policies depends on favorable answers to these questions.

Also, if there are no new penalties or risks for developing nuclear weapons-related capabilities, how likely is it that states without nuclear-capable missiles or atomic weapons will refrain from trying to acquire them? Certainly, the Greater Middle East is watching to see what, if anything, the United States and its allies might do to penalize Iran's nuclear misbehavior. Most states in the region are already hedging their nuclear bets by acquiring peaceful nuclear programs of their own. Similar dynamics are in play in the Far East in relation to North Korea's nuclear weapons program. Beyond these two cases, there is the general worry that the enforcement of nuclear nonproliferation lacks any teeth.

These questions suggest the need for an additional set of arms control and nonproliferation measures to complement the current set, an additional set that does not depend so much upon the legally binding agreement of any one state. Rather than expect international treaties on nuclear weapons material production and testing to come into force and merely *hope* that progress on this front will somehow persuade nonweapons states to keep clear of nuclear related activities, why not instead promote limits that would begin to constrain both nuclear weapons and non-nuclear weapons states at the same time? Rather than waiting for Iran, Pakistan, India, North Korea, and Egypt to ratify the Comprehensive Test Ban, why not use the implicit ban on nuclear testing contained in the Nuclear Nonproliferation Treaty to secure an immediate agreement among civilian nuclear supplier states to block nuclear trade with any NPT nonweapons state that tests? Once agreement on this has been reached, an additional agreement might be sought to expand such trade restrictions to *any* state that tests. Why not proceed with the Fissile Material Control Initiative, which would have an immediate (albeit initially modest) impact on both nuclear weapons states and nonweapons states, while simultaneously pushing the Fissile Material Cut-off Treaty, which would only affect nuclear weapons countries?

In addition, it would be useful to tie existing nuclear controls to controls over nuclear-capable missiles. Currently, violators of the NPT and states that withdraw from the treaty, while still in violation, are not prohibited from receiving nuclear-capable missile technology and assistance from missile technology supplying states. It would be useful to eliminate this loophole with the adoption of an automatic cutoff of access to goods controlled by the MTCR by these nuclear violators.

Such nuclear violators are also free to test nuclear-capable missiles, as North Korea recently did, launching them into airspace outside of their borders. Under current international law, all of this is legal. Yet, such missiles are ideal for carrying nuclear warheads, and their development is meant to intimidate. Should there be an international norm, as there is with piracy and slave trading, giving states with the technical power to shoot such objects out of international air space (e.g., the United States, Russia, Israel, and soon Japan, NATO, and China) as "outlaw" objects? Finally, if progress is made on creating additional limits on ballistic missile deployments (e.g., global INF, etc.), should violators of these understandings also be banned from receiving controlled missile and controlled nuclear goods?

The third basic principle is that international nuclear inspectors need to distinguish between nuclear activities and materials they can reliably safeguard against being diverted to make bombs, and those that they cannot. This distinction should be publicly announced. The NPT is clear that all peaceful nuclear activities and materials must be safeguarded — that is, inspected in a manner that can reliably prevent them from being diverted to make nuclear weapons. Most NPT states have fallen into the habit of thinking that if they merely declare their nuclear holdings and allow international inspections, they have met this requirement.

This view is dangerously mistaken. After the nuclear inspection gaffes in Iraq, Iran, Syria, and North Korea, we now know that the IAEA cannot reliably detect covert nuclear activities early enough to allow others to intervene to prevent possible bomb making. We also now know that inspectors annually lose track of many bombs' worth of nuclear weapons-usable plutonium and uranium at declared nuclear fuel-making plants. Privately, IAEA officials admit that the agency cannot assure continuity of inspections for spent and fresh fuel rods at more than half of the sites that they inspect. Finally, we know that declared plutonium and enriched uranium can be made into bombs, and their related production plants converted so quickly (in some cases, within hours or days) that no inspection system can offer timely warning of a bomb-making effort. Yet, any true safeguard against military nuclear diversions must reliably detect them early enough to allow outside powers to intervene to block a bomb from being built. Anything less is only monitoring that might, at best, detect military diversions *after* they occur.

In light of these points, it would be useful for the IAEA to concede that it cannot safeguard all that it inspects. This would finally raise first-order questions about the advisability of allowing the stockpiling of plutonium, highly enriched uranium, and plutonium-based reactor fuels in the belief that these materials and activities can be safeguarded. At the very least, it would suggest that nonweapons states ought not to acquire these materials or facilities beyond what they already have. These points are important enough to raise before, during, and after the May 2010 NPT Review conference.

In this regard, the United States and other like-minded nations might independently assess whether the IAEA can meet its own inspection goals; under what circumstances (if any) these goals can be met; and, finally, whether these goals are technically sound. The U.S. House of Representatives last year approved legislation to require the executive to make such assessments routinely and to report their findings. Similar legislation has been proposed in the Senate.[11]

The fourth basic principle is that greater attention must be paid to comparing costs and discouraging the use of government financial incentives for commercialization projects, especially nuclear power, in order to assure safe, economically competitive forms of clean energy. Supporters of nuclear power insist that its expansion is critical to prevent global warming. Yet, they almost always downplay or ignore the nuclear weapons proliferation risks associated with this technology's further spread. It may be impossible to prevent the spread of nuclear power if it turns out to be the cheapest, quickest way to provide low or no-carbon energy, but given the security risk associated with nuclear energy, no government should pay extra to promote it.

Moreover, offering additional government financial incentives specifically geared to building more commercial nuclear plants and their associated fuel-making facilities will only increase the difficulty of accurately comparing nuclear power with nonnuclear alternatives. Not only do such subsidies mask the true costs, they tilt the market against less subsidized alternatives. The most dangerous forms of civilian nuclear energy and nuclear fuel making in most nonweapons states and large power reactor projects in war-torn regions like the Middle East — turn out to be poor investments as compared to much safer alternatives.[12]

There are several ways to mitigate such market distortions. The first would be to get as many governments as possible to open all large civilian energy projects in their countries to international competitive bidding. This procedure is already in place in a number of countries. The problem is that when states want to build large energy-producing facilities, they limit the competition to nuclear bids rather than open the competition to any energy option that could meet the applicable set of environmental and economic criteria. Limiting the competition in this way ought to be discouraged internationally.

Most advanced nations, including the United States, claim to back the principles of the Energy Charter Treaty and the Global Energy Charter for Sustainable Development. These international agreements are designed to encourage all states to open their energy sectors to international bidding to assure that all energy options are considered, and that the various subsidies and ancillary costs associated with each are identified and reflected in the price of what is being proposed. Promoting adherence to these rules is essential if the United States and other states are serious about reducing carbon emissions in the quickest, least costly manner.

Such states should thus reference and enforce the principles of the Energy Charter Treaty and the Global Energy Charter for Sustainable Development as part of the follow-on to the understandings reached at Copenhagen, Denmark. In addition, states that elect to build a nuclear plant, when less costly nonnuclear alternatives would clearly make more sense, ought to be flagged by an economic competitiveness monitoring body qualified to oversee large international energy project transactions. Such uneconomic nuclear picks (e.g., several proposed Middle Eastern nuclear projects) might also be referred to the IAEA for further investigation.[13]

As a complementary effort, the world's advanced states could work with developing countries to create non-nuclear alternatives for addressing their energy and environmental needs. In the case of the United States, this would simply entail implementing existing law. Title V of the Nuclear Nonproliferation Act of 1978 requires the Executive Branch to do analyses of key countries' energy needs and identify how these needs might be addressed with nonfossil, non-nuclear energy sources. Title V also calls on the executive branch to create an alternative energy cadre to help developing nations explore these alternative options. To date, no president has chosen to implement this law. Some members of Congress have indicated that they would like to remedy this omission by requiring Title V country energy analyses (and independent assessments of these analyses) to be performed as a precondition for U.S. approval of any additional U.S. nuclear cooperative agreements.[14] As with most of the other suggestions already made, the United States can act on this idea without waiting for the full development of any international consensus.

ENDNOTES - CHAPTER 5

1. International Panel on Fissile Materials, "Global Fissile Materials Report 2008," October 2008, available from *www.ipfmlibrary.org/gfmr08.pdf*; and Andrei Chang, "China's Nuclear Warhead Stockpile Rising," *UPIAsia.com*, April 5, 2008, available from *www.upiasia.com/Security/2008/04/05/chinas_nuclear_warhead_stockpile_rising/7074*.

2. See, e.g., Henry S. Rowen, "This 'Nuclear-Free' Plan Would Effect the Opposite," *The Wall Street Journal*, January 17, 2008. For additional technical background, see David Kay, "Denial and Deception Practices of WMD Proliferators: Iraq and Beyond," Brad Roberts, ed., *Weapons Proliferation in the 1990s*, Cambridge, MA: MIT Press, 1995; Victor Gilinsky, *et al.*, *A Fresh Examination of the Proliferation Dangers of Light Water Reactors*, Washington, DC: NPEC, 2004, available from *www.npec-web.org/Essays/20041022-GilinskyEtAl-lwr.pdf*; and Andrew Leask, Russell Leslie, and John Carlson, *Safeguards As Design Criteria – Guidance for Regulators*, Canberra: Australian Safeguards and Non-proliferation Office, September 2004, available from *www.asno.dfat.gov.au/publications/safeguards_design_criteria.pdf*.

3. Data for this chart was drawn from the Natural Resources Defense Council, "Russian Nuclear Forces 2007," *Bulletin of the Atomic Scientists*, March-April 2007, available from *thebulletin.metapress.com/content/d41x498467712117/fulltext.pdf*; and Robert S. Norris and Hans M. Kristensen, "U.S. Nuclear Forces, 2008," *Bulletin of the Atomic Scientists*, March-April 2008, available from *thebulletin.metapress.com/content/pr53n270241156n6/fulltext.pdf*.

4. Source: Frank Von Hippel *et al.*, International Panel on Fissile Material, *Global Fissile Material Report, 2009*, pp. 11, 16, available from *www.fissilematerials.org/ipfm/site_down/gfmr09.pdf*.

5. *Ibid.*

6. Graphs developed for NPEC by Sharon Squassoni, available from *www.npec-web-org/Frameset.asp?PageType=Projects*.

7. *Ibid.*

8. See, e.g., Robert Einhorn, "Controlling Fissile Materials and Ending Nuclear Testing," Presentation before the International Conference on Nuclear Disarmament, Oslo, Norway, February 26-27, 2008, available from *www.ctbto.org/fileadmin/user_upload/pdf/External_Reports/paper-einhorn.pdf.*

9. See the Henry J. Hyde, United States-India Peaceful Atomic Energy Cooperation Act of 2006, "Implementation and Compliance Report," available from *frwebgate.access.gpo.gov/cgi bin/getdoc.cgi?dbname=109_cong_bills&docid=f:h5682enr.txt.pdf.*

10. On these points, see Peter Lavoy, "Islamabad's Nuclear Posture: Its Premises and Implementation," Henry Sokolski, ed., *Pakistan's Nuclear Future: Worries beyond War*, Carlisle, PA: Strategic Studies Institute, U.S. Army War College, 2008, pp. 129-166; and General Feroz Khan, "Reducing the Risk of Nuclear War in South Asia," September 15, 2008, available from *www.npec-web.org/Essays/20090813-khan%20final.pdf.*

11. See Section 416 of the House State Authorization Act of 2010 and 2011, "Implementation of Recommendations of Commission on the Prevention of WMD Proliferation and Terrorism," available from *www.govtrack.us/congress/billtext.xpd?bill=h111-2410.*

12. See, e.g., Peter Tynan and John Stephenson, "Nuclear Power in Saudi Arabia, Egypt, and Turkey—How Cost Effective?" February 9, 2009, available from *www.npec-web.org/Frameset.asp?PageType=Single&PDFFile=Dalberg-Middle%20East-carbon&PDFFolder=Essays;* Frank von Hippel, "Why Reprocessing Persists in Some Countries and Not in Others: The Costs and Benefits of Reprocessing," April 9, 2009, available from *www.npec-web.org/Frameset.asp?PageType=Single&PDFFile=vonhippel%20%20TheCostsandBenefits&PDFFolder=Essays;* Doug Koplow, "Nuclear Power as Taxpayer Patronage: A Case Study of Subsidies to Calvert Cliffs Unit 3," available from *www.npec-web.org/Frameset.asp?PageType=Single&PDFFile=Koplow%20-%20Calvert Cliffs3&PDFFolder=Essays.*

13. For more on these points, see Henry Sokolski, "Market Fortified Non-proliferation," *Breaking the Nuclear Impasse*, New York: The Century Foundation, 2007, pp. 81-143, available from

nationalsecurity.oversight.house.gov/documents/20070627150329. pdf. More on the current membership and investment and trade principles of the Energy Charter Treaty and the Global Energy Charter for Sustainable Development is available from www. encharter.org and *www.cmdc.net/echarter.html.*

14. See Letter from Congressmen Brad Sherman, Edward Markey, and Ileana Ros-Lehtinen to Secretary of State Hillary Clinton, April 6, 2009, available from *bradsherman.house.gov/pdf/ NuclearCooperationPresObama040609.pdf.*

PART IV

THE NUCLEAR NONPROLIFERATION TREATY
AND NUCLEAR SAFEGUARDS – ARTICLE III

CHAPTER 6

PEACEFUL NUCLEAR ENERGY AND THE NUCLEAR NONPROLIFERATION TREATY*

Eldon V. C. Greenberg

The variety of formulations written into Article I and II restricting transfer of and access to nuclear weapons and other nuclear explosive devices must be read to mean that the Treaty negotiators intended, to the maximum extent possible, that the Nuclear Nonproliferation Treaty's (NPT) restrictions would halt proliferation by any means.[1] In Article I, nuclear weapon states, after making their basic nontransfer pledge, undertake "not in any way to assist, encourage or induce any non-nuclear-weapon State to manufacture or otherwise acquire nuclear weapons or nuclear explosive devices, or control over such weapons or explosive devices." In Article II, non-nuclear weapon states party to the NPT, after making their basic nonreceipt pledge, undertake "not to manufacture or otherwise acquire nuclear weapons or other nuclear explosive devices"; and "not to seek or receive any assistance in the manufacture of nuclear weapons or other nuclear explosive devices." The reach of these prohibitions, particularly those in Article I, is poten-

---

*Taken from "Application of NPT Prohibitions To 'Civilian' Nuclear Equipment, Technology and Materials Associated with Reprocessing and Plutonium Use," 9th in the Nuclear Control Institute's "NPT/95" series "NPT at the Crossroads: Issues Bearing on Extending and Strengthening the Treaty," 1993. The chapter has been edited slightly for consistency with material elsewhere in the present book.

tially to any activity designated as "nuclear" since, as Mason Willrich has pointed out, "[a]lmost any kind of international nuclear assistance is potentially useful to a nuclear weapons program.[2]

Squared against Articles I and II is equally expansive language in Article IV. Article IV speaks of an "inalienable right of all the Parties to the Treaty to develop research, production and use of nuclear energy for peaceful purposes. . . ." Hypothetically, any nuclear energy application denominated as "peaceful" would escape the prohibitions of Articles I and II. Indeed, it has sometimes been suggested that Article IV reflects a "straightforward bargain" in the Treaty, with the weapon states trading nuclear economic benefits to nonweapon states in exchange for the enhanced security provided to weapon states under Articles I and II.[3] But clearly it makes no sense to interpret Article IV in such a fashion, for to do so would be to undercut the fundamental purpose of the Treaty to halt proliferation, primarily through the prohibitions of Articles I and II.

The key to the harmonization of Articles I and II with Article IV lies in the connecting language found in Article IV, para. 1, "in conformity with."[4] It is possible to read this phrase as meaning no more than the obvious, namely, that a weapon state cannot transfer to a nonweapon state or assist such a state in obtaining a weapon or other nuclear explosive device as such and, by the same token, a nonweapon state cannot manufacture or otherwise obtain such a weapon or device on its own or with the assistance of others. This, in fact, has been the "unexceptional" interpretation put on the language by several commentators.[5]

In such a reading of the NPT, the phrase is simply necessary because, if there were not a cross-reference to Articles I and II in Article IV, then the provisions could indeed be read in a conflicting manner. For example, a party could transfer or acquire a nuclear explosive device for allegedly peaceful purposes, and claim in so doing that it was merely acting consistently within its "inalienable right" under Article IV. The cross-reference language in Article IV, para. 1, assures that this cannot be done, but accomplishes no more. Under such a formal reading of the Treaty, Article IV would be subject to the obligations of Articles I and II only insofar as the transfer and acquisition of nuclear weapons or nuclear explosive devices as such were concerned. All other nuclear energy applications would be permissible. In effect, the Treaty would be read through an exclusively "explosives lens."

The implications, however, of this connecting language can be read more broadly. At some point, particular assistance or activities may become so risky, even though they do not involve the transfer and acquisition of weapons or explosives as such, that they can no longer be deemed in conformity with the requirements of Articles I and II, even though by their stated terms they are for peaceful power applications only. Under such a "pragmatic" reading of the Treaty, the "inalienable right" in Article IV, para. 1, and the obligation to "facilitate," and the "right to participate" in Article IV, para. 2, remain subordinate to the prohibitions of Articles I and II, if the practical consequences of the assistance or activity, whether its purpose is denominated peaceful or not, are likely to lead to the proliferation of nuclear weapons. In short, there may be activities other than final assembly and production of a "bomb," "warhead," or other nuclear explosive "device" covered by the prohibitions of Article I and II.

Such an approach makes complete sense in light

of the overall purpose of the NPT to halt proliferation. If risks are great, if there can be no reasonable civilian justification for particular forms of assistance or activities, and if there can be no certainty that safeguards would be effective with respect to such assistance or activities, then a presumption should arise under the Treaty that such assistance or activities are not for a permissible, peaceful purpose but are rather for a weapons or explosive purpose and therefore in violation of Articles I and 11.[6] Only in this way can there be any assurance that the NPT's objectives will be achieved.

The case for a pragmatic reading of the NPT is well stated in a 1979 report by Albert Wohlstetter and others to ACDA:

> Now Article IV of the NPT refers to the undertaking by all parties to the Treaty "to facilitate" and the right of all parties "to participate in the fullest possible exchange of equipment, materials and scientific and technological information for the peaceful uses of nuclear energy." Indeed, it refers to such rights to the peaceful pursuit of nuclear energy, in the language of 18th century natural law, as "inalienable." The contention was made by many of the delegates to the Iran Conference on Transfer of Nuclear Technology at Persepolis in the spring of 1977 that this "inalienable right" includes the stocking of plutonium or other highly concentrated fissile material and was therefore violated by President Carter's proposal to delay commitment to unrestricted commerce in plutonium.

* * * * *

> However, Article IV explicitly states that the inalienable right of all parties to the Treaty to the peaceful use of nuclear energy has to be in conformity with Articles I and II, and it is these Articles that are what make the Treaty a treaty against proliferation. In Article I the

nuclear weapons states promise not to transfer or "in any way to assist, [or] encourage . . . any nonnuclear weapons state to manufacture" nuclear explosives. If the "fullest possible exchange" were taken to include the provision of stocks of highly concentrated fissile material within days or hours of being ready for incorporation into an explosive, this would certainly "assist" an aspiring nonnuclear weapons state in making such an explosive. No reasonable interpretation of the Nonproliferation Treaty would say that the Treaty intends, in exchange for an explicitly revocable promise by countries without nuclear explosives not to make or acquire them, to transfer to them material that is within days or hours of being ready for incorporation in a bomb. Some help and certainly the avoidance of *arbitrary* interference in peaceful uses of nuclear energy are involved. However, the main return for promising not to manufacture or receive nuclear weapons is clearly a corresponding promise by some potential adversaries, backed by a system to provide early warning if the promises should be broken. The NPT is, after all, a treaty against proliferation, not for nuclear development.[7]

As Arthur Steiner wrote in a supporting paper, rejecting the notion of the NPT as a simple, "straightforward bargain":

Such an interpretation could be taken to imply that, in exchange for an absolute renunciation of the right to acquire nuclear explosive devices, non-weapons states have the absolute right to receive any and all nuclear assistance short of the provision, by outside aid or by their own efforts, of nuclear explosive devices. This interpretation is dubious, for the common sense interpretation of the Treaty, as well as the explicit text of Article IV, is that the latter is subordinate to, and to be interpreted in conformity with Articles I and II. It is, after all, a nonproliferation treaty. The provision of certain types of nuclear technology that defeat the objective of nonproliferation by bringing a non-weapons

109

state recipient within days or hours of a weapon, cannot be an objective toward a nonproliferation treaty.[8]

To sum up, it is most appropriate to read Articles I and II in light of the recognition that there is a spectrum of activity relating to nuclear weapons, ranging from basic to theoretical physics at one end to the final production, assembly, and deployment of operational weapons at the other, and that there is a need to apply the Treaty at the right point and in the right circumstances to prevent weapons proliferation. Articles I and II should be understood as intended to cover not just the transfer and acquisition of a bomb, but also technology transfer or other kinds of assistance or independent activities in nonweapon states short of final production and assembly of a weapon which, as a practical matter, would mean that such state would have the bomb. By the same token, the rights and obligations in Article IV must be read in a limited fashion, so as to exclude the possibility that such a result could occur in the name of fulfilling such obligations or exercising Treaty rights.

THE HISTORY OF THE NPT

Several elements of the history of the NPT tend to support the case for a pragmatic reading of the Treaty. These include: (1) the efforts of the negotiators to establish a comprehensive, loophole-free agreement primarily aimed at enhancing security; (2) the assumptions of the negotiators with respect to the economics of certain "Power" applications; (3) the negotiators' expectations concerning the role of safeguards; and (4) the recognition of the negotiators that per se rules (i.e., generalized rules applied without consideration for specific circumstances) concerning permissible activities or assistance were inappropriate.

A Comprehensive, Loophole-Free Treaty to Enhance Security.

From the outset, it was understood that assistance and activities subject to the Treaty's restrictions would have to be broadly defined if the Treaty were to be effective. Thus, the so-called "Irish Resolution" of the United Nations (UN) General Assembly, which launched the negotiations in December 1961, called upon all nations to reach an agreement under which weapon states would refrain, *inter alia*, "from transmitting the information necessary for [nuclear weapons] manufacture to States not possessing such weapons," and nonweapon states would agree "not to manufacture or otherwise acquire control of such weapons."[9]

As the negotiations got underway, the explicit goal of the negotiating parties, as set down by the UN General Assembly, was to develop an agreement "void of loop-holes which might permit nuclear or non-nuclear Powers to proliferate, directly or indirectly, nuclear weapons in any form."[10] The emphasis in General Assembly Resolution 2028 on restricting the spread of nuclear weapons "directly or indirectly" and "in any form" would appear to reflect an understanding that proliferation under the guise of peaceful power applications should be treated no differently than unabashed and explicit weapons proliferation.[11]

While some have suggested that the non-nuclear weapon states were simply looking for economic benefits (to be embodied in Article IV), not security enhancement, in negotiating the NPT,[12] the better view is that security concerns of all the parties were among the primary motivating factors leading to conclusion of the NPT.[13] Consequently, one can conclude, "Given the officially expressed primary importance of national security questions to the majority of the nations of the world in their appraisal of the NPT, it would be surprising indeed if very many of them wanted their potential adversaries to be in a position to possess nuclear weapons in a matter of days or even hours."[14] Assistance and activities which would put potential adversaries in precisely such a position cannot therefore be subject to any obligation or right in Article IV.

Finally, at several points during the negotiation of the NPT, proposals which would have expanded the duty of weapon states to aid nonweapon states to develop peaceful applications of nuclear energy were rejected. Mexico, for example, proposed an amendment to Article IV, para. 2, to establish an explicit "duty" to aid which was defeated.[15] And in the final debates at the UN Eighteen Nation Disarmament Committee (ENDC), the Spanish delegation proposed that Article IV "refer specifically to the entire technology of reactors and fuels,"[16] but this amendment, too, was rejected. Such history leads to a simple conclusion: "It seems quite clear . . . that it was not the intent of the framers of the NPT to create an obligation to supply any and all forms of nuclear energy with a single exception of actual explosive devices."[17]

The logic of the NPT does not support the idea that either weapons or nonweapons states wish to have their security reduced by unrestricted commerce in especially dangerous forms of nuclear energy. The history of the negotiations leading to the NPT shows that several attempts to make the provision of all types of nuclear energy an obligation were considered and rejected. The evidence is overwhelming that the

"straightforward bargain" is a dangerous myth.[18]
Assumptions Concerning Economic Viability.

The NPT was also premised upon certain assumptions with respect to the economic (and presumably technical) merit of nuclear power applications. Indeed, the negotiators' views might best be characterized as reflecting hopes for rather than assumptions about the future of nuclear energy. To the extent those hopes have been dashed, the operation of the Treaty should be different than originally anticipated.

There is no question that during the course of the negotiation of the NPT the parties, reflecting the conventional wisdom of the day,[19] considered that civilian reprocessing and plutonium recycling, first for conventional reactors and then for breeders, would someday be a normal part of any nation's nuclear fuel cycle. The U.S. representatives to the ENDC, for example, repeatedly indicated that permissible transfers under the NPT would include equipment for "processing" and "production" of fissionable material, as well as for the "use" of such material.[20] The UN General Assembly, in considering the final Treaty document and commending it to member states for ratification, specifically stated that it was:

> *Convinced* that, pursuant to the provisions of the Treaty, all signatories have the right to engage in research, production and use of nuclear energy for peaceful purposes and will be able to acquire source and special fissionable materials, as well as equipment for the processing, use and production of nuclear material for peaceful purposes.[21]

That the Treaty parties' understandings related to expectations, not absolute guarantees, however, is made clear by the history of the NPT before the United States Congress.[22] Thus, in hearings before the Senate Foreign Relations Committee in 1968, Glenn Seaborg, Chairman of the Atomic Energy Commission, spoke of his expectations about future uses of plutonium.[23] Other witnesses in their statements likewise spoke, for example, of "look[ing] forward to a world in which plutonium will be readily available in very large quantities in all industrially advanced states and in many developing states."[24] These expectations, presumably premised on anticipated, real economic needs, have, as pointed out above,[25] largely proven to be false. In such circumstances, the Treaty should not be interpreted as creating an obligation to facilitate or a right to participate in reprocessing and plutonium use. To the contrary, it is more appropriate to view the Treaty as creating the presumption today that assistance or activities relating thereto have more to do with weapons than with peaceful purposes and, therefore, generally would fall within the prohibitions of Articles I and II.[26]

Expectations Concerning the Role of Safeguards.

Even if it were the case that a particular nuclear application had no reasonable economic or technical justification, it might be argued that where it is subject to safeguards, the application should still be permissible under the Treaty.[27] After all, it may be contended, the Treaty itself provides a mechanism, if there is any doubt, to determine whether the assistance or activity is permissible or not. In the words of Mason Willrich, "[T]he application of safeguards to all peaceful nuclear assistance to non-nuclear weapon states, as required by Article III, provides a way to establish and clarify the peaceful purpose of most international nuclear assistance."[28]

Yet there is another way to interpret the NPT. The NPT negotiators contemplated that safeguards had more than a merely formal role to play. If that role cannot be effectively fulfilled with respect to particular assistance or activities, then perhaps, in the presence of other factors (e.g., risk or lack of economic viability), such forms of assistance or activities should fall within the Treaty's prohibitions.

The stated "exclusive" purpose of the safeguards system provided for in Article III is for "*verification* of the fulfillment of [a party's] obligations assured under this Treaty with a view to *preventing* diversion of nuclear energy from peaceful purposes. . . ."[29] As ACDA Deputy Director Fisher stated to the ENDC in January of 1968, "[T]he safeguards article . . . will *verify* important treaty obligations and thereby serve as an important instrument for reducing tensions and increasing trust."[30] Likewise, in describing the Treaty to the UN General Assembly, Ambassador Arthur Goldberg emphasized in April 1968 that "safeguards . . . have but one function: to verify the treaty obligation that nuclear material shall not be diverted to nuclear weapons. . . ."[31] If the verification function cannot be performed, the legitimacy of the particular form of assistance or activity to which the safeguards cannot be effectively applied must become dubious.

During the course of congressional deliberations on the NPT, it was made clear that, in evaluating the Treaty, congressional assumptions related to the future, not the present, effectiveness of safeguards. Critics of the NPT made much of the absence of effective safeguards in 1968 and 1969. Thus, for example, Congressman Craig Hosmer stated, "Neither the IAEA [International Atomic Energy Agency] nor anyone else has the remotest notion what constitutes a normal loss of uranium or plutonium in the peaceful industrial process. Therefore, there is not the slightest possibility of any inspectors spotting illegal diversions because they can't even be told when their suspicion should be aroused."[32] Supporters of the NPT responded to such criticisms by stating essentially that the United States had "confidence that the IAEA, by building upon its solid, though modest, foundation of experience in the field of safeguards, will be able to carry out the increased responsibilities assigned to it by the treaty."[33] Even the strongest supporters of the NPT recognized, however, that for the system to work, safeguards would have to be improved.[34] The Senate Foreign Relations Committee, which produced two reports on the Treaty,[35] while expressing doubts about the current effectiveness of safeguards, sided with the optimists and opted for the assumption that safeguards would work in the future. Thus, the Committee's reports, after acknowledging the arguments concerning the pros and cons of the IAEA safeguards system in 1968 and 1969, stated:

> Admittedly, the implementation of the treaty raises uncertainties. The reliability and thereby the credibility of international safeguards systems is still to be determined. No completely satisfactory answer was given the committee on the effectiveness of the safeguards systems envisioned under the treaty. Moreover, the committee was not given a completely satisfactory answer as to what the signatory nations will do if the International Atomic Energy Agency fails to work out mutually satisfactory agreements with individual states or associations of States within the time prescribed by the treaty. The committee hopes that the optimism of the administration will be borne out and

that successful agreements with the IAEA will be concluded without difficulty or delay. Nevertheless, the committee notes that the Euratom States have unanimously agreed that the treaty will only be ratified after a satisfactory verification agreement has been reached between Euratom and the IAEA.

The committee is fully aware of the potential problems in the safeguards field. But it is equally convinced that when the possible problems in reaching satisfactory safeguards agreements are carefully weighed against the potential for a worldwide mandatory safeguards system, the comparison argues strongly in favor of the present language of the treaty.

The committee concludes that the treaty is in the best interest of the United States. The committee is mindful, however, that this treaty is certainly no cure-all for the problems of nuclear proliferation. The success of the agreement will depend on its wide acceptance particularly by those countries with the national capability to manufacture nuclear weapons. Success will also depend on the acceptance and credibility of the safeguards provisions.[36]

Finally, the Senate debates on the NPT confirm that ratification was premised upon assumptions with respect to future effectiveness of safeguards. Thus, for example, Senator Fulbright, Chairman of the Foreign Relations Committee, noted that the credibility and reliability of agency safeguards were still to be determined, but that he was satisfied that in the future the IAEA would be able to accomplish its tasks.[37] Likewise, other Treaty supporters, such as Senator Evan Bayh, expressed the view that, while the IAEA might have shortcomings in 1969, these "could be remedied by appropriate increases in manpower, funding and applied research."[38]

Given the serious questions which exist concerning the ability to safeguard effectively now or in the foreseeable future certain forms of assistance and activities, such as those related to reprocessing and plutonium recycling,[39] it is reasonable to conclude that the contemplated verification function of Article III cannot be fulfilled today. The IAEA's lack of authority to "prevent" diversions of weapons-usable plutonium, despite the provisions of Article III, para. 1, fortifies this conclusion. Therefore, if other factors, e.g., risk or lack of economic or technical justification, are also present, the presumption should again arise that the particular assistance or activity runs afoul of the prohibitions of Articles I and II.

Recognition of the Inappropriateness of Per Se Rules Concerning Permissible Assistance or Activities.

As noted above, there is some NPT negotiating history which might be interpreted as standing for the proposition that any safeguarded, "controlled fission" applications are per se outside the prohibitions of Articles I and 11.[40] Yet, consistent with its nonproliferation purposes, the NPT creates no per se rules with respect to acceptable uses and, indeed, allows a pragmatic interpretation of its prohibitions.

That this is the case was made clear during Senate consideration of the NPT. During the 1968 Senate hearings, Senator Case asked Secretary of State Rusk, "Where do you draw the line between a nuclear explosive device and something in which a non-nuclear nation may work in research and development under another provision of the treaty?"[41] Both Secretary of State Dean Rusk and ACDA Director William Foster initially indicated in response that work on anything which would lead to "an uncontrolled nuclear reaction available to non-nuclear weapon states" would be prohibited.[42] Mr. Foster then submitted for the record the following detailed response:

> The treaty articles in question are Article II, in which non-nuclear-weapon parties undertake "not to manufacture or otherwise acquire nuclear weapons or other nuclear explosive devices," and Article IV, which provides that nothing in the Treaty is to be interpreted as affecting the right of all Parties to the Treaty "to develop research, production and use of nuclear energy for peaceful purposes ... in conformity with Articles I and II of this Treaty." In the course of the negotiation of the Treaty, United States representatives were asked their views on what would constitute the "manufacture" of a nuclear weapon or other nuclear explosive device under Article II of the draft treaty. Our reply was as follows:

> While the general intent of this provision seems clear, and its application to cases such as those discussed below should represent little difficulty, the United States believes it is not possible at this time to formulate a comprehensive definition or interpretation. There are many hypothetical situations which might be imagined and it is doubtful that any general definition or interpretation, unrelated to specific fact situations could satisfactorily deal with all such situations.[43]

Some general observations can be made with respect to the question of whether or not a specific activity constitutes prohibited manufacture under the proposed treaty. For example, facts indicating that the purpose of a particular activity was the acquisition of a nuclear explosive device would tend to show noncompliance. (Thus, the construction of an experimental or prototype nuclear explosive device would be covered by the term "manufacture" as would be the production of components which could have relevance only to a nuclear explosive device.) Again, while the placing of a particular activity under safeguards would not, in and of itself, settle the question of whether that activity was in compliance with the treaty, it would of course be helpful in allaying any suspicion of noncompliance.

It may be useful to point out, for illustrative purposes, several activities which the United States would not consider to be per se violations of the prohibitions in Article II. Neither uranium enrichment nor the stockpiling of fissionable material in connection with a peaceful program would violate Article II so long as these activities were safeguarded under Article III. Also clearly permitted would be the development, under safeguards, of plutonium fuel power reactors, including research on the properties of metallic plutonium, nor would Article I contravene the development or use of fast breeder reactors under safeguards.[44]

At first blush, the Foster statement might be taken to indicate that any number of risky activities — e.g., "uranium enrichment," "stockpiling of fissionable material," "development . . . of plutonium fuel power reactors," or "research on the properties of metallic plutonium" — would be permissible as long as they were "safeguarded." However, the real thrust of the Foster statement is different. First, Foster notes that if "facts indicated that the purpose of a particular activity was the acquisition of a nuclear explosive device," then that activity may well be considered not in compliance with the Treaty. As noted above, where there is no reasonable economic or technical justification for an assertedly peaceful use, then a presumption should arise that the purpose is not legitimate under the NPT. At the same time, while there are repeated references to safeguards, Foster stresses that "the placing of a particular activity under safeguards would not, in and of itself, settle the question of whether the activity was in compliance with the Treaty." In other words, there is not a per se rule that application of safeguards alone means that Articles I and II do not apply. Finally, Foster's references to various activities which might be permissible under safeguards are preceded by the remark that the United States simply "would not consider [such activities] per se to be violations of the prohibitions in Article II."[45] The Foster statement thus plainly leaves open the possibility that such activities could be considered violations of the NPT's prohibitions, if, for example, they were not for a legitimate purpose or if there were evidence that safeguards could not be effectively applied.

CONCLUSION

Adrian Fisher, one of the chief U.S. NPT negotiators, stated several years after the Treaty's ratification that the NPT "does not require us to do something foolish."[46] Another way of putting it is that the NPT must not be read as requiring actions which may increase, rather than reduce, the risk of proliferation. At the same time, given the lessons learned from past proliferation—particularly India's development of a nuclear explosive device utilizing the facilities purportedly dedicated to its "peaceful" civilian programs—it would, in interpreting the NPT's restrictions, seem appropriate to err on the side of caution or restraint and apply such restrictions to facilities and materials which pose unacceptable proliferation risks with no reasonably discernible civilian nuclear power benefits now or in the foreseeable future.[47]

121

To accomplish this result, the distinction between permissible and impermissible activities must come down ultimately to quite pragmatic considerations. Activities must not be considered free from the Treaty's prohibitions just by virtue of being denominated "peaceful," "civilian," "power," or "research." The Treaty must be interpreted as viewing proliferation through something more than an "explosives lens." Rather, depending upon the facts and circumstances, assistance and activities relating to declared "peaceful," "civilian," "power," or "research" purposes may be subject to the NPT's restrictions if an evaluation of all the facts and circumstances, including such factors as economic or technical justification or effectiveness of safeguards, would indicate that the legitimacy of the assistance and/or activity is questionable. Such a pragmatic, rather than a formalistic reading of the Treaty, is most consistent with its overriding purpose of stemming the proliferation of nuclear weapons.

In the specific case of reprocessing and plutonium use — given the risks, economic and technical questions, and safeguards weaknesses associated therewith — it is appropriate to conclude today that assistance (and/or indigenous activities relating thereto) in non-weapon states should generally be exempt from the obligation to "facilitate" and the "right to participate" in Article IV of the NPT and should instead fall within the scope of the prohibitions of Articles I and II of the NPT.

ENDNOTES - CHAPTER 6

1. As one commentator has stated, "The prohibitive sense of the words 'any', 'whatsoever', and 'otherwise' allows no exception." Shaker, *The Nuclear Non-Proliferation Treaty*, 1980, p. 235.

2. Mason Willrich, The Treaty on Non-Proliferation of Nuclear Weapons: Nuclear Technology Confronts World Politics, *Yale Law Journal*, Vol. 77, No. 8, (July 1968), pp. 1447-1519, p. 1447.

3. See, e.g., *The Times* (London), March 23, 1978, reporting on the decision of Mr. Justice Parker in the British inquiry into reprocessing at the Windscale facility.

4. While the phrase "in conformity with" appears only in Article IV, para. I, it would also seem to modify the rights and obligations set forth in Article IV, para. 2. If the right to develop peaceful uses of nuclear energy is subject to Articles I and II, so, too, must be the obligation to "facilitate" and the "right to participate" in peaceful applications of atomic energy. Otherwise, Article IV, para. 2, would be in potential opposition to the restrictions of Articles I and II.

5. Willrich, *Non-Proliferation Treaty: Framework for Nuclear Arms Control* 127, 1969; Willrich, *The Treaty on Non-Proliferation of Nuclear Weapons*; Shaker, *The Nuclear Non-Proliferation Treaty*.

6. Likewise, as noted above, if there is a known or reasonably suspected intent to divert, Treaty prohibitions should come into play.

7. Wohlstetter *et al.*, *Towards a New Consensus on Nuclear Technology*, ACDA Report No. PH-78-04-832-13, July 6, 1979, pp. 34-35. The same report goes on to state:

> If, in fact, technological transfers can bring a "nonnuclear weapon state" within weeks, days or even hours of the ability to use a nuclear explosive, in the operational sense that "nonnuclear weapon state" will have nuclear weapons. The point is even more fundamental than the fact that effective safeguards mean timely warning. A necessary condition for having timely warning is that there be "a substantial elapsed time. But if there is no substantial elapsed time before a government may use nuclear weapons, in effect it has them. pp. 36-37.

8. Steiner, "Article IV and the 'Straightforward Bargain'"

(PAN Paper 78-832-08), in *ibid.*, Vol. II (Supporting Papers).

9. G. A. Res. 1665 (XVI), December 4, 1961.

10. G. A. Res. 2028 (XX) (Nov. 19, 1965), reprinted in ACDA, *Documents on Disarmament*, 1965, pp. 532-534.

11. There is. It should be noted that some contrary indication that the Treaty negotiators considered that power applications were quite distinguishable from weapons or explosives uses and therefore permissible, with little limitation, under the Treaty. Thus, ACDA Director Foster, in describing U.S. proposals to the First Committee of the General Assembly, on November 9, 1966, stated, "[P]eaceful applications of energy derived from controlled and sustained nuclear reactions – that is, reactions stopping far short of explosions, in the exact use of that term – have nothing to do with nuclear weapons. Development work relating to such controlled and sustained nuclear reactions would not – I repeat: would not – be affected by having the prohibitions of a non-pro-liferation treaty also encompass peaceful nuclear explosives." A/C.I/PV.1448, reprinted in ACDA, *Documents on Disarmament, 1966*, p. 721. Likewise, Secretary of State Rusk's characterization of the Treaty, adopted by the Senate Foreign Relations Commit-tee, as "dealing only with what is prohibited . . . [:] bombs and warheads . . . [and] other nuclear explosive devices. . . ." might be taken in the same vein. See Hearings on the Treaty on the Non-Proliferation of Nuclear-Weapons before the Senate Foreign Re-lations Committee, 90th Cong., 2d Sess. 5 (1968) (Statement of Secretary of State Rusk) (hereinafter 1968 Hearings); S. Ex. Rep. No. 9, 90th Cong., 2d Sess. (1968), reprinted in ACDA, *Documents on Disarmament, 1968*, pp. 642, 644 (hereinafter 1968 Senate Re-port); S. Ex. Rep. No. 91-9, 91st Cong., 1st Sess. (1969), reprinted in ACDA, *Documents on Disarmament, 1969*, pp. 78, 80 (hereinaf-ter 1969 Senate Report).

12. Eldon V. C. Greenberg, *The NPT and Plutonium*, Washing-ton, DC: Nuclear Control Institute, 1993, p. 18.

13. See e.g., Steiner, "Article IV and the ' Straightforward Bargain'" (PAN Paper 78-832-08), in Wohlstetter, *et al.*, *Towards a New Consensus on Nuclear Technology*, Vol. II (Supporting Papers) ACDA Report No. PH-78-04-832-33, July 6, 1979. See also Jensen,

Return From the Nuclear Brink: National Interest in the Nuclear Non-proliferation Treaty, 1974, pp. 1-2, 129, 133.

14. *Ibid.*

15. See Statement of the Representative of Mexico to the ENDC, September 17, 1967, ENDC/PV.331, reprinted in *ACDA, Documents on Disarmament*, 1967, pp. 395, 397-398. For a general discussion of this proposed amendment, see Willrich, *Non ·Proliferation Treaty: Framework for Nuclear Arms Control*, 1969, pp. 131-132.

16. See Spanish Memorandum to the ENDC Co-Chairmen, February 8, 1968, ENDC/PV.361, reprinted in *ACDA, Documents on Disarmament*, 1968, pp. 39-40.

17. Steiner, "Article IV and the 'Straightforward Bargain'" (PAN Paper 78-832-08), in Wohlstetter, *et al.*, *Towards a New Consensus on Nuclear Technology*, Vol. II (Supporting Papers) (ACDA Report No. PH-78-04-832-33), July 6, 1979.

18. *Ibid.*

19. Greenberg, p. 7.

20. E.g., Statement of ACDA Deputy Director Fisher to the ENDC, July 28, 1966, ENDC/PV.277, reprinted in *ACDA, Documents on Disarmament*, 1966, pp. 483-485.

21. G.A.Res. 2373 (XXII), June 12, 1968, reprinted in *ACDA, Documents on Disarmament*, 1968, pp. 431-432.

22. In its discussion of the history of the NPT, this memorandum occasionally relies upon the record of consideration of the Treaty by the U.S. Senate in 1968 and 1969. While in some sense this is *post facto* legislative history, coming after completion of the negotiations, nonetheless the comments made on the Treaty during Senate deliberations generally reflect interpretations reached by the negotiating parties and are most helpful in illuminating the intent of the Treaty.

23. 1968 Hearings, pp. 98, 120.

24. *Ibid.*, p. 212 (Statement of Mason Willrich).

25. Greenberg, pp. 7-11.

26. It is, of course, sometimes argued that, even if economic justification is lacking, reprocessing and plutonium use can be rationalized on a civilian basis as necessary to achieve "energy independence" or "energy security" or as a tool to manage nuclear waste. See Hearings before the Subcommittees on Arms Control International Security and Scientific Affairs and on International Economic Policy and Trade of the House Foreign Affairs Committee on Plutonium Use Policy, 99th Cong., 1st Sess., July 24, 1985, Statement of Ambassador-At-Large Richard T. Kennedy. However, the former ground is far too subjective a benchmark upon which to rely in determining what constitutes permissible assistance or activities under the NPT—virtually anything can be justified in the name of "energy independence"—while the latter ground has been repeatedly shown to be without technical merit. See Feiveson and von Hippel, "Nuclear Energy Without Reprocessing," Paper presented at the Soviet-U.S. Symposium. on Energy Conservation, Institute for High Temperatures," Soviet Academy of Sciences, Moscow, June 6, 1985.

27. There is, it should be noted, some negotiating history to the effect that the NPT simply establishes a bright line between safeguarded and unsafeguarded activities and, "if the activity is safeguarded and ostensibly for peaceful purposes," then it is "in conformity with" Articles I and II. Thus, the Dutch Representative to the General Assembly stated in May 1968:

> My delegation interprets article I of the draft treaty to mean that assistance by supplying knowledge, materials and equipment cannot be denied to non-nuclear-weapon States until it is clearly established that such assistance will be used for the manufacture of nuclear weapons or other nuclear devices. In other words, in all cases where the recipient parties to the Treaty have conformed with the provisions of Article III, there should be a clear presumption that the assistance rendered will not be used for the manufacture of nuclear weapons and other explosive devices.

A/C.1/PV.1561, reprinted in ACDA, *Documents on Disarmament*, 1968, pp. 295-296. The Dutch position was endorsed by the Belgians and Luxembourgers. *Ibid*. Similarly, the Australians emphasized that "knowledge, materials and equipment [cannot] be denied . . . until it is clearly established that such activity or supply will be used for the manufacture of nuclear weapons or other nuclear explosive devices." Statement by the Australian Representative to the General Assembly, May 17, 1968, A/C.1/PV.1570, reprinted in ACDA, *Documents on Disarmament*, 1968, pp. 362-366. In fact, the U.S. Ambassador to the UN, Arthur Goldberg, stressed to the General Assembly that virtually nothing could be denied under the Treaty, unless it was clearly for weapons purposes:

> The whole field of nuclear science associated with electric power production is accessible now, and will become more accessible under the Treaty, to all who seek to exploit it. This includes not only the present generation of nuclear power reactors, but also that advanced technology, which is still developing, of fast breeder power reactors which, in producing energy, also produce more fissionable material than they consume.

Statement of Arthur Goldberg to the First Committee of the General Assembly, May 15, 1968, A/C.1/PV.1568, reprinted in ACDA, *Documents on Disarmament*, 1968, pp. 336, 344.

28. Willrich, *The Treaty on Non-Proliferation of Nuclear Weapons: Nuclear Technology Confronts World Politics*. See also Shaker, *The Nuclear Non-Proliferation Treaty*. Even under this formulation, it might be noted, where there is assistance to a non-NPT party in the absence of full-scope safeguards, facility-specific safeguards alone would not be enough to establish definitively a peaceful purpose.

29. NPT, Article III, para. 1 (emphasis added).

30. 77 ENDC/PV.357, reprinted in ACDA, *Documents in Disarmament*, 1968, pp. 11, 14 (emphasis added).

31. Statement of Ambassador Goldberg to the General Assembly, April 26, 1968, A/C.1/PV.1556, reprinted in ACDA, *Doc-*

uments on Disarmament, 1968, pp. 221,226.

32. 1968 Hearings, p. 164.

33. Statement of Glenn Seaborg, Chairman, Atomic Energy Commission, in Hearings on the Treaty on the Non-Proliferation of Nuclear Weapons before the Senate Foreign Relations Committee, 9lst Cong., 1st Sess. 313, 1969.

34. E.g., Statement of Glenn Seaborg in 1968 Hearings, pp. 99-100. See also Statement of Congressman Chet Holifeld, in *ibid.*, p. 155, "[S]afeguards have not as yet been developed to the point that I am satisfied."

35. There are two Senate reports on the NPT because, while the Senate Foreign Relations Committee approved the Treaty in 1968, the 90th Congress did not act upon it before its term expired. Thus, when the 91st Congress convened in 1969, it was necessary for the Committee to consider the NPT once again.

36. 1968 Senate Report, reprinted in ACDA, *Documents on Disarmament*, 1968, pp. 642, 656 (emphasis added). See also 1969 Senate Report. reprinted in ACDA, *Documents on Disarmament*, 1969, pp. 78, 95-96.

37. 115 Cong. Rec. 5739, March 10, 1969.

38. 115 Cong. Rec. 6207-6208, March 12, 1969.

39. Greenberg, pp. 11-13.

40. *Ibid.*, pp. 17, 25, 50.

41. 1968 Hearings, p. 38.

42. *Ibid.*, p. 39.

43. *Ibid.*

44. *Ibid.*

45. *Ibid.*

46. See Hearings on S.1439 before the Senate Committee on Government Operations, 94th Cong., 2d Sess. 141, 1976.

47. Such risks include not only "overt proliferation" by a nation determined to exercise a weapons option, but "latent proliferation" by a nation with no weapons intent today but which, through the accumulation of large stocks of separated plutonium, may acquire the means rapidly to manufacture weapons in the future in a time of regional or global crisis.

CHAPTER 7

SPREADING THE BOMB
WITHOUT QUITE BREAKING THE RULES (1976)*

Albert Wohlstetter

The basic problem in limiting the spread of nuclear weapons is that in the next 10 years or so, many countries, including many agreeing not to make bombs, can come within hours of a bomb without plainly violating their agreement—without "diverting" special nuclear material and, therefore, without any possibility of being curbed by "safeguards" designed to verify whether material has or has not been diverted.

This development would lower the political and economic price of nuclear weapons and at the same time greatly increase the incentives to acquire them. The legal acquisition of concentrated fissile material by regional powers will increase the desire of regional adversaries to do the same. Such a development is encouraged by the incoherence and carelessness of the policies of the United States and other nuclear exporters which allow material easily turned into bombs by government nuclear laboratories to be used or produced during the course of civilian research or the generation of electricity.

The problem in the present export rules can be made vivid by a comparison. Under these rules a nonweapon

---

*Originally published in *Foreign Policy*, Vol. 25, Winter 1976, pp. 88-94.

state can come closer to explosing a plutonium weapon today without violating an agreement not to make a bomb than the United States was in the spring of 1947, when the world considered us not only a nuclear power, but *the* nuclear power. The plutonium bombs of the time were primitive in design and crated in knockdown form. The very bulky high explosives had to be glued together piece by piece with slow-drying adhesives to form an implosion system. The fusing and wiring circuits were much more primitive than those commercially available today, and even a skilled team would have required several days to put a weapon together. In the spring of 1947, moreover, we had no skilled teams. Yet some believe our nuclear force to have been the main obstacle to an adversary reaching the English Channel, and others believe it to have been the backup for "atomic diplomacy." It should make suppliers thoughtful that their nuclear exports might bring a no-weapon state closer to exploding a plutonium bomb today than the United States was in 1947.

THE INCOHERENCE OF CURRENT U.S. POLICIES

From the outset of the nuclear age, it has been clear that designing a bomb and getting the nonnuclear components are much easier than getting fissile material in high enough concentration for an explosive. Research on bomb design and testing of nonnuclear bomb components are not prevented by agreements on nuclear cooperation, and can proceed in parallel with the accumulation of fissile material. Fissile uranium (in particular, uranium-235) or fissile plutonium (especially plutonium-239) concentrated enough to need no isotope separation[1], and only a modest amount of chemical separation are then the main hard steps on the way to a nuclear bomb.

The fresh fuel used in the present generation of power reactors is either natural uranium, which is almost all uranium-238 with less than 1 percent of the fissile isotope uranium-235, or low enriched uranium with only 3 to 4 percent of uranium-235. Such fresh fuel with less than 20 percent of uranium-235 cannot be used in an explosive without isotopic separation. But the irradiated or "spent" uranium fuel contains, along with other by-products, significant quantities of plutonium which result from the absorption of neutrons by the uranium-238. The plutonium so generated along with electricity has upward of 70 percent of the fissile isotopes of plutonium and requires no isotopic, but only chemical separation to be used in an explosive. Some "critical experiments" use large amounts of plutonium and uranium in metal form needing little further change.

To avoid putting fissile, that is, readily fissionable, material into the hands of no-weapon states, we deny licenses on facilities for isotope separation which could produce highly enriched uranium. So also on reprocessing plants for chemically separating plutonium. In the nuclear suppliers group, according to news accounts, we argue in principle against any other country making such exports even under International Atomic Energy Agency (IAEA) safeguards. While we so far have not won on the general principle, we have successfully opposed French sales of reprocessing plants to Taiwan and South Korea. And though not successful in our opposition, we say we objected to the German sale of enrichment and reprocessing plants to Brazil, as well as to the French sale of a reprocessing plant to Pakistan. We used to refuse to license the export of uranium enriched to more than 20 percent in uranium-235, whatever the inspection arrangements. All of this recognizes, sometimes explicitly, that safeguards imply timely warning and that material that is weeks, days, or hours from incorporation in a bomb therefore cannot be effectively safeguarded.

On the other hand, we have for some time exported to no-weapon states, for use in research, both separated plutonium and highly enriched uranium, which bring them closer to the bomb than do the facilities for separating such material. For example, from mid-1968 to spring of 1976, we exported 697 kilograms of highly enriched uranium and 104 kilograms of separated plutonium to Japan and 2,710 kilograms of highly enriched uranium and 349 kilograms of separated plutonium to the Federal Republic of Germany.

And we continue to offer nuclear assistance to countries that plan to acquire fissile material, and even to a country like India which has already detonated a nuclear explosive in defiance of explicit Canadian and U.S. statements over the past decade that no nuclear explosive is exclusively peaceful within the meaning or their agreements on nuclear cooperation. We say that that is what our agreements have always meant (and it is indeed their commonsense implication),[2] and we try to make this obvious meaning explicit in new agreements. Nonetheless, for old agreements we content ourselves with statements of U.S. unilateral understandings on this subject, and continue nuclear exports to countries that have refused to endorse our unilateral interpretation.[3]

The State Department assures the Congress that such unilateral understanding is binding enough, but after the Indians made a nuclear explosive using Canadian and U.S. peaceful assistance, we denied that the Indians had violated anything but the Canadian unilateral understanding and went through extraordinary contortions to hide the fact that they had used U.S. heavy water. We raised no objections when the French sold a reprocessing plant to Japan. Indeed, in 1972, before that sale, we had authorized U.S. companies to sell a reprocessing plant to Japan under stricter safeguards than the Japanese were willing to accept, but apparently no stricter than those they actually accepted later for the French sale.

Our policies at that time did not recognize, as they do now, that the sale of reprocessing plants is mistaken even if safeguarded. The South Koreans observe that we treat Japan differently from them when it comes to reprocessing. The French comment sardonically that we make a great fuss about the sale of a reprocessing plant to Pakistan, even though our representative to the IAEA approved the Agreement between Pakistan, France, and the IAEA on the transfer and safeguarding of that plant. And apparently not all American officials, and evidently not the most important ones, opposed the West German sale to Brazil in tones audible at the highest level of the German government. Chancellor Schmidt told the press in June 1975, that he regretted criticism by U.S. journalists and politicians but that "he knew of no criticism by the U.S. government."

We get then the worst of both worlds: In the end we refused to supply reprocessing or enrichment facilities to the Brazilians, knowing that though nominally civilian, such facilities could bring Brazil close to a bomb. But because we never formulated a coherent policy explaining that, it was easy for the Federal Republic to tell itself that we were simply sore losers in

135

a business deal and that clinching the deal by giving the Brazilians a "sweetener" in the form of the principal ingredient of a nuclear explosive was perfectly all right.

Our agreements on nuclear cooperation abound in clauses that presume that the importing country will separate and recycle plutonium and that stocks of plutonium may in principle be effectively safeguarded. Moreover, we have talked of separating and recycling plutonium as if they were essential to the future of nuclear power both here and abroad, and have allowed the myth to persist that power-reactor plutonium cannot be used as an explosive. We have recently made the recycling of plutonium a key initiative in our energy conservation program. The Nuclear Regulatory Commission (NRC) has only recently shown signs of considering the international consequences of recycling to be a factor in the U.S. decision to license it domestically. As for uranium, sometime in the 1960s our attention wandered, and we began to ship highly enriched uranium to no-weapon countries. We appear to have shipped some five tons overseas--perhaps 300 bombs worth of readily fissionable material. Our confusion has been durable and bipartisan.

HOW WE GOT INTO THIS FIX

The extensive fundamental overlap of the paths to nuclear explosives and to civilian uses of nuclear energy has been recognized since the mid-1940s.[4] The "heart of the problem" of international control, according to Robert Oppenheimer, was "the close technical parallelism and interrelation of the peaceful and the military applications of atomic energy." We have almost from the start said that the military and civilian atoms were substantially identical yet, paradoxically, that we wanted to stop one and to promote the other. The paradox was present in the Truman-Atlee-King Declaration of October 1945, and we made our most valiant effort to reconcile these opposing aims in the Acheson-Lilienthal Report and the Baruch Plan of 1946.

The Acheson-Lilienthal Report tried to resolve the dilemma by proposing to "denature" plutonium: that is, to spoil it as an explosive. This was to be accomplished by leaving the fuel to be irradiated in the reactors long enough so that the fissile isotope, plutonium-239, generated in the uranium fuel rods would in turn generate a large portion of higher isotopes of plutonium and, in particular, a large fraction of plutonium-240, which had serious drawbacks from the standpoint of the art of weapons design of the time. The idea had been advanced in March 1945 by Leo Szilard quite tentatively. (The troubles with plutonium-240 had been discovered only in the summer of 1944.) The Franck Report proposed denaturing less cautiously in June 1945.

Discussion was necessarily muted and limited by the requirements of secrecy, by the bounds of the current state of the art, and by the limitations of current understanding of that state of the art. The initial report was predicated on the belief that denaturing would interpose the high barrier of isotopic separation between the use of plutonium for civil and military ends. This, given the elaborate mechanism of international control called for in the Acheson-Lilienthal Report, would assure some 2 to 3 years warning. The report itself exhibited some uncertainty and ambivalence[5] about the hope for denaturing, and the hope was almost immediately modified by a committee of distinguished Manhattan Project scientists to suggest that such plutonium could be used in a weapon, but would be very much less effective.[6] Even the qualifications immediately introduced, we now know, were not strong enough. Yet the initial hope for denaturing has generated a long and inconsistent trail[7] of statements which still have their effect in encouraging the belief that plutonium left in the reactor long enough to become contaminated with 20 to 30 percent of the plutonium-240 or plutonium-242 would be unusable or, at any rate, extremely ineffective when used in a nuclear explosive. Since power reactors operated "normally" were expected for reasons of economics to achieve maximum "burnup" of fuel by leaving the fuel rods in the reactor long enough to so contaminate the rods, a kind of denaturing was hoped for as a result of standard procedures. However, this hope turned out to be a slender reed.

The Baruch Plan would have given sovereign states control only of safe civilian activities. They would have gotten all of their fissile material in denatured form, separated from spent fuel in plants owned by an international authority. That authority was to have monopoly of all dangerous activities; that is, all those that could quickly be turned to the manufacture of explosives. The plan rejected as unworkable any reliance on inspection rather than on ownership and control of dangerous activities.

The Soviets turned down the Baruch Plan. Since then we have come to rely on exactly the scheme regarded as unworkable by the authors of the Acheson-Lilienthal Report and the Baruch Plan. We rely in essence only on accounting and inspection of dangerous activities in no-weapon states. We are encouraged to do so by remnants of the belief that plutonium from a

138

power reactor is not very dangerous.

But why was it important that plutonium be made safe for civilian use? The short answer is that we were powerfully impelled after the horrors of Hiroshima to believe that nuclear energy had a constructive use in electric power as spectacular as its use in military destruction. And we believed, on the basis of our initial understanding of the scarcity of uranium, that plutonium was essential to the future of nuclear electric power. The known reserves of natural uranium in the late 1940s were a mere 2,000 short tons. Since natural uranium contains only a tiny fraction of the fissile isotope, uranium-235, converting the more abundant uranium-238, which is not itself fissile, into fissile plutonium seemed a logical way to extend the scarce supply of fissile material for electric power. (From the first, we had contemplated using plutonium not only in breeders, but also in present day reactors.)

And the natural impulse to find civilian use for this enormous force led statesmen frequently to talk as if the civilian use were a substitute for the military one: The more we used atoms for peace, the less we would use them for war. We subsidized the spread of civilian nuclear technology not simply in the hope for spectacular economic benefits, but as if it were a decisive measure of nuclear disarmament. We dispersed "research" reactors in the Third World as a substitute for sending a symbolic "atomic peace ship" around the world rather than as a matter of hard economics for development, and were embarrassed to find that we had made it a matter of international prestige to have a research reactor, even for countries that had no trained personnel to use it. We made concessionary loans for power reactors almost as tenuously based in economics, and we did this as if they were necessarily advancing the cause of peace. Oppenheimer was quite right in saying that, unlike the Acheson-Lilienthal Report or the Baruch Plan, the Atoms for Peace program had no "firm connection with atomic disarmament" and that its bearing on the prospect of nuclear war was "allusive and sentimental" rather than "substantive and functional." This symbolic use of atomic energy antedated the Atoms for Peace program and relates to our earliest habits of talking about promoting the peaceful uses of the atom as if they would automatically displace the military use.

However, it can be said of the pioneers of the nuclear age that though they sometimes talked as if there were a dichotomy, they also saw that the heart of the problem was a large overlap between civilian and military applications of nuclear energy, and they grasped very firmly the point that keeping the two sorts of activities separate means more than simply detecting a violation of an agreement. It means early detection of the approach by a government toward the making of a bomb in time for other governments to do something about it. This principle has been reaffirmed recently by the president, by the assistant administrator for national security of the Energy Research and Development Administration (ERDA), and by the inspector general of the IAEA. But, in practice, the point has a way of getting lost in the middle reaches of both national and international bureaucracies.

It was only to be expected that over 2 decades of Atoms for Peace programs would result in the formation of large groups of professionals in industry, in nuclear engineering departments of universities throughout the world, in governments, and in regional and international agencies. All of these groups have a strong interest in the "enlargement and acceleration" of the use of nuclear energy and a much milder concern with such long-term problems as the disposal of radioactive waste or the spread of nuclear explosives. They tend to identify any restraints to control the dangers of proliferation as simply—dread word—"antinuclear." The hostility has been worsened by some of the extremists of the environmentalist movement, who seem dedicated to stopping and dismantling all civilian nuclear power rather than controlling its dangers and encouraging the development of safe forms of nuclear and nonnuclear energy. The nuclear energy faction inside large industrial corporations in turn feels embattled by any attempt at further restriction, precisely because reactor manufacture has so far involved great business losses in spite of subsidy. The nuclear debate degenerates into a dog fight between extremes, with the accusations by Squeaky Fromme and the Manson Family about a nuclear power conspiracy almost mirrored in the dark hints by the beleaguered industrial bureaucracy.

For example, delegates to a meeting in Vienna, Austria, last spring of the International Union of Producers and Distributors of Electrical Energy suggested that the holdups in separating plutonium to "close" the fuel cycle are due to "subversive elements" at work among groups opposing nuclear development.[8] At a conference in Düsseldorf, Germany, earlier that week the chief executive of VEBA, a leading West German energy concern, indicated that the nuclear opposition was heavily backed with cash "from across the border."[9] But, from the standpoint of reactor manufacturers whose profits are all still in the future, less sales promotion and a more sober look at the social and even the entrepreneurial risks would be salutary for the industry itself. Treating as the enemy all doubters of nuclear market and cost-benefit studies encourages badly timed investments and the present industry troubles.

However we got into our present fix, we still have to ask what the fix portends for the future of proliferation, if we do nothing.

IS THE SPREAD LIKELY?

Past predictions of immediate spread have, for the most part, been false alarms. So, immediately after the war, scientists who had figured in the Manhattan Project predicted that, unless there were very drastic international controls, bombs would spread rapidly. Harold Urey forecast a half dozen countries entering the nuclear club in as few as 5 years. Irving Langmuir predicted that Russia would get nuclear weapons very quickly, but would be beaten in the race by Canada and England. And the general public reflected this pessimism. Intelligence estimates in 1948 were more hopeful (excessively so in predicting when the Soviet Union would get the bomb), but official predictions have had their ups and downs.

A second flurry of alarm came in the late 1950s as the military potential of the Atoms for Peace programs began to be visible. Officials predicted, for example, that not only Canada and Sweden would get nuclear weapons in the early 1960s but, unless there were a multilateral nuclear force, West Germany would too. Perhaps the best known study done then was by the American Academy of Arts and Sciences and the National Planning Association (NPA): it suggested that without international control there might be as many as 10 new nuclear powers in 5 years. This study was summed up somewhat incautiously by C. P. Snow's famous statement in 1960 that all physical scientists ". . . *know* that for a dozen or more states, it will only take perhaps 6 years, perhaps less" to acquire fission and fusion bombs. Nothing of the kind happened. By comparison with these early alarms, the actual increase in the number of countries testing nuclear explosives has been very slow. Three additional countries tested at intervals of 8, 4, and 10 years in the 22 years following the British nuclear explosion.

There is a lesson to be drawn from a close examination of these past apocalyptic predictions. They assumed essentially that, in the absence of some quite extreme and politically implausible change in circumstance, countries that could get nuclear weapons would do so, and would do so more or less in the order of their technical and industrial competence. The incentives and drawbacks for proceeding with a nuclear weapons program were in all essentials neglected. However, political will is the key, rather than mere competence. The demand for weapons was softened by a system of working alliances and explicit or implicit guarantees that applied to most of the then likely prospects for an independent nuclear capability. The price and risks in undertaking a nuclear weapons program were also higher than most of the prophets had recognized. It is important today, as then, to look soberly at incentives and disincentives for the spread and how they might be affected. We should not easily assume inevitability.

Some students of proliferation, however, observe that three countries tested in the first decade, two in the second, one in the third, and are made excessively cheery by the diminishing sequence. But changes are taking place beneath the placid surface, which is presently undisturbed by new countries testing weapons.

These changes are much less cheering. Under the present rules, civilian nuclear energy programs now under way assure that many new countries will have traveled a long distance down the path leading to a nuclear weapons capability. The distance remaining will be shorter, less arduous, and much more rapidly covered. It need take only a smaller impulse to carry them the rest of the way. There is a kind of Damoclean overhang of countries increasingly near the edge of making bombs.

For convenience, distinguish three conditions in which plutonium might be found in the course of generating nuclear electric power. The first is the accumulation of plutonium in irradiated or "spent" uranium fuel which is now a normal by-product of any operation of our current reactors. The second condition, much closer to being usable in a nuclear weapon, would be that of plutonium in fresh mixed plutonium and uranium oxide fuel rods. Even if a country did not separate plutonium or manufacture such mixed oxide fuel rods itself, it could have plutonium in this second form in reloads of mixed oxide fuel at the input end of reactors. Plutonium in the third condition would be found already separated in the form of plutonium dioxide or plutonium nitrate. In this form, it could be found at the output end of a separation plant or at the input end and in stocks-in-process in facilities that manufacture mixed plutonium and uranium fuel rods. Plutonium in these three conditions comes successively closer to a nuclear explosive. The last two conditions need occur only if plutonium recycling becomes general.

At present, our agreements on cooperation in general leave title to the spent fuel and all its products in the importing country. For governments accumulating the spent fuel, the barrier to obtaining a high enough concentration of fissile plutonium will be the need to separate the plutonium chemically. This is a less formidable obstacle than isotopic separation, the facility for which costs billions of dollars using present techniques and would take years to construct. Nonetheless, chemical separation is a substantial barrier and perhaps the most important one remaining, if nuclear suppliers do not secure the return of spent fuel. Getting spent fuel is a considerable stride along the road to nuclear weapons, compared to the position of the weapon states which started from scratch. But spent fuel still needs to be reprocessed, and that involves delay and then remote manipulation of extremely toxic, radioactive substances, facilities with six or seven feet for shielding, lead glass windows, etc. Tons of spent fuel must be handled to produce kilograms of plutonium.

At the other extreme is the plutonium that would be stored at the output or "back" end of reprocessing plants and at the input or "front" end of plants fabricating plutonium or "mixed oxide" fuel. Such plutonium in the form of plutonium dioxide or plutonium nitrate could be converted to plutonium metal using generally known methods and without remote handling equipment or extensive shielding and the like, but only a glove box. It should take no more than a week in a facility covering 3,600 square feet and costing about $1,400,000.

Plutonium would also be found, if it is recycled, in fresh unirradiated fuel rods at the input end of the reactor. Extracting plutonium from such mixed oxide fuel would be very much easier than taking it out of the irradiated spent uranium fuel. Plutonium is more concentrated in the mixed oxide fuel rods (4.5 percent compared to .7 percent). Unlike irradiated fuel, it is not highly radioactive and would require no delay, no "hot cells" with heavy shielding, no remote manipulation, and no removal of fission products. A facility for separating 5 kilograms per day and converting it to plutonium nitrate might exist in a 1,400 square foot laboratory and might cost $235,000. This is trivial by comparison with the cost of a facility for deriving comparable quantities of plutonium nitrate from the spent uranium fuel. The latter might cost from $75 million to $100 million. The difference is important, because today many proposals would ban separating plutonium in no-weapon states, but not recycling it in mixed plutonium and uranium fuel. So, for example, early drafts of U.S. agreements of cooperation with Egypt and Israel.

We can measure the advance toward the ability to manufacture nuclear explosives implicit in recent civilian nuclear electric programs, as of 1975, by showing first the number of countries, including the present weapon states, that would have enough separable but possibly unseparated plutonium for a few bombs between now and 1985. Second, the large number of countries with various quantities of plutonium in fresh reloads of unirradiated plutonium fuel if plutonium recycling should become general, even if these countries do not themselves separate plutonium or manufacture plutonium fuel rods. Third, the number of countries that have planned to have a capability to separate that much plutonium by 1985. The results of these three sets of calculations are displayed respectively in Figure 1, Table 1, and Figure 2.

Figure 1
The overhang of countries with enough separable plutonium for primitive or small military forces
Vertical scale: number of countries

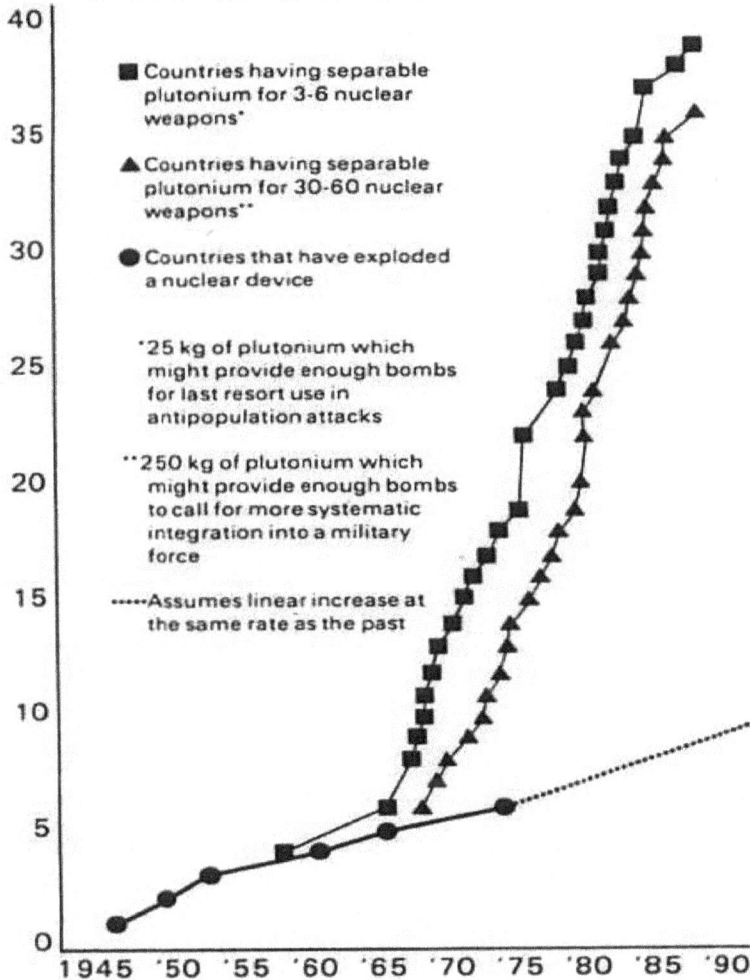

■ Countries having separable plutonium for 3-6 nuclear weapons*

▲ Countries having separable plutonium for 30-60 nuclear weapons**

● Countries that have exploded a nuclear device

*25 kg of plutonium which might provide enough bombs for last resort use in antipopulation attacks

**250 kg of plutonium which might provide enough bombs to call for more systematic integration into a military force

·····Assumes linear increase at the same rate as the past

147

Table 1
Plutonium Available from Reloads of Mixed Plutonium and Uranium Oxide (MOX) Fuel in the Early 1990s*

	kg of Pu[a] (Plutonium)	Number of Bombs' Worth[b]
Austria	400	46
Belgium	2,800	325
Brazil	500	58
West Germany	11,700	1,357
India[c]	360	42
Iran	3,200	371
Italy	2,100	244
Japan	9,000	1,044
South Korea	900	104
Mexico	800	93
Netherlands	400	46
Philippines	1,000	116
Spain	5,600	650
Sweden	4,800	557
Switzerland	3,200	371
Taiwan	3,200	371
Yugoslavia	500	58
Egypt	700	81

* *Using only indigenously produced plutonium and assuming that one reload is always kept at each reactor. Any country without its own MOX fuel fabrication facilities could justify stocking one reload. A single MOX reload might contain 350-900 kg of plutonium (40 to 104 bombs worth). Countries that fabricate MOX fuel would have still more plutonium available in process.*

[a] *Assuming 580 kg per 1,000 megawatt boiling water reactor reload and 770 kg per 1,000 megawatt pressurized water reactor reload, linear scaling for other reactor sizes. See U.S. Atomic Energy Commission, Generic Environmental Statement Mixed Oxide Fuel (GESMO), Vol. III, August 1974, p. IV C-65.*

[b] *8.62 kg Pu per bomb assuming 5kg fissile Pu/bomb and assuming MOX Pu is 58 per cent fissile Pu.*

[c] *The figures for India are the result of direct calculation.*

The first thing to be said about the numbers in these charts is that they are very large. Chemical separation of plutonium and the enrichment of uranium are civilian activities which have long been regarded as "normal," if not yet operational, parts of the nuclear electric fuel cycle. They may sometimes and in some places be discouraged by various ad hoc national policies, but they have not been subject to a clear-cut international or universal national prohibition by supplier countries. The problem of inhibiting or reducing the size of this burgeoning capacity is not merely then a matter of an improved watch, to see that clearly agreed prohibited line is not crossed. Among other things it would involve defining and moving such a clearly agreed boundary to preclude activities which cannot provide adequate warning. And for whatever dangerous activities remain on the permissible side of the agreed boundary, we need to elaborate a consistent national policy to discourage them and encourage other safer alternatives.

The second thing to be said is that this large growth is not inevitable. It presumes the carrying through of plans, negotiations, and constructions not yet firmly committed; some, like the Korean and Taiwan separation plants, have had setbacks. The growth, moreover, is open to further influence, a subject for the elaboration of policy of supplier as well as recipient governments. But American influence on the policies of various importing and exporting countries is limited by the confusion and arbitrariness of our policy on access to fissile material. Figures 1 and 2 and Table 1 are not unconditional forecasts, but indications of what may happen if conditions are not altered. The gist of these Figures is that, under the present rules of the game, any of a very large number of countries may take these further long strides toward the production of nuclear weapons in the next 10 years or so without violating the rules—at least no vigorously formulated, agreed-on rules.

These paths toward producing weapons are in addition to paths which exploit the weakness of sanctions against breaking the Treaty on Non-Proliferation of Nuclear Weapons (NPT) or bilateral rules, and in addition to paths open to those governments which have not ratified the NPT. Extending the NPT to more countries or increasing the efficiency of "safeguards" or physical security measures would not, therefore, block these paths. The recent interest in measures against diversion, while useful in itself, distracts attention from the steady spread of production capacities within the rules.

Some part of the stocks of fissile material might always be diverted within the limits of error of material unaccounted for by any inspection system. In the future, when these stocks are very large, diverting even a small percentage would yield sizable absolute amounts. This tends therefore to be the focus of most attention. Yet it is much less important than the possibility of piling up significant stocks of fissile material legally, without diversion, for use later in explosives.

I have distinguished for convenience four kinds of nuclear explosive capacity. The first is the sort of capacity which has been much in the public eye in the last year or two, due especially to the efforts of Dr. Theodore Taylor to make clear its dangers. It would consist in the manufacture of a crude device derived from stolen fissile material, perhaps not using plutonium metal, but plutonium dioxide powder, yielding as little as 10 or 100 tons of energy, and designed for terrorist use by some nongovernmental group, or possibly even a single individual. It might use poorly separated material and be dangerous not merely if exploded in anger, but to store and handle.

The second capacity would rely on a few explosives, perhaps implosion weapons in the kiloton (kt) or greater range. They might be used by governments as a desperate last resort threat against populations (or transferred by some governments to terrorists). The third capacity I have taken arbitrarily as consisting in perhaps 50 such devices, enough to call for plans to incorporate them into a military force. The fourth would be much more sophisticated. It is the kind that an industrial power like Japan might contemplate, if it made the decision to become a military nuclear power in the 1980s or 1990s. It would require very sophisticated fission and fusion weapons with predictable yields and with more advanced and protected delivery capabilities.

This chapter focuses especially on the second sort of capability. It imposes no stringent requirements for delivery. (These requirements are very stringent for a middle power to get a serious and responsible force in the 1980s.) I do not, however, mean to imply that the capacity to produce a few bombs for use as a last resort will actually realize the hopes some government might place in it. It is likely to be extremely inflexible, vulnerable, and available only for suicidal use. Nonetheless, some governments might take this route.

However, the nuclear energy bureaucracy, and statesmen informed by it, have been cheerfully arguing that the recycling of plutonium will not make the spread of weapons more likely. Their arguments are residues of the initial faith in denaturing. They are saying that power reactor plutonium would be contaminated in normal reactor operations and abnormal operations would be quickly detected and punished; that power reactor plutonium cannot be used as an explosive; or if so used, it would be ineffective, with generally low yields and highly variable ones; that only sophisticated nuclear weapon countries like the United States and the Soviet Union, with many years in the business, could so derive weapons that have any genuine military use; and finally, with a touch of bathos, that power reactor plutonium is anyway less than optimal for weapons.

It is surprising that the faith in denaturing of plutonium, however plausible initially, could have survived for more than 3 decades. Since this belief explicitly or implicitly rationalizes so much carelessness, it is important, before putting it to rest, to offer some current examples. "Both Framatome and French officials," according to *Nucleonics Week*, June 3, 1976, "deny the [South African] deal is conducive to weapons building. 'The worst way to make a bomb is to buy an LWR (light water reactor) for 5 billion francs,' commented Leny Abourdarham [also of Framatome] added, 'To get clean Pu-239 from our type of reactor, you'd have to lower the burnup rate and discharge the reactor not once a year but about twice a month.' The higher the burnup the more contaminated the spent fuel is with Pu-240." The new French foreign minister, while ambassador to the United Nations (UN), told the Security Council flatly that plutonium so derived "could not be used for military purposes."[10] In Germany, officials of Kraftwerk Union have suggested that weapons-grade plutonium must be 98 percent pure plutonium-239, and that anything less could be used not in a military weapon, but only in "terrorist explosive devices" of low and uncertain yield, which in any case would be extremely hard for terrorists to make.[11] The Swedish government committee on radioactive wastes (the Aka Committee) reports that "The plutonium . . . produced in Swedish power reactors contains as much as 25 percent to 30 percent of plutonium-240 [and] . . . can only be utilized in weak and probably unreliable nuclear charges of highly questionable military value."[12]

In the United States, the president of the Atomic Industrial Forum says that if nuclear reactors are "run on an economic fuel cycle--that is, long irradiation times--the plutonium produced is readily used only for making explosive devices which are hardly military weapons."[13] He goes on to suggest that only very sophisticated weapons countries like the United States and the Soviet Union are able to overcome the difficulty by special design. The Forum's Committee on Nuclear Export Policy concludes that we should promote peaceful nuclear electric power only to the extent consistent with the goal of eliminating proliferation, but they do not think that should impose much constraint, since, ". . . power reactors are not a practical or economic vehicle for producing weapons-grade plutonium. The processing of fuel from a power reactor at low irradiation levels would be costly and revealing of intentions, thus jeopardizing the supply of new fuel. On the other hand, the use of reactor-grade plutonium of high irradiation levels for weapons purposes presents formidable technical challenges."[14]

And finally American government officials in agencies granting loans and subsidies to countries like India which have or propose to get reprocessing plants take comfort from the fact that, "While the plutonium produced by these reactors could be used in an inefficient and unsophisticated explosive program, it is not optimum material for explosive uses because of the high percentage content of the nonfissionable plutonium isotope plutonium-240."[15]

But all of this is quite misleading. For one thing, a no-weapon country can operate a power reactor so as to produce significant quantities of rather pure plutonium-239 without violating any agreements or incurring substantial extra expense. This would involve departing from theoretical "norms" for reactor operation, but a look at the actual operating record of reactors in less developed countries suggests how theoretical these norms are. Even in America in the early 1970s, leaking fuel rods caused Commonwealth Edison to discharge the initial core of its Dresden-2 reactor early, with nearly 100 bombs-worth of 89 to 95 percent pure fissile plutonium.[16] (In India, as of September, 1975, 97 percent of the fuel discharged from its Tarapur reactors had leaked.)

Countries like Pakistan and India, with smaller electric grids and poorer maintenance, have operated much less and much more irregularly than the steady 80 percent of the time originally hoped for; and have irradiated their fuel and contaminated the plutonium in it less. Since it is neither illegal nor uncommon to operate reactors uneconomically, governments may derive quite pure plutonium-239 with no violation nor much visibility.

What is more, there is plainly a considerable latitude in the degree of purity actually required for explosives. The discussion in the European nuclear industry frequently assumes that weapons-grade plutonium must be 98 percent pure plutonium-239.[17] In this country, however, under present classification guidance, the fact that plutonium containing up to and including 8 percent plutonium-240 *is* used in weapons is unclassified as is the fact that more than 8 percent plutonium-240 (reactor-grade) *can* be used to make nuclear weapons.

Most significantly, 20 years of Atoms for Peace programs have dispersed well-equipped and well-staffed nuclear laboratories among non-nuclear weapons states throughout the world. (For example, by 1974 the United States alone had trained 1,100 Indian nuclear physicists and engineers. The shah of Iran plans to have 10,000 trained.) Many of these laboratories would be quite capable of designing and constructing an implosion device and of studying its behavior by non-nuclear firings. It is true that if they were to use power reactor plutonium with 20 to 30 percent of the higher isotopes, they would be likely to obtain a lower expected yield and a greater variation in possible yields than if they should use more nearly pure plutonium-239. (Of course, a non-nuclear component could fail, but this has nothing to do with the grade of plutonium used.) However, they could build a device which, even at its lowest yield level, would produce a very formidable explosion. This may be seen from the record (now public) of the characteristics of the Nagasaki plutonium bomb.

THE FAT MAN AND THE LITTLE BOY

The first American implosion design, "Fat Man," was used in the Trinity test and the Nagasaki bomb. It had a finite probability of predetonating even though it used an extremely high percentage of plutonium-239. Plutonium-239 itself emits neutrons spontaneously, though five orders of magnitude less so than an equal quantity of plutonium-240. More important, though the Trinity and Nagasaki devices used exceptionally pure plutonium-239, they had a significant fraction of plutonium-240. They had a definite chance, then, of detonating prematurely, that is, between the time the rapidly assembling fissile material first became critical and the time that it might have arrived at the desired degree of supercriticality; and the less supercritical, the lower the yield.

In a memorandum to General Farrell and Captain Parsons immediately after the Trinity test, and before the use of Fat Man at Nagasaki, Oppenheimer wrote,

As a result of the Trinity shot we are led to expect a very similar performance from the first Little Boy (the gun-assembled uranium weapon used at Hiroshima) and the first plutonium Fat Man. The energy release of both of these units should be in the range of 12,000 to 20,000 tons and the blast should be equivalent to that from 8,000 to 15.000 tons of TNT. The possibilities of a less than optimal performance of the Little Boy are quite small and should be ignored. The possibility that the first combat plutonium Fat Man will give a less than optimal performance is about 12 percent. There is about a 6 percent chance that the energy release will be under 5,000 tons, and about a 2 percent chance that it will be under 1,000 tons. *It should not be much less than 1,000 tons unless there is an actual* malfunctioning of some of the components. . . ." (italics added)[18]

Indeed General Leslie Groves, like Oppenheimer writing between the Trinity test and the actual use of the implosion weapon at Nagasaki, anticipated an increase in the fraction of plutonium-240 in later weapons. He wrote,

There is a definite possibility, 12 percent rising to 20 percent as we increase our rate of production at the Hanford Engineer Works, with the type of weapons tested that the blast will be smaller due to detonation in advance of the optimum time. *But in any event, the explosion should be on the order of thousands of tons.* The difficulty arises from an undesirable isotope which is created in greater quantity as the production rate increases (italics added).[19]

The essential point to be made is that even if a device like our first plutonium weapon were detonated as prematurely as possible—at a time when the fissile material was least supercritical—its would still be in the kt range. Apart from a modest degradation in the quality of the fissile material employed, and hence in the size of the expected yield, all that a higher fraction of plutonium-240 in such a first implosion device could do is increase the probability of obtaining a yield smaller than the optimal, but still as large or larger than that already enormously destructive minimum.

The lowest yield of such a weapon can by no stretch of the imagination be called "weak." Moreover, by comparison with the average or even the maximum yield possible in that implosion design (or by any standard), it would by no means be contemptible. In fact, only 7 months before Trinity, the first implosion weapons were expected to yield much *less* than one kt.[20]

A reduced yield would not mean a proportionate reduction in damage. The area destroyed by blast overpressure diminishes as the two-thirds power of the reduction in yield, and the reduction in prompt radiation—which is the dominant effect on population of a low-yield weapon—is even smaller. (If the expected yield were eight kts, and the less probable but actual yield were "merely" one kt, the blast area would be reduced not by seven-eighths, but only by three-fourths and the region in which persons in residential buildings would receive a lethal dose of prompt radiation would only be halved.) The lethal area would still be nearly a square mile.

Variability in yield would be a drawback for an advanced industrial country preparing the sort of force I have referred to as of interest to an industrial power like Japan in the 1980s or 1990s. Such a power might want a theater weapon that minimized collateral damage if only for the protection of its own troops. However, for a last resort weapon used against a distant population, it is important only that the of the yield be formidable; and if in fact more destructive energy is released than anticipated, this would only reinforce the destruction intended.

Finally, the variations in damage due to differences in the purity of the plutonium are likely to be much less than the variation in damage due to the differing operational circumstances in the use of the weapon. The Nagasaki plutonium implosion bomb had an estimated yield of 21 kts. The Hiroshima uranium gun weapon is now estimated to have released 14 kt. Yet, due to differences in terrain, weather, accuracy of delivery, and the distribution of population, the Hiroshima bomb killed twice as many people as the Nagasaki weapon.

As for the argument that military men would never use a device whose result was not precisely predictable, this is not very persuasive. If so, military men would hardly ever enter battle. The uncertainties of surviving ground attack, of penetrating air defense, and of delivering weapons on target are cumulatively larger than the uncertainties in the yield of a bomb made with power-reactor plutonium. Plans for delivering the first nuclear weapons were going forward before any test, and during a period when the Manhattan Project scientists had highly varied estimates of their yield. In sum, no one should believe that power-reactor plutonium can be used only in a feeble device too unreliable to be considered a military weapon, or that recycling plutonium is therefore safe.

Recently, as some of the examples I have cited suggest, the bureaucracy has taken a slightly different tack: power-reactor plutonium can be used as an explosive, it is admitted, but would-be nuclear countries will not use it that way. They can get better plutonium more cheaply and easily by buying reactors specifically for the purpose of producing plutonium and not for generating electricity. However, if one already has paid for an electric power reactor, the relevant economic figure is not the total, but the marginal, or extra, cost to get bomb material, given the fact that one has paid anyway for the reactor. In fact, if recycling is accepted as essential for the fuel cycle, the cost of separation plants would be charged to the generation of electricity and would involve no incremental cost for getting separated plutonium for weapons. Getting impure plutonium in this way would be nearly costless. Getting a significant quantity of rather pure plutonium would involve some fuel and operating costs, but these would be small by comparison with the expense of a program to produce and separate plutonium exclusively for weapons.

The more important costs are political for any program designed overtly to get plutonium for a weapon. That could be why the Pakistanis, the Koreans, the Taiwanese, and others deny that they are doing any such thing. It would hurt them militarily, economically, and politically. They can more easily get the financial and technical assistance and trading relations necessary for a power reactor. The political costs would be high for the exporting country too.

Finally, what the bureaucracy seems to miss altogether is that a no-weapon state under the present rules can proceed down the path toward making a weapon without deciding to do so in advance. It does not have to start out as a "would-be nuclear country." It can change its mind or it can make up its mind later. It does not have to get a production reactor.

Of course, a production reactor might be disguised as a vague sort of "research" reactor, though this is likely to yield smaller quantities of plutonium. In fact, the rules governing research reactors and "critical experiments" have been even more careless and need tightening even more than those governing power reactors. But this second line of argument is hardly a cheery confirmation that the rules make the spread unlikely. It has the opposite sense. It has led industry representatives to suggest that the spread is inevitable "sooner or later," and we will just have to live with it.[21]

WOULD THE SPREAD TO MORE COUNTRIES BE BAD?

As we and other supplier countries continue to subsidize the export of materials, equipment, and information needed for making nuclear explosives, the bureaucrats in industry and government associated with these programs tend more and more to tell themselves and everyone else that the spread of nuclear explosives may not be so bad after all: governments that get nuclear weapons will themselves behave more cautiously; their nuclear weapons will inspire caution in their neighbors; this in turn might free the United States from the burden of defending some troublesome allies.

However, the spread of nuclear weapons to many countries will disperse not only instruments of deterrence and prudent behavior, but also means of coercion and reckless or deliberate devastating attack. Not all threats of nuclear aggression will be neatly offset and canceled by convincing promises of nuclear response. The risks will rise very high. In unstable parts of the world, the disasters possible in short conflicts will increase enormously. In the Middle East, for example, before outside powers could stop the conflict, as a result of an exchange involving a few bombs, the Arabs might suffer several million and the Israelis a

160

million dead in contrast with the thousands killed in the October war. In a conventional war, it takes a very long time or huge resources to kill the number of people that would be destroyed by a few nuclear weapons in a matter of hours. The spread of nuclear weapons will reduce our ability to control events. It will have a dissolvent effect on alliances, expose our own forces overseas to huge new risks, and ultimately impose large costs in shaping our own offense and defense to protect the continental United States against small terror attacks by national, as well as subnational groups. Even distant small powers using freighters and short-range missiles, such as the Soviet SCUD, will be within system range of the United States. Even if such a development were, as it is claimed, inevitable "sooner or later," later would be better than sooner, and less better than more.

WHAT CAN WE DO TO LIMIT OR SLOW THE SPREAD?

The characteristic view in the bureaucracy is that we have no leverage. We cannot prevent foreign suppliers from selling nor importers from buying nuclear technology on terms even less constraining then ours. It is unfair, then, to burden our nuclear exporters. Besides, we can retain our influence on no-weapon states only by continuing to supply them with nuclear services, equipment, and materials without interruption.

There is an obvious muddle in the bureaucracy's view that we cannot influence events on the one hand, but on the other, we do have an important influence that we can retain only by continuing to export and--to make the muddle muddier--by continuing to export to buyers, no matter what their behavior, no matter what moves they make toward nuclear explosives. For the bureaucracy, in short, we can retain our leverage only it we never use it. A lever is a form of abstract art rather than a tool giving us a mechanical advantage.

All this is plainly disingenuous: We have talked of the inevitable while actively promoting nuclear energy in no-weapon states in forms that permit access to readily fissionable material, subsidizing the financing of these sales, giving away research reactors with highly enriched uranium cores, assisting "critical experiments" that involve hundreds of kilograms of separated plutonium and highly enriched uranium, urging that no-weapon states recycle plutonium, training engineers from no-weapon states in how to separate plutonium, arguing for domestic recycling as an essential to the future of all nuclear electric power, and in general setting an example to no-weapon states that suggests that the stocking of fissile material is both necessary and safe.

The State Department argues that we must supply nuclear services, equipment, and material "reliably"-- by which it means that we should supply them steadily and indiscriminately to importers who do and to those who do not live up to an obligation to avoid getting explosives, or materials quickly convertible to nuclear explosives. Such "reliable" supply, it claims, will enable us to influence the importers. Exactly the opposite of the truth. Importers will be influenced to stay away from stocks of explosive material only if it costs them something not to do so, and only if our threats or sanctions are taken seriously. The Indian use of Canadian and American help for "peaceful uses only" to make nuclear explosives illustrates the point marvelously. The Indians guessed right in not taking the constraint seriously. Their explosion inspired only ingenious apologies for them in our State Department.

One token of our lack of seriousness is the piece-meal way we decide on licensing exports without considering the cumulative effect of our own and other suppliers' individual decisions in enabling an importing country to set explosive material. For example, we limit the amount of highly enriched uranium in the core of an individual research reactor we have given away, but place no constraint on the total amount of highly enriched uranium the importing country might gather from several sources. In this and other ways, we set a confused and incoherent example for other suppliers.

But other supplying countries have an interest in avoiding the spread of weapons to more states. The French government does not like the prospect of Spanish nuclear weapons, and neither the Germans nor the French could afford explicitly to use bombs as sweeteners for reactor sales, even if they wanted to. The French and Germans point out correctly that they now impose more stringent safeguards on exports than the IAEA requires, but they do not recognize, nor do we point out, that safeguards cannot be effectively applied to fissile material only a few hours away from a bomb; that is, such "safeguards" cannot give timely warning. The principal precondition for us to influence other suppliers as well as importers is a clear, consistent policy: a set of signals which are green on some activities, red on others. We now flash red, yellow, and green on practically everything.

But there are clear signals we can send and effective levers we can press. On the political and military side, we can help countries defend themselves against nonnuclear attack without resort to nuclear weapons. Our military sales program should be designed to discourage a nuclear defense and to make non-nuclear defenses more effective. And our alliance policy can strengthen guarantees against nuclear adversaries. For example, we can supply the South Koreans with improved short-range surface-to-air missiles and short-range precision guided nonnuclear weapons, and discourage their attempts to convert Nike Hercules into 200-mile surface-to-surface rockets which would be effective only with nuclear warheads and only against population targets.

On the economic side, we can design our export and export financing policy to affect an importing country's energy program considered as a whole, not piecemeal, by encouraging the use of nonnuclear energy and of comparatively safe forms of nuclear energy and by discouraging or penalizing the dangerous forms of nuclear energy that permit access to fissile stocks.

The effectiveness of the levers at our disposal can be illustrated by the extreme sensitivity of various programs in the no-weapon states of the Third World (where the impending spread is now most threatening) to simple alterations in the terms of financing. Korea, for example, has drastically cut back its nuclear program in response to a slight hardening in Canadian and American financial terms. And the effectiveness of our political and military levers is illustrated by the cancellation of the Korean reprocessing plant.

In sum, statements that we have no leverage mean that we do not want to press the levers we have, that we are not serious about proliferation. We do not think about the international consequences of digging ourselves deeper into a commitment to recycle plutonium, for example, by bailing out Allied General from its costly investment in reprocessing at Barnwell. We prefer to hang on to some quite inessential outworn conceptions of the nuclear fuel cycle and we are moving toward competing with the French and the Germans by giving away para-bomb capabilities.

Other governments have reason to doubt our claim that we unequivocally oppose proliferation. But actions against proliferation do cost something. It is only fair to ask whether they are worth the cost.

WILL SLOWING THE SPREAD COST MORE THAN IT IS WORTH?

Slowing the spread means reducing the demand for nuclear weapons by intelligent policies of alliance and of military sales and assistance. It means reducing the supply of nuclear weapons materials by sensible nuclear energy policy for our domestic as well as our foreign sales. On the supply side in particular restrictions are often thought of as depriving us and other suppliers of enormous market benefits and imposing energy shortages on all of us, including the Third World countries now in the market for nuclear energy that is at least overtly civilian.

Nuclear energy has an important role to play, but its positive contributions will not make the difference between heaven and hell on earth. Its benefits have been puffed up from the start in ways that have greatly distorted its performance and made national energy programs follow something much less than the best path and timing for introducing nuclear energy into the total energy mix. A more sober program would benefit the security interests of the United States and ultimately the economic interests of the industry. Without the extensive conversion of uranium-238 into plutonium and the separation of plutonium from spent fuel, we can have enough coal and enough of the fissile isotope uranium-235 at reasonable prices to last us well into the second quarter of the 21st century. By then we should be able to make an intelligent transition to the use of abundant or renewable resources: a safe and economic breeder; or a safe form of fusion; or solar energy, whether in the form of solar electric power, biomass, or some other. We have time.

The contrary claim that we need immediately to add to the reserves of uranium-235 by the extensive use of separated plutonium in the current generation of light water reactors, and that we should now contract into the early use of the plutonium breeder, is based on bad economics. It ignores the way an increase in market prices generates a larger supply of specific scarce resources (by making them worth finding and exploiting), or a supply of substitutes, and at the same time reduces the demand.

In fact, the nuclear industry has suffered chronically from premature commitments based on exaggeration of energy demand, the demand for electric power, in particular the demand for nuclear electric power, and the derived demand for uranium and for enrichment services. This exaggeration applies to overseas as well as to domestic demand. And the impression of crisis has been encouraged further by understatements of the supply that might be made available at various prices and by the discouragement of supply that has followed from the wild swings in demand when excessive hopes have been deflated. In 1975, the AEC predicted 450 electric gigawatts (GWe)[22] of nuclear capacity operating in the United States in 1985. In 1970, it predicted 300 GWe by that date. Today, on the basis of actual construction and orders, the Federal Energy Administration (FEA) expects 145 GWe or less. Given varied technical assumptions appropriate for the dates when the forecasts were made,[23] these predictions imply a cumulative need respectively for about one million, 500,000, or 220,000 tons of fresh uranium yellow cake, if there is no recycling. The 80,000 tons that would be needed annually by the year 1985, if the AEC's 1970 nuclear power forecasts were right and we did not recycle, far exceeds the supply of low cost uranium that might be available at that time. The 33,000 tons that would be needed to fulfill the more sober FEA schedule during the year 1985 is quite in line with what is in prospect. ERDA has estimated that a rate of 33,000 tons can be available in the early 1980s at the low forward cost of $15 per pound.[24]

Much the same can be said about inflated forecasts of the need for uranium enrichment services; and about the longer-term forecasts until the end of the century for both uranium and enrichment. European, Japanese, and Third World nuclear power forecasts have been similarly inflated. In 1957, Euratom forecast about 15 GWe of nuclear power in 1967 and about 50 GWe in 1975. In actuality there was 1.6 GWe in 1967, and at the end of 1976 there will be only about 12.2 GWe.[25] The Japanese in 1970 expected 60 GWe by 1985. They have officially cut this to 49 GWe and some Japanese experts expect it to be as low as 30 GWe.

The nuclear bureaucracy believes that overstating demand is much less harmful than understanding it.[26] This is not so. The exaggeration has severely damaged both national policy and the profitability of industry. Exaggerated uranium demand biased decisions toward plutonium recycling in the current reactors as well as in breeders. The inflated domestic demand for enrichment led us in 1974 to ban any new enrichment commitments to foreigners. This led to the present scramble overseas to get enrichment capabilities independent of the United States with an obvious resulting loss of U.S. control. Inflated market expectations have also cost the industry money. Chrome-premature commitment has meant, in the United States, a loss to General Electric of $500 million to $600 million on 13 turnkey contracts; a loss of $.5 to $2 billion by Westinghouse depending on how it settles the legal claims of public utilities on its forward sale of uranium that it used to sweeten its reactor sales. Royal Dutch Shell and Gulf Oil, the two owners of General Atomic, have lost over one billion dollars on the latter's high temperature gas-cooled reactor.

It is hard to disentangle losses on commercial nuclear sales in company statements that, in general, merge those losses with profits on fossil fuel plants, military nuclear sales, or other industrial products. But it appears that Babcock and Wilcox, and Combustion Engineering, the other two major U.S. reactor manufacturers, have suffered respectively a cumulative loss on nuclear sales of about $100 million and $150 million; for 1976 each will have an estimated $10 million pre-tax loss. General Electric's pre-tax loss on nuclear sales in 1976 will be about $40 million. AEG Telefunken, part owner of Kraftwerk Union, lost DM 685 million ($274 million) on nuclear sales in 1974, and expected losses in "three-figure millions" marks in 1975.[27] It is harder to determine Framatome's losses. As for reprocessing of light water reactor fuel, though very little has been performed, the losses have been impressive. General Electric's Morris, Illinois, plant, which cost $64 million, had to be abandoned without ever going into operation.[28] The Allied General Nuclear Services plant at Barnwell owned by Allied Chemical, Royal Dutch Shell, and Gulf Oil, originally estimated to cost about $50 million actually has cost $250 million so far, and may take about a billion dollars in total to complete in accordance with current requirements. Getty's Nuclear Fuel Service plant in West Valley, New York, shut down for modification after about $30 million in gross sales. It might require some hundreds of millions just to dispose of the radioactive waste from its previous work. Getty wants to cancel some $180 million in reprocessing contracts it has accepted, since it estimates it will take $600 million to fulfill the contracts within regulatory requirements. The government-owned plant in Windscale, England, had troubles with the head end. The Eurochemic plant in Belgium has been shut down, and Europeans now judge that the recycling of plutonium will exceed the cost of getting fresh uranium fuel and that if reprocessing should be necessary for waste disposal, it will require subsidies from public utilities.[29]

In general, it is plain that for the nuclear industry as a whole, profitability is still a vision of the future. Immense losses could be avoided by greater realism.

The collapse of expectations in domestic markets unfortunately has led to an aggressive campaign to sell to the less-developed countries (LDCs), where, in general, nuclear power is least economic: Nuclear electricity is highly capital intensive, efficient only in very large sizes and requires continuing highly sophisticated maintenance. The LDC reactor market, which the industrial powers might fight to share, is quite small, and the market for reprocessing plants is even smaller--1 or 2 percent of the reactor market. The heavily subsidized initial sales have been made on terms which worsen the problem of proliferation without any realistic prospect that the ambitious LDC long-term nuclear programs will be fulfilled. Yet in the

169

past the French have talked of sales to the Third World of plutonium breeders which are more damaging and even less plausible for LDCs than the present generation of reactors which they will exceed in capital costs, diseconomies of small scale, and sophistication.

The most urgent issue, if we are to restrict access to fissile material, is the use of plutonium as a fuel in current reactors. This has been argued for on grounds that it would (1) save a lot of money, (2) save much scarce uranium, (3) be essential for permanent disposal of radioactive wastes, and (4) be required to get the plutonium breeder on present schedules. None of this is true. On Point 1, the estimates of costs for separating plutonium and making it into fuel rods have multiplied 10-fold in 10 years and are still highly uncertain and in controversy. On Vince Taylor's calculations, they exceed the estimated costs of fresh uranium fuel rods. Most important, even if plutonium separation were costless, it could make only a 1 or 2 percent difference in the delivered kilowatt hour cost of nuclear electricity.

As for Point 2, the conservation argument should be related to the economics: We are not impelled to extract plutonium from spent uranium fuel any more than we are presently moved to extract the enormous quantities of uranium from sea water. It depends on the costs. Fissile material is present in spent fuel in more concentrated form than in ore, but, by comparison with uranium ore, it is enormously radioactive. There are cheaper ways of getting uranium, by mining and even by a change in U.S. enrichment policy. (In unpublished work, Vince Taylor of PAN Heuristics has shown that the apparent uranium shortage of the 1980s has been effectively created not only by inflated projections of nuclear power and the derived demand for uranium but also by U.S. policies that (1) envision adding substantially over the next 10 years to an already immense government stockpile--worth $8 billion at current prices--of enriched and natural uranium, (2) leave an excessive amount of uranium-235 in the waste streams of the enrichment plants, thus inflating the amount of natural uranium that must be fed into the plants, and (3) force customers to stick to schedules for delivering uranium for enrichment which they contracted for before the recent substantial cut backs in nuclear power programs both here and abroad.) But even if one were absurdly optimistic about the costs of using plutonium fuel for light water reactors, the private cost savings would be trivial. The political and social costs plainly dominate.

As for Point 3, plutonium separation would remove most of the longest-lived radioactive actinides, and so, it has been hoped, would economize in packaging and compacting wastes. However, spent uranium fuel can be stored without reprocessing and recent study indicates that the process of separation will contaminate much of the equipment, filters, solvents, etc., used and that the total volume and heat content of the waste so created and of the spent plutonium fuel which will require remote handling and geologic isolation will exceed those of the unreprocessed spent fuel.

On Point 4, the present schedule calls for ERDA recommendations on a commercial breeder in 1986. If the decision is positive, it is hoped that the first commercial breeder will start operating in the mid-1990s. We can, therefore, defer the decision on plutonium separation for at least 5 years.[30] In fact, the spent fuel would cool enough in that period to make separation easier, and the savings would nearly pay for the storage costs. This fourth argument is, however, revealing. It is motivated in good part by a desire to force a positive decision on a commercial plutonium breeder--another case of premature commitment. The domestic U.S. decision on plutonium separation has obvious international implications and it is these that will impose the largest political and social costs.

POLICIES

The last year has seen a salutary ferment about changing policy so as to discourage nuclear proliferation. Proposals range from David Lilienthal's recommendation, at one end, to stop all nuclear exports, through the bureaucracy's, at the other, which suggests that we continue pretty much as we are. Rather than engage in a detailed analysis of this wide range of proposals, I will set down summarily a program indicated by my argument so far.

ON THE DEMAND SIDE

Slowing the spread of nuclear weapons means reducing the demand for them, as well as restricting the supply of nuclear weapons material. Political and military policy on alliances, on nuclear guarantees, and on non-nuclear military sales and assistance should be directed to help in nonnuclear defense against non-nuclear threats and to provide nuclear guarantees against threats of nuclear coercion or attack. I have illustrated the sort of thing needed in my earlier remarks about South Korea. But such a policy has to be shaped country-by-country and does not lend itself to easy summary.

ON THE SUPPLY SIDE

1. Deny access to readily fissionable material. We need to state as a general guide for U.S. domestic as well as export policy that it is our plain purpose to deny access by individual terrorists, either here or abroad, and to deny access by governments of no-weapon states to nuclear materials that can be readily converted to explosive use. This principle should be the basis for our negotiations in the suppliers group where we will then be able to say we not only advocate it but illustrate it. The general principle has implications spelled out in many more detailed policy suggestions.

2. Delay for at least 5 or 10 years any decision to separate plutonium in the United States.

3. Press actively for fuel cycle designs which would eliminate access to highly enriched uranium or chemically separated plutonium in power reactors and research reactors. Up to now, this has not been part of any design criterion.

4. Continue to deny export licenses for isotope enrichment facilities and plutonium separation plants.

5. Provide to any no-weapon state low enriched uranium services at nondiscriminatory prices provided that the importer agrees (a) not to acquire further enrichment facilities or plutonium separation facilities, (b) to place all its nuclear facilities under IAEA safeguards, (c) not to acquire nuclear explosives, and (d) not to acquire fissile material quickly convertible to explosive use. We should make new commitments for the sale of nuclear technology only under these conditions. Though we have no shortage of enrichment capacity, it may be prudent to expand our enrichment capacity because it is critical for exercising control,

and for assuring supplies of low-enriched uranium to importers who live up to their agreements. We should alter our perverse enrichment policy which has done much to create the appearance of a shortage of uranium and of enrichment. We should first start to reduce our $8 billion stock of natural and low-enriched uranium; second, permit customers to cancel or defer dates for delivering uranium to be enriched; and third, start operating our enrichment plants, subject to capacity constraints, so as to minimize the amount of uranium needed to produce nuclear fuel for our customers.

6. Where we supply low enriched uranium to no-weapon states, either lease it or otherwise arrange for its return. (The Soviet Union apparently does this.) Spent fuel so returned would make up a small percentage of the enormous radioactive wastes from our military program and our own domestic power program.

7. In the future, when centrifuge or laser separation facilities might otherwise become widespread, consider transfers of enrichment technology to an international or multinational center that would provide only low enriched uranium (and not plutonium fuel) services to no-weapon states. However, do not encourage plutonium separation in such centers with or without the fabrication of mixed plutonium and uranium oxide fuel. If such centers shipped out separated plutonium to no-weapon states, it would be immediately available for explosives. And plutonium is much more easily separated chemically from fresh unirradiated mixed oxide fuel than from spent fuel. Low enriched uranium is not an explosive, however, plutonium separated from reactor fuel is.

8. Deny further assistance for critical experiments in national laboratories of no-weapon states, since

these experiments involve access to unirradiated or only lightly irradiated readily fissionable material. Where warranted, provide for U.S. or possibly multinational or international facilities for the conduct of critical experiments by no-weapon states.

9. Deny licenses for the export to no-weapon states of research reactors with highly enriched uranium cores or significant plutonium output unless the total nuclear program for an importing country will not permit it to derive enough readily fissionable materials for weapons.

10. Change Export-Import Bank policy so that its loans and the private loans it guarantees will support rather than defeat the preceding recommendations.

11. Offer further financial and technical assistance to IAEA to improve safeguards, but alter trilateral agreements to permit and require IAEA to report on the location, size, and chemical and physical composition of all stocks of readily fissionable material monitored under these agreements. The improvements in IAEA inspection to detect violations will be useful if, and only if, export agreements are altered so that accumulating readily fissionable material becomes a violation, whether accounted for or not. Presently, IAEA centers its attention on the "limits of error in material unaccounted for" (LEMUF) without reporting on the legal accumulation of explosive materials.

The best maxim to keep in mind is that of Florence Nightingale: "Whatever else hospitals do, they shouldn't spread disease." On these complex issues, it has been all too easy to advance resounding programs to slow the spread of weapons which actually speed it. That is how we got into the present fix, as did Atoms for Peace and some of the incompatible clauses of the NPT. Using the 18th century language of natural law from our Declaration of Independence, the NPT asserts the "inalienable right" of all countries to peaceful nuclear energy--which includes, some exporters apparently feel, reprocessing. We have then the new natural right to Life, Liberty, and the Pursuit of Plutonium.

And now most recently each side in the last presidential campaign showed how the multinational form can distract from substance in slowing the spread. Each sometimes contemplated not only the return of spent uranium fuel but using multinational centers for making and distributing fresh mixed plutonium and uranium oxide fuels. Yet, plutonium for use in explosives is much more easily extracted from the fresh mixed oxides than from the spent uranium fuel. The word "multinational" tends to give many opponents of the spread a warm feeling all over, unless it is followed immediately by the word "corporation." But this cure would simply spread the disease. Here it is essential to focus our aim precisely on the substance rather than the symbol. Multinational centers for the distribution of bomb material will not help.

ENDNOTES - CHAPTER 7

1. Isotopes of the same heavy element, such as uranium-235 and uranium-238, undergo the same chemical reactions at almost the same reaction rates and therefore cannot be separated by any known conventional chemical means, but so far only by an expensive, difficult, and time-consuming physical process that exploits slight differences in atomic mass. The fissile isotopes are those that are readily fissionable by slow or thermal neutrons as well as fast neutrons.

2. U.S. Senate, Committee on Government Operations, Hearings on S. 1439. testimony by Robert J. McCloskey, Department

of State, June 16, 1976, p. 811.

3. Indeed, we attached a "related note" to our agreement with Spain of March 20, 1974, which said, "It is understood that the material subject thereto will not be used for any nuclear explosive device, regardless of how the device itself is intended to be used. . . ." We signed the note, but Spain did not.

4. For a more extended analysis, see Chap. III, *Moving Toward Life in a Nuclear Armed Crowd?*, a Pan Heuristics report to the Arms Control and Disarmament Agency. A revised edition will be published by the University of Chicago Press.

5. For example, it said ". . . the development of more ingenious methods . . . which might make this material effectively usable is not only dubious, but is certainly not possible without a very major scientific and technical effort," pp. 26-27, but also unequivocally that "the limit between what is safe and what is dangerous . . . will not stay fixed" in "what is sure to be a rapidly changing technical situation," p. 10. U.S. Department of State, Publication 2497, March 15, 1946.

6. The committee included Robert Oppenheimer and C. A. Thomas, who, among the authors of the Acheson-Lilienthal Report, were the two qualified to speak on the subject. Its statement was issued on April 9, 1946.

7. The ambivalence and inconsistency were present at the start. Like Leo Szilard, who had been cautious about denaturing a few months earlier, Glenn Seaborg, whose team had discovered plutonium in 1941, signed the final draft of the Franck Report which stated flatly that "denaturalization of pure fissionable isotopes . . . [would] make them useless for military purposes." Yet Seaborg, commenting on early drafts, had written, "Can't denature 49 by dilution with stable isotopes." "Forty-nine" was the wartime code for the element 94, plutonium. The James Franck papers, University of Chicago Regenstein Library.

8. "Nuclear Experts Give Warning on Build-up of Untreated Waste Fuel," *The Times*, London, May 25, 1975.

9. Guy Hawtin, "East Bloc Aids Bonn Anti-Nuclear Groups,"

Financial Times, London, UK, May 22, 1976.

10. Address by Louis de Guiringaud, June 19, 1976, New York: Service de Presse et d'Information, 1976, No. 76/95, p. 3. In September 1976, the French cabinet reconsidered such dangers, though not as a result of any clear message from the State Department. Michel Tatu, *Le Monde*, September 9, 1976.

11. Dr. G. Hildebrand, Lecture, "The Fuel Cycle and the Export Situation," to visiting embassy representatives at the Kraftwerk Union plant in Mülheim, West Germany, April 10, 1976.

12. "Spent Nuclear Fuel and Radioactive Waste," Statens Offentlige Utredningar, Document No. 32, Stockholm, Sweden: Libervorlag, 1976, p. 43.

13. Carl Walske, "Nuclear Energy Environment in the United States," Paper presented at a conference in Madrid, Spain, May 4, 1976.

14. The Atomic Industrial Forum's Committee on Nuclear Export Policy, *U.S. Nuclear Export Policy*, July 21, 1976, p. 3.

15. Letter to Congressman Findley from Denis M. Neill, Assistant Administrator for Legal Affairs, Agency for International Development, Department of State, August 18, 1975.

16. The spent fuel had 13 kg of plutonium that was 95 percent, 110 kg that was 93 percent, and 331 kg that was 89 percent purely fissile.

17. Hildebrand.

18. Memorandum from Oppenheimer to Farrell and Parsons, July 23, 1945, Top Secret, Manhattan Engineering District Papers, Box "14," Folder 2, Record Group 77, Modern Military Records, National Archives, Washington, DC, Declassified in 1974.

19. Memorandum to the Chief of Staff by General Leslie Groves, July 30, 1945, Top Secret, Manhattan engineering District Papers, Box "3," Folder 5B. Declassified in 1972.

20. See Richard G. Hewlett and Oscar F. Anderson, Jr., *The New World, 1939/1946, Volume I, A History of the United States Atomic Energy Commission*, University Park, PA: The Pennsylvania State University Press. 1962, p. 321.

21. See, e.g., Walske; and Hildebrand.

22. "GWe" is gigawatts, that is, thousands of megawatts of electrical capacity.

23. Estimates of uranium requirements vary with precise assumptions as to the percentage of uranium-235 left in the tailings by the process of enrichment, the rate of growth in reactors, the capacity factor or percentage of time the reactors are generating electricity; and such technical characteristics of reactor operation as fuel enrichment levels, fuel burnup levels, and frequency of reloads. These earlier estimates assume 80 percent capacity factors. The 1976 forecast assumes a 70 percent capacity factor. I assume .2 percent tails assay throughout.

24. John Patterson, chief of the Supply Evaluation Branch, Division of Fuel Cycle Production, "Uranium Supply Developments," Paper presented at the Atomic Industrial Forum Fuel Cycle Conference, Phoenix, Arizona, March 22, 1976. More recently, ERDA has estimated an attainable U.S. production capacity of 47,000 tons of yellow cake at the $15 cost level by 1985 and 60,000 tons by about 1990. According to *Nucleonics Week*, September 23, 1976, ERDA summed up, "The information we have today indicates that there is a good possibility that uranium will be available at reasonable prices."

25. End 1976 estimates are taken from *Nuclear News*, "World List of Nuclear Power Plants," August 1976, pp. 66-79.

26. See U.S. Congress, Joint Committee on Economics, *Review and Update of Cost-Benefit Analysis for the Liquid Metal Fast Breeder Reactor*, May 17, 1976, Washington, DC: Government Printing Office, 1976, p. 18.

27. *Financial Times*, London, UK, December 9, 1975. American loss estimates by R. Cornell of E. F. Hutton.

28. *Chemical Engineering*, January 6, 1975, p. 68.

29. *Nucleonics Week*, July 12, 1976, p. 8.

30. On ERDA's projections the plutonium then available from light water reactor fuel will be over three times more than the amount needed by breeders at the end of the century. Moreover, even ERDA's low growth projections for the breeder presume an unrealistically early and rapid build-up of commercial breeders.

CHAPTER 8

FALLING BEHIND:
INTERNATIONAL SCRUTINY OF THE
PEACEFUL ATOM*

Henry Sokolski

OVERVIEW

Some Negative Trends.

On a number of counts, the International Atomic
Energy Agency (IAEA) safeguards system appears to
be getting better. After more than a decade of no real
growth, annual funding for nuclear inspections finally
was increased in real terms from $89 million in 2003,
to $102 million in 2004, and to $108 million in 2007.
Deployment of advanced remote monitoring equipment is on the rise and implementation of new, more
intrusive inspections authority under the Additional
Protocol is moving forward. In the future, nuclear
power might expand, but most of this expansion will
take place in nuclear weapons states or countries that
are so trustworthy that it could be argued that few,
if any, additional nuclear inspections may be needed.
As for additional safeguards requirements — e.g., inspections in India, North Korea, or Iran — they might
well be met with additional contributions when and if
they arise. From this perspective, current safeguards
budgeting and planning could be viewed as being adequate to the task for years to come.[1]

---

*Originally published in Henry Sokolski, ed., *Falling Behind:
International Scrutiny of the Peaceful Atom*, Carlisle, PA: Strategic
Studies Institute, U.S. Army War College, 2008, pp. 3-61.

It could, that is, until other, less positive trends are considered. Of these, perhaps the most important deal with the number of significant quantities of nuclear material that the IAEA must safeguard to prevent it from being diverted and directly fashioned into bombs. This number is not only growing, but growing a rate far faster than that of the IAEA's safeguards budget. The amount of separated plutonium (Pu) and highly enriched uranium (HEU) — both nuclear fuels that can be fashioned into bombs in a matter of hours or days — that the IAEA inspects, for example, has grown more than six-fold between 1984 and 2004 while the agency's safeguards budget has barely doubled (see Figure 1). Meanwhile, the number of nuclear fuel fabrication and fuel making plants (facilities that are by far the easiest to divert nuclear material from) has grown in the last 2 decades from a mere handful to 65. Then, there is the number of other plants containing special nuclear material that the IAEA must safeguard: it has roughly tripled to more than 900 facilities today.[2]

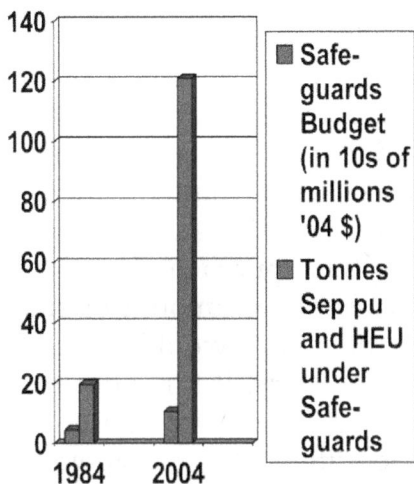

Figure 1. IAEA Safeguards Spending vs.
Mounting Weapons Usable Material Stockpiles.

From 1984 to 2004, IAEA safeguards spending roughly doubled $105 m in constant '04 dollars.

Amounts of HEU and separated Pu, meanwhile, grew nearly 6-fold — enough to make 12,000 to 21,000 crude nuclear weapons

These trends have forced the IAEA to work their inspections staff much harder. Over the last 20 years, the number of days IAEA inspectors have been in the field has nearly doubled from 60 to 70 days to 125 to 150.[3] This doubling has not only cost more money, it is one of the reasons (along with unreasonable employment and contracting rules) for a hollowing out of IAEA's experienced inspections staff. This hollowing out is expected to become acute. As noted by the U.S. Government Accountability Office, about 50 percent, or 30 out of 75, of the IAEA's senior safeguards staff are expected to retire by 2011.[4]

One way to address this inspections crunch is to have the IAEA simply inspect less. This could be done legally by implementing the Additional Protocol. In fact, limiting the number of routine safeguards inspections is one of the incentives the IAEA currently offers countries to sign up to the Additional Protocol. Once a country has ratified the Additional Protocol and the IAEA has established that there "is no indication of undeclared nuclear material activities for the state as a whole," the agency can reduce the number of routine nuclear inspections it makes of that country's nuclear materials and facilities significantly.[5]

The trouble with taking this approach, though, is that initially it actually *increases* the amount of staff time and resources that the IAEA would have to spend to safeguard a given country. It turns out that determining whether or not a country has no undeclared nuclear materials activities takes considerable safeguards staff resources.[6] Over the entire lifetime of a nuclear facility (i.e., 20 to 50 years), then, applying integrated safeguards might reduce the total amount of staff time needed to safeguard a particular set of nuclear plants slightly, but in the first few years, more, not less, staff time and safeguards resources would be consumed.[7]

Also, the Additional Protocol authorizes the IAEA to conduct wide area surveillance inspections. These would be extremely useful in the case of Iran or North Korea. They also would require significant additional safeguards staff and funding (by one estimate made for the Nonproliferation Education Center [NPEC] by a seasoned former IAEA inspector, perhaps an increase in funding constituting as much as 30 percent of the IAEA's entire current safeguards budget[8]). So far, the IAEA has done nothing to establish such an inspections capability.

Finally, relying heavily on integrated safeguards may be unsound in principle. As already noted, they require the IAEA to determine that the country in question has no undeclared nuclear material. Yet, the IAEA's safeguards staff itself has admitted that it cannot yet be relied upon to discover covert nuclear fuel-making facilities in the hardest cases (e.g., Iran). Also, reducing the frequency of on-site inspections increases the risks that a member state might divert materials to make bombs without the IAEA finding out until it is too late.

In a detailed study completed for NPEC late in 2004 on the proliferation risks associated with light water reactors, several scenarios were presented under which fresh and spent nuclear fuel rods might be diverted to make nuclear weapons fuel in covert reprocessing or enrichment plants in a matter of days or weeks without tipping off IAEA inspectors[9] These scenarios were subsequently validated independently by key officials working within the IAEA's Standing Advisory Group on Safeguards, the U.S. Department of State, and the Los Alamos National Laboratory.[10]

That a country could evade IAEA inspectors in diverting entire fuel rods is disquieting. One would assume that the current crop of IAEA remote nuclear monitoring equipment could be counted upon entirely to warn against such diversions. In fact, they cannot.[11] Most of the currently deployed remote sensors, in fact, do not allow the IAEA even to know from day to day whether these systems are activated. This is a serious shortcoming. Over the last 6 years, the agency has learned of camera "blackouts" that lasted for "more than 30 hours" on 12 separate occasions. What's worse, it only learned of these blackouts *after* inspectors went to the sites and downloaded the camera recordings as they are required to do every 90 days.[12]

Under new proposed "integrated safeguards" procedures, such "downloading," moreover, would occur as infrequently as every 12 months—a period within which a state could conceivably make a nuclear weapon unbeknownst to the IAEA.[13] The IAEA staff recently proposed to correct this inspections gap by accelerating implementation of near real-time monitoring using satellite communication connections. This effort, though, is still being implemented at an excruciatingly slow pace due to a lack of funds.[14]

Structural Problems.

The current gap in the IAEA's near-real time monitoring capabilities may be worrisome but it, at least, can be addressed if additional safeguards funding is made available. Far more intractable is the IAEA's inability to detect diversions in a timely manner from nuclear fuel-making plants. As already noted, NPEC's earlier study on the proliferation dangers associated with light water reactors highlighted the relative ease with which states might build covert reprocessing plants or divert spent civilian fuel to accelerate undeclared uranium enrichment efforts.

Additional NPEC commissioned research detailed just how poorly IAEA safeguards have performed at nuclear fuel plants in Europe and Japan. In his study, "Can Nuclear Fuel Production in Iran and Elsewhere Be Safeguarded against Diversion,"[15] Dr. Edwin Lyman highlights several examples. At a fuel fabrication plant at Tokai-mura in Japan making mixed-oxide (MOX) fuel out of powdered uranium and nuclear weapons-usable separated plutonium, the IAEA could not account for 69 kilograms of plutonium. This is enough to make at least nine nuclear weapons (assuming the IAEA's 8 kilograms per weapon estimate) or twice that figure (assuming the U.S. Department of Energy's more accurate 4 kilograms per crude nuclear weapon figure). Only after the passage of 2 years, the expenditure of $100 million, and the disassembling of the plant could the operator claim that he could account for all but 10 kilograms (i.e., one to two bombs worth).[16]

Dr. Lyman details a similarly disturbing incident involving MOX scrap in Japan where at least one bomb's worth of weapons-usable plutonium went missing and another accounting discrepancy at a Japanese reprocessing plant at which the IAEA lost track of between 59 and 206 kilograms of bomb-usable plutonium (and was able to determine this only years *after* the material initially went unaccounted for). Add to these discoveries the many bombs' worth of material unaccounted for (MUF) annually at reprocessing plants in France and the United Kingdom (UK) where the IAEA has employed its very latest near-real time monitoring techniques, and there is cause for alarm.[17]

The picture relating to safeguarding centrifuge enrichment plants is not much brighter. Even at plants where IAEA monitoring and inspectors are on site, there will be times in between inspections during which remote monitoring might be defeated. There also is the constant problem of the operator giving false design, production, or capacity figures.[18]

In any case, the times between a decision to divert and having enough material to make a crude bomb (assuming the IAEA's high estimate of 25 kilograms of highly enriched uranium being required to make one weapon) are so short, even an immediate detection of the diversion, which is by no means assured, would generally come too late to afford enough time to prevent bombs from being made. In the case of a small commercial-sized plant, a bomb's worth could be made in as little as 18 hours to 12 days (depending on whether natural or slightly enriched uranium is used as feed).[19]

SAFEGUARDS ASSUMPTIONS

Exacerbating this safeguards gap is the IAEA's overly generous view of how much material must be diverted to make a bomb (referred to by the IAEA as a "significant quantity") and how long it might take to convert this material into a nuclear weapon (known as the "conversion time"). Most of these IAEA estimates were made over 30 years ago. To reassess their accuracy, NPEC commissioned Thomas Cochran, chief nuclear scientist at the Natural Resources Defense Council (NRDC), to make new determinations. His analysis and conclusions were revealing. The IAEA estimates it would take eight kilograms of separated plutonium and 25 kilograms of highly enriched uranium to make a crude bomb. Cochran found these estimates to be too high by a minimum of 25 percent and a maximum of 800 percent, depending on the weapons expertise employed and the yield desired (see Figure 2).[20]

Yield (kt)	WEAPON-GRADE PLUTONIUM (kg) Technical Capability			HIGHLY-ENRICHED URANIUM (kg) Technical Capability		
	Low	Medium	High	Low	Medium	High
1	3	1.5	1	8	4	2.5
5	4	2.5	1.5	11	6	3.5
10	5	3	2	13	7	4
20	6	3.5	3	16	9	5

Values rounded to the nearest 0.5 kilogram.

Figure 2. NRDC Estimate of the Approximate Fissile Material Requirements for Pure Fission Nuclear Weapons.

When presented with these figures, senior IAEA safeguards staff did not dispute them. Instead they argued that the "exact" amount of diverted nuclear material needed to make a crude bomb was not important. Instead, what mattered most was the IAEA's ability to detect microscopic amounts of weapons usable materials since securing such environmental samples was the factor most likely to put an inspected party in the international spotlight.[21]

The potential downside of taking this approach, however, is significant. It is these estimates, along with the agency's projections of how long it takes a proliferator to convert uranium and plutonium materials into bombs (i.e., conversion times), that the IAEA uses to determine how often it should conduct its inspections of different nuclear facilities. If these estimates are too high, the frequency of inspections needed to detect military diversions risks being egregiously low. Certainly, what the IAEA defines as desirable "detection times" — the maximum time that may elapse between the diversion of a significant quantity of nuclear material and the likely detection of that diversion — should correspond (according to the IAEA's own guidelines) to the agency's estimated conversion times. If they do not, IAEA-inspected countries could count on being able to divert a crude weapon's worth of nuclear material and fashioning it into a bomb before the IAEA could either detect the diversion or have any chance of taking appropriate action to block bomb making.

This worry seems quite legitimate when one considers how high the IAEA's 30-year old significant quantity estimates appear to be and then looks at how generous the IAEA's estimated conversion times are (see Figure 3).

Beginning Material Form	Conversion Time
Pu, HEU, or ^{233}U metal	Order of days (7-10)
PuO$_2$, Pu(NO$_3$)$_4$ or other pure Pu compounds, HEU or ^{233}U oxide or other pure U compounds, MOX or other nonirradiated pure mixtures containing Pu, U (^{233}U + ^{235}U $\geq$ 20%), Pu, HEU, and/or ^{233}U in scrap or other miscellaneous impure compounds	Order of weeks (1-3)*
Pu, HEU, or ^{233}U in irradiated fuel	Order of months (1-3)
U containing <20% ^{235}U and ^{233}U, Th	Order of months (3-12)

*This range is not determined by any single factor, but the pure Pu and U compounds will tend to be at the lower end of the range and the mixtures and scrap at the higher end

Figure 3. Conversion Times.[22]

Using the history of the Manhattan Project as a benchmark, the IAEA's first set of estimates regarding the amount of time (7 to 10 days) needed to convert separated plutonium or HEU or U233 metal were judged by Dr. Cochran to be the correct order of time. The key reason why is that in 1945, the plutonium and enriched uranium for the first American bombs had to be shipped thousands of miles from where they were produced to where the material was fashioned into nuclear weapons. This transport took several days. If a country making nuclear weapons did not have to ship these distances, the conversion time could be much shorter. However, the conversion times could still be on the order of a day or more.

The IAEA's estimates of how long it would take (1 to 3 weeks) to convert fresh plutonium-uranium fuels (known as mixed oxide fuels or MOX) do not fare as well. Here, Dr. Cochran points out that it would take no more than a week and possibly as little as a few days to convert these materials into metal bomb components. Instead of a matter of weeks, he concludes that the correct conversion time should be measured in a matter of days.

As for the IAEA's conversion time estimates of 1 to 3 months for plutonium, HEU, or U233 contained in irradiated spent reactor fuel, these were also judged to be accurate *only* if the country possessing these materials did not have a covert or declared reprocessing or enrichment plant. If the country in question did, then it could possibly convert the spent fuel into bombs in a matter of weeks rather than months.

Finally, Dr. Cochran agreed with the IAEA's low end estimated conversion time of 3 months for low enriched uranium but, with the increased international availability of gas centrifuge uranium enrichment technology, found the IAEA's high end estimate of 12 months to be totally unwarranted. In fact, as already noted, a country might well be able to convert low enriched uranium into a bomb in a matter of weeks or less.[23]

The policy ramifications of these overly generous IAEA estimates are significant. They directly impact what the IAEA's detection goals should be. In three cases — the conversion of low enriched uranium, the conversion of plutonium, HEU, and U233 metal conversion — the order of time associated with the IAEA estimates is correct. In another three cases, however — the conversion of plutonium, HEU, and U233 in MOX (and conversion of these materials in spent fuel and of low enriched uranium if the inspected country has a covert or declared nuclear fuel-making facilities) — the IAEA's estimates are egregiously high. IAEA conversion times are measured in months when they should be measured in weeks and in weeks when they should be measured in days.

As a result, the IAEA's timeline detection goals in many cases are dangerously high. More important, the agency's current detection goals give the mistaken impression that the IAEA can detect military diversions before they result in bombs or even early enough to prevent the diversion from succeeding when this clearly is not the case. Dr. Cochran's analysis highlights that timely detection of plutonium, HEU, and U233 in metal and in fresh MOX is simply not possible. He concludes that countries that do not yet have nuclear weapons should not be allowed to stockpile or produce these materials. He reaches the same conclusion regarding the agency's ability to detect diversions of plutonium, HEU, and U233 in spent fuel in nonweapons states that may have a declared or covert enrichment or reprocessing plant. In these cases, the problem is not that the IAEA's timeliness detection goals are too liberal; it is the IAEA's claims that timely detection is possible at all (see Figure 4).

MATERIAL	IAEA Conversion Time	Cochran/NPEC Commissioned Estimate	Official IAEA Timeliness Detection Goal	Cochran Conclusions and Recommended Timeliness Detection Goals
Pu, HEU, U233 in metal form	Order of days (7-10)	Order of days (7-10)	1 month	Timely detection is not possible
In fresh MOX	Order of weeks (1-3)	Order of days (7-10)	1 month	Timely detection is not possible
In irradiated spent fuel	Order of months (1-3)	Order of months (1-3), if reprocessing - enrichment plant on tap (7-10 days	3 months	For countries with covert or declared nuclear fuel-making plants, timely detection is not possible
Low enriched uranium	Order of months (3-12)	Order of weeks to months	1 year	For countries with covert or declared enrichment plants, timely detection is not possible

Figure 4. IAEA Detection Times.

To some extent, these critical conclusions are gaining official support. As the IAEA's former director for safeguards recently explained, when it comes to nuclear fuel making, the IAEA is must rely on its limited ability to ascertain the inspected country's military intent.[24] Even the director general of the IAEA conceded that once a country acquires separated plutonium and HEU, the IAEA must start relying on these states' continued peaceful intentions, which could change rapidly. Unfortunately, the IAEA's Board of Governors and major governments, including the United States, do not yet appreciate the full implications of these points.

If the IAEA cannot provide timely detection of

diversions of weapons-usable HEU and plutonium from centrifuge enrichment, spent fuel reprocessing, and other fuel-making plants, how can it claim that it is "safeguarding" such facilities in Brazil, the Netherlands, Germany, and Japan? How can it effectively safeguard an Indian reprocessing plant (as is being currently proposed by the Indian government as a way to allow for the reprocessing of foreign fuel for use in an unsafeguarded Indian breeder reactor)? What of the idea of promoting regional nuclear fuel-making centers in nonweapons states, such as Kazakhstan? How might the IAEA prevent diversions?[25]

What of other more ambitious missions for the IAEA? If one cannot keep track of many bombs' worth of nuclear weapons-usable material produced annually at declared civilian nuclear fuel-making plants, or assure that the plants themselves would not be taken over by nonconforming parties, how much sense does it make to encourage the IAEA to oversee an even more difficult to verify military fissile production cut-off treaty?[26] Finally, there is the question of large research reactors and nuclear power plants, which require lightly enriched fuel to produce significant quantities of plutonium. If the IAEA cannot reliably ferret out covert nuclear fuel-making programs, how safe is it to export the necessary machinery to new countries particularly in war-torn regions such as the Middle East?

The questions here are all intentionally rhetorical. Yet, many experts and officials within the IAEA and the U.S. and other governments actively support at least one or more of the questionable nuclear initiatives referred to. This needs to change. One of the Cochran report's key recommendations is to encourage governments and the IAEA to reassess the agency's estimates of what constitutes a significant quantity along with the conversion times for various materials and what the proper detection goals should be for the agency. The most important part of this reassessment is clarifying precisely what nuclear materials and activities—i.e., militarily significant diversions—IAEA inspections cannot be counted on to detect in a timely fashion. These activities and materials include plutonium, HEU, and U233; making MOX; enriching uranium with centrifuges; reprocessing and fabricating plutonium-based fuels; and operating large research or power reactors in nonweapons states that might have covert or declared nuclear fuel-making plants.

For these nuclear activities and materials, the IAEA would do well simply to declare that the agency can monitor, but not safeguard them—i.e., that it can surveill these facilities and materials loosely but not assure detection of their possible military diversion in a timely fashion. Such an honest announcement would be helpful. First, it would put governments on notice about how dangerous the conduct of certain nuclear activities most closely related to bomb making actually are. Second, it would encourage countries to demand more monitoring and physical security of these unsafeguardable nuclear materials and activities. The primary aim in increasing such security and monitoring would not be to block diversions so much as to increase the chance of at least detecting them after they had occurred. This would help to deter such deeds and to limit further the risks of nuclear theft or sabotage. It is difficult to determine what the optimal level of monitoring and physical security might be for this purpose. But a good place to start would be to upgrade physical security at nuclear facilities handling or producing nuclear weapons-usable materials to those standards currently employed at the most secure nuclear weapons production and storage facilities.

FUNDING

As already noted, the IAEA's inspections of safe-guardable nuclear materials and activities could be enhanced in a number of ways. More near-real time monitoring could significantly enhance the agency's ability to detect the diversion of fuel rods. Retention and increasing the numbers of experienced nuclear inspectors could help assure that the IAEA actually meets its temporal detection goals and is able to analyze remote sensing information and imagery properly. Full support for the IAEA's environmental sampling activities would enable it to replace its aging Safeguards Analytical Laboratory and help the IAEA shorten the time needed to analyze samples from months to weeks or days. Much needed work to develop new safeguarding research capabilities and equipment could proceed much more quickly if more funds were made available[27] Similarly, with proper funding, the IAEA could muster reserve inspections staff and resources to meet unexpected demands and to provide the agency with deployable wide-area surveillance capabilities.

The first step to address these current gaps is simply to admit that they exist. For years, the IAEA has avoided doing this publicly. At the very outset of NPEC's investigations, early in 2005, the IAEA's safeguards planning staff briefed NPEC that it believed safeguards funding for the mid-term (i.e., the following 5 years) was sufficient. It conceded that it had given little or no thought to what funding agency safeguards might require beyond this period.

Fortunately, in the last 2 years, the agency's approach to safeguards planning has improved. Most recently the IAEA's director general highlighted the agency's lack of safeguards funding to deal with urgent inspections requirements associated with monitoring the shutdown of the reactor in North Korea. In a statement he made July 9, 2007, Dr. El Baradei explained that the IAEA was having difficulty obtaining the nearly 4 million euros needed to cover the monitoring costs. He went on to note:

> The DPRK case clearly illustrates the need for the agency to have an adequate reserve that can be drawn upon to enable it to respond promptly and effectively to unexpected crises or extraordinary requests, whether in the areas of verification, nuclear and radiological accidents, or other emergencies. The agency's financial vulnerability is also demonstrated by our current cash situation, which indicates that unless some major donors pay their outstanding contributions by the end of next month, the agency will have to draw from the Working Capital Fund in order to continue operations. *And unless contributions are received by September, that Fund would be depleted.* Finally, let me stress that the recent process of preparing and getting approval for the programme and budget for the next biennium has once again highlighted the urgent need for adequate resources to ensure effective delivery of the entire programme that you have requested. As I made clear during the last Board, even with the budget originally proposed by the Secretariat, the agency remains under-funded in many critical areas, a situation which, if it remains unaddressed, will lead to a steady erosion of our ability to perform key functions, including in the verification and safety fields.

At the conclusion of this statement, the director general then announced that he had initiated a study to examine the IAEA's "programmatic and budgetary requirements" over the "next decade or so." In addition, he announced his intention to create a high level panel to study options for financing the agency's requirements.[28]

The director general's announcement accords almost precisely with the recommendations Dr. Thomas Shea made to a select group of U.S. and European officials, including Dr. El Baradei's top scientific advisor, Andrew Graham, at an NPEC-sponsored conference held in Paris, France, on November 13, 2006.[29] In his brief, "Financing IAEA Verification of the NPT," Dr. Shea argued that North Korea "provides a clear justification" for additional safeguards funding and that to secure it the Director General "should convene a council of wise men to assist in determining how best to respond in this matter."[30]

As has been noted, the IAEA's funding is based on a United Nations (UN) formula that weights a donor country's gross domestic product and other factors. This formula may be sensible for raising general funds, but for nuclear safeguards purposes, it produces several anomalies. Countries with no large reactors (e.g., Italy) are sometimes asked to pay in more than countries that have a score or more of them (e.g., the Republic of Korea). The UN assessment method also overlooks the actual inspections requirements imposed by particular nuclear facilities that are significantly higher than the norm. Nuclear fuel-making plants of any type, reactors that are fueled on-line, and fast reactors all impose additional inspection challenges that are significantly more stringent than other types of nuclear facilities. Inspecting or monitoring these facilities costs much more than it does for other nuclear plants, yet the operator or owner pays no premium to cover these additional expenses.

Finally, because the IAEA's current approach to assessing its members for contributions fails to raise enough money for the Department of Safeguards, the agency must depend on additional voluntary contributions of cash and technical assistance. Almost all of the voluntary contributions come from the United States (amounting to roughly 35 percent of the IAEA's safeguards budget.). That so much of the safeguards budget is paid for voluntarily by the United States is politically awkward since the agency's most challenging inspections cases — e.g., India, Iran, North Korea, Taiwan, and South Korea — are all of special interest to Washington.[31]

Dr. Shea suggests several ways to increase funding for safeguards — ranging from setting up an endowment to selling bonds. All of them are worth pursuing but one of his ideas is particularly deserving: The customer (i.e., the inspected party) should pay. There already is a precedent for doing this. Taiwan, which the IAEA does not recognize as being an independent sovereign nation, does not pay as other nations do but instead pays what the IAEA estimates it costs the agency to inspect Taiwan's plants.

The Shea report recommends that the United States take the lead in getting the IAEA to help fund its safeguards activities with a user fee. The United States should continue to make its voluntary contributions but instead of making them as it currently does, Washington should justify them as representing a specific percentage cost associated with generating nuclear electricity annually in the United States. Japan, which also makes voluntary contributions, should be urged to do likewise. Agreement might subsequently be reached on an international standard, and this surcharge should be tacked on to the cost of electricity or other products these civilian plants produce. The last step would be to make the surcharge obligatory and assign all of the funds so raised to the IAEA's Department of Safeguards.

In addition to these funds, the agency should consider assessing an additional charge for the monitoring of unsafeguardable nuclear materials or facilities (e.g., nuclear fuel-making plants and nuclear weapons or near-nuclear weapons-usable fuels, etc.). Finally, an additional fee might be levied against nuclear facilities or plants that are particularly costly to the IAEA in meeting its own timeliness detection goals (e.g., for reactors fueled on-line).

RIGHTS

Some countries, of course, are likely to bridle at these proposals, arguing that imposing surcharges would interfere with their right to peaceful nuclear energy. These arguments, however, should be rejected. The exercise of one's right to develop, research, and produce peaceful nuclear energy hardly extends to not paying what it costs to safeguard these activities against military diversion. Also, the premise behind the argument for nonpaying represents a dangerously distorted view of the nuclear rules, viz., that so long as a state can claim a nuclear material or activity has some conceivable civilian application, it has a right to so engage even if they are unprofitable commercially, bring their possessor to the very brink of having bombs, or cannot be safeguarded against military diversion. The danger of this over-generous interpretation of the NPT is obvious: It risks, as UN General Secretary Koffi Anan explained to the 2005 NPT review conference, creating a dangerous world full of nuclear fuel-producing states that claim to be on the right side of the NPT, but are, in fact, only months or even days from acquiring nuclear weapons.[32]

Luckily, as research conducted for NPEC makes clear, this interpretation of the NPT is wrong.[33] The NPT makes no mention of nuclear fuel making, reprocessing, or enrichment. Spain, Romania, Brazil, and Mexico all tried in the late 1960s to get NPT negotiators to make it a duty under Article IV for the nuclear supplier states to supply "the entire fuel cycle" including fuel making, to nonweapons states. Each of their proposals was turned down.[34] At the time, the Swedish representative to the NPT negotiations even suggested that rules needed to be established to *prevent* nations from getting into such dangerous activities since there seemed to be no clear way to prevent nations from quickly fabricating bombs by diverting either the fuel or the fuel-making plants to such a purpose.[35] The Swedes were certainly were not interested in protecting uneconomical measures that are unnecessary and that could bring states to the brink of having bombs.[36]

A clear case in point was the NPT's handling of peaceful nuclear explosives, which turned out to be so dangerous and impossible to safeguard that the treaty spoke only of sharing the "potential benefits" of peaceful nuclear explosives that would be supplied by nuclear weapons states. No effort, however, was ever made to request or to offer such nuclear explosives because they were so costly to use as compared to conventional explosives and no clear economic benefit could be found in using them.[37]

Finally, in no case did the framers of the NPT believe that the "inalienable right" to develop, research, or produce peaceful nuclear energy should allow states to contravene the NPT restrictions designed to prevent the proliferation of nuclear weapons. These restrictions are contained in Articles I, II, and III of the treaty. Article I prohibits nuclear weapons states from "assist[ing], encourag[ing], or induc[ing] any non-weapons state to manufacture or otherwise acquire" nuclear weapons. Article II prohibits nonweapons states from acquiring in any way nuclear explosives or seeking "any assistance" in their manufacture. Together these two prohibitions suggest that the NPT not only bans the transfer of actual nuclear explosives, but of any nuclear technology or materials that could "assist, encourage or induce" nonweapons states to "manufacture or otherwise acquire" nuclear explosives.[38]

If there was any doubt on this point, the NPT also requires all nonweapons states to apply inspection safeguards against all of their nuclear facilities and holdings of special nuclear materials. The purpose of these nuclear inspections, according to the treaty, is "verification of the fulfillment of its obligations assumed under this Treaty with a view to preventing diversion of nuclear energy from peaceful uses to nuclear weapons."[39] It was understood at the time of the treaty's drafting that it was hoped a way could be found to assure such safeguards. It, however, was not assumed that such techniques already existed.[40]

CONCLUSION

It would be useful to remind members of the IAEA of these points. The most direct and easiest way to begin is to make clear what can and cannot be safeguarded—i.e., what can and cannot be monitored so as to detect a military diversion *before* it is completed.

Beyond this, the IAEA should requie the owner,

operators, and customers of nuclear facilities to bear the costs associated with monitoring and safeguarding them. The hope here would be that the poor economics associated with large nuclear power reactors and nuclear fuel-making plants might persuade some nations to reconsider the desirability of acquiring them. Making sure that the full external costs of IAEA inspections are carried by each inspected party would be useful. The NPT, after all, is dedicated to sharing the "benefits" of peaceful nuclear energy, not conducting money-losing programs that bring countries to the brink of having bombs.[41]

ENDNOTES - CHAPTER 8

1. This line of argument was actually presented to NPEC's executive director in a private briefing by the IAEA safeguards planning staff in Vienna early in 2006.

2. For data on the IAEA's safeguards budget obligation in current — not constant — U.S. dollars, see *The Agency's Accounts for 1984*, GC(XXIX)/749, Vienna, Austria: IAEA, August 1985, p. 26; and *The Agency's Accounts for 2004*, GC(49)/7, p. 47. For data on the amount of nuclear material safeguarded by the IAEA, *see Annual Report for 1984*, GC(XXIX)/748, Vienna, Austria: IAEA, July 1985, p. 63; and *Annual Report for 2004*, GC(49)/5, Annex, Table A19.

3. Private interviews with safeguards staff and former IAEA safeguards inspectors at the Los Alamos National Laboratory, Los Alamos, New Mexico, May 12, 2005.

4. See Gene Aloise, Director, Natural Resources and Environment, U.S. Government Accountability Office, "Nuclear Nonproliferation: IAEA Safeguards and other Measures to Halt the Spread of Nuclear Weapons Materials," testimony before the Subcommittee on National Security, Emerging Threats and International Relations, Committee on Government Reform, House of Representatives, September 26, 2006.

5. For a more detailed discussion of the Additional Protocol, see Richard Hooper, "The IAEA's Additional Protocol," *Disarmament Forum* "On-site Inspections: Common Problems, Different Solutions," No. 3, 1999, pp. 7-16, available from *www.unidir.ch/bdd/fiche-article.php?ref_article=209*.

6. For example, in the case of Japan, the IAEA needed 5 years to determine that it had no undeclared nuclear material activities, and estimates that it will need about as much time to make the same determination for Canada. See *Nuclear Nonproliferation*, Washington, DC: U.S. Government Accountability Office (US-GAO), pp. 12-13.

7. According to IAEA internal analyses, the average lifetime savings in safeguards resources likely from implementing integrated safeguards may be no more than 5 percent. See C. Xerri and H. Nackaerts on behalf of the ESARDA Integrated Safeguards Working Group, "Integrated Safeguards: A Case to Go Beyond the Limits: Consequences of Boundary Limits Set to the Reduction of 'Classical Safeguards Measures on Efficiency and Resources Allocation in Integrated Safeguards'" produced in 2003 for the IAEA, available from *esarda2.jrc.it/bulletin/bulletin_32/06.pdf*. For an official overview of the various safeguards resources required to implement the Additional Protocol, see Jill N. Cooley, "Current Safeguards Challenges from the IAEA View," an IAEA document produced in 2003, available from *esarda2.jrc.it/events/other_meetings/inmm/2003-esarda-inmm-Como/1-paper%20pdf/1-1-040127-cooley.pdf*.

8. See Garry Dillon, "Wide Area Environmental Sample in Iran," available from *www.npec-web.org/Essays/WideAreaEnvironmentalSampling.pdf*.

9. See Victor Gilinsky, Harmon Hubbard, and Marvin Miller, *A Fresh Examination of the Proliferation Dangers of Light Water Reactors*, Washington, DC: The Nonproliferation Policy Education Center, October 22, 2004, reprinted in Henry Sokolski, ed., *Taming the Next Set of Strategic Weapons Threats*, Carlisle, PA: Strategic Studies Institute, U.S. Army War College, 2006, available from *www.npec-web.org/Frameset.asp?PageType=Single&PDFFile=20041022-GilinskyEtAl-LWR&PDFFolder=Essays*.

10. See, e.g., Andrew Leask, Russell Leslie, and John Carlson, "Safeguards As a Design Criterion—Guidance for Regulators," Canberra, Australia: Australian Safeguards and Non-proliferation Office, September 2004, pp. 4-9, available from *www.asno. dfat.gov.au/publications/safeguards_design_criteria.pdf.*

11. For more detailed discussion of how fuel diverted from different commercial and research reactors could help accelerate a country's covert bomb program, go to Appendix II of this report.

12. See J. Whichello, J. Regula, K. Tolk, and M. Hug, "A Secure Global Communications Network for IAEA Safeguards and IEC Applications," IAEA User Requirements Document, May 6, 2005.

13. The problem of states "losing" fuel rods, it should be noted, is not limited to countries intent on diverting them to make bombs. The U.S. civilian nuclear industry, which has a clear industrial interest in keeping track of its nuclear fuel, has had difficulty keeping proper account of all of it. On this point, see *NRC Needs to Do More to Ensure Power Plants Are Effectively Controlling Spent Fuel,* GAO O5-339, Washington, DC: U.S. Government Accountability Office, April 2005, available from *www.gao.gov/new. items/d05339.pdf.*

14. Only about a third of the facilities the IAEA currently has remote sensors at have near-real-time connectivity with Vienna or other regional headquarters, and almost all of these facilities are in countries that are of minimal proliferation risk. This information was presented at a private IAEA Department of Safeguards briefing of NPEC's executive director at Vienna, Austria, at IAEA Headquarters, January 30, 2006.

15. See Edwin Lyman, "Can Nuclear Fuel Production in Iran and Elsewhere be Safeguarded Against Diversion," presented at NPEC's Conference "After Iran: Safeguarding Peaceful Nuclear Energy" held in London, UK, October 2005, available from *www. npec-web.org/Frameset.asp?PageType=Single&PDFFile=Paper05092 8LymanFuelSafeguardDiv&PDFFolder=Essays.*

16. This incident received only scant public attention. See Bayan Rahman, "Japan 'Loses' 206 kg of Plutonium," *Financial Times*, January 28, 2003, available from *news.ft.com;servlet/ ContentServer?pagename=FT.com/StoryFT/FullStory&c=StoryFT&c id=1042491288304&p=10112571727095.*

17. *Ibid.* Also see "Missing Plutonium 'Just on Paper,'" *BBC News*, February 17, 2005, available from *news.bbc.co.uk/1/hi/ uk/4272691.stm*; and Kenji Hall, "Missing Plutonium Probe Latest Flap for Japan's Beleaguered Nuclear Power Industry," *Associated Press* (Tokyo), January 28, 2003, available from *www.wise-paris. org/index.html?/english/othersnews/year_2003/othersnews030128b. html&/english/frame/menu.html&/english/frame/band.html.*

18. These points have been long recognized by outside experts. See Paul Leventhal, "Safeguards Shortcomings — A Critique," Washington, DC: NCI, September 12, 1994; Marvin Miller, "Are IAEA Safeguards in Plutonium Bulk-Handling Facilities Effective?" Washington, DC: NCI, August 1990; Brian G. Chow and Kenneth A. Solomon, *Limiting the Spread of Weapons-Usable Fissile Materials*, Santa Monica, CA: RAND, 1993, pp. 1-4; and Marvin Miller, "The Gas Centrifuge and Nuclear Proliferation," *A Fresh Examination of the Proliferation Dangers of Light Water Reactors*, Washington, DC: NPEC, October 22, 2004, p. 38.

19. See *ibid.*; also see the comments of the former chairman of the IAEA's Standing Advisory Group on International Safeguards, John Carlson, Australian Safeguards and Non-Proliferation Office, "Addressing Proliferation Challenges from the Spread of Uranium Enrichment Capability," Paper prepared for the Annual Meeting of the Institute for Nuclear Materials Management, Tucson, Arizona, July 8-12, 2007. Copy on file at NPEC.

20. See Thomas B. Cochran, "Adequacy of IAEA's Safeguards for Achieving Timely Warning, " paper presented before a conference cosponsored by NPEC and King's College, "After Iran: Safeguarding Peaceful Nuclear Energy," October 2-3, 2005, London, UK, available from *www.npec-web.org/Frameset.asp?Pag eType=Single&PDFFile=Paper050930CochranAdequacyofTime&PD FFolder=Essays.*

21. Interview of senior advisors to the IAEA Director Gen-

eral, IAEA Headquarters, Vienna, Austria, January 17 2005, and January 30, 2006.

22. *IAEA Safeguards Glossary,* 2001 Ed., Paragraph 3.13, Vienna, Austria: IAEA. Figure 2 here is identified as Table I in the glossary.

23. Cf. the low-end conversion time estimates for low enriched uranium of John Carlson in note 19 above, which for a small commercial enrichment facility range between 18 hours and 12 days.

24. See the testimony of Pierre Goldschmidt before a hearing of the House Subcommittee on National Security and Foreign Affairs of the House Committee on Oversight and Government Reform, "International Perspectives on Strengthening the Nonproliferation Regime," June 26, 2007, Washington, DC, available from the subcommittee upon request.

25. See Ann MacLachian, Mark Hibbs, and Elaine Hiruo, "Kazakh Buy-in to Westinghouse Seen as Win-Win for Kazakhs, Toshiba," *Nucleonics Week,* July 12, 2007, p. 1; and Kenneth Silverstein, "As North Korea Gives Up Its Nukes, Kazakhstan Seeks a Nuclear Edge," *Harper's Magazine,* July 2007, available from *harpers.org/archive/2007/07/hbc-90000549.*

26. On the challenges of verifying a military fissile production cut-off treaty, see Christopher A. Ford, "The United States and the Fissile Material Cut-off Treaty," presented at the Conference on "Preparing for 2010: Getting the Process Right," Annecy, France, March 17, 2007, available from www.state.gov/t/isn/rls/other/81950.htm.

27. For a detailed discussion of what specific new safeguards capabilities the IAEA Department of Safeguards is investigating, see N. Khlebnikov, D. Parise, J. Whichello, "Novel Technology for the Detection of Undeclared Nuclear Activities," IAEA-CN148/32, presented at the IAEA Conference on Safeguards held in Vienna, Austria, October 16-20, 2006, available from *www. npec-web.org/Frameset.asp?PageType=Single&PDFFile=20070301-IAEA-NovelTechnologiesProject&PDFFolder=Essays.*

28. See IAEA Director General Dr. Mohamed El Baradei, "Introductory Statement to the Board of Governors," July 9, 2007, Vienna, Austria, available from *www.globalsecurity.org/wmd/library/news/dprk/2007/dprk-070709-iaea01.htm*.

29. See Thomas E. Shea, "Financing IAEA Verification of the NPT," paper presented at a conference sponsored by the Nonproliferation Policy Education Center and the French Foreign Ministry, "Assessing the IAEA's Ability to Verify the NPT," November 12-13, 2006, Paris, France, available from *www.npec-web.org/Essays/20061113-Shea-FinancingIAEAVerification.pdf*.

30. *Ibid.*

31. See U.S. GAO, *Nuclear Nonproliferation*, pp. 34-40.

32. See UN Secretary General Kofi Annan, Statement to the Nuclear Nonproliferation Treaty Review Conference, May 2, 2005, UN Headquarters, New York, available from *www.acronym.org.uk/docs/0505/doc11.htm*.

33. Robert Zarate, "The NPT, IAEA Safeguards and Peaceful Nuclear Energy: An 'Inalienable Right,' But Precisely To What?" presented at "Assessing the IAEA's Ability to Safeguard Peaceful Nuclear Energy," a conference held in Paris, France, November 12-13, 2006, available from *www.npec-web.org/Frameset.asp?PageType=Single&PDFFile=20070509-Zarate-NPT-IAEA-PeacefulNuclear&PDFFolder=Essays*.

34. See "Mexican Working Paper Submitted to the Eighteen Nation Disarmament Committee: Suggested Additions to Draft Nonproliferation Treaty," ENDC/196, September 19, 1967, U.S. Arms Control and Disarmament Agency, *Documents on Disarmament, 1967*, Publication No. 46, Washington, DC: U.S. Government Printing Office, July 1968, pp. 394-395; "Romanian Working Paper Submitted to the Eighteen Nation Disarmament Committee: Amendments and Additions to the Draft Nonproliferation Treaty," ENDC/199, October 19, 1967, in *ibid.*, pp. 525-526; "Brazilian Amendments to the Draft Nonproliferation Treaty," ENDC/201, October 31, 1967, in *Ibid.*, p. 546; and "Spanish Memorandum to the Co-Chairman of the ENDC," ENDC/210, February 8, 1968, in U.S. Arms Control and Disarmament Agency, *Documents on Disarmament, 1968*, Publication No. 52, Washington, DC: U.S. Gov-

ernment Printing Office, September 1969, pp. 39-40.

35. See "Statement by the Swedish Representative [Alva Myrdal] to the Eighteen Nation Disarmament Committee: Nonproliferation of Nuclear Weapons," ENDC/PV. 243, February 24, 1966, in U.S. Arms Control and Disarmament Agency, *Documents on Disarmament, 1966*, Publication No. 43, Washington, DC: U.S. Government Printing Office, September 1967, p. 56.

36. See Eldon V. C. Greenberg, "NPT and Plutonium: Application of NPT Prohibitions to 'Civilian' Nuclear Equipment, Technology and Materials Associated with Reprocessing and Plutonium Use," Washington, DC: Nuclear Control Institute, 1984 (Rev. May 1993).

37. See *Report of Main Committee III*, Treaty on the Nonproliferation of Nuclear Weapons Review and Extension Conference, May 5, 1995, NPT/CONF.1995/MC.III/1, Sec. I, para. 2, emphasis added, available from *www.un.org/Depts/ddar/nptconf/162.htm*, which states:

The Conference records that the potential benefits of the peaceful applications of nuclear explosions envisaged in article V of the Treaty have not materialized. In this context, the Conference notes that the potential benefits of the peaceful applications of nuclear explosions have not been demonstrated and that serious concerns have been expressed as to the environmental consequences that could result from the release of radioactivity from such applications and on the risk of possible proliferation of nuclear weapons. Furthermore, no requests for services related to the peaceful applications of nuclear explosions have been received by IAEA since the Treaty entered into force. The Conference further notes that no State party has an active programme for the peaceful application of nuclear explosions.

38. See Greenberg, "NPT and Plutonium"; and Henry D. Sokolski and George Perkovich, "It's Called *Non*proliferation," *Wall Street Journal*, April 29, 2005, p. A16.

39. NPT, Art III, para. 1.

40. For example, see "British Paper Submitted to the Eighteen

Nation Disarmament Committee: Technical Possibility of International Control of Fissile Material Production," ENDC/60, August 31, 1962, Corr. 1, November 27, 1962, U.S. Arms Control and Disarmament Agency, *Documents on Disarmament, 1962*, Publication No. 19, Vol. 2, Washington, DC: U.S. Government Printing Office, November 1963, pp. 834-852.

41. On these points, see Henry Sokolski, "Market-based Non-proliferation," testimony presented before a hearing of the House Committee on Foreign Affairs, "Every State a Superpower? Stopping the Spread of Nuclear Weapons in the 21st Century," May 10, 2007.

Part V

THE RIGHTS AND BENEFITS OF PEACEFUL NUCLEAR ENERGY — ARTICLES IV AND V

CHAPTER 9

IT'S CALLED NONPROLIFERATION*

Henry Sokolski and George Perkovich

Iran's Foreign Minister Kamal Kharrazi has just stated in no uncertain terms that if today's talks with France, Britain, and Germany fail, there will be "no choice but to restart" his country's uranium-enrichment program. The Iranian people, he says, "believe it is their inalienable right to have access to this technology for peaceful purposes."[1]

Iranian negotiators recognize the leverage that nuclear "rights" give them; so they say that the only issue is to establish the procedures under which they will exercise their rights to operate enrichment centrifuges. In February, Hassan Rohani, Iran's national security council secretary, offered to open up Iran's enrichment plants to even more intrusive inspections than those now currently allowed. If this was not acceptable, he suggested that Iran would be willing merely to run a pilot enrichment plant that he claimed would be too small to make even one bomb's worth of highly enriched uranium. He even offered to allow the U.S. to buy up to one-half of Iran's entire nuclear program to build confidence that Iran's program would only be used for peaceful purposes.

These offers are beguiling. They are also bad. The reasons why, though, are likely to remain obscure so

---

*Originally published in the *Wall Street Journal*, April 25, 2009, available from *online.wsj.com/article/SB111474293254420461.html*.

long as our diplomats continue to agree with Mr. Kharrazi that all states that are not in violation of the Nuclear Nonproliferation Treaty (NPT) have a right to make nuclear fuel, and that such activity can be monitored to prevent quick diversions to make bombs. In fact, there is no such right, and nuclear fuel-making of the sort Iran is planning to engage in still cannot be safeguarded in any meaningful way.

The NPT's history and common sense clarify why the right to peaceful nuclear energy is qualified. First, the NPT, to which Iran is a signatory, is a nuclear nonproliferation treaty, not a nuclear bartering tool. If it authorized states to get all they needed to come within days of having a nuclear arsenal, perversely it would be no more than a legal cover for proliferation. A state could be fully compliant with the NPT so long as it declared all of its nuclear activities and avoided taking the final step (which in extreme cases would take no more than hours or days) of assembling the nuclear weapons-usable materials it had into bombs.

Second, if there are different ways to interpret a contract, the one that lends the greatest support to its provisions and prime intent is the one any sound lawyer or judge must back. Unfortunately, nuclear promoters and diplomats have disobeyed this sensible rule. When it comes to the NPT, they read the treaty's "inalienable right" to develop "peaceful nuclear energy" as being absolute. This is what leads them to conclude that a state has a right under the treaty to get everything up to but not including a complete nuclear weapon so long as it continues to claim that its nuclear activities are peaceful and there is no clear international determination otherwise.

This reading of the treaty, besides making a hash of the NPT's intent to block bomb makers, is simply wrong. Article IV of the NPT makes clear that non-nuclear weapons state members are free to exercise their right to develop peaceful nuclear energy, but only if they do so "in conformity" with the NPT's nonproliferation restrictions. Which restrictions are these? The first is the stipulation in Article II that nonweapons states are "not to seek or receive any assistance in the manufacture of nuclear weapons." The other is the requirement in Article III of the treaty that all nonweapons states must place all of their civil nuclear activities under International Atomic Energy Agency (IAEA) nuclear safeguards—i.e., nuclear inspections geared "to preventing diversion of nuclear energy from peaceful uses to nuclear weapons."[2]

Nuclear activities and materials that cannot be safeguarded, then, cannot count on being protected by the NPT. Centrifuge enrichment of uranium for power reactors, which can be switched to produce weapons-grade uranium overnight; chemical separation of weapons-usable plutonium from spent reactor fuel; and the fabrication of weapons-usable plutonium and highly enriched uranium (HEU) reactor fuels, all fall into this category.

The following recent examples betray the inherent limitations of IAEA efforts to try to safeguard such plants. Earlier this year, the United Kingdom (UK) publicly admitted to having "lost" nearly 30 kilograms—or five crude nuclear devices' worth—of weapons-usable plutonium at its commercial reprocessing facility. The year before, the British reported 19 kilos had gone missing. Japan, meanwhile, announced in early 2003 that it had lost 206 kilos of plutonium at its pilot reprocessing plant. These losses, it claimed, occurred over the previous 15 years. This revelation came after the Japanese had already admitted to hav-

215

ing lost 70 kilos at an entirely different plutonium fuel fabrication plant.

All of these facilities were under the IAEA's watchful eyes. What's more frightening, the IAEA found all of these losses to be within permissible limits: Inspectors assumed the material simply was "lost in the plant's pipes." This is not the margin of safety needed to ensure that all safeguarded nuclear activities are solely for peaceful purposes, as required under the NPT. With facilities like these and with uranium enrichment and HEU fabrication plants, the IAEA should admit that it cannot yet know if and when a bomb's worth of bomb-usable material might have been stolen. It also should admit that a state could divert these activities and the materials they produce to make a bomb well before the IAEA or any outside power could step in to block it.

WHAT, THEN, DOES THIS RECOMMEND?

First, unless there is a clear economic imperative to proceed with these dangerous nuclear fuel-related activities, the security reasons for holding back should take precedence. The burden of proof should clearly be on those who seek to expand such activities to demonstrate clear civilian benefits and market economic competitiveness in comparison with alternatives. Reprocessing plutonium for civilian use, fabricating HEU or plutonium-based fuels, building new enrichment capacity to expand now beyond the world's already large surplus of uranium-enrichment capacity, are unnecessary to promote peaceful nuclear energy today and, in most cases, are clear money losers.

This suggests adoption of some variant of President Bush's or IAEA Director General Mohamed El

Baradei's proposed curbs on these activities. Certainly, nuclear industry can well afford to put the further addition of any new net capacity to make enriched uranium or to recycle plutonium-based fuels on hold for several years. The European Union (EU) has already signed on board to some kind of limits. This pause could be used to try to establish just what nuclear activities and materials the IAEA can and cannot truly safeguard against quick diversion.

Second, using the time gained from this pause, the United States and others should return to the NPT's original, commonsensical intent regarding what is peaceful, what is protected, and what is dangerous and should be curbed as much as possible. In this regard, Congress, and especially the U.S. Senate, should ask for clarification of what nuclear activities are allowed under what circumstances under Article IV of the NPT and why.

Certainly, it makes no sense for the United States to be disputing with Iran and other would-be bomb makers if we share their views on how much is allowed under the rules. Indeed, if we cannot get others to return to the NPT's original, tougher view of what peaceful nuclear energy means, our current campaign to prevent Iran from going nuclear will not only fail, but will make the rules all but meaningless.

ENDNOTES - CHAPTER 9

1. See Susanna Loof, "Iran Will Restart Uranium Enrichment if European Talks Fail, Foreign Minister," *Associated Press*, April 28, 2005, available from *www.accessmylibrary.com/article-1G1-135697037/iran-restart-uranium-enrichment.html*.

2. See Articles II and III of *The Treaty on the Non-Proliferation of Nuclear Weapons*, available from *www.state.gov/www/global/arms/treaties/npt1.html*.

CHAPTER 10

THE THREE QUALIFICATIONS
OF ARTICLE IV'S "INALIENABLE RIGHT"*

Robert Zarate

To be sure, Article IV of the NPT recognizes the "inalienable right" of signatories to peaceful nuclear energy. However, it also explicitly imposes two qualifications on the "nuclear energy for peaceful purposes" to which NPT signatories have an "inalienable right." Signatories shall develop "research, production and use" of peaceful nuclear energy (1) "without discrimination" and (2) "in conformity with articles I and II of this Treaty."[1] Moreover, when the NPT's Article III defines the purpose of comprehensive safeguards by the IAEA as the *"verification of the fulfillment of [signatory] obligations assumed under this Treaty* with a view to preventing the diversion of nuclear energy from peaceful purposes to nuclear weapons and other nuclear explosive devices,"[2] it effectively establishes (3) "conformity with Article III" as a third qualification. These three qualifications, when understood in relation to the treaty's preamble and main text, not only narrow the scope of "nuclear energy for peaceful purposes" to which signatories have an "inalienable right," but also establish criteria that signatories must meet in order to exercise this right.

---

*Originally published as a part of "The NPT, IAEA Safeguards and Peaceful Nuclear Energy: An 'Inalienable Right,' But Precisely to What?" Henry Sokolski, ed., *Falling Behind: International Scrutiny of the Peaceful Atom*, Carlisle, PA, Strategic Studies Institute, U.S. Army War College, 2008, pp. 221-290.

To begin, paragraph seven of the NPT's preamble lays out the principle that addresses the special meaning of Article IV's first qualification, "without discrimination," within the context of the treaty.[3] That paragraph affirms:

> the principle that *the benefits* of peaceful applications of nuclear technology, including any technological by-products which may be derived by nuclear-weapon States from the development of nuclear explosive devices, should be available for peaceful purposes to all Parties of the Treaty, whether nuclear-weapon or non-nuclear weapon States.[4]

To be clear, neither this principle (which hereinafter I refer to as the "benefits-without-discrimination" principle), nor any other part of the NPT, ever expressly requires that any specific *nuclear technology*, or any specific *peaceful application* of nuclear technology, be made available to all signatories, but rather that only *the benefits* of a given nuclear technology's peaceful application be made available somehow. In essence, this principle recognizes that some nuclear technologies and some peaceful applications of nuclear technology — to take an extreme example, so-called "nuclear explosions for peaceful purposes" in civilian mining, excavation, or canal-digging operations — may be too uneconomical, too proliferative, and too unsafeguardable to permit non-nuclear-weapon states to acquire and use them. Thus, when Article IV's first qualification applies this principle to peaceful nuclear energy, it appears to permit, in principle, the denial of a given nuclear technology or a given nuclear technology's peaceful application to a signatory as long as the benefits of the denied nuclear technology's peaceful application are made available somehow.

Article IV's second qualification requires that the development of "research, production and use" of peaceful nuclear energy be "in conformity with articles I and II" of the NPT. These two articles articulate the NPT's main prohibitions against the direct and indirect proliferation of nuclear weapons by treaty signatories. Article I prohibits nuclear-weapon signatories from giving nuclear weapons and other nuclear explosive devices, or control over such devices, to "any recipient whatsoever," and also forbids them from "assist[ing], encourag[ing], or induc[ing]" any non-nuclear-weapon state "to manufacture or otherwise acquire" nuclear explosive devices.[5] Article II correspondingly prohibits non-nuclear-weapon signatories from receiving nuclear explosive devices, or control over such devices, and also forbids them from building or acquiring in any way nuclear explosive devices, and from receiving or seeking "any assistance in the manufacture" of such devices.[6] Article IV's second qualification therefore effectively narrows the scope of "nuclear energy for peaceful purposes" to which signatories have an "inalienable right" under Article IV, since peaceful nuclear energy "in conformity with articles I and II" excludes *not only* nuclear explosive technology for peaceful or non-peaceful purposes, *but also* other nuclear technology and assistance that could "assist, encourage or induce" non-nuclear-weapon states "to manufacture or otherwise acquire" nuclear explosive technology.[7]

Furthermore, the NPT's Article III requires each non-nuclear-weapon signatory to conclude a comprehensive safeguard agreement with the IAEA:

> for the exclusive purpose of *verification of the fulfillment of its obligations assumed under this Treaty* with a view to preventing the diversion of nuclear energy

221

from peaceful purposes to nuclear weapons and other nuclear explosive devices.[8]

By requiring non-nuclear-weapon signatories to submit to full-scope IAEA safeguards to verify the fulfillment of their obligations under Articles I and II, as well as other parts of the NPT, Article III effectively establishes a third legally-binding qualification on the "nuclear energy for peaceful purposes" to which signatories have an "inalienable right" under Article IV. That is, to develop "research, production and use" of peaceful nuclear energy "in conformity with articles I and II" necessarily implies full "conformity with Article III."[9] Thus, Article IV's third qualification appears to recognize the "inalienable right" of a signatory to peaceful nuclear energy only when the signatory's nuclear activities are *effectively* safeguardable by the IAEA, and the signatory complies fully with its obligations under Article III of the NPT and related IAEA comprehensive safeguards agreements.[10]

ARTICLE IV'S THREE QUALIFICATIONS AND NUCLEAR EXPLOSIONS FOR PEACEFUL PURPOSES

With respect to "nuclear explosions for peaceful purposes," the majority of the NPT negotiators understood that, at the time of their negotiations and for the foreseeable future, nuclear explosive technology in civilian projects not only lacked clear and immediate economic benefits, especially when compared to non-nuclear alternatives; but also possessed an unacceptable risk of nuclear proliferation since such technology *could not be effectively safeguarded by the IAEA*. Hence, the final text of the NPT denies non-nuclear-weapon signatories access both to nuclear explosive technology and its peaceful applications.

In conformity with the preamble's "benefits-without-discrimination" principle, though, the NPT's Article V outlines the framework by which non-nuclear-weapon signatories could avail themselves of "the potential benefits" of nuclear explosive technology's peaceful application, if such economic benefits should ever materialize. The relevant part of Article V reads:

> Each Party to the Treaty undertakes to take appropriate measures to ensure that, in accordance with this Treaty, under appropriate international observation and through appropriate international procedures, *potential benefits* from any peaceful applications of nuclear explosions will be made available to non-nuclear-weapon States Party to the Treaty on a *non-discriminatory basis* and that the charge to such Parties for the explosive devices used will be as low as possible and exclude any charge for research and development. Non-nuclear-weapon States Party to the Treaty shall be able to obtain such benefits, pursuant to a special international agreement or agreements, through an appropriate international body with adequate representation of non-nuclear-weapon States. . . .[11]

As the NPT's negotiation history reveals, many of the non-nuclear-weapon states represented at the ENDC did not view either the denial of nuclear explosive technology and its peaceful applications, or Article V's framework for providing the "potential benefits" of the denied nuclear explosive technology's peaceful applications, as discriminatory per se.[12] For example, in late January 1968 Polish delegate Mieczyslaw Blusztajn remarked to the ENDC:

> I should like once again to stress that *the right of all countries to conduct peaceful nuclear explosions is not at*

stake. The only matter to be settled is the procedure and the conditions to be observed so that countries which forgo the manufacture of nuclear devices shall not be deprived of *the benefits* that may be derived from the use of nuclear explosives.[13]

Bulgarian delegate Kroum Christov echoed the Polish delegate's sentiments:

> [I]t seems to us quite clearly impossible to admit and to include in the non-proliferation treaty the right to manufacture nuclear devices and to carry out nuclear explosions. *There is no question in this case of denying a right; nor should the prohibition of all activity of this nature be regarded as an infraction of that right.* Account is taken of a state of facts which, for reasons which cannot be refuted and which have been explained here at length, renders the manufacture of nuclear devices incompatible with a non-proliferation treaty.[14]

In retrospect, the efforts of NPT negotiators to limit the spread of nuclear explosive technology for peaceful purposes proved to be well-founded. Indeed, the "potential benefits" of so-called peaceful nuclear explosives ("PNEs") never materialized as non-nuclear explosive alternatives for mining, excavation, and canal-digging operations emerged as safer and more economical choices.[15] In fact, in May 1995 the quadrennial NPT review conference reached the following conclusions about PNEs:

> The Conference records that *the potential benefits* of the peaceful applications of nuclear explosions envisaged in article V of the Treaty *have not materialized.* In this context, the Conference notes that the potential benefits of the peaceful applications of nuclear explosions have not been demonstrated and that serious concerns have been expressed as to the environmental consequences that could result from the release of

radioactivity from such applications and on the risk of possible proliferation of nuclear weapons. Furthermore, no requests for services related to the peaceful applications of nuclear explosions have been received by IAEA since the Treaty entered into force. The Conference further notes that no State party has an active programme for the peaceful application of nuclear explosions.[16]

Moreover, though the *Comprehensive Nuclear-Test-Ban Treaty* has not entered into force, it has nonetheless established an international norm against the use of nuclear explosions, whether for non-peaceful or allegedly peaceful purposes.[17]

By prohibiting non-nuclear-weapon states from developing, accessing, and using so-called peaceful nuclear explosive devices, the NPT reinforces the importance of the following principle: When the IAEA cannot effectively safeguard the nuclear material involved in an allegedly peaceful application of nuclear technology, then the NPT does not protect the right of states to develop, access, or use that allegedly peaceful application of nuclear technology.

ARTICLE IV'S THREE QUALIFICATIONS AND NUCLEAR ENERGY FOR PEACEFUL PURPOSES

In conformity with Article IV's three qualifications, then, both (a) the "benefits-without-discrimination" principle of the NPT's preamble, and (b) the framework by which Article V allows non-nuclear-weapon signatories to avail themselves of the "potential benefits" of nuclear explosive technology's peaceful applications without providing them actual access to the technology or its peaceful application, can be applied to enrichment, reprocessing, and other sensitive nuclear fuel-making activities. Under a sustainable reading of the NPT, it is both plausible and consistent for governments to interpret Article IV as affirming the "inalienable right" of nuclear signatories to develop "research, production and use" of nuclear fuel-making only to the extent that such nuclear fuel-making activities: (1) are economically beneficial in accordance with the treaty's preamble (Article IV's first qualification); (2) possess a low risk of proliferation in accordance with Articles I and II (Article IV's second qualification); and (3) are *effectively* safeguardable and undertaken in full compliance with NPT and IAEA safeguard obligations in accordance with Article III (Article IV's third qualification).[18] Moreover, it is both plausible and consistent with the treaty to forbid signatories from developing, acquiring, and using nuclear fuel-making technologies (especially those related to nuclear materials that the IAEA cannot effectively safeguard) that can assist them in manufacturing nuclear weapons under some circumstances — at the very least, when they fail to comply with their obligations under the NPT's Article III and related IAEA safeguards agreements — as long as the benefits of peaceful applications of such nuclear fuel-making technologies are made available to them.[19]

As the NPT's negotiation history reveals, ENDC delegations from both nuclear-weapon states and non-nuclear-weapon states viewed nuclear fuel making in a manner similar to nuclear explosives for peaceful purposes: that is, as potentially aiding and even constituting the manufacture of nuclear weapons. For example, in September 1962 British delegate Sir Michael Wright told the ENDC:

The thing which is unique to a nuclear weapon is its

warhead. And what is there in a nuclear warhead that is found in no other weapons? . . . It is the fissile material in the warhead; that is to say, the plutonium and uranium-235, the two fissile materials now most commonly used in nuclear weapons.

If we are to deal effectively with nuclear weapons, we must concentrate on the fissile material which every nuclear weapon has and which no other weapon has.[20]

In another example, in February 1966 Swedish delegate Alva Myrdal argued before the ENDC:

[T]o block the road to nuclear weapon development as early as possible . . . what we are facing is a long ladder with many rungs, and the practical question is: on which of these is it reasonable and feasible to introduce the international blocking? . . . *To prohibit just the final act of "manufacture" would seem to come late in these long chains of decisions.* . . . Could a middle link be found on which the prohibitory regulation should most definitely be focused?[21]

A month later, during a speech to the ENDC, Burmese delegate U. Maung Maung Gyi answered Myrdal's question:

An undertaking on the part of the non-nuclear weapon Powers not to manufacture nuclear weapons would in effect mean forgoing the production of fissionable material . . . and such production is the first essential step for the manufacture of these weapons and constitutes an important dividing line between restraint from and pursuit of the nuclear path.[22]

Proponents of the per se right or unqualified per se right reading of Article IV might counter the NPT's sustainable reading by claiming that Article IV's second paragraph necessarily obliges signatories to transfer any and all nuclear technology, materials, and assistance — including nuclear fuel making — in an unqualified and unfettered manner. The relevant part of that paragraph states:

> All the Parties of the Treaty undertake to facilitate, and have the right to participate in, the fullest possible exchange of equipment, materials and scientific and technological information for the peaceful uses of nuclear energy.[23]

It is important to note, though, that this paragraph is carefully worded to call not for "the fullest exchange," but rather for only "the fullest *possible* exchange," and thus actually encourages NPT signatories to exchange nuclear technology, materials, and know-how with great care, caution, and restraint.[24] In May 2005, during a speech to the quadrennial NPT review conference, Christopher Ford (at the time the Principal Deputy Assistant Secretary of State for Verification, Compliance and Implementation) elaborated this point:

> The use of the term "fullest possible" is an acknowledgement that cooperation may be limited. Parties are not compelled by Article IV to engage in nuclear cooperation with any given state — or to provide any particular form of nuclear assistance to any other state. The NPT does not require any specific sharing of nuclear technology between particular State Parties, nor does it oblige technology-possessors to share any specific materials or technology with non-possessors.[25]

"[T]o conform both to the overall objective of the NPT — strengthening security by halting nuclear proliferation — and to any Article I and III obligations," Ford added, "supplier states must consider whether certain types of assistance, or assistance to certain countries, are consistent with the nonproliferation purposes and obligations of the NPT, other interna-

tional obligations, and their own national requirements." NPT signatories, Ford concluded,

> should withhold assistance if they believe that a spe-
> cific form of cooperation would encourage or facilitate
> proliferation, or if they believe that a state is pursuing
> a nuclear weapons program in violation of Article II, is
> not in full compliance with its safeguards obligations,
> or is in violation of Article I.[26]

Moreover, by establishing no *per se* obligation or duty
of nuclear exporters to give any specific nuclear technology, material or assistance, Article IV's second
paragraph suggests that nuclear importers, at the
same time, have no reciprocal *per se* right to receive
or otherwise acquire any specific nuclear technology,
material or assistance.[27]

In sum, the analysis in this chapter suggests that
the NPT does not affirm the "inalienable right" of
signatories to nuclear materials and activities that the
IAEA cannot effectively safeguard. In fact, this ex-
plains why the treaty prohibits non-nuclear-weapon
signatories from developing, accessing, or using so-
called "nuclear explosions for peaceful purposes," the
most military-relevant of civilian applications of nuclear technology. Instead, the NPT appears to establish three qualifications of Article IV which condition
the extent to which signatories have an "inalienable
right" to develop and use peaceful nuclear energy —
key qualifications being a signatory's full compliance
with its obligations under the NPT and IAEA comprehensive safeguards agreements, and the actual
ability of the IAEA to administer *effective* safeguards
on nuclear materials in a given civilian application of
nuclear technology. But while the NPT may be understood as prohibiting non-nuclear-weapon signatories

from unsafeguardable nuclear materials and activities, the treaty also provides for mechanisms by which nuclear-weapon signatories can provide, individually or through multilateral frameworks, *the benefits* of proscribed, unsafeguardable peaceful applications of nuclear technology in a nondiscriminatory manner to non-nuclear-weapon signatories in full compliance.

ENDNOTES - CHAPTER 10

1. *The Treaty on the Non-Proliferation of Nuclear Weapons* (NPT), Art. IV, para. 1, available from *www.state.gov/www/global/arms/treaties/npt1.html*.

2. NPT, Art. III, para. 1, emphasis added.

3. The NPT's negotiation history confirms that the "benefits-without-discrimination" principle is meant to be understood in relation to Article IV. In August 1967, when American delegate William Foster (along with Soviet delegate Alexey Roshchin) introduced the first version of what we know today as Article IV, he said that the article's two paragraphs "are *specific elaborations of the principle stated in the preamble* 'that the benefits of peaceful applications of nuclear technology should be available for peaceful purposes to all Parties . . . whether nuclear-weapon or non-nuclear-weapon States'." See "Statement by ACDA Director [William] Foster to the Eighteen Nation Disarmament Committee: Draft Nonproliferation Treaty," ENDC/PV. 325, August 24, 1967, *Documents on Disarmament, 1967*, Washington, DC: U.S. Arms Control and Disarmament Agency, p. 345, emphasis added.

4. NPT, preamble, para. 7, emphasis added.

5. NPT, Art. I.

6. NPT, Art. II.

7. Albert Wohlstetter and colleagues stressed this point in studies conducted for a number of U.S. government agencies in the 1970s. In a 1979 report for ACDA, for example, they argued,

"Article IV explicitly states that the inalienable right of all parties to the Treaty to the peaceful use of nuclear energy has to be in conformity with Articles I and II . . . [T]hese Articles are what make the Treaty a treaty against proliferation." See Albert Wohlstetter, Greg Jones, and Roberta Wohlstetter, *Towards a New Consensus on Nuclear Technology*, Vol. 1, 1979, PH 78-04 - 832-33, a summary report prepared for the U.S. Arms Control and Disarmament Agency, Contract #AC7 NC-106, Los Angeles, CA: Pan-Heuristics, July 6, 1979, pp. 34-35. A few years later, Eldon V. C. Greenberg reiterated this point in a legal memorandum on the NPT's relation to plutonium fuel-making and use:

There is, in short, a dynamic tension in the Treaty between its prohibitions and its injunctions to cooperate in peaceful uses of nuclear energy. An analysis of the language and history of the NPT, and particularly the key phrase "in conformity with [articles I and II]" in Article IV, paragraph 1, which is the link between the Treaty's promises and its prohibitions, tends to support the conclusion that Articles I, II and IV must be read together in such a way that assistance or activities which are ostensibly peaceful and civilian in nature do not as a practical matter lead to proliferation of nuclear weapons. The NPT, in other words, can and should be read as permitting the evaluation of such factors as proliferation risk, economic or technical justification, and safeguards effectiveness in assessing the consistency of specific or generic types of assistance and activities with the Treaty's restrictions, to ensure that action is not taken in the guise of peaceful applications of nuclear energy under Article IV which in fact is violative of the prohibitions of Articles I and II.

See Eldon V. C. Greenberg, "The NPT and Plutonium," Washington, DC: Nuclear Control Agency, 1993, p. 10.

8. NPT, Art. III, para. 1, emphasis added.

9. It is of interest to note that both the 2000 NPT Review Conference and 2006 summit of the Non-Aligned Movement released a politically-binding final document affirming that "nothing in the Treaty shall be interpreted as affecting the inalienable right of all the parties to the Treaty to develop research, production and use of nuclear energy for peaceful purposes without discrimination and in conformity with articles I, II *and* III of the Treaty."

See 2000 Review Conference of the Parties to the Treaty on the Non-Proliferation of Nuclear Weapons, *Final Document,* NPT/CONF.2000/28 (Parts I and II), p. 8, para. 2, available from *disarmament2.un.org/wmd/npt/finaldoc.html;* and Fourteenth Summit Conference of the Heads of State or Government of the Non-Aligned Movement, *Final Document,* NAM 2006/Doc.1/Rev. 3, September, 16, 2006, para. 95. I am grateful to Andreas Persbo, a nuclear law and policy researcher at the Verification Research, Training and Information Centre ("VERTIC") in London, UK, who first drew my attention to this passage of the 2000 NPT Review Conference's *Final Document.*

10. *Cf.* Henry D. Sokolski and George Perkovich, "It's Called *Non*proliferation," *Wall Street Journal,* April 29, 2005, p. A16, available from *http://www.npec-web.org/Frameset.asp?PageType=Single&PDFFile=OpEd50429ItsCalledNonprolife&PDFFolder=OpEds;* and George Perkovich, "Defining Iran's Nuclear Rights," Washington, DC: Carnegie Endowment for International Peace, September 7, 2006, available from *www.carnegieendowment.org/npp/publications/index.cfm?fa=view&id=18687>.*

11. NPT, Art. V, emphases added.

12. Exceptions included Brazil, the government of which had argued before the ENDC that non-nuclear-weapon states should be allowed to develop peaceful nuclear explosive devices. For example, see "Brazilian Amendments to the Draft Nonproliferation Treaty," ENDC/201, October 31, 1967, U.S. Arms Control and Disarmament Agency, *Documents on Disarmament, 1967,* Publication No. 46, Washington, DC: U.S. Government Printing Office, July 1968, p. 546.

13. ENDC/PV. 359 (January 25, 1968), p. 6, emphasis added, available from *www.hti.umich.edu/e/endc/.*

14. ENDC/PV. 360 (January 30, 1968), p. 7, emphasis added, available from *www.hti.umich.edu/e/endc/.*

15. On the comparative economics and proliferation dangers of PNEs, see Thomas Blau, *Rational Policy-Making and Peaceful Nuclear Explosives,* Doctoral Dissertation, Department of Political Science, University of Chicago, December 1972.

16. *Report of Main Committee III*, Treaty on the Nonproliferation of Nuclear Weapons Review and Extension Conference, May 5, 1995, NPT/CONF.1995/MC.III/1, sec. I, para. 2, emphasis added, available from *www.un.org/Depts/ddar/nptconf/162.htm*.

17. *Comprehensive Nuclear-Test-Ban Treaty*, Opened for signature, September 24, 1996, 35 I.L.M. 1430, available from *www.state.gov/www/global/arms/treaties/ctb.html*.

18. Here, I use what I view to be Article IV's three qualifications on the "nuclear energy for peaceful purposes" to which NPT signatories have an "inalienable right," to elaborate Eldon V. C. Greenberg's argument for the specific facts and circumstances under which peaceful nuclear energy should not be permissible:

If the [proliferation] risks are great, if there can be no reasonable civilian justification for particular forms of assistance or activities, and if there can be no certainty that safeguards would be effective with respect to such assistance or activities, then a presumption should arise under the Treaty that such assistance or activities are not for a permissible, peaceful purpose but are rather for a weapons or explosive purpose and therefore in violation of Articles I and II. Only in this way can there be any assurance that the NPT's objectives will be achieved.

See Greenberg, p. 13.

19. *Cf.* Eldon V. C. Greenberg's legal memorandum on the NPT and plutonium fuel-making, which argues:

[T]he distinction between permissible and impermissible activities must come down ultimately to quite pragmatic considerations. Activities must not be free from the Treaty's prohibitions just by virtue of being denominated "peaceful," civilian," power" or "research." The Treaty must be interpreted as viewing proliferation through something more than an "explosive lens." Rather, depending upon the facts and circumstances, assistance and activities relating to declared "peaceful," civilian," "power" or "research" purposes may be subject to the NPT's restrictions, if an evaluation of all the facts and circumstances, including such factors as economic or technical justification or effectiveness of safeguards, would indicate that the legitimacy of the assistance and/or activity is questionable. Such a pragmatic, rather than a formalistic reading of the Treaty, is most consistent with the overriding purpose of stemming the proliferation of nuclear weapons.

See Greenberg, "The NPT and Plutonium," p. 24.

20. ENDC/PV. 82 (September 7, 1962), p. 37, emphasis added, available from *www.hti.umich.edu/e/endc/*. See also "British Paper Submitted to the Eighteen Nation Disarmament Committee: Technical Possibility of International Control of Fissile Material Production," ENDC/60, August 31, 1962 (Corr. 1, November 27, 1962), in U.S. Arms Control and Disarmament Agency, *Documents on Disarmament, 1962*, Publication No. 19, Vol. 2 of 2, Washington, DC: U.S. Government Printing Office, November 1963, pp. 834-852.

21. "Statement by the Swedish Representative [Alva Myrdal] to the Eighteen Nation Disarmament Committee: Nonproliferation of Nuclear Weapons," ENDC/PV. 243, February 24, 1966, in U.S. Arms Control and Disarmament Agency, *Documents on Disarmament, 1966*, Publication No. 43, Washington, DC: U.S. Government Printing Office, September 1967, p. 56, emphasis added.

22. ENDC/PV. 250, March 22, 1966, p. 28, emphasis added, available from *www.hti.umich.edu/e/endc/*.

23. NPT, Art. IV, para. 2, emphasis added.

24. As strategist Albert Wohlstetter and colleagues argued in a 1979 report for the U.S. Arms Control and Disarmament Agency:

If the "fullest possible exchange" were taken to include the provision of stocks of highly concentrated fissile material within days or hours of being ready for incorporation into an explosive, this would certainly "assist" an aspiring nonnuclear weapons state in making such an explosive. No reasonable interpretation of the Nonproliferation Treaty would say that the Treaty intends, in exchange for an explicitly revocable promise by countries without nuclear explosives not to make them or acquire them, to transfer to them material that is within days or hours of being ready for incorporation into a bomb. . . . The NPT is, after all, a treaty against proliferation, not for nuclear development.

See Wohlstetter *et al.*, *Towards a New Consensus on Nuclear Technology*, pp. 34-35.

25. Christopher Ford, "NPT Article IV: Peaceful Uses of Nuclear Energy," Statement of the Principal Deputy Assistant Secretary of State for Verification, Compliance and Implementation, to the 2005 Review Conference of the Treaty on the Nonproliferation of Nuclear Weapons, New York, NY, May 18, 2005, available from *www.state.gov/t/vci/rls/rm/46604.htm*.

26. *Ibid.*

27. According to Henry D. Sokolski,

[The Principal Deputy Assistant Secretary of State for Verification, Compliance and Implementation] had attempted, to my knowledge, to get more cleared than what he was able to say [at the 2005 NPT Review Conference]. What he was able to say and what was cleared was that the United States at least is under no duty or obligation under Article IV to supply enrichment and reprocessing technologies to anyone. I think what he wanted to say might have included that countries really don't have a *per se* right to acquire this from others or to develop it even indigenously, but that was not approved.

See "Statement of Henry D. Sokolski," in *Assessing "Rights" Under the Nuclear Nonproliferation Treaty*, a hearing before the Subcommittee on International Terrorism and Nonproliferation, Committee on International Relations, U.S. House of Representatives, 109th Cong., 2nd Sess., Serial No. 109-148, March 2, 2006, Washington, DC: U.S. Government Printing Office, 2006, p. 28, available from *www.foreignaffairs.house.gov/archives/109/26333.pdf*.

CHAPTER 11

NUCLEAR TECHNOLOGY RIGHTS AND WRONGS: THE NUCLEAR NONPROLIFERATION TREATY, ARTICLE IV, AND NONPROLIFERATION*

Christopher A. Ford

In diplomatic circles associated with the Nuclear Nonproliferation Treaty (NPT), it is widely believed that Article IV of the Treaty unquestionably protects the "inalienable right" of non-nuclear weapons states to develop any sort of nuclear technology they wish, short of actual nuclear weapons, provided that it is subjected to International Atomic Energy Agency (IAEA) safeguards and used only for "peaceful" purposes. This belief, however, is false. The text of Article IV itself does not preclude that interpretation, but such an understanding is in no way supported by the text, nor by the negotiating history of the NPT, and is in fact inconsistent with this history and with the structure of the Treaty.

The meaning of the Treaty's peaceful use provisions has been debated for many years between (a) those who advocate technology-access rights per se, and (b) those who read the NPT as reflecting a strong commitment to sharing nuclear benefits but as treating specific claims to technology access as policy questions to be determined on a case-by-case basis,

---

* Available from *www.npec-web.org/Essays/20090601-Ford-NuclearRightsAndWrongs.pdf*.

informed by considerations such as the ability of safe-guards to provide timely warning of misuse. Of these two camps, the latter, the "safeguardability" school offers the stronger argument.

The policy-focused, benefits-sharing approach advanced by "safeguardability" theorists is not only more consistent with the Treaty's text and negotiating history, but also quite consonant with long-standing themes in the international community's struggle with nuclear technology issues since the dawn of the nuclear age. By contrast, theories of access rights would require concluding, against the evidence, that these long-standing themes were suddenly and ut-terly repudiated during the NPT's drafting. Worse, access rights would turn Article IV into a mechanism for undermining the rest of the Treaty by facilitating the spread of the (fissile material production) tech-nologies that are critical to making nuclear weapons. This is not merely unwise and untenable as a matter of public policy, it is, in fact, an inferior answer as a matter of legal interpretation. The safeguardability approach, however, reconciles the text of Article IV with the rest of the Treaty, with its negotiating record, and with long-standing international approaches to nuclear technology. While both views of Article IV may be "legally available," the policy-privileging safeguardability interpretation is far superior, both substantively and legally.

Significant consequences follow from properly un-derstanding safeguardability as the best framework for understanding nuclear technology "rights" under the peaceful use provisions of the NPT. First, IAEA nuclear safeguards must be the focus of great attention and detailed study, particularly with regard to their ability to provide an adequate warning of misuse in sufficient time to permit the international community to mount an effective response. This is a critical factor, for upon considerations of effective safeguardability will hinge whether claimants in fact possess the "right" to nuclear "benefits" in any particular technological form. Second, the international community must develop a rational and defensible standard for assessing the real economic and developmental benefit offered by nuclear technologies—not merely in their own right but also vis-à-vis non-nuclear alternatives—in order to allow possible the exercise of informed policy judgment to determine the form that "benefit"-sharing should take.

INTRODUCTION

Contemporary diplomatic debates regarding the NPT have become conspicuous for the disagreements they reflect not merely over nonproliferation *policy*, which is somewhat expected, but also over the fundamental *meaning* of key portions of the Treaty itself. One of the most interesting debates over the meaning of the NPT today concerns Article IV of the Treaty: its provisions concerning the peaceful uses of nuclear energy. On one side, representing the seeming preponderance of diplomatic opinion on the subject—as well as, it must be said, no small amount of acquisitive self-interest by nuclear technology "have-not" countries—are the advocates of an interpretation that sees Article IV through the lens of technology access rights. On the other side stand those more focused upon vindicating the Treaty's *nonproliferation* components (Articles I, II, and III), and who think that the NPT's commitment to nonproliferation may on occasion require *refusing* requests for technology sharing, or concluding that *certain* capabilities are simply not able to be possessed safely by non-nuclear weapons states *at all* – even for "peaceful" purposes.

These debates have acquired both great salience and all too much venom as a result of Iran's decision to adopt the movement for Article IV "rights," while secretly pursuing a program of uranium enrichment and plutonium reprocessing in violation of not just its nuclear safeguards commitments under Article III but also – given the apparently now general agreement that Iran's nuclear program was designed to give it the ability to build nuclear weapons – of Article II. The diplomatic confrontation has been especially acute since the embarrassing public revelation in August 2002 of much of Iran's hitherto clandestine nuclear program.

This chapter outlines the contentious debates underway today concerning Article IV, and it outlines the history of the international community's efforts to grapple with the challenge of nuclear technology control. This chapter discusses the problematic text and ambiguous negotiating history of Article IV itself, and then it offers an alternative view to the *access-privileging* which underlies the conventional wisdom of much of today's diplomatic community. In place of the rigid *rights-fetishism* of what has now become Article IV's conventional interpretation, I argue for a *policy-privileging* understanding of that provision – one that embodies a strong ethic of *benefits*-sharing but without any commitment to the sharing or permitting the possession of any particular nuclear technology.

This approach, I argue, is the best way to reconcile the confusing text of Article IV and the complexity of its negotiating history, and the one most substantively consistent with the long history of how key players struggled with the challenge of technology control in the years leading up to the drafting of the Treaty. Most importantly, while competing interpretations may also be legally available, I contend that the policy-privileging, benefits-sharing approach is the best interpretation of Article IV to make it consistent with the rest of the NPT—thus ending the dangerous and indeed regime imperiling opposition that has been developing between the Treaty and its peaceful use provisions under the more rights-focused view.

THE GREAT ARTICLE IV DEBATE

The NPT deals with the issue of peaceful nuclear uses in two places, both of which we shall see are highly relevant. In the Preamble, it affirms:

> the principle that the benefits of peaceful applications of nuclear technology, including any technological by-products which may be derived by nuclear-weapon States from the development of nuclear explosive devices, should be available for peaceful purposes to all. . . ."[1]

Article IV adds detail to this idea, declaring in its two paragraphs that:

> (1) Nothing in this Treaty shall be interpreted as affecting the inalienable right of all the Parties to the Treaty to develop research, production and use of nuclear energy for peaceful purposes without discrimination and in conformity with Articles I and II of this Treaty;

> (2) All the Parties to the Treaty undertake to facilitate, and have the right to participate in, the fullest possible exchange of equipment, materials and scientific and technological information for the peaceful uses of nuclear energy. Parties to the Treaty in a position to do so shall also cooperate in contributing alone or

together with other States or international organizations to the further development of the applications of nuclear energy for peaceful purposes, especially in the territories of non-nuclear-weapon States Party to the Treaty, with due consideration for the needs of the developing areas of the world.[2]

While everyone seems to agree that the NPT embodies a strong commitment to sharing the benefits that nuclear technology can bring to mankind, making sense of exactly what the notably unspecific phrasing of Article IV actually *requires* as a matter of law is quite contentious. As it turns out, this issue is also of quite considerable importance—which is why Article IV issues have emerged as a contentious and significant arena of debate and discussion in contemporary diplomatic and policy circles.

The Stakes.

To put it crudely, the issue is of importance because of the potentially enormous cost of getting the answer wrong. Nuclear energy technology has presented great challenges to the international community for many decades, and governments have always struggled to walk a tightrope between the benefits it might bring and the dangers it so clearly might also present. I once summarized this tension when I was in an official capacity when I stated that,

> [n]uclear energy . . . has always had a Janus-faced aspect, offering humankind both great peril and extraordinary promise." Nuclear weapons scientist Robert Oppenheimer's well-known quotation from the *Bhagavad-Gita* upon witnessing the first nuclear weapons test drew from a verse which, in its entirety, references not just the destructive power of Death, but

also the creative power that forms the origin of things yet to be. Nuclear technology is like that: it embodies a nearly unbelievable power to destroy, but at the same time an extraordinary power to create — to enrich our lives, to provide the electric power by which we may read at night, to produce potable water from the ocean's brine, to help cure deadly diseases, and to enable science and industry to advance in innumerable ways that can improve the quality of life for people in all societies."[3]

Nuclear technology has been significantly advanced since the magnitude of this challenge first became apparent, but it has long been quite clear — and remains at least as true as ever — that some balance must be struck between the two faces of the nuclear Janus-god. Our efforts to exploit nuclear technology for good must always be tempered by an awareness of, and consideration for, the dangers inherent in such knowledge. Clearly, getting the answer wrong could have terrible implications, either in impeding technological and economic developments that might otherwise bring enormous benefits to mankind or, worse, in leading to an increased likelihood of global instability and indeed nuclear warfare by facilitating the proliferation of nuclear weapons capabilities.

In recent years, in fact, the stakes have been rising. On the one hand, in the face of increasing global energy needs and increased worries about how to control the impact of fossil fuel combustion on climate change, there has been much talk of a "nuclear renaissance." Electricity generation by means of nuclear power reactors has been described by many as an important part of the solution to the world's 21st-century energy security and climate change dilemmas. Many governments around the world have proclaimed an interest in developing nuclear reactor programs,[4] supplier states are currently taking advantage of a recently-agreed exception to the rules of the Nuclear Suppliers Group (NSG)[5] in order to seek lucrative contracts with the energy-hungry state of India, and even some environmentalists are reportedly rethinking their long-standing opposition to nuclear power in light of fossil fuel-related climate change.[6]

On the other hand, it has also become increasingly clear that the spread of nuclear technology — or at least of certain types of nuclear capability — can have grave proliferation and global security implications. Since the early 1990s, and culminating with that country's test of a nuclear weapon in October 2006, it has been apparent that North Korea used the pursuit of a "peaceful" nuclear reactor program as cover for its weapons development efforts. Since early 2004,[7] moreover, it has been publicly known that renegade Pakistani nuclear scientist and smuggler A. Q. Khan played an extraordinary role for many years in providing uranium enrichment and other technology to the nuclear weapons development programs of a number of problematic regimes around the world, including Libya, North Korea, and Iran. Most dramatically, from an Article IV perspective, controversies over the discovery of Iran's long-secret nuclear program have engaged diplomats, policymakers, and observers alike in fierce disputes over precisely what ostensibly "peaceful" nuclear capabilities Iran can safely be permitted to employ.

These latter developments have sparked renewed interest in how to handle the potential proliferation challenges of the spread of uranium enrichment and plutonium reprocessing (a.k.a. ENR) technology as part of the full nuclear fuel cycle. As official U.S. statements have explained it,

> the ubiquitous availability of uranium enrichment ca-
> pability—or its analogue, plutonium production and
> reprocessing—also necessarily entails a capability to
> develop nuclear weapons. The basic physics and oper-
> ating principles of nuclear weapons have been known
> publicly for many years now, and it has long been un-
> derstood that the greatest technical barrier to massive
> and widespread proliferation has been the difficulty
> of acquiring sufficient quantities of weapons-usable
> fissile material. Anyone who can enrich (or reprocess)
> can overcome this hurdle to weapons development—
> helping open the door to the incalculable dangers of a
> proliferated world.[8]

Spreading availability of ENR thus threatens to con-
front the international community with a growing
number of states becoming what the Director General of the IAEA has called "virtual nuclear weapons
states."[9] Most observers plausibly assume that a world
in which many countries are in a position to develop
nuclear weapons with little or no notice would be a
profoundly unstable one, and that the spread of ENR
could likely undermine—and here one might go so far
as to say "destroy"—the nonproliferation regime.

To help forestall such potentially destabilizing effects, various supplier states, and the IAEA itself, have
advocated approaches to providing would-be reactor-
operating states with reliable sources of nuclear fuel.
The idea behind these proposals is to obviate any perceived need for such states to independently pursue
nuclear fuel-making by means of acquiring enrichment or reprocessing capabilities. The United States,
for instance, has proclaimed its desire to

> work . . . with the producer states and the IAEA to

245

> develop broad cooperative programs for fuel-supply
> assurances . . . [through] a reliable system of fresh fuel
> supply and spent-fuel management services, [and] to
> build upon and reinforce the efforts currently under-
> way [at the IAEA] in Vienna to create a reliable fuel
> supply system that might include an IAEA overseen
> fuel bank as a supply of "last resort."[10]

The aim of such efforts is "to provide such attractive and responsible cooperative alternatives that countries offered the chance to participate will choose to forego involvement with ENR."[11]

Presumably out of deference to the diplomatic sensitivities of such a persuasive exercise—that is, either because they think there *do* exist ENR rights under the NPT but that such things are most prudently not spoken of, or because it would irritate technology seeking diplomatic partners to point out that their legal arguments are illusory—many Western countries have gone to considerable trouble to avoid taking a position on the actual legal meaning of the Treaty's peaceful use provisions. At the 2005 NPT Review Conference, for instance, a working paper offered by several Western governments carefully refrained from spelling out what Article IV actually entails, instead stressing that whatever rights it *may* enshrine are not ones that countries necessarily *have* to act upon. "States may choose individually not to exercise all their rights," the paper carefully noted, "or to exercise those rights collectively."[12]

In a similar vein, the European Union (EU) tap-danced around the question by declaring that "[t]he right to peaceful uses of nuclear energy remains undisputed," but without describing what it actually means to have such a right. Instead, the EU's working paper on the subject merely pleaded the policy merits of "multilateralizaton/guarantees of access to the fruits of the most sensitive parts of the nuclear fuel cycle." The EU hoped, in other words, that a system of fuel-supply assurances — that is, for ensuring that states' needs for nuclear fuel were reliably met without any need for them to develop enrichment or reprocessing — would be seen as an acceptable "means of *implementing* the right [described in Article IV] . . . while at the same time avoiding the risks of proliferation."[13]

To the extent that the fuel-supply based "enticement" approach works,[14] it may succeed in avoiding a real reckoning with the legal meaning of the peaceful use provisions of the NPT. If it does not, however — and it must here be admitted that the principal (and most urgent) target of such fuel-supply blandishments, Iran, has to date shown no interest whatsoever in giving up its emerging nuclear weapons "option" — it will not be possible to avoid struggling with Article IV. If countries cannot be bribed out of any desire to possess ENR technology in the first place, it will be necessary to take a position on what specifically, any such "rights" actually are, and the fate of the nonproliferation regime may hang upon the outcome.

The Contenders.

It would be an oversimplification to describe there being only two or three camps in the broad and conceptually messy international debates that have been developing over peaceful use benefits under the NPT. Nevertheless, it may be convenient to divide the protagonists into two broad categories.

1. The Technology-Seekers. Countries that are, for various reasons, less concerned with preventing nuclear weapons proliferation than with using the NPT

as a tool to spur technology transfers from nuclear suppliers — that is, from the privileged "have" states of the modern international system, none of whom are more resented than the five powers who are also recognized by the NPT itself as the only States Party to the treaty permitted to possess nuclear weaponry[15] — see in Article IV a potentially powerful weapon. After all, if indeed it was the case that the NPT recognizes or conveys nuclear technology-access "rights," what could be more appropriate than insisting upon what one is owed *as of right*?

Some states thus defend a view of Article IV that gives nonpossessors a right to develop — or perhaps even to be *given* — the full range of nuclear-related technology short of actual weaponization techniques, provided that they promise to use all of it exclusively for peaceful purposes and subject their activities to IAEA safeguards. The "inalienable right" of Article IV is often brandished as an absolute trump card that is expected to make nonproliferation risks (which are, after all, merely *policy* considerations) take a back seat. As the People's Republic of China revealingly phrased it in a paper delivered to the 2005 NPT Review Conference, "[n]on-proliferation efforts should not undermine the legitimate rights of countries, especially the developing countries, to the peaceful uses of nuclear energy."[16]

Some governments have even attempted to use Article IV to undermine nonproliferation export controls. Cuba, for instance, argued at the 2005 Review Conference that "the unilateral restrictions put in place by some States parties to the Treaty" have "impeded other States parties' peaceful uses of nuclear energy." In fact, the very existence of "export-control regimes . . . which, in practice, seriously hamper the inalienable right of all States to use for peaceful purposes the various nuclear-related resources and technologies available" was entirely "unacceptable." In short, Cuba said, nonproliferation export controls were "a violation of the Treaty, and should cease."[17]

Given Iran's efforts since 2002 to defend its previously secret but now well-known nuclear program, its long-standing noncompliance with IAEA safeguards, and its defiance of legal requirements imposed by the United Nations (UN) Security Council to suspend enrichment and reprocessing-related activity, it is perhaps not surprising that the clerical regime in Tehran has taken an extreme view of Article IV. However, Iranian officials did not just develop their strong view of Article IV only after Iran was embarrassingly revealed in August 2002 to be pursuing a secret nuclear program aimed at uranium enrichment and the construction of a heavy-water reactor ideally suited for plutonium production. In fact, Iran apparently staked out these Article IV claims years earlier — at a time when its secret nuclear efforts still remained unknown to the world, apart from accurate but unheralded warnings from arms control verification and compliance experts in the United States.[18]

As Etel Solingen has recounted, before the 1995 NPT Review and Extension Conference, "Iran threatened to withdraw from the NPT because of imputed U.S. violations of Article IV granting members full access to equipment, materials, and scientific and technological information for peaceful purposes."[19] Iran's emphasis in 1995, upon its purported "right" to whatever "peaceful" nuclear technology it wanted, was likely no coincidence. It was that year that Russia and Iran agreed to a nuclear cooperation agreement that led to the construction of the current nuclear reactor

at Bushehr and apparently included a side protocol —
subsequently canceled (and then denied) by Russia in
the face of international pressure — for the construction of a gas centrifuge plant for the enrichment of
uranium.[20]

The Russian deal was not the clerical regime's first
effort to acquire fissile material production capabilities. It had secretly begun experiments with uranium
conversion as early as 1981, imported uranium yellow-
cake as early as 1982, started a gas centrifuge program
at least as early as 1985, obtained centrifuge designs
and other information beginning at least in 1987 (from
the smuggling network run by Khan), carried out plutonium separation experiments beginning in 1988, began experiments with creating neutron sources [usable
in nuclear weapons triggers] from polonium in 1989,
and imported its first supply of uranium hexafluoride
centrifuge feedstock in 1991[21] — from China, no less: a
fellow believer in the merely secondary importance of
nonproliferation. None of this activity was reported
to the IAEA as required by Iran's nuclear safeguards
agreement; it only came to light during the investigations that followed the press leaks of August 2002.

At any rate, in the years after the public revelation
of these secret efforts, Iran stepped up its Article IV
campaigning. It is not simply that Iran has defended
its development of ENR capabilities in Article IV
terms. Iran also asserts that supplier states are legally
required to *make available* whatever technology it de-
sires for the peaceful purposes it claims. In April 2008,
for instance, Iran's representative declared that "[r]
estrictions imposed by nuclear suppliers" for nonproliferation reasons were "[c]lear violations of Article
IV obligations . . . in depriving the States parties from
[sic] the exercise of their inalienable right."[22] Article IV,

in other words, is seen as a potent weapon for Iran's fight against "nuclear apartheid,"[23] by which Tehran means an international system in which not everyone is allowed to have whatever nuclear technologies they wish.

At an NPT meeting in May 2009, the Iranians offered even more aggressive arguments, defending an absolutist vision of Article IV and describing it not merely as one pillar of the NPT but as the "very foundation of the Treaty."[24] (So important is technology-promotion to the NPT, in fact, that this principle seems in Iranian minds to have overridden the nonproliferation conformity requirement in the last 10 words of the first paragraph of Article IV.[25] "[N]o State party," claimed the Iranian delegation, "should be limited in exercising its rights under the Treaty based on allegations of non-compliance.") Denouncing nuclear export controls as "a clear violation" of the Treaty, Iran even claimed the right to "compensation" for the effect of nonproliferation rules in "hampering" Iran's "peaceful nuclear activities."[26]

Perhaps more than any other single factor, the Iranian case — including Iran's use of assertions about Article IV to excuse its nuclear provocations — has helped drive and exacerbate the tensions surrounding today's debates over the peaceful use provisions of the NPT. Despite Iran's brazenly self-exonerating involvement in advancing such arguments, many countries apparently now really do think Article IV "means that states have a *per se* right to any and all nuclear technology and materials, including nuclear fuel-making technology and weapons-usable nuclear fuels."[27]

2. The Nonproliferators.

a. Government Positions. It is somewhat strange that, given the enormous importance placed upon

Article IV claims by Iran and its apologists, a more clearly articulated and defended counterargument has not developed in diplomatic circles. This is surely not because other governments accept Iranian and Cuban claims at face value: the 45 members of the Nuclear Suppliers Group presumably do *not* believe that maintaining nuclear export controls makes them violators of the NPT. Moreover, it has been explicit U.S. policy since President George W. Bush's speech at the National Defense University in February 2004 to oppose the spread of ENR technology to "any state that does not already possess full-scale, functioning enrichment and reprocessing plants."[28] The policy positions of all these governments preclude agreement with Iranian-style interpretations of Article IV. Why then, has there never been an official articulation of a counter-argument?

No doubt part of the answer for this relative silence lies in some governments' worries that offering arguments to debunk extremist proliferation-facilitating interpretations of Article IV would irritate the delicate diplomatic sensibilities of governments whom we hope to persuade to accept multinational fuel-supply assurances in lieu of ENR development. Bush Administration Energy Secretary Samuel Bodman, for instance, once declared that he felt it was "unproductive often to talk in terms of rights."[29] The danger of such reticence is, however, that—as I have elsewhere warned—it risks "ced[ing] the intellectual field to the proliferators" because even the most tendentious of arguments may be believed "in the absence of clear rebutting arguments."[30]

In fact, however, the situation seems to be worse than that. The United States has sometimes seemed confused on the subject of Article IV's specific meaning. To be sure, U.S. officials have articulated a clear rebuttal of Iranian-style arguments, based upon that provision's *second* paragraph, that the NPT requires specific technology transfers. The United States has clearly and publicly rejected any notion that export controls or any other sort of supplier discretion in making potentially proliferation facilitating transfers is in any way problematic under the Treaty. As I explained it to the 2005 NPT Review Conference,

> Paragraph 2 of Article IV calls on parties 'to facilitate ... the fullest possible exchange' of technology for the peaceful uses of nuclear energy. The use of the term 'fullest possible' is an acknowledgement that cooperation may be limited. Parties are not compelled by Article IV to engage in nuclear cooperation with any given state — or to provide any particular form of nuclear assistance to any other state. The NPT does not require any specific sharing of nuclear technology between particular States Party, nor does it oblige technology-possessors to share any specific materials or technology with non-possessors. Indeed, to conform both to the overall objective of the NPT — strengthening security by halting nuclear proliferation — and to any Article I and III obligations, supplier states must consider whether certain types of assistance, or assistance to certain countries, are consistent with the nonproliferation purposes and obligations of the NPT, other international obligations, and their own national requirements. They should withhold assistance if they believe that a specific form of cooperation would encourage or facilitate proliferation, or if they believe that a state is pursuing a nuclear weapons program in violation of Article II, is not in full compliance with its safeguards obligations, or is in violation of Article I.
>
> . . . While compliant State[s] Party should be able to avail themselves of the benefits that the peaceful use of nuclear energy has brought to mankind, the Treaty establishes no right to receive any particular nuclear

technology from other States Party—and most especially, no right to receive technologies that pose a significant proliferation risk.[31]

With regard to the *first* paragraph of Article IV,
however—the location of the portentous and much-
cited phrasing about the "inalienable right" of States
Party to develop nuclear energy—the United States
has excelled at sending foolishly mixed messages. As
noted above, President George W. Bush made it U.S.
policy in February 2004 to oppose any further spread
of ENR technology. Unless it was to be U.S. policy to
deprive other states of what international law permits them—a position that American representatives
denied[32]—President Bush's position would certainly
seem at least to *imply* that adopting such a policy
was not an NPT violation. Nor, so far at least, has the
Obama Administration changed U.S. policy to one of
supporting or acquiescing in ENR proliferation, which
is presumably what one would expect from any country believing nonweapons states to have a real legal
right to such capabilities. One might presume, therefore, that the United States still does not think that
Article IV creates or describes any sort of a "right" to
specific technologies irrespective of proliferation risk.
Moreover, U.S. officials have offered explications
of Article IV that rebut Iranian style arguments that
the NPT provides or enshrines a legal right to uranium
enrichment and/or plutonium reprocessing. In the official U.S. exegesis on Article IV that I presented to the
2005 NPT Review Conference, for example, the United
States declared that although some have asserted that
"any State Party . . . has a specific right to develop the
full nuclear fuel cycle, and that efforts to restrict access to the relevant technologies is inconsistent with

the NPT," it was in fact the case that "[t]he Treaty is silent on the issue of whether compliant states have the right to develop the full nuclear fuel cycle. . . ."[33]

A U.S. working paper, also presented in 2005, underlined this point about Article IV's indeterminacy, declaring that "the NPT neither guarantees nor prohibits the acquisition of a particular nuclear fuel cycle facility."[34] These U.S. presentations also stressed the importance under the NPT of sharing the *benefits* that nuclear technology can bring—phrasing that pointedly stopped short of endorsing legal rights to all of the underlying technology used to produce such benefits.[35] In 2004, Under Secretary of State John Bolton made the fundamental Article IV point in a characteristically concise way: "The Treaty provides no right to such sensitive fuel cycle technologies."[36]

The U.S. bureaucracy, however, seems to have had trouble keeping its story straight. On the heels of the relatively clear pronouncements of 2004 and 2005, much confusion ensued when, in 2007, the U.S. Department of Energy included in one of its publications a comment taking precisely the *opposite* position. According to the Energy Department at that time, "[o]ne challenge we face is that all nations that have signed the NPT retain the right to pursue enrichment and reprocessing for peaceful purposes in conformity with article I and II of the Treaty."[37] This claim—which endorsed the conceptual core of the Iranian and Cuban position that the development of proliferation facilitating ENR technology is a matter of *legal right* — quickly came under criticism from the U.S. Congress. In July 2007, for instance, the leadership of the Foreign Affairs Committee in the House of Representatives wrote to Secretary of State Condoleeza Rice declaring it "a mistake" to assert the existence of ENR rights and asking for clarification.[38]

When it came, however, the requested clarification was anything but clear. The State Department's reply—not with the signature of Secretary Rice, but of Jeffrey Bergner, the Assistant Secretary for Legislative Affairs, provided after a delay of 4 months—merely restated existing U.S. *policy* against transferring ENR technology, and asserted merely that ENR capabilities were "not necessary in order for states to harness nuclear energy for peaceful purposes."[39] It entirely avoided answering the question posed: whether the Energy Department's interpretation of Article IV represented the considered view of the U.S. Government as a whole.[40] Arguably, the official U.S. positions articulated at the 2004 and 2005 NPT meetings still remained U.S. policy, for the Bergner letter certainly did not repudiate them. In the wake of the Energy Department's remarkable endorsement of an Iranian-style reading of Article IV, however, the Bergner response understandably left things seeming rather confused.

In his widely-reported (but not necessarily widely understood) April 2009 nuclear policy speech in Prague, President Barack Obama did not do too much to clarify the situation. On the one hand, Obama played to the perceived grievances of developing nations—and Iranian clerics—unhappy with his predecessor's approach to nuclear technology control by stressing that "no approach will succeed if it's based on the denial of rights to nations that play by the rules." On the other hand, the actual "right" to which he referred was apparently *not* one that included unqualified access to technology irrespective of proliferation risk. Quite the contrary, in fact, Obama specified no more than that "the right of every nation that renounces nuclear weapons" has the right to "access peaceful power without increasing the risks of proliferation."[41]

The Prague speech seems to have been received around the world as a repudiation of Bush-era policies. Despite its conciliatory tone, however, it seems with regard to Article IV issues to have been closer to a reaffirmation of the approach propounded by John Bolton and others (including this author) during the Bush administration. The "right" Obama described was merely to "access power" rather than specifically to access *technology*, and even this was further qualified by the requirement that its exercise not increase proliferation risk. It is far from clear what, if anything, the new president will wish, or be able, to do with regard to nuclear technology control—and whether it will turn out to be helpful or harmful to nonproliferation that there is apparently such a gap between what people *assume* he said in this regard and what he actually did.[42] Nevertheless, it is at least *potentially* significant that Obama seems to have offered the most recent official articulation of the "safeguardability" perspective.

The Americans are not alone. A French working paper presented to the third Preparatory Committee meeting for the 2005 NPT Review Conference, for instance, clearly repudiated the notion of *per se* technology access rights. The French paper noted that "[d]eveloping peaceful uses of nuclear energy . . . does not require, in the large majority of cases, sensitive and potentially proliferating technologies," but it implied that should a conflict occur between the objective of peaceful development and the requirements of nonproliferation, the latter should prevail. Technology access, it stressed, "should only be envisaged in the light of the existence of a set of conditions relevant to the global non-proliferation regime and NPT objectives."[43] Paris pledged to offer the developing world "[i]ncreased access to *non*-sensitive technologies" — in fact, "guarantees of access" — but it carefully phrased this promise so as *not* to promise access to *sensitive* ones.[44] The paper made clear, moreover, that no co-operation should be pursued with any state "for which the IAEA cannot provide sufficient assurances that their nuclear program is devoted exclusively to peaceful purposes," with any state where there was "an 'unacceptable risk of diversion,'" or when it was "impossib[le] for the Agency to carry out its mission."[45]

Apart from such by-implication treatment of the underlying Article IV legal issues, however, governments concerned about the proliferation risk of spreading ENR technology either have remained studiously quiet about the legal import of Article IV, or have simply appeared confused. Despite the fact that governments have been so shy about offering a detailed and *official* account of the specifically *legal* case[46] against an Iranian-style "rights"-based view of Article IV, however, notable observers of NPT issues — experts spanning the conventional political spectrum — have been offering just such legal arguments for years.

b. Outside Experts. In a 1976 paper prepared for the U.S. Arms Control and Disarmament Agency (ACDA), seminal Cold War nuclear theorist Albert Wohlstetter warned of the dangers of allowing dual-use civilian nuclear technology to spread. This, he said, was creating "[a] kind of growing legitimate — but Damocletian — 'overhang' of countries increasingly near the edge of making bombs" that would make nuclear safeguards "increasingly irrelevant."[47] Wohlstetter warned of the dangers of a situation in which, "in return for their (revocable) promise not to make or accept nuclear explosives," nonweapons states would continue to acquire "civilian technologies that would carry them a long distance on the road to nuclear explosives."[48]

Wohlstetter characterized the NPT as being fundamentally — and dangerously — ambiguous about peaceful uses, reflecting a broader confusion he felt to have been partly engendered by early rhetoric about the presumed — but, he stressed, notably "exaggerated" — benefits of nuclear power for the developing world.[49] The Treaty was, he said,

> a highly ambiguous and uncertain set of compromises, reflecting but not resolving . . . dilemmas about national sovereignty and the problem of encouraging civilian nuclear energy while discouraging military nuclear energy.[50]

This confusion lay at the root of the regime's problems with technology, for "the present rules of the game" permitted countries to "take . . . long strides towards nuclear weapons capability in the next 10 years or so without violating the rules — at least no rigorously formulated, agreed on rules."[51]

The other side of this ambiguity, however, was that interpreting the NPT in a sensible and sustainable way was not prohibited. Wohlstetter argued that "[t]he line drawn between safe activities that are permitted under agreement and dangerous prohibited activities needs to be redrawn and clearly defined to make safeguards relevant."[52] In his view, there was no sharp distinction between "safe" and "dangerous" activities, with the result that the advisability of spreading technology should be assessed according to its impact upon "the shrinking critical time" needed to make a nuclear weapon.[53] He warned that the nonproliferation regime faced stresses because of early assumptions about the "simple dichotomies" between safety and danger, and that "sensible decision making and international bargaining in this field" required more.[54] In particular, Wohlstetter observed that it would be necessary to "persuad[e] less developed countries to forego national capabilities" in certain risky technological areas.[55]

Wohlstetter's analysis focused in particular upon chemical reprocessing of plutonium, which he argued in some detail was not merely "uneconomic" but in fact simply *could not* be safeguarded in such a way as to provide timely warning of misuse and therefore "creates unjustifiable risks."[56] His point was a broader one of principle, however, not merely a technology-specific risk assessment. His basic idea was that if the nonproliferation regime were to make any sense, and indeed to survive, consideration of proliferation risk had to be a part of *all* technology-access decisions[57] — and that there thus could be no *per se* right to technology.

Wohlstetter's argument in 1976 was framed more in policy and economic terms than in legal ones. In 1979, however — in another report prepared for ACDA — he sharpened his already implicit legal conclusion. Wohlstetter noted there that if the "fullest possible exchange" provisions of Article IV(2) were taken to include "the provision of stocks of highly concentrated fissile material within days or hours of being ready for incorporated into an explosive," this would "certainly 'assist' an aspiring nonnuclear weapons state in making such an explosive" — thus violating the "assistance" prohibition of Article I.

> No reasonable interpretation of the Nonproliferation Treaty would say that the treaty intends, in exchange for an explicitly revocable promise by countries with-

out nuclear explosives not to make or acquire them, to transfer to them material that is within days or hours of being ready for incorporation into a bomb. Some help and certainly the avoidance of *arbitrary* interference in peaceful uses of nuclear energy are involved. However, the main return for promising not to manufacture or receive nuclear weapons is clearly a corresponding promise by some potential adversaries, backed by a system to provide early warning if the promises should be broken. The NPT is, after all, a treaty against proliferation, not for nuclear development.[58]

Further articulation of these ideas was offered by Arthur Steiner, Eldon Greenberg, Paul Leventhal, Leonard Weiss, and others. Steiner, for instance, rejected the "dubious" idea that "non-weapons states have the absolute right to receive any and all nuclear assistance" short of actually obtaining nuclear explosive devices. He interpreted Article IV as being necessarily "subordinate to, and to be interpreted in conformity with Articles I and II."[59] Examining the legislative history of the Treaty, Steiner declared that:

"[i]t seems quite clear . . . that it was not the intent of the framers of the NPT to create an obligation to supply any and all forms of nuclear energy with a single exception of actual explosive devices. The logic of the NPT does not support the idea that either weapons or non-weapons states wish to have their security reduced by unrestricted commerce in especially dangerous forms of nuclear energy. . . . The evidence is overwhelming that the 'straightforward bargain' [of weapons-relinquishment in return for unrestricted access to technology for peaceful purposes] is a dangerous myth.[60]

This conclusion was not surprising to Steiner:

It is, after all, a nonproliferation treaty. The provision

261

of certain types of nuclear technology that defeat the objective of nonproliferation by bringing a non-weapons state recipient within days or hours of a weapon cannot be an objective ... [of] a nonproliferation treaty.[61]

Eldon Greenberg's subsequent paper on the subject for the Nuclear Control Institute[62] — which approvingly quoted both Wohlsteter and Steiner — also analyzed the NPT's treatment of "nuclear equipment, technologies and materials . . . ostensibly for peaceful purposes in denominated civilian nuclear power programs."[63] (As it had been with Wohlstetter's argument, Greenberg's specific focus was plutonium reprocessing, but his legal point was not limited to this particular technology.) He described there being "a dynamic tension in the Treaty between its prohibitions and its injunctions to cooperate in peaceful uses of nuclear energy." Greenberg concluded, however, that the NPT's language and history — and in particular, the "in conformity with" language that qualifies the "inalienable right" described in Article IV(1) —

> tend[s] to support the conclusion that Articles I, II, and IV must be read together in such a way that assistance or activities which are ostensibly peaceful and civilian in nature do not as a practical matter lead to proliferation of nuclear weapons. The NPT, in other words, can and should be read as permitting the evaluation of such factors as proliferation risk, economic or technical justification and safeguards effectiveness in assessing the consistency of specific or generic types of assistance and activities with the Treaty's restrictions, to ensure that action is not taken in the guise of peaceful applications of nuclear energy under Article IV which in fact is violative of the prohibitions of Articles I and II.[64]

Greenberg apparently did not think that this conclusion was legally *compelled* by the NPT. Arguing against the view that any technology short of actual weapons could be permitted to nonweapons states as long as this technology was subjected to IAEA safeguards, he stressed that "there is another way to interpret the NPT."[65] Specifically, it was "reasonable to interpret the Treaty" as prohibiting even notionally "civilian" uses where "safeguards under Article III of the Treaty are not effective."[66]

Greenberg did *not* think safeguards could be effective, especially with regard to plutonium reprocessing. He contended, following Wohlstetter, that there were "serious questions" about "the ability to safeguard effectively now or in the foreseeable future certain forms of assistance and activities, such as those related to reprocessing and plutonium recycle." As a result, "it is reasonable to conclude that the contemplated verification function of Article III cannot be fulfilled today."[67] Accordingly, Greenberg felt that "the presumption that the particular assistance or activity runs afoul of the prohibitions of Articles I and II should again arise."[68]

As this example indicates, Greenberg's was necessarily a strong position against "bright line" rules with regard to technology access. He was quite explicit about this, writing that "the NPT creates no *per se* rules with respect to acceptable uses and, indeed, allows a pragmatic interpretation of its provisions."[69]

> Since questions with respect to the economics and safeguardability of . . . [specific nuclear technologies] are essentially factual in nature, judgments with respect to the applicability of the NPT's prohibitions can and should be made on a case-by-case basis, in light of al the facts and circumstances surrounding particular nuclear assistance or activities.[70]

As he later summed up his view, it was:

> perfectly legitimate to evaluate such factors as pro-
> liferation risk, economic or technical justification and
> safeguards effectiveness in determining whether spe-
> cific or generic types of assistance or activities should
> be regarded as permissible under the NPT.[71]

Significantly, proliferation risk was first and foremost among the factors that needed to be considered, for— as Greenberg pungently put it—"the NPT 'does not require us to do something foolish'."[72]

> At some point, particular assistance or activities may
> become so risky, even though they do not involve the
> transfer and acquisition of weapons or explosives as
> such, that they can no longer be deemed in conformity
> with the requirements of Articles I and II, even though
> by their stated terms they are for peaceful power ap-
> plications only.[73]

Similar arguments, citing Greenberg, were subse-quently advanced by Paul Leventhal at the Nuclear Control Institute, who argued that the "conformity" qualifications upon the "right" described in Article IV(1) meant that weapons-usable fissile materials "can be banned [for nonweapons states] under the ex-isting terms of the Treaty" because "IAEA safeguards are clearly inadequate" to provide effective assuranc-es against their misuse.[74] Writing upon the 50th an-niversary of President Dwight Eisenhower's "Atoms for Peace" speech, Leonard Weiss also criticized "the notion that the NPT requires nuclear weapon states to share technology for producing separated fissile material with non-weapon states," and decried "the early euphoric embrace of Atoms for Peace, when the spread of nuclear technology was unaccompanied by adequate consideration of proliferation risks."[75] Additionally, in a 1996 discussion of Article IV, Weiss argued that while international disputes over the meaning of its provisions have yet to reach "formal resolution," IAEA safeguards "cannot be *effectively* carried out at this time for enrichment and reprocessing facilities" and that therefore those who transfer such technology might "find themselves in violation of Article I."[76]

This line of reasoning is also reflected in the writing of Henry Sokolski of the Nonproliferation Policy Education Center (NPEC)—who edited the volume in which Weiss' 1996 analysis appeared. In 1996, for instance, Sokolski argued that:

> the NPT's framers understood that some forms of civil nuclear energy(*e.g.*, weapons-usable nuclear fuels and their related production facilities) were so close to bomb making that sharing them might not be in 'conformity' with Articles 1 and 2.[77]

Also casting doubt upon the ability of IAEA safeguards to provide timely warning of diversion, Sokolski cautioned that if the NPT were to have "worth . . . in the decade ahead," it would be necessary to focus upon the Treaty's "original concerns" as a *nonproliferation* instrument and "correct for its current deficiencies"[78] in that it was all too often being interpreted as a technology-privileging agreement. Fidelity to the original intention of the Treaty, said Sokolski, meant rejecting the idea that a nonweapons state has "a 'peaceful' right to acquire all it needs to come within days of having a bomb." Instead, he said, it must be accepted that "although nations should be free to develop peaceful nuclear energy . . . whether or not a particular activity met this criterion depended upon a number of factors" — including whether this application could be safeguarded in a way that provided timely warning of misuse.[79]

In contemporary debates — that is, in the wake of the revelations about Iran that bubbled forth after 2002 — NPEC has continued to propound this counterpoint to Iran's rights-privileging reading of Article IV. Specifically, Sokolski has continued to argue the need to:

> reinterpret existing rules to eliminate the mistaken belief that all forms of civilian nuclear activity, including those that bring states within days of acquiring nuclear weapons, are guaranteed.[80]

As Sokolski suggested before a congressional subcommittee in 2006, if the international community wishes to ensure the continued validity of the NPT regime, it should not "make our past mistakes [in interpreting Article IV] hereditary by grandfathering dangerous nuclear activities in . . . nonweapons states."[81]

In 2008, NPEC researcher Robert Zarate published a specifically legal analysis of Article IV which picked up the various themes — including the emphasis upon *safeguardablity* — stressed by Wohlstetter, Steiner, Greenberg, and Sokolski, and which built upon research into the NPT's negotiating history undertaken by Paul Lettow in May 2005.[82] Zarate contended that the NPT, "at a minimum," can be interpreted as "not recognizing the 'inalienable right' of signatories to nuclear materials, technologies, and activities that the IAEA cannot effectively safeguard."[83] He argued further that:

> "the [International Atomic Energy] Agency cannot

provide—even in principle—timely warning of a non-nuclear-weapon state's diversion of weapons-ready nuclear materials from civilian applications to nuclear weapons or unknown purposes; it must tolerate, under its current accounting methods, large amounts of unaccounted nuclear material at facilities that handle such material in bulk form before even beginning to suspect a diversion; and it appears to lack adequate financial resources to carry out many of its safeguarding activities effectively."[84]

Because Article III requires safeguards on nuclear activities in nonweapons states—and because to read the Treaty any other way would make Article III incoherent—"the NPT may be understood as prohibiting non-nuclear weapon signatories from unsafeguardable nuclear materials, technologies, and activities."[85]

Surveying its negotiating history, Zarate argued that Article IV is perfectly consistent with a reading that interprets the "inalienable right" as being qualified in three ways. First, peaceful use applications must be "economically beneficial in accordance with the treaty's preamble. Second, they must possess a low risk of proliferation in accordance with Articles I and II. Third, they must be "effectively safeguardable and undertaken in full compliance with NPT and IAEA safeguard obligations in accordance with Article III."[86]

The view that adopting a *per se* rule of technology access rights under Article IV is to *misinterpret* that provision of the Treaty—or at least that the NPT *need not*, and for quite sound nonproliferation reasons *should not*, be interpreted in that fashion—has increasingly been picked up elsewhere in the nonproliferation community. It was, for instance, adopted in a 2007 Council on Foreign Relations study of nuclear energy issues written by Charles Ferguson. Subtitled

"Balancing Benefits and Risks," Ferguson's report discussed the proliferation risks attendant to nuclear fuel making, and described certain critical problems of applying nuclear safeguards to such technologies.[87] Among other things, Ferguson warned that "greater efforts are needed . . . to limit the spread of fuel-making technologies"[88] and declared that "the NPT's right to peaceful nuclear technologies" should be "properly interpret[ed]" to make clear that "[t]his right . . . comes with the responsibility to maintain adequate safeguards" and that the NPT does not "specifically" guarantee "nuclear fuel-making facilities as part of that right."[89]

The Commission on the Prevention on the Prevention of Weapons of Mass Destruction Proliferation and Terrorism also seems, by implication, to have taken such a view of Article IV in its final report published in 2008. One of its key recommendations on nuclear non-proliferation was "to prevent the spread of uranium enrichment and plutonium reprocessing technologies and facilities to additional countries," and it urged the United States to "work to orchestrate an international consensus to block additional countries from obtaining these capabilities."[90] This recommendation seems to have been based upon the Commission's concerns about "the inherent difficulty of reliably detecting dangerous illicit nuclear activities in a timely fashion." Some of these difficulties, the Commission warned, "are not likely to be remedied no matter how much the IAEA's resources are increased." In particular, this was the case with "detecting military diversions from nuclear fuel cycle activities."[91] Since such capabilities could not be safeguarded, their acquisition had to be prevented—and the Commission apparently saw no legal problem with doing so.

The Congressional Commission on the Strategic Posture of the United States seems to have reached a similar conclusion in late 2008. Its Interim Report warned that nuclear proliferation stood at a "tipping point," beyond which a "cascade" of proliferation might occur, and it noted that the IAEA had not been given the support it needed to provide adequate protection of fissile materials.[92] The terse report did not offer a legal analysis of the NPT, but it made clear that the Commission had reached a grim conclusion about how well the Treaty has hitherto generally been interpreted as a barrier to proliferation. To wit, it declared that the NPT's "effectiveness has been undermined by errors in how it has been interpreted and by failures of enforcement by the UN Security Council."[93] (It urged the United States to work to fix such interpretive errors at the 2010 NPT Review Conference.) The Commission's final report, released in 2009, emphasized that the "further globalization of nuclear expertise" will "inevitably increase the risks of possible diversion to illicit purposes."[94] It did not discuss the "right" discussed in Article IV beyond reiterating the NPT's requirement that it be limited to peaceful uses (i.e., "in conformity with Articles I and II of this Treaty"), but the Commission urged governments to agree to "limit access to enrichment and reprocessing technologies, and the facilities that employ them, to the maximum extent possible."[95]

Arguments consistent with, or explicitly supportive of, a "safeguardability" reading of Article IV have thus been offered for many years. (This is a history of critical analysis to which I myself would have already added a voice, had I not in 2007 been refused clearance by the State Department's Office of the Legal Advisor to make similar points even in an essay drafted as my "personal views."[96]) To sum up the "safeguardability" perspective, the vague text of Article IV is read as embodying no more than an elaboration upon the idea expressed in the NPT Preamble about sharing the *benefits* of nuclear technology.[97] Safeguardability recasts the legal analysis of Article IV, turning claims of a rights-based discourse on their head by rejecting the idea that the NPT discusses peaceful use "rights" in any sense *other* than affirming a right to the *benefits* of nuclear technology. Through this lens, sharing of the technology itself, or of nuclear materials, is not a question of *right* at all but rather of *policy*: whether or not such access can be given in a way consistent with the overarching purpose of the Treaty in preventing the proliferation of nuclear weapons. To be sure, possessors have the obligation to work to help *all* of mankind, and not just *some* of it, benefit from nuclear know-how.

Nevertheless, proliferation risk trumps peaceful use "rights" where sharing specific technologies is concerned. The most forgiving form of the safeguardability argument might simply deny the existence of ENR "rights." This would effect a *de-legalization* of the NPT's peaceful use discourse,[98] leaving specific technology-sharing questions to be resolved on a case-by-case basis as a matter for technically-informed policy choice. As we have seen, many authors have criticized the adequacy of IAEA safeguards, questioning the Agency's ability — at least with its current resources, or by some accounts *at all* — to provide genuinely timely warning of the diversion of particular types of nuclear technology. This line of argument runs back through the critiques of plutonium reprocessing offered by Wohlstetter, Steiner, and Greenberg, which have been echoed by some experts today, and indeed expanded to cover uranium enrichment and even the operation of light water nuclear reactors.[99] The simple "de-legalization" form of the safeguardability critique would hold simply that there is no *right* to such technology, and that as a matter of *policy*, right-thinking members of the international community should work to stop the spread of any capabilities that cannot adequately be safeguarded, because of the proliferation risks that they entail. (As noted above, this is about as far as we got within the U.S. State Department in 2004 and 2005, with our interagency-cleared remarks about Article IV and ENR.[100])

But one might perhaps go further. A stronger form of the safeguardability critique—already suggested by at least some of the authors surveyed above—would build upon *factual* assessments of unsafeguardability toward a legal conclusion of such technologies' *impermissibility*. Such arguments tend to note that the possession of inadequately safeguarded materials or facilities raises Article III compliance problems, while Article I requires nuclear weapons states, at least, to avoid assisting nuclear weapons efforts in nonweapons states. If it is indeed the case that the IAEA *cannot* adequately safeguard certain nuclear activities, some authors have thus suggested that these should be understood as being *prohibited* by the NPT for states not already lawfully having nuclear weapons. This is a potentially dramatic conclusion, for it would raise questions not only about the impermissibility of *spreading* capabilities such as uranium enrichment and reprocessing, but also about the *existing* fact of their possession by nonweapons states (e.g., plutonium bulk-handling facilities in Japan).

Such a "strong form" of the safeguardability argument, however, has its weaknesses as a question of legal interpretation. It is easier and usually more plausible, for instance, to read a vague committee-drafted text as ducking a contentious issue than to interpret its ambiguity as a sharp prohibitory stand. It is also problematic to build a general technology-prohibition argument—however substantively sensible such a position might be—so heavily upon inferences from the weapons-assistance ban of Article I, which by its terms applies only to nuclear weapons states, and at least arguably does *not* prohibit nonweapons states from assisting others' nuclear weapons programs.[101]

Either way, however, the distinctiveness of the safeguardability reading of the NPT's peaceful use provisions is in its transformation of the debate from a policy-*trumping* discourse of "rights" into a policy-*privileging* arena for technically-informed substantive judgments involving the consideration of such things as specific safeguards capabilities and the time needed for an effective response to the detection of a violation. Safeguardability approaches to technology access, in other words, tie themselves to a calculus of proliferation risk—a focus that their defenders suggest is entirely appropriate, and indeed quite necessary, under a *nonproliferation* treaty.

A PREHISTORY OF NUCLEAR TECHNOLOGY CONTROL

Despite the recently increased salience of Article IV debates in the struggles over Iranian proliferation challenges, the conceptual lines have long been fairly clearly drawn. What, however, are we to make of all this? One useful way to help approach the NPT's treatment of peaceful use issues is to understand the context of the broader problem of technology control that has been keenly understood—and was approached in characteristic ways—from the very earliest years of the international community's struggle to come to grips with the implications of the nuclear age.

Struggling With Janus: The Acheson-Lilienthal Era.

The idea of ensuring broad international participation in the *benefits* that nuclear technology can bring to mankind, yet while trying to avoid spreading knowledge and capabilities related to its destructive aspects, goes back to the dawn of the nuclear age. It has always been understood that nuclear technology is in no way always a good, and that its spread requires qualification commensurate to the risks. For this reason, it was recognized at the beginning of mankind's struggle with these nuclear tensions that a commendable focus upon spreading the *benefits* of nuclear power did not necessarily imply any commitment to spreading *all* nuclear know-how—and indeed that a genuine commitment to nuclear benefits *did* necessarily imply careful attention to what specific capabilities should *not* be spread.

In a Joint Declaration in November 1945, for instance, U.S. President Harry Truman, British Prime Minister Clement Attlee, and Canada's Prime Minister Mackenzie King stressed their belief in sharing what they called "the fruits" of nuclear scientific research. They noted, however, that "[t]he military exploitation of atomic energy depends, in large part, upon the same methods and processes as would be required for industrial uses," and suggested pointedly that it would be counterproductive to share technology in the absence of effective "and enforceable" safeguards.[102]

Crucially, moreover, it was also understood from the start that the types of nuclear know-how that should *not* be shared were *not* limited solely to those involved in endstage manufacture of nuclear weaponry. Actual bomb making skills clearly *should* not be shared, of course, but as the Joint Declaration suggested, a sane approach to managing the tension between the destructive and creative powers of nuclear technology required attention to the degree to which safeguards could control the proliferation risks of shared technology.

The idea that certain nuclear capabilities and activities were inherently dangerous, and that they should *not* be shared or spread more widely, dates from the very earliest years of the international community's struggle with nuclear energy. Even as scientists and policymakers scrambled to figure out how to share nuclear *benefits* more widely in the name of socioeconomic progress, those aspects of nuclear technology that were common to *both* weapons work and to peaceful uses were naturally the focus of special concern and attention. They were widely, and quite explicitly, regarded as being something that needed to be controlled: something to which access should be restricted unless and until approaches could be developed that could preclude their exploitation for weapons-related work.

The idea that some technologies and activities were inherently "dangerous," for example, was a fundamental aspect of the U.S. Government's famous "Baruch Plan" — which in 1946 called for the creation of an International Atomic Development Authority to exercise "[m]anagerial control and ownership of all atomic-energy activities potentially dangerous to world security." Specifically, the proposed Authority was to exercise *exclusive* control over "intrinsically dangerous activities" such as "the production of fissionable materials," including "all plants producing fissionable materials."[103] In addition to "all facilities for the production of U-235, plutonium and other such fissionable materials," the Authority was therefore to have control over all fissile materials themselves, "wherever present in potentially dangerous quantities." Sharp restrictions upon access to such capabilities — which the Baruch Plan proposed in the form of exclusive international control — were necessary because "all the initial processes in the production of these fissionable materials . . . are identical whether their intended use or purpose is beneficent or dangerous."[104]

Nor was it expected that the category of intrinsically dangerous activities was one that would remain fixed for all time. To the contrary, there was no fixed line between "safe" and "dangerous" nuclear technologies. It was expected that as technology developed — or our understanding of nuclear risks matured — this category might change. Because of the need to flexibly define intrinsic danger according to the best understanding of the time, it was thus considered necessary to give the proposed International Atomic Development Authority the authority to define, and redefine, the categories of technology requiring international control.[105] The Authority needed "the power to determine, and adjust from time to time, in accordance with increased knowledge, the dividing line between 'safe' and 'dangerous' activities as new conditions demand."[106]

The issue of nuclear technology-access, in other words, was not to be a matter of legal "rights," but rather a scientifically-informed question of nonproliferation *policy*. It was very important that "the benefits" derived from atomic energy research and development be available to all mankind,[107] but the specific issue of *technology*-access had always to be subordinated to nonproliferation considerations. As the United States put it at the time, it was "important" to share nuclear benefits, but it was a "prime purpose" of the proposed authority to "prevent national development or use of atomic armament."[108] What could not *safely* be shared must *not* be.

It was therefore central to the scheme that technology-access policy hinge upon whether, and the degree to which, the wider spread of specific nuclear know-how was consistent with preventing proliferation in light of the best available understanding of what could be made "proliferation proof" in protecting against weapons-related exploitation. To officials at the time, fuel-cycle technology was clearly "intrinsically dangerous" and consequently unshareable, but this was not a conclusion written in stone. The key insight was that *nothing* should be permitted outside the exclusive control of the proposed Authority that could be exploited for weapons development. A rigorously-defined notion of *safeguardability*, in effect, was the litmus test of technology access for *any* national government.

The Baruch Plan was the outgrowth of an extensive U.S. review of nuclear policy that culminated in the so-called Acheson-Lilienthal Report of March 1946, which had provided the intellectual underpinnings for the approach proposed by Bernard Baruch to the UN Atomic Energy Commission later that year. While U.S. officials were well aware that "the only *complete* protection for the civilized world from the destructive use of scientific knowledge lies in the prevention of war,"[109] the authors of the Report clearly felt that there were better and worse ways to reduce the tremendous dangers presented by nuclear technology short of achieving complete world peace.

The Baruch Plan's distinction between "safe" and "dangerous" nuclear activities—with only the former being appropriately left in national hands—derived from the Acheson-Lilienthal Report.[110] That study argued that, for the sake of global security, an international control authority must be given "exclusive jurisdiction to conduct all intrinsically dangerous operations in the [nuclear] field." The line between safe and dangerous, as we have seen, was "not sharp and may shift from time to time in either direction." (It would be, said the Report, up to the Atomic Development Authority "continually to reexamine the boundary between dangerous and nondangerous activities.")[111] "In our view, any activity is dangerous which offers a solution either in the actual fact of its physical installation, or by subtle alterations thereof, to one of the three major problems of making atomic weapons: (1)The provision of raw materials, (2)The production in suitable quality and quantity of the fissionable materials plutonium and U 235, and (3)The use of these materials for the making of atomic weapons."[112]

Interestingly, the Report considered even nuclear power generation—which was not in fact then possible, because "existing plants are not designed to operate at a sufficiently high temperature for the energy to be used for the generation of electrical power"—to be an intrinsically dangerous nuclear activity.[113] (It reached this conclusion, moreover, despite the initial belief of its drafters that techniques of "denaturing" uranium and plutonium in reactor fuel could "render materials safer" so that they "do not readily lend themselves to the making of atomic explosives."[114] The fact that this assumption about denaturing was already under question at the time the document was

277

released—leading the U.S. Government to re-release the Report with an explanatory press release noting that it "does not contend nor is it in fact true, that a system of control based solely on denaturing could provide adequate safety"[115]—simply highlighted the conclusion. Another technology emphatically noted as "dangerous" was the production of fissile material itself: uranium isotopic separation and reactor operation for plutonium production. Such activities were clearly "intrinsically dangerous operations, " and the Report argued pointedly that fissile material production "may be regarded as the *most* dangerous [type of activity], for it is through such operations that materials can be produced which are suitable for atomic explosives."[116]

The analysis underpinning the Report reflected great skepticism about the utility of a control system in which nations remained free to undertake nuclear activities that would be useful both for peaceful applications and for weapons development, even if some international inspectorate could be created in an effort to monitor activity for possible impermissible weapons-related work. An "agency with merely police-like powers attempting to cope with national agencies otherwise restrained only by a commitment to 'outlaw' the use of atomic energy for war"[117] would be, the Report argued, inherently inadequate. For an inspection system to be feasible, the Report noted, safeguards mechanisms must:

> provide unambiguous and reliable danger signals if a nation takes steps that do or may indicate the beginning of atomic warfare. Those danger signals must flash early enough to leave time adequate to permit other nations—alone or in concert—to take appropriate action.[118]

Yet the activities involved in developing atomic energy for peaceful purposes and those used in developing it "for bombs" were too "interchangeable and interdependent," and the potential consequences of military diversion too great, for any stable regime to rely simply upon national government good faith backed by some sort of inspections. It was simply not possible, the Report's authors believed, for safeguards to ensure the requisite timely warning: "[i]f nations or their citizens carry on intrinsically dangerous activities it seems to us that the chances for safeguarding the future are hopeless."[119]

The Report's explanation is worth quoting at length, for, if correct, it would have fateful implications for today's Article IV debates.

> From this it follows that although nations may agree not to use in bombs the atomic energy developed within their borders the only assurance that a conversion to destructive purposes would not be made would be the pledged word and the good faith of the nation itself. This fact puts an enormous pressure upon national good faith. Indeed it creates suspicion on the part of other nations that their neighbors' pledged word will not be kept. This danger is accentuated by the unusual characteristics of atomic bombs, namely their devastating effect as a surprise weapon, that is, a weapon secretly developed and used without warning. Fear of such surprise violation of pledged word will surely break down any confidence in the pledged word of rival countries developing atomic energy if the treaty obligations and good faith of the nations are the only assurances upon which to rely.
>
> . . . We have concluded unanimously that there is no prospect of security against atomic warfare in a system of international agreements to outlaw such weapons controlled only by a system which relies on inspection and similar police-like methods. The reasons sup-

porting this conclusion are not merely technical, but primarily the inseparable political, social, and organizational problems involved in enforcing agreements between nations each free to develop atomic energy but only pledged not to use it for bombs. National rivalries in the development of atomic energy readily convertible to destructive purposes are the heart of the difficulty. So long as intrinsically dangerous activities may be carried on by nations, rivalries are inevitable and fears are engendered that place so great a pressure upon a system of international enforcement by police methods that no degree of ingenuity or technical competence could possibly hope to cope with them.

. . . We are convinced that if the production of fissionable materials by national governments (or by private organizations under their control) is permitted, systems of inspection cannot by themselves be made "effective safeguards . . . to protect complying states against the hazards of violations and evasions."

. . . The efforts that individual states are bound to make to increase their industrial capacity and build a reserve for military potentialities will inevitably undermine any system of safeguards which permits these fundamental causes of rivalry to [continue to] exist. In short, any system based on outlawing the purely military development of atomic energy and relying solely on inspection for enforcement would at the outset be surrounded by conditions which would destroy the system.

. . . [T]he facts preclude any reasonable reliance upon inspection as the primary safeguard against violations of conventions prohibiting atomic weapons, yet leaving the exploitation of atomic energy in national hands.[120]

The Report thus emphasized that *"an otherwise uncontrolled exploitation of atomic energy by national governments* will not be an adequate safeguard" and that the "necessary preconditions for a successful scheme of inspection . . . *cannot be fulfilled in any organizational arrangements in which the only instrument of control is inspection.*"[121] It did not mince words:

> It is not possible to devise an atomic energy program in which safeguards independent of the motivation of the operators preclude the manufacture of material for atomic weapons."[122] This conclusion about the unavoidable inadequacy of any inspection-based system of safeguards which allowed fissile material production capacity to remain in national hands formed the basis for the U.S. conclusion that an international agency be created with exclusive prerogatives to engage in those "activities which it is essential to control because they are dangerous to international security."[123]

For these very reasons, the Acheson-Lilienthal Report also made clear that the national government's access to nuclear technology could not be made a question of *legal right*. Such "rights" would undermine the control system by preventing the kinds of restrictions that would be required in order to preserve international peace and security. The Report deemed it "essential" for any "workable system of safeguards" to "remove from individual nations or their citizens the legal right to engage in certain well-defined activities in respect to atomic energy . . . [that are] intrinsically dangerous because they are or could be made steps in the production of atomic bombs."[124] Only if technology access were a *policy* question — indexed, in effect, to proliferation risk — could a workable regime survive. A *rights*-based discourse about fissile material production and stockpiling was understood to be fundamentally incompatible with global security in the nuclear age.

United Nations Endorsement. Though these conclu-

281

sions were resolutely opposed by the Soviet Union and its communist allies—Moscow, of course, being then hard at work developing its own nuclear weapons on the basis of information pilfered from the Manhattan Project, and thus none too keen on a system that would remove weapons-making technology from national governments' hands—the basic outlines of the Baruch Plan were endorsed by considerable majorities in the young UN. The first report of the UN Atomic Energy Commission (UNAEC) in 1946 emphasized:

> the intimate relation between the activities required for peaceful purposes and those leading to the production of atomic weapons; most of the stages which are needed for the former are also needed for the latter. . . . [T]he productive processes are identical and inseparable up to a very advanced state of manufacture.[125]

This made international control of such capabilities imperative. This identity and inseparability of the productive processes for nuclear fuel and nuclear weapons material made fuel-cycle technology effectively unsafeguardable: these were *not* capabilities that could safely be left in national hands.[126]

Interestingly, the UNAEC did not follow the United States in endorsing the idea of giving the proposed international Authority *carte blanche* in making the sort of risk based policy determinations that would be necessary in setting the specific contours of permissible nuclear "benefit"-sharing. This was not, however, out of any concern that the Authority would be too strict in drawing the line against peaceful use applications that entailed proliferation risks. Instead, the Commission seems in part to have feared that the Authority might be too *lenient*: "[i]f the agency were free to decide the rate of production of nuclear fuel and were to embark upon a policy of production exceeding recognized or actual beneficial uses . . . the conditions of world security would be greatly affected."[127] The UNAEC, in other words, was concerned to ensure that global nuclear policy was not made *so* solicitous of requests for peaceful uses that it threw nuclear weapons proliferation considerations to the winds.

Noting "the conflict between the requirements of security and those of preparing for large-scale application of peaceful developments" of nuclear energy, the UNAEC recommended that the proposed Authority keep fuel production "at the minimum required for efficient operating procedures necessitated by actual beneficial uses, including research and development."[128] (Remember also that this discussion only occurred within a framework that presupposed the Authority's exclusive right to engage in fissile material production: even *internationally*-controlled production was thus understood to risk creating nonproliferation problems, and had to be kept to the bare minimum possible consistent with what was actually "beneficial.") In approaching the objective of sharing the "benefits" of nuclear technology, therefore, the Commission seems to have perceived a linkage between the idea of "actual beneficial uses" and "the conditions of world security." Nuclear "benefits" could not be approached independently of the issue of preventing states from developing nuclear weapons.

THE PRIMACY OF SECURITY

The UNAEC was quite firm that international control of nuclear energy was needed because the proliferation risks would be intolerable if each state were to claim the "right" to determine whether, and how much, fissile material to produce. Such a "right" was entirely inconsistent with global security.[129] As the Commission put it,

> if the right to decide upon the number and size of such facilities and upon the size of the stockpiles of source material and nuclear fuel situated on their territory were left to nations, the control measures provided for in the [UNAEC's] first report would not, if applied alone, eliminate the possibility of one nation or group of nations achieving potential military supremacy, or, through seizure, actual military supremacy.[130]

As the Commission envisioned it, the proposed international Authority would define what was "dangerous" within the scope of parameters set by the international convention establishing it.

What would be permitted to national governments was a *policy* decision to be made with an eye to the global security impact — in terms of nuclear weapons proliferation — of permitting access to any particular type of technology or nuclear capability.

"Dangerous activities or facilities are those which are of military significance in the production of atomic weapons. The word "dangerous" is used in the sense of "potentially dangerous to world security." In determining from time to time what are dangerous activities and dangerous facilities, the international agency shall comply with the provisions of the treaty or convention which will provide that the agency shall take into account the quantity and quality of materials in each case, the possibility of diversion, the ease with which the materials can be used or converted to produce atomic weapons, the total supply and distribution of such materials in existence, the design and operating characteristics of the facilities involved, the ease with which these facilities may be altered, possible combinations with other facilities, scientific and technical advances which have been made, and the degree to which the agency has achieved security in the control of atomic energy."[131]

As had the U.S. officials that were promoting the Baruch Plan, the UNAEC understood that this essentially *policy* question was also one that could change over time.

> The dividing line between dangerous and non-dangerous activities will change from time to time. Many factors will be involved, and these factors will vary from one installation to another.[132]

The bottom line, however, was that the UN recommended that proliferation impact—and the closely related criterion of safeguardability—be made the keys to determining what technology can and should be permitted to national governments.

Thinkers of the period were painfully aware of what we might today call the problem of the latent or virtual nuclear weapons programs afforded by possession of nuclear fuel-making capabilities. As U.S. Secretary of State Dean Acheson put it, the true measure of atomic armament available to a country was to be found less in what it actually had put into a bomb than in the amount of fissionable material which has been produced and is currently being produced there. It was the essence of the U.S. and UN approach, therefore, to ensure that "no nation would be permitted to possess the means with which weapons could be made"—namely, fuel-production technology.[133]

This approach, it was recognized, would not be without cost. The UNAEC recognized that there was "conflict between the requirements of security and those of large-scale development and use of atomic energy for peaceful purposes." Security measures, for instance, might retard the development of nuclear energy, while the production and stockpiling of nuclear fuel — however useful that might be for reactor operation — "would hardly be consistent with security." Nevertheless, at least for the foreseeable future, the Commission stressed that "[i]n regard to the specific proposal for future production and stockpiling of nuclear fuels, it appears that at the present time policy should be dictated primarily by security considerations."[134] Where peaceful uses appeared inconsistent with preventing proliferation, in other words, security considerations must be paramount: sharing the benefits of nuclear technology was important, but not more important than preventing nuclear weapons development.

According to the Commission, the international Authority should "make every effort to widen the activities involving nuclear fuels and key substances permitted to nations, *as conditions warrant*," and should "be guided by the general principle that nuclear fuel is intended for beneficial use." Nevertheless, "[d]angerous facilities shall be provided for nations *only* as world conditions of security warrant *and* where economic justification exists."[135] Significantly, moreover, these two conditions were described as both being necessary: to be permissible, such technology access had to be *both* consistent with security — i.e., nonproliferation, to use the modern term — *and* economically justified. Meeting merely one of these criteria was insufficient.

It Was Not About "Rights" — And It Could Not Be. As had also been the case for the Acheson-Lilienthal Report and the Baruch Plan, the UN proposals were the antithesis of a "rights"-based approach to technology access. Indeed, the key protagonists in developing these U.N. proposals flatly rejected the idea that this was or could be an issue of state "rights." The potential implications of nuclear weapons development were too dire to permit this to be a matter of national government discretion. In order to prevent, as it were, a weapons proliferation tragedy of the commons,[136] making any specific technology access a matter of *right* was out of the question. As Canada, China, France, the United Kingdom (UK), and the United States put it in their joint statement of October 1949,

> The development and use of atomic energy even for peaceful purposes are not exclusively matters of domestic concern of individual nations, but rather have predominantly international implications and repercussions.
>
> The development of atomic energy must be made an international cooperative enterprise in all its phases.[137]

As the UN Atomic Energy Commission saw it, preventing unrestricted national technology access rights was the only way to "bring the benefits of atomic energy to all nations, and at the same time ensure reasonable security against atomic war and, particularly provide a warning of any preparations for a surprise atomic war."[138] For benefits-sharing to be consistent with international peace and security, it had to be a *policy*-driven, not a *rights*-driven process.

The Soviet Counteroffensive: A "Right" to Chase the Bomb.

Majorities in the new UN organization supported

the UNAEC plan, endorsing it, and for a number of years describing the Commission proposals as being the only sensible approach offered to the challenge of dealing with nuclear technology.[139] Eager to acquire its own nuclear weapons, however, the Soviet Union mounted a fierce diplomatic campaign against it—a campaign striking, to 21st century eyes, for its similarities to the propaganda campaign undertaken by the Islamic Republic of Iran against U.S.-led efforts to impose nonproliferation-driven limits upon nuclear technology sharing.

Then secretly working to develop their own atomic weapons as rapidly as possible, the Soviets professed outrage at the UN plan for nuclear energy control. Developing themes that would be enthusiastically resurrected by the clerical regime in Tehran when confronted years later with international outrage over *Iran's* analogous nuclear efforts, and with American efforts to limit the spread of enrichment and reprocessing technology, the Soviets attacked the UN plan for being affront to national sovereign rights. The proposals were, they said, an American plot to monopolize control of nuclear energy—in effect, a conspiracy of the nuclear "haves" against the nuclear "have nots."

According to then-Ambassador Andrei Gromyko, for instance, the UN plan was "directed against the independence of other States," and was designed "to secure the monopoly position of one country [the United States] in the field of atomic energy." Denouncing the inevitability of "one-sided decisions" by the Authority, Gromyko declared that the Union of Soviet Socialist Republics (USSR) would refuse to allow "the fate of its national economy to be handed over to this organ."[140] Foreign Minister Andrei Vyshinsky similarly denounced "the notorious Acheson-Baruch-Lilienthal plan" as being "no more than a mockery of international control" which would function as "an American control organ."[141] Moscow's U.N. Ambassador, Jacob Malik, echoed that the UN proposals were a plan not for international control but for national monopolization: a plot whereby "the United States monopolistic big capital" would somehow come to "own all atomic energy-producing plants and all raw material extracted throughout the world."[142]

As a diplomatic counter-punch, Moscow advanced its own competing plan for the control of nuclear energy. This plan would *not* have restricted nations' ability to pursue activities the UNAEC had described as "dangerous" (e.g., producing fissile material), instead opting to place its reliance entirely upon periodic[143] inspections by an international organ that reported to the UN Security Council. As this subordination to the Council indicated, of course, the Soviet plan would also have made action against violations subject to a UN Security Council vote, with the natural opportunity for a veto by any permanent member (e.g., the Soviet Union).[144]

Moreover, in yet another parallel to modern-day diplomatic offensives by Iran — a country that has itself benefited from being thus far subject to enforcement action only by international organs largely hamstrung by consensus or veto procedures (i.e., the IAEA Board of Governors and the UN Security Council) — the Soviets stressed the importance of technology-sharing to empower "have-nots," emphasized the need to consider the unrestricted pursuit of nuclear technology as a *legal right*, and wrapped all these issues together with a strong emphasis upon the need of existing nuclear weapons possessors (i.e., the United States) to disarm before any progress could be made. Moscow's proposals to the UNAEC, for example, declared that a control plan could only be agreed if nuclear weapons were prohibited *first*[145] — and that all signatories to such a weapons prohibition convention "must have a right to carry on unrestricted scientific research activities in the field of atomic energy."[146]

Within 2 years of first making these proposals, the Soviets detonated their first atomic bomb.[147] With the benefit of hindsight, therefore, Moscow's pursuit of unrestricted nuclear technology-access rights for ostensibly peaceful purposes is revealed as the dangerous fraud that it really was. Its outrageousness lies not in the fact merely that the Soviet proposals were *incompatible* with the UN plan for nuclear energy control. More fundamentally, those proposals were offered in order to *subvert* that plan, and to make the prevention of nuclear weapons proliferation — and indeed the world's nuclear disarmament, as envisioned in the Acheson-Lilienthal Report and the Baruch framework — quite impossible. This is a lesson that modern-day policymakers should not forget.

Retreat Into Inspection-Driven Safeguards.

In the face of the Soviets' diplomatic counter-offensive — and after 1949, Moscow's own possession of atomic weaponry — the UN plan stagnated, and was eventually abandoned. By 1953, President Eisenhower had obviously given up on the grand American idea of entirely removing "dangerous" applications of nuclear energy from national hands. This was not to say that Washington had given up on the idea of preserving international peace and security as much as possible against the threat of nuclear warfare by working to prevent the *further* spread of nuclear weapons capabilities, of course: that effort continues to the present day. The United States, however, reluctantly fell away from the dream of international control, and eventually into support for a decidedly second-best regime of inspection-driven safeguards, upon at least *some* nuclear technologies, under a new IAEA.

In his famous Atoms for Peace speech to the UN, Eisenhower observed that while at one time the United States had enjoyed a monopoly upon nuclear technology, "the knowledge now possessed by several nations will eventually be shared by others — possibly all others."[148] To help make the best of what therefore must clearly seemed to be — in light of his country's previous analyses and proposals — a rather bad situation, he proposed the creation of the IAEA, and urged the governments "principally involved, to the extent permitted by elementary prudence, to begin now and continue to make joint contributions from their stockpiles of normal uranium and fissionable materials" to the Agency under safeguards to be devised against surprise seizure by countries in which such materials were being stored or used.[149]

Secretary of State Acheson had reemphasized in 1952 that "no system of inspection alone, be it periodic or continuous, can insure the effective prohibition of atomic weapons,"[150] and in 1954 U.S. representatives were still promoting proposals at the UN that would have involved the creation of a UN Disarmament and Atomic Development Authority responsible, *inter alia,* for "for the control of atomic energy to the extent necessary to ensure effective prohibition of nuclear weapons and use of nuclear materials for peaceful purposes only."[151] (These 1954 proposals still envisioned an Authority itself possessing the power to suspend the supply of nuclear materials to a violator state, and to close down plants utilizing nuclear materials there.[152]) Nevertheless, ambitious Baruch-era thinking was clearly falling by the wayside.

The Disarmament Nexus.

One of the casualties of the collapse of these early efforts to come to grips with controlling access to intrinsically dangerous nuclear technologies was arguably any hope of containing the emerging and accelerating nuclear arms race between the United States and the Soviet Union, let alone of achieving genuine nuclear disarmament. Because fuel-making capabilities were inherently dual-use in nature — and thus were, according to Acheson-Lilienthal reasoning, fundamentally unsafeguardable by any IAEA-style inspection-based regime — and because there no longer existed any chance of removing such capabilities from at least *some* nations' hands, nuclear disarmament was coming to seem quite out of the question. What possessor country, after all, would bind itself to forego nuclear weapons if its neighbors' compliance with such a prohibition could not be assured? This connection between control of nations' access to fissile material production capabilities and the prospects for disarmament is one that we forget at our peril in 21st-century debates over NPT Article IV issues.

By the mid-1950s, at any rate, *both* Cold War adversaries — and the Western allies, for that matter — seem to have come to think in similarly pessimistic terms about the problems of controlling nuclear technology. With the only safeguards now available being the inspection of *nationally*-owned and -controlled nuclear facilities, U.S. authorities evinced increasing skepticism that the actual elimination of nuclear weapons capabilities could be achieved any more effectively than the acquisition of such capabilities could be precluded for anyone having access to an intrinsically dangerous technology such as fuel making. President Eisenhower said that the United States would be happy to reduce armaments in conjunction with other nations if an effective verification mechanism could be found, but he added pointedly that "[w]e have not as yet been able to discover any scientific or other inspection method which would make certain of the elimination of nuclear weapons."[153]

Notwithstanding their eagerness to score rhetorical points against the United States for being too reluctant—on account of the numerical superiority of the Warsaw Pact in Central Europe[154]—to abandon nuclear weapons, even the Soviets now seemed largely to agree. Soviet representatives described the challenge of nuclear technology control as being "particularly difficult," noting that "[t]his danger is inherent in the very nature of atomic production." Echoing earlier American pronouncements in the Acheson-Lilienthal Report and the Baruch Plan, as well as the conclusions of the UN Atomic Energy Commission, the Soviets now conceded that

> production of atomic energy for peaceful purposes can be used for the accumulation of stocks of explosive atomic materials, and moreover, in ever greater quantities. This means that States having establishments for the production of atomic energy can accumulate, in violation of the relevant agreements, large quantities of explosive materials for the production of atomic weapons. The danger of this state of affairs becomes still more apparent if account is taken of the fact that, where the corresponding quantities of explosive atomic materials exist, production of actual atomic and hydrogen bombs is technically fully feasible and

can be effected on a large scale.[155]

Accordingly, there would exist "possibilities beyond the reach of international control for evading this control and for organizing the clandestine manufacture of atomic and hydrogen weapons," even if there were "a formal agreement on international control." In such a situation, Moscow now warned, the security of States Party to a nuclear control treaty "cannot be guaranteed, since the possibility would be open to a potential aggressor to accumulate stocks of atomic and hydrogen weapons for a surprise attack on peace-loving States."[156] Arguments that had earlier been used by the West in favor of international control of nuclear energy, however, were now marshaled, in effect, to demonstrate the futility of treaty constraints.

The harm done to the cause of disarmament by failing to control weapons-facilitating nuclear technology soon became a major theme of the Eisenhower Administration's approach to UN disarmament discussions. The international community's failure to sufficiently assume control over access to the sort of intrinsically dangerous technologies identified in the Acheson-Lilienthal, Baruch, and UNAEC proposals, in other words, was dooming disarmament.

Citing the existence of a "barrier of science which prevents us at this moment, on the admission of the Soviet Union, the United States and every other delegation represented at this table, from making nuclear disarmament the safe hope for the world that we would wish it to be,"[157] U.S. officials argued "[t]he present impossibility of establishing an effective inspection and control method that would completely account for nuclear weapons material." This meant, they said, that it was not possible to account for all nuclear weapons material, and that "the amount of unaccountability is of such magnitude as to be an unacceptable unknown quantity of vast destructive capacity."[158]

According to British Foreign Secretary Harold MacMillan, the "difficulties which have arisen in connection with the control of nuclear weapons and the materials of which they are made" helped explain why disarmament proposals were stuck:

> ... [I]f we are in earnest about disarmament, we cannot go on admitting on the one hand that there are possibilities of evasion beyond international control, and proposing on the other hand the total abolition of nuclear weapons as our ultimate goal, but it would be misleading to pretend that it is a realizable goal in our present state of scientific knowledge. ... I cannot agree on behalf of Her Majesty's Government, and I would not expect other Governments to agree, to abolish all our nuclear weapons as long as there is no assurance that every other state is doing the same. ... [T]hese thermo-nuclear weapons are now so deadly that the slightest margin of error or deception could be decisive for the fate of nations. The risks involved are quite unacceptable in present conditions. ... [S]ome of the concepts of *total* nuclear disarmament which we have been using are quite out-off-date in the world as it is today and that we only mislead people by clinging to them.[159]

The United States, France, Canada, and the United Kingdom agreed, moreover, that it had by this point become essentially "impossible to account for *past* production of nuclear material" by states possessing fuel-making capabilities,[160] which underlined MacMillan's basic point. As the Americans described it, at least, Moscow's decision to torpedo the Baruch Plan had therefore doomed mankind to a stalemate on nuclear disarmament and the specter of a nuclear arms race. According to a White House publication in October 1956, both of these ills "stemmed largely from the repeated rejections by the USSR of the Baruch proposals of 1946-47 for putting all atomic energy under international control."[161]

After Eisenhower appointed Harold Stassen to serve as his new Special Assistant to the President for Disarmament, Stassen led an interagency review of these issues which reached the grim conclusion that—on account, *inter alia*, of these problems of nuclear technology control and "the extreme importance of providing against surprise attack"—the United States should *not* agree even to a moratorium on hydrogen bomb (thermonuclear weapon) testing. As U.S. Ambassador James Wadsworth later explained to the UN Disarmament Commission, "in the absence of agreement to eliminate or limit nuclear weapons under proper safeguards, continuation of testing is essential for our national defense and the security of the free world."[162] Given the pessimistic conclusions of so many participants about the effective safeguardability of the nuclear fuel cycle, Wadsworth's qualification could easily be read as nothing less than an indictment even of the *possibility* of arms control and disarmament, now that more and more countries possessed the nuclear fuel cycle.

The United States subsequently retreated from such heights of skepticism, of course, supporting the establishment of the IAEA (as advocated by Eisenhower himself in 1953) and its development at the center of a global system of safeguards for the peaceful use of nuclear energy. Disarmament prospects fared less well during this period as the United States and Soviet Union built increasingly large arsenals and the

UK (1952), France (1960), and China (1964) joined the nuclear weapons club. With regard to peaceful uses, however, the world was for a time content to make do with the inspection-driven regime of safeguards upon nationally-controlled peaceful nuclear activities.

Thinking about Technology Control.

Thus did the world end up gradually converging upon the institutionalized system of inspection-driven IAEA safeguards — a system which acquired additional legal import with the advent of the NPT, Article III of which required non-nuclear weapons states to accept IAEA safeguards "with a view to preventing diversion of nuclear energy from peaceful uses to nuclear weapons or other nuclear explosive devices."[163] Unfortunately, this was precisely the sort of regime that the Acheson-Lilienthal Report had warned would be entirely unable to preserve security in a world of widespread nuclear access to intrinsically dangerous capabilities such as fuel making. As Albert Wohlstetter once grumbled, in the wake of the Soviets' rejection of the Baruch Plan,

> we have come to rely on exactly the scheme regarded as unworkable by the authors of the Acheson-Lilienthal report and the Baruch Plan. We rely in essence only on accounting and inspection of dangerous activities in non-weapon states.[164]

The shift to inspection safeguards thus highlighted the importance of limiting access to such technologies — which, in turn, naturally necessitated *not* making their acquisition a matter of legal *right*.

President Eisenhower's Atoms for Peace speech gave a bit of a window into how it was anticipated that such a system might operate. As recounted above, he envisioned "elementary prudence" — that is, nonproliferation policy — as governing the degree to which the IAEA should be entrusted with nuclear materials and technology for sharing, under strict safeguards, with governments receiving international cooperation in nuclear peaceful uses. The materials and technology that were to be shared would come from the countries principally involved in nuclear work. The system, in other words, was imagined to revolve around a finite number of supplier states with extensive nuclear know-how, which would feed as much knowledge and material as was *prudent*, in light of the obvious security risks, into an international cooperative network run under IAEA auspices and under a system of inspection-related safeguards.

For a while, this appears to have been felt satisfactory. Nevertheless, the problem of technology control always lurked in the wings. This problem — so pointedly outlined at the very outset of the nuclear age by the Acheson-Lilienthal Report — could largely be ignored during the IAEA's first decades, because for many years it was apparently felt that is was unlikely that many (or indeed perhaps any) additional countries would acquire the full nuclear fuel cycle anyway, or perhaps that at least some aspects of the cycle were not actually *too* dangerous. When such assumptions ceased to hold, however, the problem of control reemerged with a vengeance, to form the core of today's disputes over Article IV of the NPT.

U.S. Intelligence Views the Proliferation Threat. For some understanding of why it was felt acceptable for so long to rely upon IAEA inspections notwithstanding the problems long predicted with such an approach, it may be useful to examine how proliferation security threats were perceived at the time. A good window into such perceptions can be found in declassified proliferation-related U.S. National Intelligence Estimates (NIEs) from the 1950s and 1960s, which have become available in recent years. Specific detailed conclusions based upon intelligence information cannot be expected to have influenced decisionmaking on proliferation and nuclear technology issues outside the then limited number of recipients of such classified documents. Nevertheless, the old NIEs do provide a valuable window upon broader understandings among the expert community at the time with regard to the *type* of activities that presented proliferation risks, and how the (very public) global spread of nuclear technology could affect the security environment.

Clearly, the U.S. intelligence community worried about proliferation threats. In 1957, for instance, an NIE warned that "up to 10 countries" could produce at least "a few nominal (20-40 kt) nuclear weapons using only native resources" within a decade (i.e., by 1967) by means of exploiting "civilian atomic energy program[s] encompassing fairly large reactor and processing facilities" such as by producing weapons "clandestinely through concealed diversion of plutonium from inspected power plants."[165] In the wake of Eisenhower's Atoms for Peace speech to the UN, the potential proliferation implications of the spread of nuclear energy seem to have been clearly understood. An NIE in 1958 warned that "[n]uclear know-how applicable to reactor technology is rapidly being spread throughout the world by national and international programs for the peaceful development of nuclear energy," especially "dual-purpose reactors which generate both power for peaceful purposes and plutonium."[166]

Interestingly, however—as this phrasing about dual-purpose reactors suggested—the focus of this concern was mainly plutonium reprocessing, not uranium enrichment. As the 1957 NIE put it, "[n]uclear weapons could be produced clandestinely through concealed diversion of plutonium from inspected power plants." To have a large and diverse nuclear weapons program would take "specialized facilities" such as "large plutonium producing reactor and isotope separation plants if U-235 is to be obtained." But "particularly for production of U-235," this was so difficult and expensive that only a few countries, it was felt, could "by themselves achieve such a program over the next decade."[167]

The principal perceived weapons proliferation threat, it seemed, was thus related to plutonium, not uranium weapons. This point was underlined by the 1958 NIE, which made the same basic points about how the main danger was expected to be plutonium, not U-235.[168] Even France, clearly a likely potential weapon developer and a country rapidly building a relatively sophisticated nuclear infrastructure, was mainly only a plutonium threat in the near term.[169]

The lack of general access to fuel-making capabilities was apparently critical. A number of countries planned nuclear reactor programs—thus raising at least *potential* issues related to the diversion of plutonium chemically reprocessed out of such reactor fuel that they acquired—but they lacked the capability themselves to make uranium fuel. This enabled the supplier states to interpose proliferation-keyed restrictions that, it was felt, would allow nuclear power development on terms consistent with the maintenance of international peace and security.

According to the 1958 NIE, "[a]t present reactor fuels are available to have-not countries from major producers in the Free world only on terms intended to prevent diversion to weapon application."[170] Unless "present restrictions on the availability of fissionable materials for weapons application" were reduced[171] — or unless would-be weapons-possessors received "foreign assistance with development of isotope separation facilities or weapons design information"[172] — the risk was thus apparently felt to be a manageable one. To be sure, it was felt that

> as world uranium production and commercial sales of power reactors expand, it appears likely that, *in the absence of international controls*, even a country without direct access to natural uranium will be able to acquire uranium and produce enough fissionable material to fabricate at least a few crude weapons."[173]

Provided that a lid could be kept upon proliferation-risky technology sharing, however, the emerging nonproliferation regime was felt to be sustainable.

The assumptions behind such assessments, therefore, seemed to embody what we have seen as a safeguardability perspective. Plutonium reprocessing from reactor fuel was felt to be some danger, but the implication seemed to be that that proper safeguards could make this plutonium risk an acceptable one in light of the clear benefits that were perceived to exist from the development of electricity generation by nuclear reactors. There appears to have been for many years, as Albert Wohlstetter later put it, a widespread "belief that plutonium from a power reactor is not very dangerous."[174]

Wohlstetter traced this assumption to a technical mistake: the early comment in the Acheson-Lilienthal

Report that plutonium could be "denatured" — that is, made useless for weapons purposes — by leaving it in reactors long enough that its isotopic content of weapons-useful plutonium would become contaminated. As noted previously, the Report's authors had misgivings about the denaturing solution even as early as 1946, and worried about the potential for "public misunderstanding of what denaturing is, and of the degree of safety that it could afford."[175] Nevertheless, even the re-released text at least *sounded* optimistic about denaturing.[176] Though this initial hopefulness about denaturing as a solution was later discredited,[177] the Acheson-Lilienthal Report's treatment of the issue — in just the sort of public misunderstanding some had feared — encouraged the mistaken belief for many years that plutonium from spent reactor fuel could be made intrinsically "unusable or, at any rate, extremely ineffective when used in a nuclear explosive."[178]

Confusion over denaturing led to a belief that reactor operation entailed low proliferation risks,[179] and this in turn may have contributed to the relative equanimity with which analysts — as evidenced, for instance, in the NIEs — approached nuclear reactor promotion. Whatever the accuracy of assumptions made at the time about the fundamental safety of reactors, however, the key point for present purposes is that the policy community during the Atoms for Peace era clearly approached nuclear technology-sharing through the prism of proliferation risk: a classic safeguardability framework in which the challenges of nuclear technology control were approached through a weighing of proliferation risks and anticipated benefits.

As for the proliferation risks from uranium enrichment (as opposed to the separation of plutonium from reactor fuel), the same point holds, although the dangers presented by *that* technology were apparently then considered manageable for different reasons. In practice, enrichment seems to have been felt to present little danger because the infrastructure costs of indigenously developing this capability were so high as to make it essentially unachievable by most countries anyway.[180] According to one high-level panel of U.S. Government experts in 1964, uranium separation plants were so "expensive and difficult to operate" that this factor might in itself "deter some potential nuclear powers from considering U-235 for weapons use."[181] Its analysis of a number of "potential nuclear powers" concluded that while all were "in position to develop fission weapons from plutonium," *none* was "likely to build gaseous diffusion plants for obtaining U-235 or to develop thermonuclear weapons, however, because of the high cost and technological complexity."[182]

There was another factor that seems to have made U.S. officials more comfortable with the proliferation risks of Atoms for Peace: in the context of the intense Cold War nuclear rivalry between the United States and the Soviet Union, the highest priority was to prevent a newcomer's acquisition of a nuclear arsenal capable of upsetting the balance of power between the superpowers by posing a direct military threat of crippling nuclear attack against the United States. In a global environment in which the two predominant players and competing alliance leaders each possessed extremely large and rapidly growing arsenals and faced a real risk of massive nuclear exchanges with each other, the prospect of *some* additional countries acquiring small, "entry-level" nuclear arsenals was felt to be a secondary concern. No one wished to see proliferation, but the *real* problem would only come if someone else acquired a *substantial* nuclear capability. This was felt to allow the global security system, in effect, the ability to "absorb" at least *some* proliferation if it could not be prevented: the alarming degree of *vertical* proliferation, in other words, made the prospect of a bit of *horizontal* proliferation seem less shocking. Such conclusions made the proliferation risks of Atoms for Peace seem easier to bear.

This — to modern eyes — somewhat relaxed view of proliferation risks was by no means a secret. A number of senior U.S. officials told the U.S. Senate in the 1950s, in effect, that while some governments might indeed be able to circumvent nuclear safeguards and develop a small nuclear arsenal, this was an acceptable risk because such a tiny stockpile would pale in significance alongside the superpowers' nuclear holdings.[183] UN Ambassador Harold Stassen told the UN in 1957, in fact, that the admitted risk of "relatively minor diversions for a few weapons" was manageable because "those few weapons would be restrained, canceled out, and deterred by the remaining capability in the hands of nations on various sides."[184] The United States sought to prevent nuclear weapons proliferation, but what Washington at that point *really* feared was a so-called knock-out blow of the sort only possible at the hands of a major nuclear weapons state; preventing the acquisition of a small arsenal by a newcomer was only a secondary priority.[185]

This perspective seems to have colored the U.S. approach to safeguards and Washington's willingness to countenance proliferation risks in the dissemination of nuclear technology. U.S. officials understood that "[a]s the number of power and research nuclear reactors in a country increases, the potential for producing plutonium will increase." Accordingly, it was eventu-

ally "likely that any country will be able to obtain reactors which could be used for plutonium production
. . . [and] could theoretically acquire the technical ability to produce at least a few crude weapons."[186] Nevertheless, because such a few crude weapons would not
upset the global balance of power, it was not necessary to take heroic prophylactic steps — with the result
that Atoms for Peace could proceed notwithstanding
its potential to lead to *some* proliferation. Officials' de-
valuation of the systemic dangers presented by horizontal proliferation made Atoms for Peace seem more
reasonable.

Such views are also reflected in declassified NIEs
from the period. While U.S. intelligence did predict
"a small increase in the number of countries having
nuclear weapons,"[187] it also estimated that during the
next decade no one would be able to acquire "sufficient nuclear capabilities . . . to produce a change in
the basic world power situation" because "[t]he U.S.
and the USSR will still be so far ahead of all others [as]
to dominate the scene without much question."[188]

> In strictly military terms, the nuclear proliferation
> likely to occur over the next 10 years will almost cer-
> tainly not upset global power relationships. None of
> the prospective or potential nuclear powers will ac-
> quire capabilities which, if added to those of the U.S.
> or the USSR, would significantly affect East-West mili-
> tary relationships, or bulk large militarily as an inde-
> pendent force.[189]

Such proliferation-related geopolitical issue-
triage — with its all but explicit conclusion that *some*
proliferation need not be unduly troubling — may appear quite problematic to today's eyes, and entirely
untenable even on its own terms in today's post-Cold

War world of drastically reduced and still declining U.S. and Russian arsenals.[190] Nor can we forget that some of the assumptions that underlay relatively optimistic assessments of the proliferation risks presented by nuclear technology—about the potential of denaturing to prevent the development of plutonium weapons from reactor fuel and the degree to which uranium enrichment technology would remain out of reach for would-be proliferators—clearly have not stood the test of time. We have already noted how the denaturing hopes raised by the Acheson-Lilienthal report proved illusory. No student of modern proliferation history, moreover, can ignore the degree to which the development of efficient, centrifuge-based uranium enrichment—and its widespread proliferation since the mid-1980s by Pakistani scientist A. Q. Khan—has upended the traditional assumption that "the uranium route" to a nuclear weapon is unachievable for all but the wealthiest and most sophisticated powers.[191]

Having the advantage of hindsight in viewing older and perhaps obsolete perspectives upon proliferation risk, however, should not obscure an important point: the nuclear technology-sharing enterprise of the 1950s and 1960s was grounded in a safeguardability perspective that evaluated risks and benefits rather than operating on the basis of any kind of technology rights. We may think today that they got their facts wrong—that is, that decisionmakers of the period were operating on the basis of faulty risk analyses—but to concede this is not the same thing as to discredit the safeguardability *principle* that underlies past approaches. There is no indication that decisionmakers during this period felt that there existed any sort of hard right to nuclear technology independent of proliferation risk. To the contrary, the Atoms for Peace era seems to have proceeded on the basis of quite the opposite assumption.

ARTICLE IV OF THE NPT

It is useful to understand this "back-story" — the conceptual prehistory, as it were, of the challenge of nuclear technology control that confronted the drafters of the NPT — if one is to make sense of Article IV itself. It helps explain both that provision's actual text and the dynamics behind certain aspects of its negotiating history.

Paragraph 2: Technology Transfers.

For those interested in establishing the Treaty's intended meaning, the language of the *second* paragraph of Article IV is the easiest to explain. To recap, Article IV(2) provides that all Parties

> undertake to facilitate, and have the right to participate in, the fullest possible exchange of equipment, materials and scientific and technological information for the peaceful uses of nuclear energy.[192]

As hortatory language reflecting just the sort of generalized commitment to "benefit" sharing that is described in the NPT's Preamble,[193] Article IV(2) seems relatively straightforward.

The only reasonable reading of "the *fullest possible exchange*" is to take this phrasing as qualifying, rather than amplifying, language: it signals a *limit* rooted in real world practicalities (e.g., supplier cost, economic rationality, or proliferation risk) rather than any sort of requirement that technology transfers must continue until it is simply *impossible* to provide anything more. U.S. and other Western policy pronouncements are thus surely correct that the NPT does not actually *require* a technology-possessor to give any particular technology to any particular recipient.

A discretionary rather than mandatory reading of Article IV's language on technology transfers is also the only interpretation consistent with the clear requirement in the first paragraph of Article IV that the right to develop and use nuclear energy must be conducted in conformity with the nonproliferation obligations in Articles I and II. If they are to conform their own conduct with Article I, for instance, nuclear weapons state possessors simply *must* have broad discretion in what to share, and *cannot* transfer technology to the extent that doing so is inconsistent with nonproliferation interests.

This reading is also consistent with long-standing themes of nuclear technology control policy — stressing *benefit*-sharing but acutely aware of the potential destabilizing effect that "peaceful" technology transfers could have in facilitating nuclear weapons development — that would have been quite well known to the U.S. and Soviet officials who coordinated the NPT's drafting process. And indeed, the NPT's negotiating history bears this out: the parties rejected repeated efforts to *oblige* technology possessors to transfer technology.

Mexico, for instance proposed to make it a "duty" for technology-possessors to "contribute, according to their ability," in developing others' peaceful nuclear applications.[194] According to the Mexican ambassador,

> it is essential to establish the legal obligations of the nuclear Powers . . . to contribute to the technological development of the others, and to transfer and place

at the disposal of those countries their scientific and technological knowledge of the peaceful use of nuclear energy. We believe that the provision of such technical assistance should be made a legally-binding obligation. . . .[195]

Italy did not go quite so far, but nonetheless suggested new phrasing that would have specified an "inalienable right" to "obtain supplies of source and special fissionable materials intended for peaceful purposes."[196]

For its part, Nigeria proposed provisions that would have required nuclear weapons states to host scientific delegations from nonweapons states so that the latter could "collaborate with their scientists working on nuclear explosive devices, in order to narrow the intellectual gap" between them.[197] The repeated efforts made to specify that technology transfers must cover the full nuclear fuel cycle included a Spanish memorandum urging that the right of "participat[ing] as fully as possible in scientific and technical information for the peaceful uses of atomic energy" should be clarified in order "to refer specifically to the entire technology of reactors and fuels."[198] In the end, however, proposals to oblige fuel-cycle technology transfer were rejected.[199]

Certainly, the final form of Article IV left advocates of unrestricted technology sharing unhappy. Discussing the March 1968 treaty draft, for instance — a version that already included the "inalienable right" and "fullest possible exchange" phrasings[200] — some countries complained that it failed to ensure transfers of the full range of scientific and technical information.[201] In sum, the import of this negotiating history is clear, and it reinforces our conclusion about the highly qualified ("fullest possible") language of Article IV.

The NPT clearly does *not* require specific technology transfers.

Paragraph 1: The "Inalienable Right."

Textual Opacity and Confusion. It is the first paragraph of Article IV — the one most frequently cited in today's technology-access debates for its grand phrasing about an "inalienable right" to nuclear technology — that is the hardest to understand. States Party to the NPT, it says, have an "inalienable right . . . to develop, research, production and use of nuclear energy for peaceful purposes without discrimination and in conformity with Articles I and II."[202] More broadly phrased than Article IV(2), which deals with "cooperat[ion]" and the "exchange" of technological information between states — and thus with technology *transfer* — the first paragraph seems also to cover *indigenous development,* and is therefore potentially the more significant. "Even if you *do* have discretion in what you supply us," one might imagine an Iranian representative arguing, "we have the 'inalienable right' under the NPT to seek, develop, and retain any capability we wish for peaceful purposes." This paragraph is indeed at the core of today's Article IV debates.

Let's start at the end of the paragraph. It would seem clear enough that the phrasing in Article IV(1) about "conformity with Articles I and II" means that having signed the NPT, a nonweapon State Party no longer has *any* right, much less an inalienable one, to anything acquired or possessed in violation of these core nonproliferation obligations of the Treaty. Ironically, for all of Iran's emphasis upon its Article IV rights, the spare words of the conformity requirement

310

thus neatly dispose of Tehran's recent arguments. Having acquired its enrichment infrastructure—and set off down the road to plutonium reprocessing as well, with the commencement of construction of its heavy-water plant and the heavy-water plutonium production reactor at Arak—using designs and seed technology from Khan's smuggling network as part of a clandestine nuclear weapons program underway since the 1980s, Iran has *not* been in conformity with Article II and thus can claim no right to its fuel-cycle facilities.

Such an approach, however, raises as many questions as it answers. It is an interesting legal question, for instance, whether a country could "cure" its Article II noncompliance, and thus reacquire any right forfeited pursuant to the last 10 words of Article IV(1), merely by promising hereafter to use only for peaceful purposes what it had acquired in order to make nuclear weapons—or whether, instead, such ill-gotten gains must first be "disgorged" in the manner sometimes seen in civil litigation. (The legal doctrine of "unjust enrichment" might find relevance here, being both substantively appropriate and a marvelous *double entendre* to boot.) The former answer seems implausibly easy for any system at all concerned with preventing nuclear weapons proliferation, but even were such credulous leniency possible, Iran certainly has yet to persuade any serious observer that it has really turned over a new leaf.[203]

Nor should anyone interested in the legal meaning of these provisions forget that the conformity language of Article IV(1) refers not merely to Article II but also to Article I—that is, it would seem to impose qualifications upon the peaceful-use rights of the *nuclear weapons states* (the only ones subject to the provisions of Article I) as well as those of nonpossessors. What does this mean? Could, say, China be said to have lost its right to engage even in peaceful nuclear pursuits if it had assisted, say, Pakistan or Iran with nuclear weapons development (e.g., by supplying the nuclear weapons designs that Khan later provided to Libya and perhaps others, or by providing Iran's first uranium hexafluoride centrifuge feedstock)?

No matter who the violator might happen to be, what does it mean that the right referred to in Article IV is an inalienable one? Technically, this could mean no more than that one's peaceful use rights cannot be sold or transferred to another party, but it is hardly clear what this would actually add to the effective meaning of Article IV. (Was such transfer considered in any way a danger?) Another possibility is that inalienable essentially *does not* mean anything in particular—that is, that it was simply "color language" designed to serve the political purpose of emphasizing that the drafters thought that the right somehow to take advantage of nuclear know-how for peaceful purposes was a *very important* one.

Iran and its apologists sometimes seem to suggest that inalienability means that *nothing* can abridge the right to use any nuclear technology for peaceful purposes, but this is untenable as a matter of statutory interpretation because it would erase the conformity requirement so carefully included alongside the inalienable right phrasing. Nor would inalienability seem to impose any obstacle, in principle, to a forfeiture-implying reading of the conformity qualifications of Article IV(1). After all, history's most famous invocation of inalienable rights—the reference to "Life, Liberty, and the Pursuit of Happiness" in the U.S. Declaration of Independence—has never been taken

312

to mean that someone's right to liberty, for instance, cannot be infringed upon (e.g., by imprisonment) as the result of a sufficiently serious instance of law-breaking.[204]

It is thus not surprising, for instance, that the committee drafting the NPT rejected Romania's suggestion that the right described in what became Article IV be declared an "absolute right."[205] It could not be *truly* absolute, for — as Wohlstetter would later phrase things — this was a *nonproliferation* treaty, not a nuclear development treaty. As the Mexican ambassador to the committee drafting the NPT noted, it "could not be otherwise" than that peaceful use rights were qualified by the requirements of nonproliferation. Explaining his country's proposal for the inclusion of a peaceful use provision in the NPT that had been modeled on the approach taken in the Treaty for the Prohibition of Nuclear Weapons in Latin America (a.k.a. Treaty of Tlatelolco), the Mexican representative made clear that it was essential to limit peaceful use rights to those who were in compliance with nonproliferation rules. This

> reconciles the comprehensive and absolute prohibition of nuclear weapons, without any exception or reservation, with the rights of States members . . . to peaceful use of the atom for their economic and social development. Both principles — that of the prohibition and that of the use — are embodied in the Treaty. However, whereas the prohibition . . . is absolute and unconditional, the use — and this could not be otherwise — is subject . . . to the condition that it may not involve a violation or breach of that unrestricted prohibition.[206]

This was to be no less true for the NPT than it had been for Tlatelolco. That a limitation of the inalienable right was intended is therefore clear, and absolutist Iranian interpretations of inalienability are self-evident nonsense. Despite this understanding about what inalienable *does not* mean, however — or perhaps partly as a result of it — the specific legal import (if any) of the word remains, at the least, a question mark.

As a matter of treaty interpretation, the various issues raised by the text of Article IV are thus not easily or even necessarily coherently resolved. (This is true, furthermore, even without getting into vexing questions about *Who decides?* that are made especially pointed if Article IV is supposed to refer to hard technology rights that might be turned intermittently on or off according to their would-be possessor's conformity with nonproliferation rules.)

Then, of course, there are questions pertaining to what Article IV does *not* say. Notably, for example, Article IV does *not* specify a requirement for conformity with Article III of the NPT, though this idea was endorsed by consensus at the 2000 NPT Review Conference. It would certainly seem *reasonable* to provide that non-nuclear weapons States Party to the Treaty may not enjoy the right to possess or use nuclear material or engage in nuclear activities, even for peaceful purposes, without applying nuclear safeguards as indeed they are required to do by Article III. Why was this not done, and what might the omission imply? Could a country be in violation of the NPT by refusing all safeguards upon its nuclear activities and yet shelter behind a right to continue these activities solely on grounds that its work was not connected to a weapons program (and thus not an Article II violation)? It would be odd, at the least, to read the NPT in that fashion, and even Iran — which endlessly trumpets its purported return to safeguards compliance when arguing for its right to enrich uranium—does not seem to take such a view. But the text of Article IV provides little clue as to what we should think.

Most fundamentally, perhaps, the text of Article IV(1) is quite unhelpful in specifying what specific rights it might be thought protect in the first place. The right specified in that paragraph is the right "to develop, research, production and use of nuclear energy for peaceful purposes," but what does this entail? This vague and questionably grammatical phrasing could equally plausibly support very different readings. Does Article IV(1) refer[207] to a right merely to develop, research, produce, and use nuclear *energy* itself? Or does it say something further, about involvement with the underlying technologies that make such power production possible?

The former reading might not imply too much in terms of hard technology access privileges. (Perhaps the right to operate some kind of power reactor?[208]) If the latter reading were adopted, however, the argument for an ENR-privileging Iranian reading becomes somewhat stronger. But Article IV(1) does not make its meaning clear, and it certainly does *not* refer explicitly to the production of nuclear *fuel* – merely to that of "energy." Its eloquence at signaling the importance of peaceful uses and the existence of *some* right to partake in peaceful exploitation of the atom is in no way matched by its clarity in describing what any of this actually means in practical terms. If one insists upon looking for a hard rights-based discourse in Article IV, this ambiguity might seem strange in a document the drafters of which clearly *did* know how to write clearly, in lawyers' language, about obligation and prohibition.[209]

Negotiating History.

The negotiating history of Article IV (1) is not particularly helpful, but it may shed some light upon such conundra. There exist some statements in the record which suggest that the delegations participating in the NPT's drafting—in Zarate's words—"viewed nuclear fuel-making in a manner similar to nuclear explosives for peaceful purposes: that is, as potentially aiding and even constituting, the manufacture of nuclear weapons."[210] A British representative, for instance, stressed that "deal[ing] effectively with nuclear weapons" required "concentrating on the fissile material," while a Swedish representative remarked in 1966 that prohibiting merely the final stage of the "manufacture" of nuclear weapons was insufficient.[211] Building upon these insights, in fact, Burma's delegate declared in 1966 that

> [a]n undertaking on the part of the non-nuclear weapon Powers not to manufacture nuclear weapons would in effect mean forgoing the production of fissionable material . . . [because] such production is the first essential step for the manufacture of these weapons and constitutes and important dividing line between restraint from and pursuit of the nuclear[weapons] path.[212]

This is not necessarily to suggest, of course, that it was expected that Article IV would actually *prohibit* nuclear fuel making for non-nuclear weapons states. That fuel making was recognized as a somewhat proliferation-problematic technology, however, seems unmistakable. Perhaps for this reason, a Mexican proposal of 1966 to specify Parties' right to use nuclear energy for peaceful purposes "in any manner"[213] was not adopted.

In a sense, this is hardly surprising. In light of what we have seen of the long prehistory of the technology control problem – in which from the very dawn of the nuclear age nuclear fuel making was seen as "inherently dangerous" and as presenting special proliferation risks on account of the identity of its techniques and processes with what one would need to produce fissile material for nuclear weapons – it might in fact be more surprising had this point *not* arisen during the drafting of the NPT. To regard the drafters of Article IV as having suddenly conducted a complete *volte-face* from such insights and long-standing concerns, by drafting Article IV(1) to give countries an affirmative *right* to engage in such activity, would have been remarkable indeed.

Perhaps it is simply the case that the drafters did not think it *necessary* to be clearer about the *noninclusion* of fuel manufacture within the Article IV(1) right because they shared the apparent assumptions we have seen among U.S. intelligence analysts and others of the period that the spread of fuel-making capabilities was unlikely to present too much of a proliferation problem – provided that technology *transfers* were controlled – because such a capability was financially and technically out of reach of almost all states anyway. Certainly, as we have seen, every proposal was rejected that attempted to ensure that transfers under Article IV(2) *did* cover fissile material production technology. If it were felt that without such transfers no new states would be able to develop such capabilities in the first place, closing the door to mandatory sharing and trusting in the discretion of the then-supplier states would have left scarcely any need to labor longer over specifying the parameters of Article IV(1)'s inalienable right. As long as it did not unquestionably *include* fuel-cycle capabilities, which they ensured that it did not, that might have been seen as enough.

Some Western observers have suggested that this may have been in fact precisely what happened. They include Australian nuclear safeguards authority John Carlson,[214] but I have also argued the point. As I put it in a 2007 speech cleared by the U.S. interagency process,

> [b]ack at the time the NPT was negotiated, enrichment technology was available to very few, not widely understood, and commonly treated as tightly-controlled national security information because of its utility in producing fissile material for weapons. Enrichment technology was not expected to be widely available, so it was easy to promote "Atoms for Peace" because peaceful nuclear cooperation was seen as largely building power reactors to be run on fuel produced by the few states that already had the technology.[215]

Former Clinton Administration official Rose Gottemoeller has written, too, that "[h]istorically, economic reasons have limited the number of states possessing the full range of fuel cycle activities."[216]

A review of the negotiating history suggests little reason to believe that the drafters of the NPT ever expected technology possessors to share such things as uranium enrichment, or nonpossessors to get it if they did not. While some nonpossessors tried unsuccessfully to win agreement on participation rights that includes such technology, the delegations from technology *possessor* states who spoke favorably about international cooperative efforts seem generally to have had in mind only relatively innocuous technologies not directly related to nuclear weapons—e.g., nuclear reactors for electric power generation, or equipment related to agriculture, industry, seawater desalination, and fusion research—rather than such things as uranium production capabilities.[217]

One exception came with regard to fast-breeder reactors, the development of which, in West Germany and elsewhere, a 1967 U.S. State Department statement declared need not be impeded by the Treaty.[218] (Here we may perhaps see an example of the confused optimism about plutonium safeguards decried by Wohlstetter and others in the wake of the Acheson-Lilienthal Report's treatment of the denaturing issue.) Nevertheless, the point seems to hold with regard to uranium enrichment technology—the capability perhaps most at the center of today's diplomatic-cum-legal disputes with Iran. It may simply not have been felt necessary to provide any real clarity in Article IV(1) as to the scope of the "inalienable right."

A Reconciliation?

Clearly the temptation is great, in today's diplomatic context, to read Article IV ambitiously—to rely upon it both as a sword with which to compel the granting of countries' every wish for technology transfers, and as a shield with which to fend off efforts to limit access to capabilities that entail significant proliferation risks. Arguably, however, the best way to make both textual and substantive sense of Article IV—to sidestep and help explain the question-begging confusions and omissions of its phrasing, to lift the suggestive but all too opaque veil of its negotiating history, and to reconcile all of this with consistent themes running through the history of the international community's pre-NPT struggle with these same issues of nuclear control—is to retreat from the assumption that Article IV is really about hard technology rights at all. Perhaps the secret to understanding its specific, concrete, and invariant legal import is that it really *has* no such import, and was not intended to.

Article IV undoubtedly embodies and articulates — as the NPT's Preamble makes quite explicit — a strong commitment to ensuring that the benefits of nuclear technology are shared as widely as possible. This has always been understood as one of the major goals of the Treaty, and has been a lodestar for international nuclear cooperative efforts at least since Eisenhower's Atoms for Peace speech in 1953. In this author's view, however, the most tenable way to read Article IV essentially stops there, without wading into the conceptual and jurisprudential quicksand of trying to tease concrete, *per se* legal requirements out of its tortured syntax.

It is probably a mistake, and likely to be fruitless, to search for *any* sort of "bright line rules" for technology control within the ambit of Article IV. It would be very hard, for instance, to maintain that the NPT simply *prohibits* the possession or proliferation of nuclear fuel-making capabilities. After all, it would have been easy simply to *say* this if such had been the intention, and the drafters were not entirely strangers to the art of clear writing. Furthermore, as we have seen, even the drafting committee's co-chair, the United States, made clear in 1967 that the Treaty would not necessarily preclude even nonweapons states' development of fast-breeder reactors.[219] Nor, while it was clear enough that technology transfers would not be *mandatory*, was it established that they would necessarily *exclude* everything to do with fissile material production. (During the negotiations, moreover, Switzerland at one point spoke up to make the point — apparently without contradiction — that the Treaty would not outright prohibit "transfer[s]" of "enrichment of uranium, [or] extraction of plutonium from nuclear fuels, or manufacture of fuel elements or heavy water, when these processes are carried out for civil purposes."[220]) Except for nuclear weapons themselves — and the obviously related case of "peaceful nuclear explosions," which we will examine below — it would be hard to find a *per se* rule of technology exclusion in the NPT.

At the same time, however, it would seem that no *per se* rule of technology *inclusion* was intended either. The language of Article IV is quite notably ambiguous, and repeated efforts to make it more specific in just such ways were rejected, leaving nothing completely clear except that the drafters considered it very important to the scheme of the Treaty that — as the Preamble of the NPT nicely summarized — "the benefits of peaceful applications of nuclear technology ... should be available for peaceful purposes to all."[221] All seemed to share a genuine commitment to this principle, even as they declared their firm commitment to the overarching goal of the Treaty in preventing the further spread of what the Mexican ambassador called "these terrible weapons of mass destruction"[222] and retained an acute awareness of the fact that the dual-use nature of much nuclear technology meant that more widespread possession of some capabilities necessarily involved proliferation risks.

An obvious way, and perhaps the only way, to reconcile these elements was, in effect, to follow the path blazed by the Acheson-Lilienthal Report, the Baruch Plan, and the UN Atomic Energy Commission in adopting a vision of nuclear technology control strongly committed to the sharing of *benefits* yet approaching specific questions of technology access on a case-by-case basis with an eye to whether or not potential proliferation risks could be adequately controlled. Article IV, in other words, may be nothing more (and nothing less) than a pragmatic effort to carve out, from an instrument otherwise much concerned with specific legal requirements, a space in which nuanced *policy* judgments could be utilized to surmount the seeming tension between nonproliferation and peaceful uses. Rather than reifying the idea of technology access rights, therefore, sophisticated readers of Article IV are better advised to understand it—ironically, despite its colorful invocation of an inalienable right—as a *de-legalization* of peaceful use issues and a return to the fountainhead of today's international nuclear cooperation system: President Eisenhower's call to use atoms for peace with an eye to the elementary prudence of nonproliferation.

Let me stress that this is not the *only* way to read Article IV. For the most part, it is *possible* to read it—or at least its first paragraph—as Iran and others contend. Both a more contextually-dependent, *policy*-privileging reading and an absolutist, *rights* privileging interpretation are therefore legally available, as it were. In my view, however, the former understanding is the better one, being less plagued by the confusing text of Article IV, less confounded by the complexity of its negotiating history, and less substantively surprising and indeed contradictory in light of the long history of how key players (and the UN itself) struggled with the challenge of technology control in the years leading up to the drafting of the Treaty.

Such an approach would also be consistent with the discussion in the Preamble of the importance of sharing the *benefits* that nuclear technology can bring. This language seems clearly to reference and build upon what we have already seen to be a long-standing international discourse of benefit sharing that goes back to the earliest days of the Baruch Plan and UNAEC deliberations. The central theme of this discourse was, in effect, that specific technology sharing issues should be dealt with on a case-by-case basis — informed by proliferation risks — even as every effort is made to ensure that recipients benefit from nuclear applications even when they are themselves denied access to particular technologies.

Indeed, U.S. documents at the time explicitly described Article IV as embodying the principle of *benefit* sharing described in the Preamble. In an explanatory telegram sent to U.S. embassies and missions around the world, for instance, Article IV was described as a

> specific elaboration of the principle, stated in the preamble, "that the benefits of peaceful applications of nuclear technology . . . should be available for peaceful purposes to all Parties, whether nuclear weapon or non-nuclear weapon states."[223]

It would be at least somewhat strange to read Article IV's specific elaboration of the principle of benefit sharing in such a way as to repudiate the reason it had long been felt necessary to speak in terms of sharing *benefits* – as opposed to sharing specific *technologies* – in the first place.

This brings us to a final point. Perhaps most importantly, approaching peaceful use issues through the prism of *benefits* sharing within nonproliferation parameters is perhaps the only way to read Article IV that does not make that provision the enemy of the *rest* of the NPT. By contrast, a hard rights-reifying interpretation pits Article IV squarely against the overarching nonproliferation purpose of the Treaty. However egregious his behavior in helping shield

Iran from suffering consequences for its noncompliance until he declared it too late to stop Tehran's enrichment effort,[224] IAEA Director General El Baradei is nonetheless quite right to warn darkly of the potential consequences of a looming world full of virtual nuclear weapons states. That looming world, however, is a natural consequence of strong technology-rights readings of Article IV.

Reading the NPT's peaceful use provisions as being not about *per se* technology access rights but rather about the importance of exercising substantive policy judgment—that is, achieving a prudential balance between the benefits to be had from nuclear technology and the global security risks created by some means of achieving such sharing—thus seems like the best way to understand Article IV *as part of the NPT as a whole*, rather than just a cluster of phrases read in isolation. Such a reading may not be obligatory as a matter of statutory interpretation, but it certainly seems the wisest one.

A policy-privileging reading that sees the inalienable right of the NPT's Article IV through the prism of nonproliferation requirements is also the one most consistent with broader notions of probity in treaty interpretation that counsel signatories' fidelity to the object and purpose of a Treaty even in the period *before* their final ratification of an instrument.[225] It is also most consistent with those maxims which counsel turning to supplementary means of interpretation (e.g., negotiating history) in cases where looking merely at the text itself might leave a provision's meaning obscure or "lead to a result which is manifestly absurd or unreasonable."[226]

Civil Law legal systems and some significant international conventions also often incorporate a doctrine of abuse of rights (*abus de droit*), whereby the law will be read so as not to give any right to engage in activity that will tend to imperil such rights and freedoms.[227] As the principle was famously put in a 1961 judgment of the European Court of Human Rights,

> no person may be able to take advantage of the provisions of the Convention [for the Protection of Human Rights and Fundamental Freedoms] to perform acts aimed at destroying the aforesaid rights and freedoms.[228]

Though I managed to persuade the U.S. Government to hint at the notion in cleared remarks given to the 2005 NPT Review Conference,[229] *abus de droit* does not appear elsewhere to have been raised in an Article IV context. Nevertheless, the principle seems quite appropriate in Article IV discussions, where the danger is precisely that technology access rights purportedly recognized by the NPT's Article IV could in practice undermine the entire Treaty. It would, at the very least, be a perplexing reading of Article IV of the Nuclear Nonproliferation Treaty that facilitates that provision's use as a tool for *weakening* international protections against nuclear weapons proliferation.

The Case of Peaceful Nuclear Explosions.

Before we conclude, it is useful to mention the clearest case of the benefit sharing principle — and the way in which it did *not* necessarily entail sharing specific technologies — offered in the history of the NPT: the curious case of "peaceful nuclear explosions." As early as 1949, Soviet authorities had apparently begun professing interest in using nuclear explosions for "such peaceful purposes as moving mountains, irrigating deserts, and clearing jungles."[230] (At least as late as 1964, the Soviets still entertained ideas about "the removal of overburden from mineral deposits and the creation of waterways and harbors by means of nuclear detonation."[231]) Early on, U.S. officials ridiculed this idea, plausibly inferring that it was merely a cover for nuclear weapons ambitions. As one U.S. representative observed, after all, "if nations have devices in their possession which can level mountains, they also have in their possession devices which can level cities."[232] Nevertheless, the idea of "peaceful nuclear explosions" (PNEs) did not go away so easily.

During the course of the NPT's negotiations, in fact, countries as diverse as Brazil, Switzerland, India, and Nigeria all suggested that PNE technology should be made available to all countries under the aegis of peaceful nuclear cooperation.[233] In late 1967, for instance, Brazil proposed amending Article IV to provide an inalienable right that "include[d] nuclear explosive devices for civil uses."[234] Brazil tried again in February 1968.[235]

Giving access to the specific technology necessary to conduct PNEs, however, was entirely indistinguishable from sharing nuclear weapons technology, and was thus regarded by many other participants as being entirely out of the question within the ambit of a treaty devoted to the nonproliferation of nuclear weapons. Significantly, this did not result in an outright rejection of the *idea* of PNEs, but rather an acceptance of the importance of giving access to any *benefits* that could be derived from such explosions, yet emphatically *without* giving access to the technology. PNEs thus present, in effect, the classic example of the benefit-sharing principle as a way of serving the cause of peaceful nuclear uses *and* the cause of nonproliferation.[236]

The solution was to make clear that while PNEs were permissible and theoretically available to all Parties, only their *benefits* would be shared, with the technology itself remaining under NWS control.[237] As the United States explained this approach,

> any benefits which may emerge from the development of peaceful nuclear explosive devices should be made available to the world. As for the actual *use* of these devices, the United States has said that this service ought to be performed by the nuclear-weapon powers without discrimination for the non-nuclear-weapon powers.[238]

According to the representative of Mexico, the country that had itself first proposed the basic language that became Article IV, this solution to the PNE problem — namely, distinguishing between sharing *benefits* and necessarily sharing *technologies* — flowed naturally from "the spirit which pervades the Treaty and is expressed in the Preamble." In the event of a conflict between specific peaceful applications of nuclear technology and nonproliferation, he made it clear that one must give priority to nonproliferation. His explanation of this key insight — given here in the context of the PNE debate, but of obvious broader significance — is worth quoting in detail:

> . . . [I]f unfortunately it were necessary to choose between the manufacture of nuclear devices which, though intended for peaceful purposes, were basically identical with nuclear weapons, and the renunciation of all nuclear explosions as the only means of avoiding the proliferation of those terrible weapons of mass destruction, the spirit which pervades the Treaty and is expressed in the Preamble clearly indicates which of those two alternatives would be chosen . . . .. [That choice is] a solution which precludes the spread of

nuclear weapons and at the same time ensures that the States which . . . do not possess them are not deprived of the immense benefits which their economic development might derive from the use of nuclear explosions for peaceful purposes."[239]

This is a discourse not of *technology-access* rights but of rights to *benefits* from technology, the specific modalities of which must be assessed on the basis proliferation impact. In the end, Article V of the NPT embodied this approach quite clearly: the *benefits* of PNEs would be made available to all, but the *technological capability* to conduct such explosions would be permitted to no additional countries whatsoever.[240]

CONCLUSION: SAFEGUARDABILITY, REAL BENEFIT, AND TECHNOLOGY ACCESS

The preceding pages have argued that while a rights-privileging approach to technology access under the peaceful use provisions of the NPT and a more flexible and prudential policy-privileging interpretation are both legally available alternatives, the latter reading is by far the better one. At a minimum, the Treaty in no way *requires* a fixation upon *per se* technology access as the right described in Article IV. Eschewing the reification of technology access rights that seems to be becoming today's Article IV conventional wisdom, moreover, would return harmony to the fundamental scheme of the NPT, preventing that provision from actually undermining the instrument of which we must presume it was intended to be a constructive and coherent component. In fact, abandoning today's legally unnecessary and substantively dangerous rights-fetishism would open the door to what might end up being some very wise and principled public policymaking, in response to the challenges of reconciling the legal and substantive imperatives of nonproliferation with the international community's long-standing commitment to sharing the benefits of nuclear technology.

Delegalizing the peaceful use issue — that is, carving out conceptual space in which the operation of *policy* judgment can and should be employed — would have significant implications for how technology sharing issues are approached within the NPT regime. Specifically, it suggests at least two important areas for further research and analysis.

Safeguardability.

First, much more attention must be given to the effective safeguardability of specific nuclear technologies and capabilities. This is the logical consequence of a policy-privileging approach to Article IV. To assess whether a particular type of technology may appropriately be shared with, or should be possessed by, nonweapons states — or whether, instead, it is only the *benefits* of this technology that should be shared — it is necessary to know what proliferation risks it would actually entail. As the example of peaceful nuclear explosions demonstrates, *some* technologies may not be safely left in the hands of non-nuclear weapons states at all. The principle of benefit sharing referenced in the NPT's Preamble — and of which Article IV itself is an embodiment — is designed to accommodate this possibility, allowing for the *de facto* prohibition of nonweapons state possession of such a technology as long as possessors help make its *benefits* available in the alternative.

This approach, however, puts a premium upon

having a deep understanding of proliferation risks and safeguards possibilities, for it is the interplay between these two factors that will determine whether any particular capability — or, in the alternative, merely its *benefits* — may be shared with or possessed by non-nuclear weapons states. Such assessments will be, of course, judgment calls. As illustrated by the old assumption that denaturing would make widespread plutonium handling relatively safe, furthermore, judgments made at one time can later be understood as faulty. An answer that makes sense today may require revision tomorrow. We might, for example, discover certain capabilities to be more dangerous than once supposed, or be pleasantly surprised to learn that we had previously *over*estimated certain risks. Or perhaps we will simply devise cleverer ways of managing what seems today to be a danger so great as to preclude safe non-weapons state access to a particular technology.[241]

The contextuality — and hence impermanence — of technology-access judgments under the benefit-sharing framework of the NPT, however, is in fact more of a strength than a weakness, for it allows mistakes to be corrected, understandings to be improved, innovations to be incorporated, and a complex and changeable world to be accommodated without shattering the Treaty regime. It may be true that we do not in fact know what hindsight will reveal to be the best answer. Nonetheless, this sort of *not knowing* is no excuse to avoid making the wisest decisions we can on the basis of the best information available to us today. We should embrace this, for it is the essence of responsible public policymaking.

Because of its potentially dramatic implications with respect to technology access, exercising such judgment responsibly requires that we pay attention to the growing chorus of critiques of IAEA safeguards capabilities. This is particularly the case with regard to questions concerning the Agency's ability to adequately monitor bulk-handling facilities and large-scale enrichment operations, where even small error margins can quickly produce material accountancy uncertainties sufficient to mask the disappearance of quite notable quantities of fissile material. We should worry about criticisms that the figures used by the IAEA to define a "significant quantity" (SQ) of fissile material (i.e., the amount that one would need to manufacture a nuclear weapon) are much too high, and that the IAEA's benchmark conversion times for turning such material into a weapon—on the basis of which IAEA safeguards procedures and inspection periodicity are in large part determined—are therefore too long.[242] We should be more than slightly concerned not merely that only 89 states have thus far adopted the IAEA Additional Protocol that the Agency deems necessary to help detect undeclared nuclear activities, but indeed that the IAEA *itself* believes this Protocol to provide insufficient inspector authority in the face of denial and deception by the host government.[243]

Exercising our judgment responsibly also requires that we pay much more attention to matters such as the challenge of timely warning within the IAEA safeguards framework. Because it is obviously more important to *prevent* the diversion of material or technology into nuclear weapons than simply to *document* a proliferator's Treaty-violative *fait accompli*, the idea of timely warning is quite fundamental to the concept of nuclear safeguards. The IAEA's model for comprehensive safeguards agreements makes clear that:

the objective of safeguards is the timely detection of diversion of significant quantities of nuclear material from peaceful nuclear activities to the manufacture of nuclear weapons or of other nuclear explosive devices or for purposes unknown, and deterrence of such diversion by the risk of early detection.[244]

Timeliness, however, is not a purely technical issue. It has long been recognized that keeping civilian and military applications of nuclear energy separate means

> more than simply detecting a violation of an agreement. It means early detection of the approach by a government toward the making of a bomb in time for other governments to do something about it.[245]

This understanding of timeliness has long been the position of the U.S. Government. As we have seen, the Acheson-Lilienthal Report made clear that such timely warning was essential to any workable nonproliferation system: safeguards must provide danger signals that "flash early enough to leave time adequate to permit other nations—alone or in concert—to take appropriate action."[246] This view of timely warning has been recently reaffirmed. However unhelpful it may have been with regard to the precise meaning of Article IV, the U.S. State Department's reply to the Article IV query from Congressman Lantos nonetheless stressed "the need to ensure timely warning of diversion to non-peaceful purposes sufficient to permit an effective response."[247] Timeliness, therefore, has long been understood with an eye not simply to the specific conversion time required for a particular SQ of fissile material, but also to *the time it would take for the international community to respond to the violation detected.*

Needless to say, this makes the already demanding business of nuclear safeguards even more problematic. How much advance warning is, in fact, timely enough to permit a response to a violation? If one is to judge by the remarkable sloth of the IAEA Board of Governors in reporting *Iran's* safeguards noncompliance to the UN Security Council only 3 years after it was discovered[248] — despite such reporting being a requirement of the IAEA's own Statute[249] — genuine timeliness would seem, to put it mildly, rather hard to achieve.

Such worries are important under a policy-privileging peaceful use framework of benefits-sharing — and contemporary critiques deserve careful study to determine whether they do indeed indicate significant flaws in the safeguards framework — because of their potential implications for what technologies can safely be shared with, or possessed by, nonweapon states within the NPT regime. Some observers have already begun to draw grim conclusions. NPEC's Sokolski, for instance, argues that

> not all nuclear activities can be safeguarded — that the IAEA cannot detect military diversion from some facilities (like nuclear fuel plants) early and reliably enough to assure we can stop or deter them before any bombs are made[250]

Such critiques of IAEA safeguards, if warranted, could cut powerfully against technology-sharing, particularly with regard to ENR technology on the grounds that its possession can, in effect, allow states to proceed "to the very brink of acquiring nuclear arms — so that the final dash can be completed in a matter of . . . days."[251] As Roberta Wohlstetter pointed out many years ago in her insightful assessment of the implications of India's misuse of Atoms for Peace cooperation in order to develop the nuclear device it tested in 1974,

> a government can, without overtly proclaiming that it
> is going to make bombs (and while it says and possi-
> bly even means the opposite), undertake a succession
> of programs that progressively reduce the amount of
> time needed to make nuclear explosives, when and if
> it decides on that course. This can be done consciously
> or unconsciously, with a fixed purpose of actually ex-
> ploding a device or deferring that decision until later.
> But it is more than holding out the option. It involves
> steady progress toward a nuclear explosive.[252]

In India, this "process of drifting toward a bomb"[253]
occurred largely outside the IAEA system and the
NPT. The existence of safeguards and Article II obligations, however, may not offer much protection against
such drift—especially if no clear or detectable specific
decision is made to develop nuclear weapons until
late in the process.

Because even a country with the purest of motives can change its mind, moreover—and indeed, because acquiring the capability makes such a change of
course toward nuclear weapons easier, quicker, and
less risky[254]—the nonproliferation regime cannot rely
entirely upon safeguards even if they *are* effective in
providing timely warning of diversion during such
time as they are applied. Recognizing that there was
ultimately no way to prevent a host country's seizure
even of internationally-owned and—controlled facilities located in its territory, the Acheson-Lilienthal Report advocated locating such nuclear plants according
to strategic criteria, apparently in the hope that host
governments would be deterred from appropriating
them by the likelihood that rival nations would quickly follow suit by seizing (and presumably diverting to
weapons uses) nuclear facilities located in their *own*

respective territories.[255]

If the powerful Atomic Development Authority envisioned by the Report and the Baruch Plan was expected so nervously to contemplate the risk of seizure, how much less secure must the IAEA feel in a world in which all nuclear facilities are nationally owned and Agency inspectors work only at the pleasure of host governments? It is, after all, hardly difficult to simply expel IAEA inspectors as North Korea did in December 2002, *en route* to its nuclear test of October 2006. The international community might hope to *deter* such steps—at least if it can improve its currently woeful record of steadfastness against NPT and safeguards noncompliance—but there seems very little chance flatly to *preclude* them as a matter of safeguards methodology or design.

This is one reason why the idea of safeguardability as the touchstone of Article IV analysis has such significance. If IAEA safeguards are indeed as problematic as alleged in some modern critiques, one might be compelled to conclude, with Sokolski, that

> nuclear fuel-making activities cannot be considered 'peaceful' unless they are conducted in states that already have nuclear weapons. At the very least, it suggests that spreading fuel-making activities to new nonweapons states would be contrary to the NPT.[256]

Viewed through the prism of such safeguards critiques, in other words, the authors of the Acheson-Lilienthal Report—with their emphatic dismissal of the possibility that a safeguards system could *ever* make nationally-controlled nuclear facilities genuinely safe from a proliferation perspective—could end up having the last laugh.

This is not the place to assess the merits of current

safeguards critiques based upon materials accountancy, significant quantity estimates, presumed conversion times, timely warning, and inspector authorities in the face of determined denial and deception. The questions that have been raised, however, underscore the importance of making safeguards adequacy a subject for much more serious study and attention. The stakes are enormously high.

Real Benefits.

Another question raised by the benefit-sharing approach to NPT peaceful use issues is precisely what it means for a particular technology to be of benefit or to have a benefit worthy (or capable) of being shared at all. After all, for there to be any intelligible weighing of proliferation risk against the benefits offered by a particular technology—not to mention any coherent way of understanding how to provide such benefits to others *without* sharing that technology in the event that the proliferation risk proves unacceptable—there has to be at least *some* benefit in the offing in the first place.

If no real benefit is offered by a particular technology, in other words, it is not worth even *having* a discussion about whether any proliferation risk should be borne in its pursuit. Not even the smallest proliferation risk could possibly be justified by something that provides *no* benefit.

Having demonstrable benefits to offer is in no way dispositive with regard to the propriety of technology sharing. A judgment that a particular technology cannot or will not be properly safeguarded, for instance, could make even a very valuable application prohibitively costly from the standpoint of global security. At least with respect to technology transfers, however, a showing of real benefit is presumably *necessary* to open the policy debate, even if this is not sufficient to decide the issue: without demonstrable benefit, there is no case to plead in the court of safeguardability. (This is not to say that *indigenous* technology development efforts should be prohibited if they cannot make any coherent showing of benefit. A nonbeneficial technology that presents no proliferation risks would surely be permitted, for countries presumably retain the right to squander scarce resources upon otherwise harmless flights of fancy if they wish to do so. Economic irrationality may be quite relevant when drawing inferences about the intentions underlying an indigenous development program for purposes of Article II compliance analysis, but should not be regarded as dispositive in this regard. A safeguardability interpretation of Article IV would insist merely that neither transfer nor indigenous development be permitted to non-nuclear weapons states where this would entail significant proliferation risks.)

But what constitutes a demonstrable benefit? One would imagine that the benefit is relatively clear if the question at issue is the use of radioactive isotopes to sterilize disease-carrying tse-tse flies, or the production of isotopes in a research reactor to support medical oncology. Moreover, how is one to evaluate claims of real benefit in the context of a claim upon nuclear fuel-making capabilities, or even nuclear electricity generation itself? It takes nuclear technology of some sort to generate cancer-curing isotopes, but there are often a number of possible ways to acquire electric power. Does the availability of alternatives matter? Or their relative merits or efficiencies?

One presumably should not simply *assume* the

genuineness of benefit just because it is asserted.[257]
That is a lesson we should perhaps learn from the odd
history of the "peaceful nuclear explosions" concept.
Some delegations to the NPT's drafting committee appear to have believed that PNEs would really be valuable excavating tools. After some considerable trouble
was taken to allow for the *possibility* of providing PNE
benefits to nonweapons states, however, it turned out
that no one really wanted such services. (Whatever
legitimate interest in PNEs may once have existed, it
was apparently quickly overtaken by economic rationality and public health considerations. Alternatively,
the entire issue was nothing more than a pretext for
would-be proliferators all along—as indeed is suggested by India's disingenuous claim of peaceful intentions when it detonated its first nuclear weapon
in 1974.) With PNEs, transfer of the basic technology
itself was flatly prohibited by the NPT, and even the
benefits of PNE services ultimately ended up being
withheld, because their advantages turned out to be
illusory. It is quite doubtful that any nuclear weapons state would today provide such NPT-authorized
services even if someone could figure out a reason to
request them, but in fact no one wants such services
anyway, because their irrationality is now well-under-
stood.

Especially in light of the PNE experience, it thus
seems reasonable, in assessing the merits of particular technology and/or benefit-sharing proposals, to
consider the degree to which they make demonstrable economic sense. Particularly if a claimant wishes
the nonproliferation regime to accept any potential
increase in proliferation risk—even a small one—it
ought to be possible to show that there is a real *need*
for the thing being sought. Judging need simply by

the presence of a mere *desire* for what is requested should be insufficient. (Therein lies tautology: the issue would not have arisen if there were no desire. If requests are not simply to be rubber-stamped — which would represent the betrayal of policy judgment, rather than its exercise — something more objectively defensible must be required.) This presumably rules out requests grounded merely in

> the rhetorical identification of investments in civilian nuclear energy with economic development and catching up with the advanced countries . . . with no pretense at hard economic argument.[258]

Arguably, therefore, claimants should be expected to show that they have a real economic need for whatever it is they seek by way of international nuclear cooperation.

This idea of economic rationality as a criterion with which to evaluate technology sharing requests and as a partial basis for inferences about purpose is by no means entirely foreign to the NPT's contemporary peaceful use discourse. The U.S. working paper on Article IV at the 2005 NPT Review Conference, for example, emphasized that any nuclear fuel cycle facility being acquired by a non-weapons state "should conform to and be fully consistent with the scale of that country's nuclear programme as measured by international standards and economic factors."[259] Coming at this issue from the other side, U.S. arms control compliance assessment experts also view a nuclear program's economic *irrationality* as being one of the factors that can help suggest the likelihood of that program being intended to support nuclear weapons work in violation of Article II of the NPT. The "lack of a reasonable economic justification for this program" was explicitly noted in the long U.S. list of factors contributing to its first explicit Iranian noncompliance finding in 2005.[260]

The principle of necessary benefit has long antecedents. It was presaged in the early UN proposals to keep fuel production to the absolute minimum required for *"actual beneficial uses"* and to give access to safe forms of nuclear technology only, *inter alia*, "where economic justification exists."[261] The Acheson-Lilienthal Report itself actually suggested the idea of using market mechanisms to help allocate nondangerous nuclear facilities – that is, ones that could safely be left in national hands – in a fashion designed to ensure both that they were responsive to real needs and that nuclear applications were not inefficiently utilized vis-à-vis other energy sources. The Report's idea was to permit and support the development of safe peaceful nuclear capabilities "on the basis of competitive bidding among interested nations." Such bids, the Report said, could be limited

> to those warranted by the costs of alternative sources. . . . In this way the maximum usefulness of fissionable materials with the greatest conservation of other sources of power would be secured.[262]

The Report was quite clear that its authors believed "mankind can confidently look forward to beneficial uses" of nuclear energy.[263] Particularly in light of modern debates about the relative merits of various energy sources, however – sources which are competing both for market share and for the attentions of governments eager to maximize energy security and speed the development of non-fossil fuel sources while yet struggling in a time of economic hardship with the imperative of efficient resource-allocation –

the Report's notion of competitive cross-sectoral bidding is an idea that may deserve to be dusted off and given a second look.

In fact, it has been a requirement of U.S. law for many years, embodied in Title V of the Nuclear Nonproliferation Act of 1978, that the United States will work to assist developing nations in developing non-nuclear energy sources, and that, to this end, it should undertake "general and country-specific assessments" of the energy alternatives available to such countries.[264] Promoting non-nuclear energy sources is not necessarily the same thing as *discouraging* nuclear ones, of course. Nevertheless, especially in the context of a statute the aim of which is to ensure "more effective international controls over the transfer and use of nuclear materials and equipment and nuclear technology for peaceful purposes in order to prevent proliferation,"[265] Title V is certainly consistent with the idea that nuclear energy proposals should be undertaken only when they compare favorably to available *non-nuclear* alternatives.[266]

Nor is the United States alone in providing precedent for assessing nuclear technology issues through the prism of demonstrable economic benefit. Indeed, France has been even more explicit about the importance of tying nuclear technology-access issues to some notion of *real* benefit. A French working paper in 2005, for instance, specified that technology exports "should only be envisaged" where, among other things, there existed "an economically rational plan for developing such projects."[267] A working paper jointly presented by eight nations in 2008 as part of the preparatory process for the 2010 Review Conference also declared that international nuclear cooperation plans must "reflect economic reality and the real needs of recipient countries."[268]

Private sector experts addressing how to square the NPT's peaceful use provisions with its nonproliferation purposes have sometimes stated this point quite clearly. Many advocates of what I have termed the safeguardability approach to Article IV issues, in fact, have long argued the need to tie technology access to demonstrable benefit. Albert Wohlstetter, for example, suggested that in order to "mak[e] sensible trade-offs," a peaceful use policy consistent with the nonproliferation purposes of the NPT would also need to consider "distinctions . . . between *optimal* economic alternatives and the next best use of resources."[269] Eldon Greenberg argued similarly that technology transfers should be judged in part according to whether there existed "reasonably discernable civilian nuclear power benefits,"[270] warning that many long-standing past assumptions about the benefits of nuclear power generation "have . . . largely proven to be false." Taking aim, as had Wohlstetter, at the notion of sharing plutonium reprocessing technology—a significant issue at the time—Greenberg declared that

> [i]n such circumstances, the Treaty should not be interpreted as creating an obligation to facilitate or a right to participate in reprocessing and plutonium use. To the contrary, it is more appropriate to view the Treaty as creating the presumption today that assistance or activities relating thereto have more to do with weapons than with peaceful purposes and, therefore, generally would fall within the prohibitions of Articles I and II.[271]

Similarly, Leonard Weiss argued the impermissibility of transferring fissile material production capabilities not only "because such technology cannot be effectively safeguarded" but also because it "exhibits no compelling economic need anywhere in the world."[272] Henry Sokolski has also argued for more honest cost comparisons between nuclear power and its alternatives, suggesting that such projects should be notionally competed against each other in order to help identify projects that are uneconomical and dangerous.[273]

The merits of the specific economic case many of these safeguardability authors marshaled against plutonium recycling and the merits of the argument made by some today against uranium enrichment, or even against nuclear power *in toto*, are far beyond the scope of this chapter. Also unaddressed here will be the merits of long-standing assumptions—from the time of the Acheson-Lilienthal Report through the Atoms for Peace era and into the present day—that nuclear power *does* offer significant benefit to the developing world. The key point, however, is that advocates of policy-privileging safeguardability approaches to Article IV have long suggested, in effect, that it would be incoherent and untenable to judge proliferation risk against nuclear technology benefits without bringing into the analysis a relatively rigorous and intellectually defensible standard for assessing such benefit.

If this is so—and the idea is certainly plausible, not precluded by text of Article IV, and consistent both with the NPT's own Preamble and with long-standing themes in the international community's struggle with peaceful nuclear use issues—a requirement of demonstrable economic need could have significant implications for today's fuel cycle debates. As Gottemoeller and Arnaudo recount, for example,

> [a]ccording to traditional calculations, acquiring the full fuel cycle—the indigenous capability to enrich fissile material to produce nuclear fuel, to generate

electricity using that fuel in reactors, and to reprocess or store the spent fuel — only made sense with a large nuclear energy program. A country would have to be generating more than 25,000 megawatts of electricity in nuclear reactors — equivalent to about 15 current-generation, light water reactors — before it made economic sense to acquire the full fuel cycle.[274]

In this light, it would seem that "some of those rushing to acquire new capabilities have down played the question of the costs and risks of the full nuclear fuel cycle" to the point that they "do not appear to be making rational economic choices."[275] This author is presently in no position to assess in any useful detail the relative merits of any particular country's claim to need a nuclear power infrastructure, but a case can be made for *some* such assessment.

To be sure, it must be admitted that rejecting the simplistic, technology-focused, rights-privileging pseudo-literalism of today's Article IV conventional wisdom in favor of a more sophisticated, policy-privileging, benefits-sharing approach to peaceful nuclear uses under the NPT would place significant demands upon policymakers. It would deny them the easy option of avoiding difficult decisions by retreating behind the judgment precluding absolutisms of legal rights and *per se* rules. It would require them to work harder in understanding the issues of nuclear technology control that have challenged the international community since the beginning of the atomic era. It would require of them more wisdom in making difficult judgment calls, and oblige them to take positions for which others (and history) will hold them accountable. It would also deprive policymakers, in some countries at least, of the easy rhetorical weapon of rights denial that they have so far happily wielded

in service either of their legitimate technology-acqui-
sition policies or in support of their illegitimate nuclear weapons ambitions. For all of these reasons—and
no doubt more—a policy-privileging interpretation of
Article IV may remain unpopular in many quarters.

Such reasons to oppose a safeguardability interpretation, however, are discreditable. If we wish our
understanding of Article IV to *make sense* – and to be
one consistent with, rather than an enemy of, the rest
of the NPT—it will be necessary to adopt such a reading despite such complaints. Policymakers should not
fear having to exercise wisdom and discretion, and
they should not be permitted to avoid it.

ENDNOTES - CHAPTER 11

1. Treaty on the Non-Proliferation of Nuclear Weapons
(opened for signature July 1, 1968; entered into force March 5,
1970), 21 U.S.T. 483, 729 U.N.T.S. 161 (hereinafter NPT), from the
Preamble.

2. *Ibid.*, at Art. IV.

3. U.S. Special Representative for Nuclear Nonproliferation
Christopher Ford, "The Promise and Responsibilities of Peaceful
Uses of Nuclear Energy," remarks to 19th Annual Conference on
Disarmament Issues, Sapporo, Japan, 2007, available from *www.
state.gov/t/isn/rls/rm/92721.htm*.

4. Most notably, in recent years—and perhaps not by coincidence, largely since Iran's secret uranium enrichment efforts first
came to light in August 2002—a number of Middle East states
have announced their intention to develop nuclear power programs, in some cases including uranium enrichment. See Rose
Gottemoeller and Raymond Arnaudo, "Agreeing to Disagree on
Nuclear Rights," *Bulletin of the Atomic Scientists*, Vol. 64, No. 5,
November/December 2008, pp. 15, 17 (listing in this regard Bah-
rain, Jordan, Kuwait, Oman, Qatar, Saudi Arabia, United Arab
Emirates, and Yemen).

5. See International Atomic Energy Agency, "Communication dated September 10, 2008, received from the Permanent Mission of Germany to the Agency regarding a 'Statement on Civil Nuclear Cooperation with India,'" INFCIRC/734 (Corrected), September 19, 2008 (attaching copy of NSG decision of September 6, 2008), available from *www.iaea.org/Publications/Documents/Infcircs/2008/infcirc734c.pdf*.

6. See Jason Mark, "Atomic Dreams," *UTNE Reader*, January-February 2008, available from *www.utne.com/2008-01-01/Environment/Atomic-Dreams.aspx* (noting "strains in the environmental movement as organizations and individuals grapple with the pros and cons of using nuclear power to check carbon emissions" and describing some prominent environmental figures as having recently voiced support for nuclear power for climate change reasons).

7. Office of the Press Secretary, The White House, "President Announces New Measures to Counter the Threat of WMD," Washington, DC: National Defense University, February 11, 2004 (publicly revealing existence of Khan network). Or George W. Bush, "Remarks on Weapons of Mass Destruction," Speech at the National Defense University, Washington, DC, February 11, 2004.

8. U.S. Special Representative for Nuclear Nonproliferation Christopher Ford, "The NPT Review Process and the Future of the Nuclear Nonproliferation Regime," remarks to the NPT Japan Seminar on "How should we respond to the challenges of maintaining and strengthening the treaty regime?" Vienna, Austria, February 6, 2007, available from *www.state.gov/t/isn/rls/rm/80156.htm*.

9. IAEA Director General Mohammed El Baradei, "Addressing Verification Challenges," remarks to the Symposium on International Safeguards, Vienna, Austria, October 16, 2006, quoted in Robert Zarate, "The NPT, IAEA Safeguards and Peaceful Nuclear Energy: An 'Inalienable Right,' but Precisely to What?" in Henry D. Sokolski, ed., *Falling Behind: International Scrutiny of the Peaceful Atom*, Carlisle, PA: Strategic Studies Institute, U.S. Army War College, February 2008, p. 221.

10. Ford, "The NPT Review Process and the Future of the Nuclear Nonproliferation Regime."

11. U.S. Special Representative for Nuclear Nonproliferation Christopher Ford, "The 2010 NPT Review Cycle So Far: A View from the United States of America," remarks at Wilton Park, United Kingdom, December 20, 2007, available from *www.state.gov/t/isn/rls/rm/98382.htm.*

12. Australia, Austria, Canada, Denmark, Hungary, Ireland, the Netherlands, New Zealand, Norway, and Sweden working paper entitled "Articles III(3) and IV, preambular paragraphs 6 and 7, especially in their relationships to article III (1), (2) and (4) and preambular paragraphs 4 and 5 (Cooperation in the Peaceful Uses of Nuclear Energy)," NPT/CONF.2005/WP.11, April 26, 2005, pp. 1-2.

13. European Union, working paper entitled "Multilateralization of the nuclear fuel cycle/guarantees of access to the peaceful uses of nuclear energy," NPT/CONF.2010/pc.1/WP.61, May 9, 2007, pp. 1, 3.

14. It should be noted, in this context, that even apart from the *political* adequacy of existing fuel supply proposals in the face of radicalized non-aligned sentiment and the occasional country's nuclear weapons ambitions, some experts have questioned the technical and market feasibility of a multilateralized nuclear fuel cycle. Writing elsewhere in this volume, for instance, the World Nuclear Association's Steve Kidd offers such a critique. See also *www.npecweb.org/Frameset.asp?PageType=Single&PDFFile=20090306-Kidd-NuclearFuelMythsAndRealities&PDFFolder=Essays.*

15. See NPT, at Art. IX(3) ("For the purposes of this Treaty, a nuclear-weapon State is one which has manufactured and exploded a nuclear weapon or other nuclear explosive device prior to 1 January 1967.") and Art. II (requiring that each *non*-nuclear-weapon State Party not receive, manufacture, or otherwise acquire "nuclear weapons or other nuclear explosive devices").

16. People's Republic of China, "Peaceful Uses of Nuclear Energy," NPT/CONF.2005/WP.6, April 26, 2005, pp. 1-2.

17. Cuba, "Peaceful uses of nuclear energy," NPT/CONF.2005/WP.25, May 4, 2005, p. 1, para. 6, and p. 2, para. 7.

18. U.S. officials publicly raised NPT compliance concerns about Iran at least as early as 1993, at which point the Arms Control and Disarmament Agency declared that "Iran has demonstrated a continuing interest in nuclear weapons and related technology that causes the U.S. to assess that Iran is in the early stages of developing a nuclear weapons program." U.S. Arms Control and Disarmament Agency, "Adherence to and Compliance With Arms Control Agreements and the President's Report to Congress on Soviet Noncompliance with Arms Control Agreements," January 14, 1993 [unclassified version], p. 17.

19. Etel Solingen, *Nuclear Logics: Contrasting Paths in East Asia and the Middle East,* Princeton, NJ: Princeton University Press, 2007, p. 171.

20. See, e.g., Nuclear Threat Initiative, "Russia: Nuclear Exports to Iran: Reactors" (undated), at text accompanying notes 2 and 4, and following note 14, citing David Albright *et al.*, *Plutonium and Highly Enriched Uranium 1996: World Inventories, Capabilities, and Policies,* Oxford, UK: Oxford University Press, 1997, pp. 355-361; Andrew Koch and Jenette Wolf, "Iran's Nuclear Procurement Program," *Nonproliferation Review*, No. 5, Fall 1997, p. 127), available from *www.nti.org/db/nisprofs/russia/exports/rusiran/react.htm.*

21. See International Atomic Energy Agency, "Implementation of the NPT Safeguards Agreement in the Islamic Republic of Iran," GOV/2004/83, November 15, 2004, at pp. 8, 13, 14, 23, 31, 71, 73, and 79.

22. Ambassador of the Islamic Republic of Iran Ali Reza Moaiyeri, remarks to the Second Session of the Preparatory Committee for the 2010 Review Conference of the Parties to the Treaty on the Non-Proliferation of Nuclear Weapons, Geneva, Switzerland, April 29, 2008, p. 4, para. 4.

23. Iranian President Mahmoud Ahmadinejad, "Iran, Nuclear Power," interview by Christiane Amanpour, CNN, New York, September 17, 2005, available from *www.cnn.com/2005/WORLD/*

meast/09/17/ahmadinejad/index.html.

24. Iranian Delegation, "Statement to the Preparatory Committee of the NPT 2010 Review Conference," New York, May 12, 2009, as cited in Fars News Agency, "Iran Blasts Industrial States' Non-Compliance with NPT," May 13, 2009. Iran's legalized discourse on Article IV has developed within a broader tradition of modern Iran's predilection to "scour the international arena for examples and models" and to rely, to a sometimes startling degree, upon emulation of Western models even when emphatically decrying Western influence. (Ali Ansari, for instance, has described the "imitative quality of Iranian society and politics" as having manifested itself particularly in the ideological framework of the Islamic Revolution, not least in the rise to political power of the radicalized "principalist" clique surrounding President Ahmadinejad. See Ali M. Ansari, *Iran Under Ahmadinejad: The Politics of Confrontation*, Adelphi Paper 393, London, UK: International Institute of Strategic Studies (IISS), 2007, pp. 19-20; Laurent Muraviec, *The Mind of Jihad*, Cambridge, UK: Cambridge University Press, 2008, pp. 256-294. Iran's legalistic propaganda campaign in favor of its Article IV rights — offered in reaction to criticism of Tehran's own compliance with IAEA safeguards and Articles II and III of the NPT — may be located within this imitative tradition, right down to the Iranians' unimaginative mimicry and inversion of sometime American arguments about the centrality of nuclear nonproliferation to the Nuclear Nonproliferation Treaty.

25. NPT, at Art. IV(1) describing "inalienable right" to activities "in conformity with Articles I and II of this Treaty."

26. "Iran Blasts Industrial States' Non-Compliance with NPT."

27. Henry Sokolski, "Nuclear Policy and the Presidential Election," *The New Atlantis*, No. 21, Summer 2008, pp. 3, 10.

28. "President Announces New Measures to Counter the Threat of WMD."

29. See Energy Secretary Samuel Bodman, "Press Briefing," U.S. Department of Energy, Washington, DC, February 6, 2006,

available from *www.energy.gov/news/3171.htm*. By contrast, some current and former U.S. officials appear simply to counsel capitulation. Former Clinton Administration official Rose Gottemoeller and (apparently current) State Department lawyer Raymond Arnaudo have publicly argued for "a companion agreement to the NPT that is specifically designed to reinforce states' rights to acquire peaceful nuclear energy technologies, including the full nuclear fuel cycle." This agreement would "restate these rights in international law," while attempting to limit the potential proliferation damage of such a step merely by "reassuring states that they do not have to exercise [these rights] immediately." Gottemoeller & Arnaudo, pp. 18.

30. Christopher A. Ford, "A New Paradigm: Shattering Obsolete Thinking on Arms Control and Nonproliferation," *Arms Control Today*, Vol. 38, November 2008, pp. 12, 16.

31. Christopher A. Ford, "NPT Article IV: Peaceful Uses of Nuclear Energy,"Washington, DC: U.S. Department of State, May 18, 2005, available from *merlin.ndu.edu/archivepor/wmd/state/46604.pdf*.

32. See Bureau of International Security and Nonproliferation, *Promoting Expanded and Responsible Peaceful Uses of Nuclear Energy*, Washington, DC: U.S. Department of State, April 16, 2007, available from *www.state.gov/t/isn/rls/other/83210.htm* (denouncing as "false" the allegation by some countries that "any steps by other states to deny them any technology somehow violates their 'inalienable' rights or their rights under the NPT"). See also Ford, "NPT Article IV: Peaceful Uses of Nuclear Energy," declaring that "[n]othing could be further from the truth" than the claim by some countries that "steps by other states to deny them some technology somehow violates their NPT rights."

33. Ford, "NPT Article IV: Peaceful Uses of Nuclear Energy."

34. United States of America, "Strengthening Implementation of Article IV of the Treaty on the Non-Proliferation of Nuclear Weapons," NPT/CONF.2005/WP.57, May 23, 2005, pp. 3, 14.

35. *Ibid.*, describing Article IV as giving the "right to receive the *benefits* of peaceful nuclear development" if they are in com-

pliance with NPT nonproliferation obligations" (emphasis added); Ford, "NPT Article IV: Peaceful Uses of Nuclear Energy," ("Paragraph 2 of Article IV speaks of . . . sharing in the development of *applications* of nuclear energy for peaceful purposes. Furthermore, the Preamble to the NPT affirms the general 'principle that the *benefits* of peaceful applications of nuclear technology ... should be available for peaceful purposes to all Parties.'") (emphasis in original).

36. John R. Bolton, "The NPT: A Crisis of Non-Compliance," statement to the Third Session of the Preparatory Committee of the 2005 Review Conference of the Treaty on the Non-Proliferation of Nuclear Weapons, New York, April 27, 2004. Nor was this point entirely lost on the U.S. Congress, for in 2006 two Senators opined that "[t]he dangers are so great that the world community must declare that there is no right under the Nuclear Non-Proliferation Treaty to separate plutonium from spent nuclear fuel." Senator Richard Lugar and Senator Evan Bayh, "A Nuclear Fuel Bank Advocated," *Chicago Tribune*, October 22, 2006. In the House of Representatives, Ileana Ros-Lehtinen made a similar point. See Representative Ileana Ros-Lehtinen, "The Right to Survive: Nuclear 'Rights' Don't Trump It," *National Review Online*, October 5, 2007. The issue was also raised on the 2008 U.S. presidential campaign trail by Senator John McCain, the Republican candidate, who publicly called for the convening of an international summit in order to assess what the NPT's peaceful nuclear use rights actually entail. See Sokolski, "Nuclear Policy and the Presidential Election," p. 9. (The Democratic candidate, and eventual winner, Senator Barack Obama, appears not to have raised the issue.)

37. Office of Nuclear Energy, U.S. Department of Energy, *Global Nuclear Energy Partnership Strategic Plan*, GNEP 167312 Rev. 0, January 2007, pp. 3, available from *www.fas.org/programs/ ssp/_docs/GNEPStratPlanJan07.pdf*. In the U.S. interagency process, this statement was cleared, on behalf of the State Department, by a mid-ranking official without checking with or informing the U.S. Special Representative for Nuclear Nonproliferation or apparently any higher authority at all.

38. House Foreign Affairs Committee Chairman Tom Lantos *et al.*, letter to Condoleeza Rice, July 17, 2007, p. 1.

39. Assistant Secretary of State for Legislative Affairs Jeffrey Bergner, letter to Tom Lantos, November 19, 2007, p. 1.

40. The reason for the delay and the essential uselessness of the Bergner response was that the Bush administration was, at that point in its wilting second term, unable to reach internal agreement on the specific meaning of Article IV. One key State Department attorney assigned to cover nonproliferation issues in the Office of the Legal Advisor ("L") in effect agreed with Iran (and the U.S. Department of Energy!) to the extent that he felt that Article IV described a preexisting right to develop enrichment and reprocessing.

Such a position was unacceptable to this author, who thought it both legally permissible and substantively imperative to hew more closely to the U.S. policy positions already cleared through the U.S. interagency process and announced publicly in 2004 and 2005. Despite those earlier public declarations, however, the "L" attorney refused to clear anything similar in the 2007 reply to Congressman Lantos. This created an impasse: "L" would accept nothing suggesting that there was no "right" to ENR, while I would accept nothing that said there *was* such a right. The result was presumably disappointing to all: the Bergner letter's mere recapitulation of the vague text of Article IV. Thus did the State Department—despite having been publicly committed by the President to a policy of opposing the further spread of ENR, and having proclaimed at two official NPT meetings the non-existence of any Article IV ENR "right"—decline to conclude that U.S. policy did not violate the "rights" of countries such as Iran.

Interestingly, this was not the first time that "L" had blocked agreement upon a legal position made logically and legally inevitable by preexisting, interagency-cleared, and publicly announced conclusions related to Iran. The reader will recall that at least as early as 1993, the United States had found Iran to be seeking to develop nuclear weapons. It was not until more than a decade later, however—and after much resistance—that the same "L" attorney was finally persuaded to clear what should long since have been a rather common-sense follow-on conclusion that Iran was in violation of its Article II obligation not to try to develop nuclear weapons. Compare *Adherence to and Compliance With Arms Control Agreements and the President's Report to Congress on Soviet Noncompliance with Arms Control Agreements,* January 14, 1993, p. 17 ("Iran is in the early stages of developing

352

a nuclear weapons program"), with U.S. Department of State, *Adherence to and Compliance With Arms Control, Nonproliferation, and Disarmament Agreements and Commitments,* August 2005 (hereinafter *2005 Noncompliance Report*), p. 80, available from *www.state.gov/documents/organization/52113.pdf* (finding that "Iran is pursuing an effort to manufacture nuclear weapons, and has sought and received assistance in this effort *in violation of Article II of the NPT*") (emphasis added).

41. President Barack Obama, remarks in Prague, Czech Republic, April 5, 2009, available from *www.whitehouse.gov/the_press_office/Remarks-By-President-Barack-Obama-In-Prague-As-Delivered/.*

42. If one's objective is merely to win acclaim for change, such a gap is no doubt useful. It is less clear that encouraging such dramatic misunderstandings will provide a useful foundation for nonproliferation policy.

43. France, "Strengthening the Nuclear Non-Proliferation Regime," NPT/CONF.2005/PC.III/WP.22, May 4, 2004, p. 2, available from *www.npec-web.org/Presentations/NonPaper040504%20 UN-%20France%20-%20NPT-%20English%20Version.pdf.*

44. *Ibid.,* p. 3 (emphasis added).

45. *Ibid.,* pp. 3-4.

46. The *substantive* case is easier to make, of course. Even IAEA Director General Mohammed El Baradei—who otherwise seems to regard himself as having as his most important mission not reigning in noncompliance with the safeguards with which the international community has entrusted his agency but rather protecting Iran from the United States, See Elaine Sciolino and William J. Broad, "To Iran and Its Foes, An Indispensable Irritant," *New York Times,* September 17, 2007, (quoting El Baradei that those who contemplate war against Iran are "crazies" and describing himself as having a mission as the "secular pope" whose job is to "make sure, frankly, that we do not end up killing each other")—has warned about the dangers of a world of "virtual nuclear weapon states." See Zarate, p. 221 (quoting El Baradei). The generally agreed worrisomeness of a world in which many countries could quickly produce nuclear weapons at will

is presumably why opponents of efforts to stop the spread of ENR technology have preferred to emphasize ostensibly policy-trumping claims of an inalienable Article IV peaceful use right.

47. Albert Wohlstetter, *et al.* [as Pan Heuristics], "Moving Toward Life in a Nuclear Armed Crowd?" paper prepared for the U.S. Arms Control and Disarmament Agency, ACDA/PAB-263 PH76-04-389-14, December 4, 1975 (Revised April 22, 1976), p. 2.

48. *Ibid.*, p. 58.

49. *Ibid.*, pp. 58, 62.

50. *Ibid.*, p. 62.

51. Wohlstetter, *et al.* , p. 17; see also *ibid.*, p. 18 (declaring that "These paths of approach towards a weapons capability . . . do not break any precise, generally agreed on rules.").

52. *Ibid.*, p. 19.

53. *Ibid.*, pp. 48-54.

54. Among other problems, Wohlstetter noted that "[a]mbiguities as to what is safe and what is dangerous" make for tremendous compliance enforcement problems in the real world of international politics. See *ibid.*, pp. 5-58.

55. *Ibid.*, pp. 47-48.

56. *Ibid.*, pp. 66-72, 95.

57. *Ibid.*, p. 89 ("If our primary objective is to impede nuclear weapon development, all civilian nuclear activities are not equally desirable.").

58. Eldon V. C. Greenberg, "The NPT and Plutonium: Application of NPT Prohibitions to 'Civilian' Nuclear Equipment, Technology and Materials Associated with Reprocessing and Plutonium Use," Washington, DC: Nuclear Control Institute, 1993, pp. 13-14 (*quoting* Albert Wohlstetter *et al.*, "Towards a

New Consensus on Nuclear Technology," PH-78-04-832-13, prepared for the U.S. Arms Control and Disarmament Agency, July 6 ,1979, pp. 34-35).

59. See Greenberg, "The NPT and Plutonium," p. 14 (*quoting* Arthur Steiner, "Article IV and the 'Straightforward Bargain'" [PAN Paper 78-832-08]). Steiner's paper appeared in the supporting materials for Wohlstetter's 1979 report.

60. Steiner (quoted by Greenberg, p. 16).

61. *Ibid.*

62. Greenberg first prepared "The NPT and Plutonium" paper for the Nuclear Control Institute (NCI) in the mid-1980s, and revised it for NCI in 1993. See Eldon Greenberg, testimony before the House Subcommittee on International Terrorism and Nonproliferation, Washington, DC, March 2, 2006, p. 1, available from *www.internationalrelations.house.gov/archives/109/gre030206. pdf.*

63. Greenberg, "The NPT and Plutonium,"p. 1.

64. *Ibid.* , p. 10.

65. *Ibid.* , p. 19.

66. *Ibid.* , p. 1.

67. *Ibid.* , pp. 21-22.

68. *Ibid.* , p. 22. Greenberg held that these conclusions were particularly compelling because reprocessing did not seem to offer any meaningful economic benefit anyway, and he hinted that a finding of "non-benefit," as such, might give rise to "a presumption . . . that the purpose is not legitimate under the NPT." *Ibid.*, pp. 22-23. He did not, however, mean to suggest that a finding of nonbenefit *in itself* would necessarily trigger the nonproliferation provision. Greenberg did not think it would be *per se* unlawful to possess a non-beneficial technology provided that it could be adequately safeguarded. His point was straightforward: if a technology could not be effectively safeguarded against mis-

355

use, there was no "right" to its possession by nonweapons states. See Eldon Greenberg, interview with the author, April 2, 2009; Greenberg, "The NPT and Plutonium," p. 24 (noting that ACDA Director William Foster, in his explanation of the NPT to the U.S. Senate, left open the possibility that even activities placed under safeguards "could be considered violations of the NPT's prohibitions . . . if there were evidence that safeguards could not be effectively applied").

69. Greenberg, "The NPT and Plutonium,"p. 22.

70. *Ibid.* , p. 1.

71. Greenberg testimony, p. 1.

72. *Ibid.* , p. 24 (quoting U.S. NPT negotiator Adrian Fisher, in Hearings on S.1439 before the Senate Committee on Government Operations, 94th Cong., 2d Sess. 141, 1976).

73. Greenberg, "The NPT and Plutonium,"p. 12.

74. Paul Leventhal, "Safeguards Shortcomings — A Critique," Washington, DC: Nuclear Control Institute, September 12 ,1994, at n.16, available from *www.nci.org/p/plsgrds.htm*.

75. Leonard Weiss, "Atoms for Peace," *Bulletin of the Atomic Scientists*, Vol. 59, No. 6, November 1, 2003.

76. Leonard Weiss, "The Nuclear Nonproliferation Treaty: Strengths and Gaps" [hereinafter Weiss I], Henry Sokolski, ed., *Fighting Proliferation: New Concerns for the Nineties*, Maxwell Air Force Base, AL: Air University Press, 1996, available from *www.fas.org/irp/threat/fp/index.html*.

77. Henry Sokolski, "What Does the History of the Nuclear Nonproliferation Treaty Tell Us about Its Future?" in Sokolski, ed., *Fighting Proliferation: New Concerns for the Nineties*, at part I, ch.1, text accompanying note 61.

78. *Ibid.*, at text accompanying notes 62-65.

79. Henry A. Sokolski, "After Iran: Back to the Basics on

'Peaceful' Nuclear Energy," *Arms Control Today*, Vol. 36, April 2006, at text accompanying note, p. 3, available from *www.armscontrol. org/act/2005_04/Sokolski*.

80. Henry Sokolski, "Too Speculative?" *The New Atlantis*, Fall 2006, pp. 119, 123; Sokolski, "Nuclear Policy and the Presidential Election,"p. 9 (decrying the idea that "states have an inalienable right not just to *have* but to *make* nuclear fuel—a step, it bears repeating, that would bring them within a whisker of making a bomb").

81. Henry Sokolski, "The Nuclear Nonproliferation Treaty and Peaceful Nuclear Energy," testimony before the House Subcommittee on International Terrorism and Nonproliferation, Washington, DC, March 2, 2006, available from *www.internationalrelations. house.gov/archives/109/sok030206.pdf*.

82. *Ibid.*, p. 4, n.7 (citing Lettow paper); See also *ibid.*, p. 1., n.1 (noting that NPEC's safeguardability arguments "rely heavily upon the substantive historical and legal analyses of Albert Wohlstetter, Arthur Steiner, Eldon V.C. Greenberg, and Paul Lettow").

83. Zarate, p. 226.

84. *Ibid.*, p. 225.

85. *Ibid.*, p. 226.

86. *Ibid.*, p. 256.

87. Charles Ferguson, *Nuclear Energy: Balancing Benefits and Risks*, CFR Special Report No. 28, April 2007, pp. 16-18.

88. *Ibid.*, p. 25.

89. *Ibid.*, p. 20.

90. Commission on the Prevention of Weapons of Mass Destruction Proliferation and Terrorism, *World At Risk*, New York: Vintage Books, 2008, (hereinafter *WMD Commission Report*), p. 53.

91. *Ibid.*, p. 46.

92. Congressional Commission on the Strategic Posture of the United States, *Interim Report,* December 15, 2008, (hereinafter Congressional Commission *Interim Report*), pp. 4-5.

93. *Ibid.*, p. 10.

94. Congressional Commission on the Strategic Posture of the United States, *America's Strategic Posture,* Washington, DC: U.S. Institute of Peace Press, 2009 (hereinafter Congressional Commission *America's Strategic Posture*), p. 77; see also *ibid.*, p. 80.

95. *Ibid.*, p. 78.

96. An attorney in the Office of the Legal Advisor insisted upon deleting passages to this effect from the author's draft presentation to a conference in Paris in the summer of 2007 sponsored by the U.S. Naval Postgraduate School. Those deleted sections formed the starting point for this article.

97. NPT, from the preamble (affirming that "the *benefits* of peaceful applications of nuclear technology . . . should be available for peaceful purposes to all Parties")(emphasis added).

98. This author has elsewhere called for·disarmament debates under the NPT's Article VI to be similarly de-"legalized." See Christopher A. Ford, "Nuclear Disarmament and the 'Legalization' of Policy Discourse in the NPT Regime," remarks to the James Martin Center for Nonproliferation Studies, Washington, DC, November 29, 2007; see also Christopher A. Ford, "Christopher A. Ford responds," *Nonproliferation Review,* Vol. 15, No. 3, November 2008, pp. 418, 420 (arguing the need for "a kind of mercy killing of conventional jurisprudential wishful thinking about Article VI—not in order to 'paper over' anything, but rather precisely in order to make possible the kind of rich and constructive policy debates the world needs").

99. See, e.g., Victor Gilinsky, Marvin Miller, and Harmon Hubbard, "A Fresh Examination of the Proliferation Dangers of Light Water Reactors," October 22, 2004, available from *www.npecweb.org/Frameset.asp?PageType=Single&PDFFile=Repo*

rt041022%20LWR&PDFFolder=Reports; Edwin S. Lyman, "Can Nuclear Fuel Production in Iran and Elsewhere Be Safeguarded against Diversion?" in *Falling Behind: International Scrutiny of the Peaceful Atom*, pp. 101; Thomas B. Cochran, "Adequacy of IAEA's Safeguards for Achieving Timely Detection," in *ibid.,* p. 121; Henry Sokolski, "Assessing the IAEA's Ability to Verify the NPT," in *ibid.,* p. 3.

100. See Bolton; Ford, "NPT Article IV: Peaceful Uses of Nuclear Energy."

101. This is a drafting problem of the NPT that has been noted by others. See Weiss, ("Nothing in the treaty prohibits a non-weapon state that is party to the treaty from assisting another non-weapon state in manufacturing or otherwise acquiring the bomb.")

102. "Joint Declaration by the Heads of Government of the United States, the United Kingdom, and Canada," November 15, 1945, U.S. Department of State, *Documents on Disarmament: 1945-1959, Vol. I,* Washington, DC: Department of State Historical Office, 1960, pp. 1, 2.

103. "Statement by the United States Representative (Baruch) to the United Nations Atomic Energy Commission," June 14, 1946, in *Documents on Disarmament: 1945-1959, Volume I,* pp. 7, 10 & 14-15.

104. "United States Memoranda on the Proposed Atomic Development Authority, Submitted to Subcommittee I of the UN Atomic Energy Commission," *Documents on Disarmament: 1945-1959, Vol. I,* pp. 25, 27 (July 2, 1946 memorandum); see also *ibid.,* pp. 30, 32 (July 5, 1946 memorandum). One reason for the U.S. emphasis upon a flat prohibition upon national governments having any fuel making *capability* lay in the difficulty of verifying and enforcing compliance with any system that permitted national fissile material production for "peaceful" purposes. As one U.S. diplomat explained it, once the International Authority had been provided with exclusive authority to undertake such activity, "then the agency in the detection of clandestine activities need not be concerned with the motives of those carrying on unauthorized activities in this field, for it is the very exis-

tence of such activities that is illegal." Also, see "Statement by the Deputy United States Representative (Cohen) to Committee I of the Disarmament Commission" (May 14, 1952), *Documents on Disarmament: 1945-1959, Vol. I*, pp. 358, 362. This is a problem, of course, that bedevils the nuclear safeguards system today – and which has also been identified as a stumbling block for verifying a future Fissile Material Cutoff Treaty (FMCT). See U.S. Special Representative for Nuclear Nonproliferation Christopher Ford, "The United States and the Fissile Material Cutoff Treaty," paper delivered at conference on "Preparing for 2010: Getting the Process Right," Annecy, France, March 17, 2007, available from *www.state.gov/t/isn/rls/other/81950.htm*.

105. "United States Memoranda on the Proposed Atomic Development Authority, Submitted to Subcommittee I of the UN Atomic Energy Commission," p. 27 (July 2, 1946, memorandum).

106. United States Memoranda on the Proposed Atomic Development Authority, Submitted to Subcommittee I of the UN Atomic Energy Commission," p. 32 (July 5, 1946, memorandum).

107. United States Memoranda on the Proposed Atomic Development Authority, Submitted to Subcommittee I of the UN Atomic Energy Commission," p. 27 (July 2, 1946, memorandum).

108. United States Memoranda on the Proposed Atomic Development Authority, Submitted to Subcommittee I of the UN Atomic Energy Commission," p. 33 (July 5, 1946, memorandum).

109. Report on the International Control of Atomic Energy, March 16, 1946 (hereinafter Acheson-Lilienthal Report), Washington, DC: U.S. Government Printing Office, 1946, U.S. Department of State, Publication 2498, p. 3 (quoting Agreed Declaration of November 15, 1945, by the President of the United States and the Prime Ministers of the United Kingdom and Canada).

110. See Acheson-Lilienthal Report, p. 26 (emphasizing that "this distinction between the 'safe' and the 'dangerous' can be useful without being completely sharp or fixed for all time"); *ibid.*, pp. 26, 29 (discussing what it considers to be inherently "dangerous" activities, including U-235 enrichment "by any methods now known to us" and plutonium production, and "[t]

he operation of the various types of reactors for making plutonium, and of separation plants for extracting the plutonium"); *ibid.*, pp. 27-28 (discussing what it considers to be "safe activities").

111. *Ibid.*, pp. 32-33.

112. *Ibid.*, p. 26.

113. *Ibid.*, p. 35.

114. *Ibid.*, p. 26.

115. U.S. State Department, press release No. 235, April 9, 1946, p. 1, appended to Acheson-Lilienthal Report.

116. Acheson-Lilienthal Report, p. 35 (emphasis added).

117 . *Ibid.*, p. viii.

118. *Ibid.*, p. 9.

119. *Ibid.*, p. 30.

120. *Ibid.*, pp. 4, 8-9; See also *ibid.*, p. 21,

Take the case of a controlled reactor, a power pile, producing plutonium. Assume an international agreement barring use of the plutonium in a bomb, but permitting use of the pile for heat or power. No system of inspection, we have concluded, could afford any reasonable security against the diversion of such materials to the purposes of war. If nations may engage in this dangerous field, and only national good faith and international policing stand in the way, *the very existence of the prohibition* against the use of such piles to produce fissionable material suitable for bombs would tend to stimulate and encourage surreptitious evasions. This danger in the situation is attributable to the fact that this potentially hazardous activity is carried on by nations or their citizens.

121. *Ibid.*, pp. 5-6 (emphasis in original).

122. *Ibid.* p. 29.

123. *Ibid.*, p. viii. The Acheson-Lilienthal Report also worried about the problem of *seizure*. Because even internationally-owned and -operated nuclear facilities had to be located *somewhere*, there existed a danger that a bomb-acquisitive host government might simply take over a reactor or fuel making plant by force of arms. This, the Report recognized, could not really be prevented: "It is not thought that the Atomic Development Authority could protect its plants by military force from the overwhelming power of the nation in which they are situated." *Ibid.*, p. 47. In an interesting presaging of the idea of "countervailing reconstitution" floated by U.S. officials many years later as a potential way to deter "breakout" from a hypothetical future regime of nuclear weapons prohibition, however, the Acheson-Lilienthal Report suggested that seizure by any particular host country might be deterred by the prospect that if this occurred *other* countries would quickly follow suit in order to create a nuclear weapons balance:

The real protection will lie in the fact that if any nation seizes the plants or the stockpiles that are situated in its territory, other nations will have similar facilities and materials situated within their own borders so that the act of seizure need not place them at a disadvantage.

Ibid., p. 47; compare with U.S. Special Representative for Nuclear Nonproliferation Christopher A. Ford, "Disarmament and Non-Nuclear Stability in Tomorrow's World," remarks to the Conference on Disarmament and Nonproliferation Issues, Nagasaki, Japan , August 31, 2007, available from *www.state.gov/t/isn/rls/rm/92733.htm* (noting "the possibility that the potential availability of countervailing reconstitution would need to be a part of deterring "breakout" from a zero-weapons regime." As a result, "[t]he decisive consideration in determining the location of such plants will have to be strategic; otherwise the physical balance between nations will be impaired. In other words, the distribution of these plants throughout the world will have to be based primarily on security considerations."Acheson-Lilienthal Report, p. 48.

124. Acheson-Lilienthal Report, p. 22.

125. "First Report of the United Nations Atomic Energy Commission to the Security Council,"December 31, 1946, *Documents on Disarmament: 1945-1959, Vol. I*, pp. 50, 51, 56.

126. See also "Statement by the United States Representative (Cooper) to the General Assembly," December 12, 1950, *Documents on Disarmament: 1945-1959, Vol. I*, pp. 263, 264 ("A real and effective solution to the problem [of controlling nuclear technology] was made essential by the fact that atomic energy developed for peaceful purposes is, automatically and inescapably, adaptable to military purposes.").

127. "Second Report of the UN Atomic Energy Commission to the Security Council," September 11, 1947, *Documents on Disarmament: 1945-1959, Vol. I*, pp. 93, 97.

128. *Ibid.*, p. 98.

129. The word "nonproliferation" did not yet appear in the international lexicon. Indeed it was the concern of the UN and the American proposals not merely — as would later be the case with the NPT — to stop the spread of weapons capabilities to *additional* states, but instead to ensure that *no* national governments retained a fuel-cycle capability at all. Nevertheless, the fundamental issue would remain the same throughout the nuclear era: grave concern about the implications for peace and stability of national acquisition of nuclear weapons capabilities.

130. "Second Report of the United Nations Atomic Energy Commission," p. 96.

131. *Ibid.*, p. 99; see also *ibid.*, pp. 149-50 (offering the same basic definition).

132. *Ibid.*, p. 129.

133. "Address by Secretary of State Acheson to the First Committee of the General Assembly,"November 19, 1951, *Documents on Disarmament: 1945-1959, Vol. I*, pp. 309, 216, 326.

134. "Second Report of the United Nations Atomic Energy Commission," pp. 127-128.

135. *Ibid.*, pp. 131, 133 (emphasis added).

136. The phrase comes from a well-known 1968 article on overpopulation, in which it was suggested that individuals free to act independently in their own rational self-interest could produce a collective disaster by entirely consuming a shared resource. The example Hardin gave was that of a shared pasture that will destroyed by unrestricted livestock grazing, because as long as any of it remains ungrazed, there existed an economically "rational" reason for each villager to add another cow to the herd already using it. See Garrett Hardin, "The Tragedy of the Commons," *Science*, Vol. 162, No. 3859, December 13, 1968, p. 1243, available from *www.sciencemag.org/cgi/content/full/162/3859/1243*. For our purposes, by analogy, states with nuclear technology-access rights, acting in their own self-interest, could produce collective catastrophe by exhausting the shared resource of a world in which nuclear weapons development was precluded. As Hardin put it, "[f]reedom in a commons brings ruin to all." As he saw things, at least,

The only way we can preserve and nurture other and more precious freedoms is by relinquishing the freedom   to [consume the shared resource], and that very soon. 'Freedom is the recognition of necessity' — and it is the role of education to reveal to all the necessity of abandoning the freedom [to consume it] . . . . Only so, can we put an end to this aspect of the tragedy of the commons.

Needless to say, Hardin's analysis would surely have been grimmer still had his grazing analogy had to cope with the additional challenges faced by the nuclear nonproliferation regime — which must struggle not only with aspiring nuclear technology consumers each acting out of economic self interest for genuinely peaceful purposes, but also with the occasional consumer whose intentions are malign (i.e., who seeks to acquire nuclear weapons).

137. "Statement on Atomic Energy Control by the Representatives of Canada, China, France, the United Kingdom, and the United States," October 25, 1949, *Documents on Disarmament: 1945-1959, Vol. I*, pp. 216, 223.

138. "Second Report of the United Nations Atomic Energy Commission," pp. 129-130.

139. See General Assembly Resolution 502(VI): "Regulation, Limitation, and Balanced Reduction of All Armed Forces and All Armaments; International Control of Atomic Energy," January 11, 1952, *Documents on Disarmament: 1945-1959, Vol. I*, pp. 337, 338.

140. "Statement by the Soviet Representative (Gromyko) to the Security Council," March 5, 1947, *Documents on Disarmament: 1945-1959, Vol. I*, pp. 64, 73-74, 76.

141. "Address by the Soviet Foreign Minister (Vyshinsky) to the General Assembly [Extract]," November 8, 1951, *Documents on Disarmament: 1945-1959, Vol. I*, pp. 281-282.

142. See "Statement by the Deputy United States Representative (Cohen) to Committee I of the Disarmament Commission" (May 14, 1952), *Documents on Disarmament: 1945-1959, Vol. I*, pp. 358, 358, n. 2 (citing Disarmament Commission *Official Records: Special Supplement No.1, Second Report of the Disarmament Commission*, pp. 78 [comments by Malik]).

143. The Soviet proposals insisted upon inspection being merely *periodic*, and Moscow opposed any continuous inspector presence. "Statement on Atomic Energy Control by the Representatives of Canada, China, France, the United Kingdom, and the United States" (October 25, 1949), *in Documents on Disarmament: 1945-1959, Vol. I*, pp. 216, 219 (denouncing periodic inspections as inadequate).

144. "Soviet Proposals Introduced in the United Nations Atomic Energy Commission," June 11, 1947, *Documents on Disarmament: 1945-1959, Vol. I*, pp. 85, 86-87. As they explained it,

the question of sanctions against violators of the convention on the prohibition of atomic weapons is subject to decisions by the Security Council only. As it is known, procedure of adoption by the Council of decisions on sanctions as well as of other important decisions relating to the maintenance of international peace has been defined in Article 27 of the United Nations Charter.

"Letter from the Soviet Representative on the United Nations Atomic Energy Commission (Gromyko) to the British Representative (Cadogan)," September 5, 1947, *Documents on Disarmament: 1945-1959, Vol. I*, pp. 91, 93. As U.S. officials noted derisively, the Soviets thus wanted

an international agency whose recommendations would be subject to the veto of any one of the five Powers which are permanent members of the Security council. Such a power of veto would make any treaty unenforceable.

"Statement by the Deputy United States Representative (Osborn) to the United Nations Atomic Energy Commission" (July 20, 1949), *in ibid.*, pp. 194, 196. The other former allies from the Second World War denounced Moscow's proposals as being "so inadequate as to be dangerous" because they would "delude the peoples of the world into thinking that atomic energy was being controlled when in fact it was not." "Statement on Atomic Energy Control by the Representatives of Canada, China, France, the United Kingdom, and the United States," October 25, 1949, pp. 216, 217-18; 326; "Address by Secretary of State Acheson to the First Committee of the General Assembly," November 19, 1951, in *ibid.*, pp. 309, 326.

145. See "Letter from the Soviet Representative on the United Nations Atomic Energy Commission (Gromyko) to the British Representative (Cadogan)," p. 91 ("After the conclusion of [a] convention on the prohibition of atomic weapons, another convention can and must be concluded, to provide for the creation of an international control commission and for the establishment of other measures of control and inspection . . . ."). Later, after they had themselves acquired nuclear weapons, the Soviets modified their approach by suggesting the possibility of accomplishing a nuclear weapons ban *simultaneously* with the establishment of an international energy control mechanism. See "Statement by the Soviet Government on President Eisenhower's 'Atoms for Peace' Address," December 21, 1953, *Documents on Disarmament: 1945-1959, Vol. I*, pp. 401, 405.

146. "Soviet Proposals Introduced in the United Nations Atomic Energy Commission," p. 88.

147. See "Statement by President Truman Regarding Atomic Explosion in the Soviet Union," September 23, 1949, *Documents on Disarmament: 1945-1959, Vol. I*, pp. 207, 207 (first announcing that "We have evidence that within recent weeks and atomic explosion occurred in the USSR").

148. "United States 'Atoms for Peace'" Proposal: Address by President Eisenhower to the General Assembly," December 8, 1953, *Documents on Disarmament: 1945-1959, Vol. I*, pp. 393, 395.

149. *Ibid.*, pp. 399-400.

150. "News Conference Remarks by Secretary of State Acheson on the Revised Soviet Proposal," January 16, 1952, *Documents on Disarmament: 1945-1959, Vol. I*, pp. 342, 343.

151. See "United States Working Paper Submitted to the Disarmament Subcommittee: Methods of Implementing and Enforcing Disarmament Programs—The Establishment of International Control Organs With Appropriate Rights, Powers, and Functions,"May 25, 1954, *Documents on Disarmament: 1945-1959, Vol. I*, pp. 414-418.

152. *Ibid.*, pp. 419-420.

153. "Statement by President Eisenhower at the Geneva Conference of Heads of Government: Aerial Inspection and Exchange of Military Blueprints," July 21, 1955, *Documents on Disarmament: 1945-1959, Vol. I*, pp. 486-488.

154. See "Statement by President Eisenhower Regarding Nuclear Weapons Tests," October 23, 1956, *Documents on Disarmament: 1945-1959, Vol. I*, pp. 698, 698-701, (arguing that the United States would agree to nuclear disarmament when it could be confident of otherwise ensuring "safety from attack," but that for the time being, the continuing need for America's nuclear arsenal was still "sharply accented by the unavoidable fact of our numerical inferiority to Communist manpower").

155. "Soviet Proposal Introduced in the Disarmament Subcommittee: Reduction of Armaments, the Prohibition of Atomic

Weapons, and the Elimination of the Threat of a New War," May 10, 1955, *Documents on Disarmament: 1945-1959, Vol. I*, pp. 456, 465.

156. *Ibid.*

157. "United States Memorandum Supplementing the Outline Plan for the Implementation of President Eisenhower's Aerial Inspection Proposal, Submitted to the Disarmament Subcommittee," October 7, 1955, *Documents on Disarmament: 1945-1959, Vol. I*, pp. 523-524 (quoting comments of United Kingdom representative on October 5, 1955).

158. *Ibid.*, pp. 524-525.

159. "Statement by the British Foreign Secretary (Macmillan) at the Geneva Meeting of the Foreign Ministers," November 10, 1955, *Documents on Disarmament: 1945-1959, Vol. I*, pp. 547, 549-551.

160. "Draft Resolution Introduced in the Disarmament Commission by the United States, the United Kingdom, France, and Canada," July 3, 1956, *Documents on Disarmament: 1945-1959, Vol. I*, pp. 645-646 (emphasis added); See also "Statement by the French Representative (Moch) to the Disarmament Commission [Extract]," July 10, 1956, *Documents on Disarmament: 1945-1959, Vol. I*, pp. 658 (arguing that "[i]t is now established that past production cannot be checked with sufficient accuracy" and that "the rapid growth of stocks, already foreseeable even [when estimated by French authorities in 1952 to have an accuracy rate of only 70 to 80 percent], must therefore by now have converted the margin of error into complete and total uncertainty").

161. "White House Memorandum: Weapons Tests and Peaceful Uses of the Atom," October 23, 1956, *Documents on Disarmament: 1945-1959, Vol. I*, pp. 702, 706.

162. "White House Memorandum: Review of Disarmament Negotiations," October 23, 1956, *Documents on Disarmament: 1945-1959, Vol. I*, pp. 708, 713, 718.

163. NPT, Art. III(1).

164 . Albert Wohlstetter, "Spreading the Bomb without Quite Breaking the Rules," *Foreign Policy*, No. 25, Winter 1976, p. 88, Robert Zarate & Henry Sokolski, eds., *Nuclear Heuristics: Selected Writings of Albert and Roberta Wohlstetter*, Carlisle, PA: Strategic Studies Institute, U.S. Army War College, 2009, pp. 301, 306.

165. U.S. Director of Central Intelligence, *Nuclear Weapons Production in Fourth Countries: Likelihood and Consequences*, declassified U.S. National Intelligence Estimate, NIE 100-6-57, June 18, 1957 (hereinafter *June 1957 NIE*), pp. 1-3, para. 11.

166. U.S. Director of Central Intelligence, *Development of Nuclear Capabilities by Fourth Countries: Likelihood and Consequences*, declassified U.S. National Intelligence Estimate, NIE 100-2-58, July 1, 1958 [hereinafter *July 1958 NIE*], pp. 3, para. 13.

167. *June 1957 NIE*, p. 3, para. 12.

168. *July 1958 NIE*, p. 3, para. 14.

169. *Ibid.*, p. 4, para. 16; *ibid.* p. 1, para. 1 (estimating at least 5 years).

170. *Ibid*, p. 5, para. 21.

171. *Ibid.*

172. *Ibid.*, p. 5, para. 24.

173. U.S. Director of Central Intelligence, *Likelihood and Consequences of the Development of Nuclear Capabilities by Additional Countries*, declassified U.S. National Intelligence Estimate, NIE 100-4-60, September 20, 1960 (hereinafter *September 1960 NIE*), p. 3, para. 10 (emphasis added); See also U.S. Director of Central Intelligence, *Nuclear Weapons and Delivery Capabilities of Free World Countries other than the U.S. and UK*, declassified U.S. National Intelligence Estimate, NIE 4-3-61, September 21, 1961 (hereinafter *September 1961 NIE*), p. 3, para. 5 (making a similar point).

174. Wohlstetter, p. 306.

175. See Acheson-Lilienthal Report, p. 1 (recounting an official statement issued, after the first release of the Report on March 28, 1946, that there had been "some public misunderstanding of what denaturing is, and of the degree of safety that it could afford," and noting that it was untrue "that a system of control based solely on denaturing could provide adequate safety").

176. *Ibid.*, p. 26.

177. See Wohlstetter *et al.*, pp. 48-54. As Amory Lovins has recounted in a detailed discussion of the plutonium issue, "the assumption that power-reactor Pu [plutonium] was unsuitable for bombs was questioned with increasing force" in the early 1970s. The notion was apparently widely discredited by 1974, and indeed in 1977 the United States announced that it had indeed "successfully tested a nuclear weapon made from reactor-grade Pu." Amory B. Lovins, "Nuclear Weapons and power-reactor plutonium," *Nature*, Vol. 283, No. 5750, February 28, 1980, pp. 817-823, p. 1 (pagination from reprint in author's collection). Interest in denaturing seems perennial. Recently, an Israeli scientist has claimed to have developed an apparently new way of denaturing plutonium in reactor fuel. This, it is suggested, could declaw the plutonium by making it, if separated, "unsuitable for use in nuclear arms." See Batsheva Sobleman, "Israel: Science against nuclear proliferation," *Los Angeles Times* blog posting, March 5, 2009, available from *latimesblogs.latimes.com/babylonbeyond/2009/03/israel-science.html*.

178. Wohlstetter, p. 305.

179. *Ibid.*; See also Wohlstetter *et al.*, pp. 49, 71 (noting "some residual traces [persist] of a belief that a solution" based upon denaturing, and discussing the denaturing issue). According to Lovins, basic facts about the weapons-usability of reactor plutonium were apparently still widely — and, he argued, dangerously — misunderstood even in the late 1970s. Lovins, p. 1.

180. The technical and financial entry barriers to the enrichment business were doubly fortunate, in fact, insofar as its costliness permitted existing supplier states to continue their monopoly upon fuel making — and it was this monopoly that helped permit the emerging system of international nuclear benefit-shar-

ing to manage the risk of plutonium reprocessing, because suppliers insisted that safeguards be applied upon the nuclear fuel they provide. In any event, U.S. officials estimated that anyone desiring "a substantial [nuclear weapons] capability," including "the production of U-235," would have to spend "astronomic" amounts of money. U.S. Director of Central Intelligence, *Likelihood and Consequences of a Proliferation of Nuclear Weapons Systems*, declassified U.S. National Intelligence Estimate, NIE 4-63, June 28, 1963 (hereinafter *June 1963 NIE*), p. 5, paras. 2-3. The expense and difficulty was doubly great because ballistic missiles or other nuclear-capable delivery systems had not yet themselves proliferated: a new weapons state would have not merely to acquire nuclear explosive devices but also systems with which to deliver them.

181. Roswell Gilpatric *et al.*, "Nuclear Weapons Programs Around the World," TS 190187, December 3, 1964, declassified memorandum (hereinafter Gilpatric Report), available from *www.gwu.edu/~nsarchiv/NSAEBB/NSAEBB155/prolif-10.pdf*, p. 1.

182. Gilpatric Report, p. 9 (discussing India, Israel, Sweden, West Germany, Italy, Japan, and Canada). The Acheson-Lilienthal Report had been even more sanguine: "Whether any nation — we are excluding Great Britain and Canada — could achieve such an intensive program is a matter of serious doubt." Acheson-Lilienthal Report, p. ix; see also *ibid.*, p. 2 (noting "[s]trong arguments" that "the results attained in the United States cannot be paralleled by independent work in other nations"); *ibid.*, p. 23.

183. See Henry Sokolski, *Best of Intentions: America's Campaign Against Strategic Weapons Proliferation*, Westport, CT: Praeger, 2000, p. 32 (citing testimony); and "Atoms for Peace: A Non-Proliferation Primer?" *Arms Control*, Vol. 1, No. 2, September 1980, pp. 199-231.

184. "Statement by the United States Representative (Stassen) to the Disarmament Subcommittee: Nuclear Weapons and Testing," March 20, 1957, *Documents on Disarmament 1945-1959*, Vol. II, pp. 763, 766-767.

185. See Sokolski, *Best of Intentions*, pp. 25-29. A number of ideas for increasing the effectiveness of safeguards in prevent-

ing the diversion of fissile materials were proposed by American officials in the negotiations that led to the creation of the IAEA Statute in 1957, but these were opposed by India, France, the Soviets, and Switzerland, and were not ultimately included; *ibid.*, pp. 30-31.

186. *September 1961 NIE*, p. 3, para. 5, p. 4, para. 8.

187. *September 1960 NIE*, p. 11, para. 42.

188. *July 1958 NIE*, p. 18, para. 86. Moreover, the actual impact upon world stability of additional proliferation was understood to depend, to some degree, upon *who* got nuclear weapons. Not all potential possessors were equally worrisome. "The actual effect on the world situation is likely to depend on the country itself: the character of its government, the nature of its national aims and aspirations, the identity of its principal rivals, and the alliances and alignments in which it is involved, and the chief problems of its foreign relations." *Ibid.* p. 18, para. 87. In any event, a subsequent NIE noted, the most significant determinants of "pace and content of nuclear diffusion" were not "differences in national wealth and technical skill" but rather "national differences in political determination and strategic objectives." *June 1963 NIE*, p. 6, para. 5.

189. *June 1963 NIE*, pp. 18 para. 47. Instead, the dangers of such small-scale proliferation were felt to be limited to the "political and psychological effects of the existence of such new weapons," and possible escalation of regional problems. *Ibid.*, pp. 18-19, para. 47; see also *ibid.*, pp. 19-20, para. 50 (arguing that "[a] new nuclear power may be emboldened by the possession of nuclear weapons to a more vigorous pursuit of its objectives against enemy states, and the result may be an increase in the frequency of local crises").

190. Whether or not such conclusions were reasonable half a century ago, they would be much harder to sustain today, when U.S. and Russian arsenals have been reduced so dramatically — and they would be less tenable still if further progress were made toward nuclear weapons abolition. See Christopher A. Ford, "Five Plus Three: How to Have a Meaningful and Helpful Fissile Material Cutoff Treaty," *Arms Control Today*, Vol. 39, March 2009,

pp. 24, 33, n.23 (". . .[U]ncertainty about the possible existence of an extra handful of weapons here or there might perhaps have been acceptable in the context of a Cold War nuclear standoff between parties already possessing several thousand of such devices. The threshold of military significance arrives much more quickly where at issue is the potential arrival of a completely new player in the nuclear weapons business [today] or one country's achievement of breakout from a [future] nuclear weapons abolition regime.").

The Eisenhower Administration's argument, moreover, revolved almost entirely around the threat of *direct* nuclear attack by a future proliferator. Even though UN Ambassador Lodge conceded in 1956 that seeing the nuclear arms race "spread to more areas of the globe . . . could easily ignite a nuclear conflagration," the United States does not seem to have considered the potential impact of horizontal proliferation upon regional stability and extra-regional security relationships. See "Statement by the United States Representative (Lodge) to the Disarmament Commission," July 3, 1956, *Documents on Disarmament 1945-1959*, Vol. I, pp. 648-649.

191. Ironically, the 1961 NIE noted that such developments might indeed undercut its assumption that uranium enrichment was unachievable for most would-be proliferators. It expressly assumed that "there will be no significant technological breakthrough in the next several years which would significantly alter the complexity or economic costs of developing a nuclear capability," such as "the perfecting of the gas centrifuge process for isotope separation" in order to "require less electric power, be adaptable to small capacity production, and be more easily concealed." An advance of this kind, the NIE warned, "would increase the number of countries which could afford to produce weapons." See *September 1961 NIE*, p. 4, para. 11. Fatefully — if unknowingly — foreshadowing the wide dissemination of URENCO-developed enrichment technology by Pakistan's A. Q. Khan, which would shatter many of these assumptions, the 1961 NIE also noted in passing that West Germany was already doing research on U-235 isotope separation, "including the gas centrifuge process," which could speed up separation from uranium ore. *Ibid.*, p. 10, para. 41.

192. NPT, Art. IV(2).

193. See NPT, from the Preamble ("Affirming the principle that the benefits of peaceful applications of nuclear technology, including any technological by-products which may be derived by nuclear weapon States from the development of nuclear explosive devices, should be available for peaceful purposes to all . . . .").

194. See Mexican Working Paper submitted to the Eighteen Nation Disarmament Committee: Suggested Additions to Draft Nonproliferation Treaty, September 19, 1967, U.S. Arms Control and Disarmament Agency, *Documents on Disarmament 1967*, Washington DC: Government Printing Office, 1968 (hereinafter *Documents on Disarmament 1967*), pp. 394-395; See also U.S. Arms Control and Disarmament Agency, *International Negotiations on the Treaty on the Nonproliferation of Nuclear Weapons*, Washington, DC: U.S. Government Printing Office, 1969 (hereinafter *ACDA Negotiating History*), p. 67.

195. *Documents on Disarmament 1967*, p. 397 (remarks of Amb. Castaneda).

196. Conference of the Eighteen-Nation Committee on Disarmament, ENDC/PV.367, February 20, 1968, p. 18; see also *ACDA Negotiating History*, p. 103.

197. "Nigerian Working Paper Submitted to the Eighteen-Nation Disarmament Committee: Additions and Amendments to the Draft Nonproliferation Treaty, November 2 1967," *Documents on Disarmament 1967*, pp. 557-558; see also Zarate, pp. 246-247, 280-81, n.62.

198. Spanish Memorandum to the Co-Chairmen of the Eighteen-Nation Disarmament Committee, February 8, 1968, *Documents on Disarmament 1968*, Washington, DC: ACDA, 1969, p. 40; see also *ACDA Negotiating History*, p. 103.

199. See *ACDA Negotiating History*, p. 83; Conference of the Eighteen-Nation Committee on Disarmament, ENCD/PV.371, February 28, 1968, p. 20 (remarks of Canada's General Burns); see also U.S. State Department, *Promoting Expanded and Responsible Uses of Nuclear Energy*, April 16, 2007, available from *www.state.*

gov/t/isn/rls/other/83210.htm.

200. "Revised Draft Treaty on the Nonproliferation of Nuclear Weapons, January 18, 1968," *in ACDA Negotiating History*, pp. 150-154.

201. *Ibid*. p. 117 (comments by Nigeria), 120-123 (comments by Mexico, Chile, Australia, South Africa, and Israel). Their objections were addressed only to the extent that the final text was amended to refer to "exchange" of "equipment" and "materials" rather than just "information." See Draft Treaty on the Nonproliferation of Nuclear Weapons, May 31, 1968, *ACDA Negotiating History*, pp. 160-165; see also *ibid.*, p. 123.

202. NPT, Art.IV(1).

203. It is also worth remembering that the UN Security Council, acting pursuant to Chapter VII of the UN Charter, has imposed clear international legal obligations upon Iran to suspend its enrichment and reprocessing activities—obligations that operate quite independently of whatever the NPT's Article IV otherwise does or does not say about Tehran's right to engage in such work.

204. Zarate has also made this point. See Zarate, p. 282, n.66, as did I in internal arguments with State Department lawyers beginning in 2004.

205. "Romanian Working Paper Submitted to the Eighteen Nation Disarmament Committee: Amendments and Additions to the Draft Nonproliferation Treaty, October 19, 1967," *Documents on Disarmament 1967*, p. 525.

206. "Statement by the Mexican Representative (Garcia Robles) to the Eighteen-Nation Disarmament Committee: Latin American Nuclear-Free Zone and Nonproliferation of Nuclear Weapons, March 21, 1967," *Documents on Disarmament 1967*, pp. 162-163.

207. Whatever else it might mean, the best reading of Article IV(1) does not see that paragraph as *conferring* the "inalienable right." Its phrasing seems merely to *refer* to some preexisting

right, though the "conformity" requirements (which refer to articles of the NPT itself) are obviously a new constraint accepted by all States Party by virtue of their agreement to the Treaty's terms. The origin of such a preexisting right, however, is unaddressed. Conceivably, it comes from no place more profound or more codified than the basic assumed "right" of *any* sovereign state, in a fundamentally anarchic international system, to do *anything it wants* in the absence of positive legal constraint. Since the NPT seems expressly to limit that very right, however — thereby providing just such a positive constraint — it adds little to the discussion to make this point.

208. On the other hand, as noted previously, some nuclear experts reject the view that nuclear power plants are safeguardable in any country of whose peaceful intentions one is not already quite confident. Even, the most proliferation resistant light water reactor, they argue, comes with fresh fuel and produces plutonium-laden spent fuel that could be diverted to help make bombs without the IAEA necessarily finding out in a timely fashion. See Gilinsky *et al.*

209. Compare NPT, Arts. I, II, and III with *ibid.*, Art. IV.

210. Zarate, pp. 256-257.

211. Henry Sokolski, "The Nuclear Nonproliferation Treaty and Peaceful Nuclear Energy," testimony given before the House Committee on International Relations, Subcommittee on International Terrorism and Nonproliferation, Washington, DC, March 2, 2006, available from *www.internationalrelations.house. gov/archives/109/sok030206.pdf* (*quoting* ENDC/PV.82, September 7, 1962; "Statement by the Swedish Representative [Alva Myrdal] to the Eighteen-Nation Disarmament Committee: Nonproliferation of Nuclear Weapons," ENDC/PV.243, February 24, 1966).

212. Zarate. pp. 257, 286, n.91 (quoting ENDC/PV.250, March 22, 1966, p. 28 [statement of U. Maung Maung Gyi]).

213. "Statement by the Mexican Representative . . . March 21, 1967," p. 164; see also *ACDA Negotiating History*, p. 67.

214. See John Carlson, "Addressing Proliferation Challenges

from the Spread of Uranium Enrichment Capability," presentation by Russell Leslie, on behalf of John Carlson, to the Institute for Nuclear Materials Management Annual Meeting, Tucson, Arizona, July 9-12, 2007, PowerPoint slide 2.

215. Ford, "The NPT Review Process and the Future of the Nuclear Nonproliferation Regime."

216. Gottemoeller and Arnaudo, p. 17.

217. See *ACDA Negotiating History*, pp. 60, 125.

218. "Statement by the Department of State on Nonproliferation and Peaceful Nuclear Activities, February 20, 1967," *Documents on Disarmament 1967*, pp. 96, 96-97 (also stating that selling U.S. plutonium to EURATOM for electrical power generation purposes would be permitted).

219. The official summary of the negotiations paraphrases these statements by recounting that the United States had proclaimed that "[t]here was no area of peaceful nuclear development that would be precluded by a treaty." *ACDA Negotiating History*, p. 64. The actual U.S. statement, however, does not quite go so far. While it does emphasize that fast-breeders are not precluded, it does not make the *per se* claim quoted, and does in fact *rule out* sharing the technology involved in "peaceful nuclear explosive devices." See "Statement by the Department of State," pp. 96-97.

220. "Swiss Aide-Memoire to the Co-Chairmen of the Eighteen-Nation Disarmament Committee: Draft Nonproliferation Treaty, November 17, 1967," *Documents on Disarmament 1967*, pp. 572; see also ACDA *Negotiating History*, p. 81. (An undated U.S. document from the same period also explained to the government of Australia that the treaty would prohibit "[n]either uranium enrichment nor the stockpiling of fissionable material in connection with a peaceful program . . . so long as these activities were safeguarded under Article III. Also clearly permitted would be the development, under safeguards, of plutonium power reactors . . . .") U.S. Government, undated "Aide Memoire to the Government of Australia" [declassified version], p. 2, para. 5. Admittedly, however, this response concerned only the scope of what

activities *would violate Article II* of the NPT, and it is likely true that none of those activities constitute Article II problems if not undertaken for purposes of furthering nuclear weapons development. See *Noncompliance Report*, pp. 64-65 (setting forth U.S. standards for Article II compliance assessments). The undated U.S. document thus did not address whether or not these technologies fell within the ambit of the "right" discussed in Article IV.)

221. NPT, Preamble.

222. Quoted in *ACDA Negotiating History*, pp. 65-66.

223. U.S. Department of State, diplomatic cable entitled "Aide-Memoire on the Draft Non-Proliferation Treaty (NPT)" [declassified version], August 24, 1967, pp. 3-4.

224. See AFP, "UN Nuclear Chief Says Iran Should Stop Expanding Enrichment," June 14, 2007; Associated Press, "Iran: No Halt to Enrichment," May 25, 2007.

225. Vienna Convention on the Law of Treaties, May 23, 1969, 1155 UNT.S. 331, Art. 18(a).

226. *Ibid.*, Art. 32.

227. See Charter of Fundamental Rights of the European Union, Art. 54 ("Nothing in this Charter shall be interpreted as implying any right to engage in any activity or to perform any act aimed at the destruction of any of the rights and freedoms recognised in this Charter or at their limitation to a greater extent than is provided for herein."), available from *www.europarl.europa.eu/ comparl/libe/elsj/charter/art54/default_en.htm*; Universal Declaration of Human Rights, available from *www.unhchr.ch/udhr/lang/ eng.htm*, Art. 30 ("Nothing in this Declaration may be interpreted as implying for any State, group or person any right to engage in any activity or to perform any act aimed at the destruction of any of the rights and freedoms set forth herein.").

228. Lawless v. Ireland (E.C.H.R., Series A, No.3), July 1, 1961, available from *www.ena.lu/judgment_european_court_human_ rights_lawless_ireland_july_1961-020004456.html*, at para. 7 of discussion of law.

229. See Principal Deputy Assistant Secretary of State Christopher Ford, "NPT Article IV: Peaceful Uses of Nuclear Energy," Statement to the 2005 Review Conference of the Treaty on the Nonproliferation of Nuclear Weapons, New York, May 18, 2005, available from *www.state.gov/t/vci/rls/rm/46604.htm* ("NPT parties have the responsibility to implement Article IV in such a way that not only preserves NPT compliant parties' right to develop peaceful uses of nuclear energy, but also ensures against abuse of this right by States Party pursuing nuclear weapons capabilities").

230. "Statement by the United States High Representative (Hickerson) to the Ad Hoc Political Committee of the General Assembly, November 11, 1949," *Documents on Disarmament, 1945-1959*, pp. 225, 227.

231. Gilpatric Report, p. 3.

232. "Statement by the United States High Representative (Hickerson)," p. 227.

233. See *ACDA Negotiating History*, pp. 81, 84-86.

234. "Brazilian Amendments to the Draft Nonproliferation Treaty, October 31, 1967," *Documents on Disarmament 1967*, p. 546.

235. See Zarate, pp. 247, 281, n.64 (quoting "Brazilian Amendments to the Draft Treaty on Nonproliferation of Nuclear Weapons," ENDC/201/Rev.2, February 13, 1968).

236. In 1976, Wohlstetter observed that PNEs were "[t]he reduction to absurdity of the dichotomy" between "peaceful" and military uses. "These plowshares, in all essentials, *are* swords." Wohlstetter *et al.*, p. 46. More recently, Zarate has argued similarly that the PNE issue demonstrates the importance of the principle that "[w]hen the IAEA cannot effectively safeguard the nuclear material involved in an allegedly-peaceful application of nuclear technology, then the NPT does not protect the right of states to develop, access or use that allegedly-peaceful application of nuclear technology." Zarate, p. 255.

237. See *ACDA Negotiating History*, pp. 52, 60, 81, 84-85, 104-

379

106, 124.

238. "Statement by the Department of State on Nonproliferation and Peaceful Nuclear Activities, February 20, 1967," p. 97
(emphasis added).

239. Quoted in *ACDA Negotiating History*, pp. 65-66.

240. NPT, Art.V (providing that the "potential benefits from
any peaceful applications of nuclear explosions will be made
available to non-nuclear-weapon States Party . . . [and that] Non-
nuclear-weapon States Party to the Treaty shall be able to obtain
such benefits, pursuant to a special international agreement or
agreements, through an appropriate international body").

241. After all, even with respect to PNEs, one ambassador
centrally involved in crafting the NPT's peaceful use provisions
held out at least some hope that "technological progress" might
"one day" "make it possible to distinguish clearly between nuclear explosives for peaceful and for warlike purposes." *ACDA
Negotiating History*, p. 65 (quoting Mexican representative).

242. See Cochran.

243. The IAEA Director General has made it clear that even
the AP's new authorities are inadequate to the challenges presented by IAEA verification activities in the face of the sort of
denial and deception activities undertaken by Iran. In 2005, after
two years of work to detail Iran's covert nuclear program, the
Director General of the IAEA called upon Iran to provide cooperation and transparency above and beyond that required by the
AP. IAEA, "Implementation of the NPT Safeguards Agreement
in the Islamic Republic of Iran," GOV/2005/67, September 2,
2005, para. 50 ("such transparency measures should extend beyond the formal requirements of the Safeguards Agreement and
Additional Protocol"); See also IAEA Board of Governors, "Implementation of the NPT Safeguards Agreement in the Islamic
Republic of Iran," GOV/2006/14 (February 4, 2006), at operative
para. 1 (deeming it necessary for Iran to "implement transparency measures . . . which extend beyond the formal requirements
of the Safeguards Agreement and Additional Protocol").

244. IAEA, The Structure and Content of Agreements between the Agency and States Required in Connection with the Treaty on the Non-Proliferation of Nuclear Weapons, INFCIRC/153 (Corrected), June 1972, p. 9, para. 28, available from *www.iaea.or.at/Publications/Documents/Infcircs/Others/infcirc153.pdf*.

245. Wohlstetter, p. 307; see also Fred C. Iklé, "After Detection—What?" *Foreign Affairs*, Vol. 39, No. 2, January 1961, p. 208.

246. Acheson-Lilienthal Report, p. 9.

247. Bergner letter, p. 2.

248. See Christopher A. Ford, "The Nonproliferation Bestiary: A Typology and Analysis of Nonproliferation Regimes," *New York University Journal of International Law and Politics*, Vol. 39, No. 4, Summer 2007, pp. 937, 955.

249. See Statute of the IAEA, Art. XII(C), available from *www.iaea.org/About/statute_text.html#A1.12* ("The inspectors shall report any noncompliance to the Director General who shall thereupon transmit the report to the Board of Governors. . . . The Board shall report the non-compliance to all members and to the Security Council and General Assembly of the United Nations.").

250. Sokolski, "Nuclear Policy and the Presidential Election," p. 10. He points out, for example, that while IAEA estimates it would take only 7-10 days to convert separated plutonium into nuclear weapon, the IAEA's own detection goal is only to inspect facilities containing such material once a month. Sokolski, "Too Speculative?" pp. 122-123; Henry Sokolski, ed., *Falling Behind: International Scrutiny of the Peaceful Atom*, Carlisle, PA: Strategic Studies Institute, U.S. Army War College, 2008, pp. 3-62.

251. Sokolski, "Nuclear Policy in the Presidential Election," p. 10.

252. Roberta Wohlstetter, "The Buddha Smiles: U.S. Peaceful Aid and the Indian Bomb," *Nuclear Policies: Fuel without the Bomb*, Cambridge, MA: Ballinger, 1978, reprinted in Zarate and Sokolski, pp. 339-340.

253. *Ibid.*, p. 349.

254. *Ibid.*

255. Acheson-Lilienthal Report, p. 47.

It will probably be necessary to write into the charter it-self a systematic plan governing the location of the operations and property of the Authority so that a strategic balance may be maintained among nations. In this way, protection will be afforded against such eventualities as the complete or partial collapse of the United Nations or the Atomic Development Authority, protection will be afforded against the eventuality of sudden seizure by any one nation of the stockpiles, reduction, refining, and separation plants, and reactors of all types belonging to the Authority. . . . The real protection [against seizure] will lie in the fact that if any nation seizes the plants or the stockpiles that are situated in its territory, other nations will have similar facilities and materials situated within their own borders so that the act of seizure need not place them at a disadvantage.

256. Sokolski, "Nuclear Policy in the Presidential Election," p. 10.

257. See Roberta Wohlstetter, "The Buddha Smiles," pp. 339, 341 (noting that "[t]he identification of civilian nuclear energy with economic progress is sometimes made in self-consciously symbolic terms with no pretense at hard economic argument, but merely as an invocation to modernity").

258 . Roberta Wohlstetter, "The Buddha Smiles," p. 341.

259. NPT/CONF.2005/WP.57, p. 3, para. 14.

260. 2005 Noncompliance Report, p. 80.

261. "Second Report of the United Nations Atomic Energy Commission to the Security Council," pp. 97, 98, 131, 133 (emphasis added).

262. Acheson-Lilienthal Report, pp. 48-49.

263. *Ibid.*, p. 17.

264. Nuclear Non-Proliferation Act of 1978, Public Law 95-242 [H.R. 8638], 92 Stat. 120, March 10, 1978 (as amended by Public Law 99-661 [National Defense Authorization Act for Fiscal Year 1987; S. 2638], 100 Stat. 3816, November 11, 1986), at Title V, § 503, available from *www.nti.org/db/china/engdocs/nnpa1978.htm*.

265. Nuclear Non-Proliferation Act of 1978, at § 2(2).

266. The WMD Commission described Title V as requiring "general and country-specific assessments of the relative merits of nuclear and non-nuclear energy sources for meeting the energy needs of developing nations." *WMD Commission Report*, p. 93; see also Sokolski, "After Iran." The Commissioners, however, seem to have felt that the U.S. Government had failed to live up to the intent of Title V, and needed to do better. See *WMD Commission Report*, p. 51 (recommending that the United States "implement Title V of the Nuclear Nonproliferation Act of 1978, which requires energy assessments for developing states").

267. NPT/CONF.2005/PC.III/WP.22, p. 2.

268. Canada, Estonia, France, Republic of Korea, Poland, Romania, Ukraine, and United Kingdom, "Nuclear Power Development: Meeting the World's Energy Needs and Fulfilling Article IV," NPT/CONF.2010/PC.II/WP.40, May 9, 2008, available from *daccessdds.un.org/doc/UNDOC/GEN/G08/612/88/PDF/G0861288.pdf?OpenElement*, p. 8.

269. Wohlstetter *et al.*, p. 47.

270. Greenberg, p. 1.

271. *Ibid.*, p. 18.

272. Weiss, "The Nuclear Nonproliferation Treaty."

273. See Henry Sokolski, "Market Fortified Non-proliferation," Jeffrey Laurenti and Carl Robichaud, eds., *Breaking the Nuclear Impasse*, New York: Century Foundation, 2007, pp. 81-143.

274. Gottemoeller and Arnaudo, pp. 15, 17-18.

275. *Ibid.*, p. 18.

CHAPTER 12

ECONOMICS OF NEW NUCLEAR POWER AND PROLIFERATION RISKS IN A CARBON CONSTRAINED WORLD*

Jim Harding

INTRODUCTION

Climate change, growth in electricity demand, and persistently higher fossil fuel prices have reignited the debate over nuclear power and whether it is a safe or competitive resource inside the United States or internationally. Estimating the cost of a new U.S. reactor is a daunting exercise. The data base of advanced light water reactors underway or completed is small, almost entirely in Asia, and mostly accumulated in the 1990s—there has been significant real escalation in worldwide materials costs since 2002. The supply chain—key materials, components, skilled labor—is also extremely tight.

While the Japanese supply chain capacity is intact, U.S., Western European, and Russian industries have been largely moribund since the Three Mile Island and Chernobyl accidents. In the last several years, however, there has been a steep change. Utilities and vendors (nuclear system suppliers), both in the United States and abroad, have gone beyond computer models and extrapolation from Asian experience to real bids and real estimates.

---

*A version of this article is available from *www.npec-web.org/ Essays/20070600-Harding-EconomicsNewNuclearPower.pdf*.

Risk is reflected in contract terms, the allocation spread between vendors and utilities is often opaque. The thinly traded uranium spot market has been volatile. Electricity markets have also changed, with respect to the structure, regulation, finance, and cost and availability of competing and emerging technologies.

We do face inevitable controls on carbon emissions sometime in the future, with nuclear power obviously benefitting, whether these controls take the form of taxes or cap-and-trade approaches. One question is whether such benefits will help the nuclear industry enough.

To answer this question, we need to start by looking at probable construction or capital costs. This represents 80-90 percent of overall life-cycle cost. Other factors are important, including finance and capital cost recovery (debt, equity, taxes, and depreciation), net capital additions during operation, capacity factor, operating life, decommissioning cost, operations and maintenance, and fuel, including costs for waste management. This chapter presents two possible cases (high and low), and contrasts those results with estimates for other technologies under a range of possible carbon prices. It also offers some observations on possible worldwide growth rates for nuclear capacity, fuel cell requirements, and potential risks of weapons proliferation.

CAPITAL COST

To estimate the cost of new reactors in the United States, the best place to turn might be U.S. experience, but the data is old and not easy to interpret. Plants increased in cost at rates far exceeding general inflation.[1] The more plants we built, the more they cost, but that explanation is too simple — we had rising inflation and rising interest rates in the 1970s and 1980s, supply chain imbalances for key components and skilled labor, state and federal regulatory issues, design-as-you-build construction, siting and financing challenges, growing public opposition, and declining rates of electricity growth (see Figure 1).

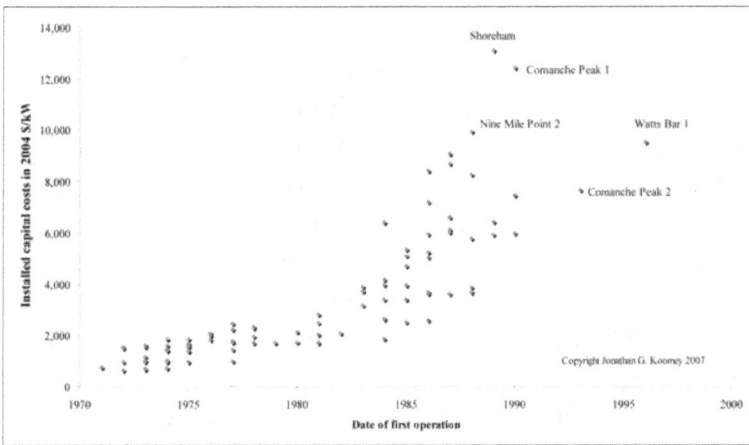

Figure 1. Capital Costs of U.S. Reactors Built between 1970 and 2000.

In the recent past, industry and government estimates for nuclear construction ranged from $1,500 to $2,100/ kilowatt (kW), expressed in various year dollars.[2] Recent bids and industry estimates, however, are far higher. In June 2009, the Ontario Power Authority declined two bids for two reactors from Atomic Energy of Canada (AECL) ($10,800/ kW) and Areva ($7,375/ kW). The latter was "non-conforming," which presumably means that substantial risk of delay and cost escalation was placed on the utility. The Electricity Supply Commission of South Africa also declined to accept bids this year, the lowest of which was reportedly $6000/kW.

A variety of studies have been conducted in recent years to test past government and industry estimates. In 2003, an MIT study rejected lower cost estimates as based on software estimates, rather than real construction experience, and for failing to include key owners' costs, including land, construction oversight, and project contingencies. The report instead relied on estimates for recently completed (1993-2002) advanced light water reactors in Japan and South Korea. Overnight costs (a common convention), not including either escalation or interest during construction, are shown in Figure 2 at date of commercial operation in real 2002 dollars.[3] We have not included the South Korean units in computing the average because of lower South Korean labor rates, though the average exclusive of these units is provided in Figure 2. MIT, however, assumed that the Asian experience could be directly imported to the United States, and that there would be zero real cost escalation or delay for U.S. reactors.

Plant	Megawatts	Date of Commercial Operation (COD)	Yen@COD	2002$s/kW	2007$s/kW
Onagawa 3	825	Jan-02	3 14E+11	2409	3332
Genkai 3	1180	Feb-94	3 99E+11	2643	3656
Genkai 4	1180	Jul-97	3 24E+11	1960	2711
KK3	1000	Jan-93	3 25E+11	2615	3617
KK4	1000	Jan-94	3 33E+11	2609	3608
KK6	1356	Jan-96	4 18E+11	2290	3167
KK7	1356	Jan-97	3 67E+11	1957	2707
Y5	1000	Jan-04	NA	1700	2352
Y6	1000	Jan-05	NA	1656	2290
Average				2354	3257

Figure 2. MIT Cost Estimates Based on Light Water Reactors in Japan and South Korea.

The chart in Figure 3 provided by the Electric Power Research Institute shows recent cost trends for large U.S.-engineered projects. After a number of years with little or no real escalation in costs, the curve has steepened to roughly 4 percent real escalation per year, mainly driven by higher costs for steel, copper, concrete, and other materials.

Construction Cost Indices
Source: Chemical Engineering Magazine, August 2006

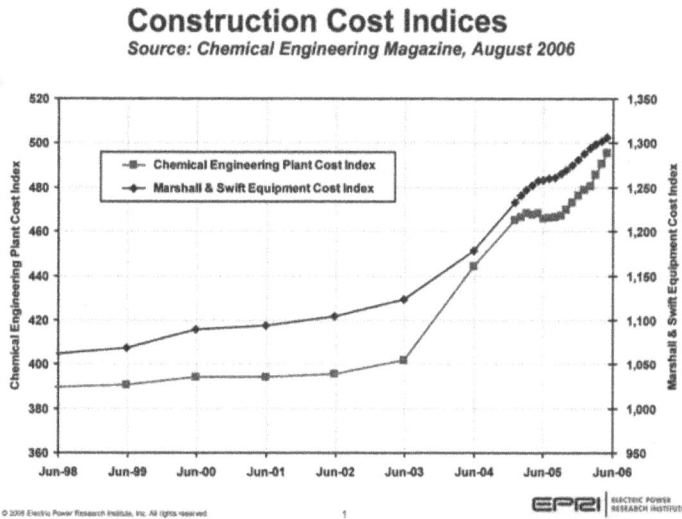

Figure 3. Cost Trends for Recent U.S.-Engineered Projects.

Some utilities believe that other indices (e.g., "heavy construction") are more appropriate though yielding higher escalation rates (e.g., American Electric Power at 7.8 percent real through 2007).[4] See Figure 4.

Commodity/Construction Material	Avg Annual Escalation from 1986 to 2003	Avg Annual Escalation from December 2003 to April 2007	Last 40 Mo Escalation at Ratio of Recent Historical Avg
Nickel	3 8%	60 3%	15 9x
Copper	3 3%	69 2%	21x
Cement	2 7%	11 6%	4 3x
Iron & Steel	1 2%	19 6%	16 3x
Heavy construction	2 2%	10 5%	4 8x

Figure 4. Escalation Rates Based on Heavy Construction.

Cambridge Energy Research Associates (CERA) has also begun to compile a power plant capital cost index based on current worldwide transactions by utilities and vendors, as shown in Figure 5. A Reuters press report indicated that the nuclear cost increase estimated by CERA was 185 percent (i.e., nearly trebling) from 2000 to 2008, or roughly 16 percent per year in nominal dollars. Escalation has been negative, however, for the past 18 months.

IHS/CERA PCCI: With and Without Nuclear Projects

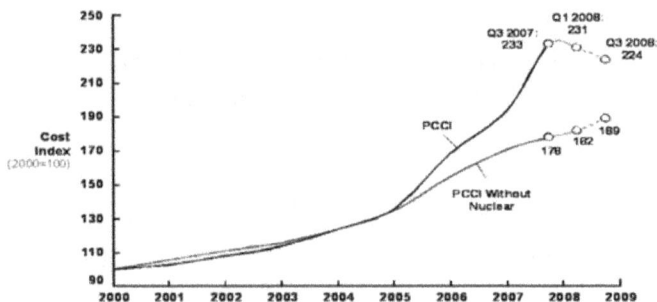

Figure 5. CERA's Worldwide Power Plant Capital Cost Index.

390

The reasons for real cost escalation are extremely complex and difficult to predict. Some key factors include volatile materials prices, mostly traded in international markets; changing value of the dollar; strong demand for construction materials, especially in China and India; supply-chain imbalances and possible scarcity pricing for suppliers, sub-suppliers, engineering-procurement-contracting (EPC) firms, and skilled labor; rising contingency insurance premiums, and/or hedging costs throughout the supply-chain; and poor or unsophisticated cost estimates from 2000-04.

In the 1970s, the usual utility practice was to get a bid for a new nuclear steam supply system (NSSS) from a vendor (then General Electric, Westinghouse, Combustion Engineering, Babcock & Wilcox, or General Atomics). The utility would typically hire an architect-engineer (e.g., Bechtel) to manage engineering design, procurement, and contracting. The current approach is different; utilities expect the vendors to hire architect-engineers and manage construction. Initially, vendors did this in the 1960s, delivering a turnkey (ready for operation) unit. While the projects being proposed today are turnkey in the sense that construction and procurement are managed by vendors instead of the utility, they are not turnkey in terms of being built for an initially agreed fixed price.

While some vendors may be willing to bid some parts of the project at a fixed price, there is little evidence of vendors being willing to bid most of the project cost at a fixed price, or as a loss leader (sold at below cost to attract future business). Bids typically include elements that are "fixed" in cost; "firm," meaning indexed to various escalators; and "variable," meaning passed through at whatever the cost turns out to be. The range in cost estimates may be substantially explained by different levels of escalation risk borne by the vendor. Vendors' bids are often not directly comparable; some may include some owners' costs (e.g., cooling towers), while others do not. Greenfield (industrial project starting from scratch on virgin land) sites are likely to be more expensive than brownfield (industrial project involving conversion of a no-longer-in-use factility), and often require substantial investments in dedicated transmission. A substantial number of recent cost estimates involve confidentiality agreements that make a thorough outside assessment and comparative analysis difficult, if not impossible.

Final completion cost is usually expressed in "mixed current dollars" at the date of commercial operation. Mixed current dollars is an unusual term. Investments are made in then current dollars, but they accrue interest from that date forward until commercial operation begins. So an investment in 2008 is in 2008 dollars, but it accumulates interest until the plant is complete. An investment in 2012 on the same plant is in 2012 dollars, but it was exposed to inflation and real escalation from 2008 to 2012, producing a sum which may be higher or lower than a 2008 investment with interest. When the plant enters service, its completion cost is the sum of early investments with interest and little inflation or escalation, plus later investments with inflation and escalation, but little interest. In the rare (if not unimaginable) case that real escalation and real interest costs are exactly zero, overnight cost equals final completion cost.

It is also possible and highly desirable, though uncommon, to state completion cost in real (discounted) constant year dollars, including real interest and real escalation during construction. This makes it possible to directly compare project estimates for completion in 2015 with those scheduled for 2020, which is otherwise a laborious task, mainly involving deconstructing cash flows, assumptions regarding interest during construction, real escalation during construction, and project contingencies.

Florida Power & Light (FP&L) recently filed testimony before the state Public Service Commission, with costs derived from the Tennessee Valley Authority's (TVA) 2005 estimate for new units at the nuclear plant site in Bellefonte, Alabama. The vendor's engineering-procurement-contracting cost estimate for Bellefonte was given as $1611/kW in 2004 dollars, not including owners' costs. FP&L escalated the Bellefonte values using a range of escalation rates and contingency assumptions, plus owners' costs.

The utility's overnight cost estimates, in 2007 dollars, included a low case estimate of $3108/kW, mid-case of $3600/kW, and high case of $4540/kW. The FP&L analysis includes $200-$250/kW in transmission integration (hooking into the regional grid) costs (see Figure 6).

Source	$/kW overnight cost
Keystone (2007)	2950
Constellation Energy (2008)	3500-4500
Eskom (South Africa, 2009)	6000
FP&L (2008)	3108-3600-4540
Duke Energy (2008)	5000

Figure 6. Transmission Integration Costs.

Figure 7 shows real and expected escalation rates used by various organizations for recent past escalation, and for estimating future escalation.

Source	2004-2007 nominal	2004-2007 real	Future	Basis
Keystone	6.0 %	3.3%	0-3.3% real	Chemical plant
AEP	10 5 %	7.8%	NA	Heavy construction
CERA	16 %	13.3%	NA	Utility generation
FP&L	10.7-20.7 %	8-18%	1-2% real	Construction indices

Figure 7. Overnight Cost (2007 Dollars, Including Real Escalation/Interest During Construction).

In general, there is little reason to think that escalation rates for nuclear power would be any lower, and could be substantially higher than for other generating resources. Long construction periods and high capital intensity exacerbate this problem. There is a spectacular difference between zero, 4 percent, and 14 percent per year cost escalation, especially for long lead time projects. See figures 8 and 9.

Real escalation	0%/year	4%/year	8%/year	14%/year
Medium case	$4050/kW	$5400/kW	$7130/kW	$9050/kW
High case	$4540/kW	$6050/kW	$8000/kW	$10150/kW

Figure 8. Levelized Cost of Energy (2007 Cents/Kwh, Including Interest and Operating Costs).[5]

Real escalation	0%/year	4%/year	8%/year	14%/year
Medium case	10.7	13.4	16.9	20.7
High case	11.7	14.7	18.6	23.0

Figure 9. Real Escalation Percentages by Year.

CONSTRUCTION TIME, LEAD TIME, AND DATE OF COMPLETION

It is very difficult to determine whether real cost escalation will continue into the future, and it clearly affects all generating options, though it is most acute for capital intensive resources. As described earlier, nuclear power faces some specific supply-chain challenges that argue against a low number. Twenty years ago, the United States had about 400 suppliers and 900 nuclear or N-stamp certificate holders (subsuppliers) licensed by the American Society of Mechanical Engineers. The numbers today are 80 and 200.[6]

Worldwide forging capacity for pressure vessels, steam generators, and pressurizers is limited to two qualified companies—Japan Steel Works and Creusot Forge—and the reactors' builders will be competing with each other as well as with simultaneous demand for new refinery equipment. Japan Steel Works prices have increased by 12 percent in 6 months, with a new 30 percent down payment requirement.[7]

Other long lead-time components, including reactor cooling pumps, diesel generators, and control and instrumentation equipment have 6-year manufacturing and procurement requirements. In the near term, reliance on foreign manufacturing capacity could complicate construction and licensing. Nuclear Regulatory Commission (NRC) Chairman Dale Klein recently indicated that reliance on foreign suppliers would require more time for quality control inspections to ensure that substandard materials are not incorporated in U.S. plants.[8]

Skilled labor and experienced contractors present another problem. A recent study by GE-Toshiba identified a potential shortage of craft labor within a 400-

mile radius of the Bellefonte site, forcing the adoption of a longer construction schedule.[9] Other sources have pointed to the potential for skilled labor shortages if nuclear construction expands.[10]

Several of these problems have clearly surfaced at the Olkiluoto 3 site in Finland, where the French vendor Areva is building a 1,600 megawatt advanced European pressurized reactor (EPR). Areva originally estimated a 4-year construction period, but the plant has fallen 18 months behind schedule, and is substantially over budget. Analysts estimate that Areva's share of the loss on the turnkey contract will exceed $1 billion. Concrete poured for the foundation of the nuclear island was found to be more porous than the Finnish regulator would accept. Hot and cold legs of the reactor cooling system required reforging.

At a recent conference in Nice, Areva official Luc Oursel indicated that the company had underestimated what it would take to reactivate the global supply chain for a new nuclear plant. In particular, they were not "100 percent assured to have a good quality of supply," were not sufficiently familiar with the "specific regulatory context" in Finland, and began building without a complete design. Some 1,360 workers from 28 different nations are now at work at the site. The project manager for STUK, the Finnish regulator, added that "a complete design would be the ideal. But I don't think there's a vendor in the world who would do that before knowing whether they would get a contract. That's real life."[11]

The industry believes that standardization and "learning curves," coupled with resolving supply chain imbalances, will drive costs lower over time. But there are chicken-and-egg problems with this conclusion. Utilities may not order new plants and equipment if capacity is limited and costs are uncertain. Suppliers may not expand production capacity if orders are not immediately forthcoming. As suggested in the comment above, vendors may not be willing to complete engineering designs before contracts are awarded. Moreover, given the structure of the U.S. utility industry, learning curves may be hard to achieve, with different utilities in different parts of the country considering standardized but different reactor designs.

The French experience most strongly suggests that rapid construction is best achieved with one utility ordering one basic design at a steady rate, keeping vendors, subsuppliers, and construction crews operating near capacity and able to move smoothly from one project to the next.[12] That model of single government vendor, coordinated procurement, and single government utility is rare, if not unique and unavailable, in today's world.

Market and regulatory issues also play a role. In most restructured U.S. markets, utilities would not be able to "rate base" new nuclear generation, and would instead need to rely on sales in the wholesale market, where trades are often thin, unpredictable, and short in duration. Plants built in that environment would have a very unfavorable financing structure (e.g., 70 percent equity and 30 percent debt).

In more traditional markets, utilities will probably be required to prepare integrated resource plans, comparing all supply and demand side options, including utility and nonutility owned generation. The utility might then be required to run a competitive procurement process that could include utility-owned nuclear generation. Regulators will probably consider cost caps, and/or annual prudence reviews, as a condition of final approval. Some states may take a more supportive and proactive position, for example by permitting utilities to recover construction work in rate base despite near-term rate impacts.[13] In other states, charging costs to customers before the plant came into service would not be acceptable or consistent with current law.[14]

The MIT study assumed a financial structure of 50 percent debt (at 8 percent) and 50 percent equity (at 15 percent), including a modest equity risk premium (3 percent) for a new nuclear plant. Those assumptions are reasonable for an investor-owned utility able to access rate base. However, a recent report by Moody's indicates that virtually any utility planning to build a large nuclear plant would almost inevitably face a rating downgrade, increasing the cost of money during construction.[15]

The 2005 National Energy Policy Act included several subsidies to jump start low carbon emission resources, the most important of which involved federal loan guarantees. In May 2007, the Department of Energy (DoE) released a second draft of its loan guarantee rules. The draft rule provides for the federal government to guarantee 90 percent of the debt, so long as the amount does not exceed 80 percent of the total project cost. DoE also indicated that it was considering a significant minimum equity stake on the part of any developer, and that guarantees should be limited to five projects that use the same technology.

Three features of the program diminish its value: first, the government-backed debt cannot be stripped from the total debt; second, the nonguaranteed fraction of debt is subordinated to the covered fraction; and finally, DoE's fiscal 2008 budget proposes $9 billion in total loan guarantees of which $4 billion would be allocated to nuclear plants and coal with carbon sequestration. A banker contacted by the trade journal *Nucleonics Week* commented that the first two features devalue the debt from a possible AAA rating to "single B or double D."[16] Four billion dollars in loan guarantees also might cover only one or two new units.

In general, most prospective nuclear builders regard these provisions as potentially valuable, but uncertain, unlikely to be sustained over the long term, and not a tipping point for a nuclear investment. Finally, it is important to emphasize that government subsidies do not reduce the cost of nuclear power; they spread risk and cost to taxpayers and reduce prices to ratepayers.

Interest during construction depends on several key factors—duration of construction, shape of outlays, the debt to equity ratio, and returns on both debt and equity. The U.S. Energy Information Administration assumes a 6-year construction period for a new reactor. Some vendors believe it can be done in 4 years. The MIT base case was 5 years.

OPERATING, MAINTENANCE, AND FUEL COSTS

One of the most important parameters affecting lifecycle cost is reactor performance, or capacity factor. U.S. average nuclear capacity factors have increased from below 60 percent during most of the 1980s to nearly 90 percent in the post-2000 period.[17] Some of the increase is attributable to changes in technical specifications for equipment to operate within a wider range and to higher fuel enrichments. The first reduces the number of equipment related reactor trips and shutdowns. The second reduces the number of refueling outages. It may also be true that outages are more frequent in early years ("teething") and later years ("aging"). A reasonable lifetime range for future units is 75 to 85 percent.

Advanced light water reactors may have lower operations and maintenance costs than current units, based on the use of more passive safety systems. Including capital additions (essentially capitalized operations and maintenance), the current U.S. average is about \$100-\$120/kW-year, inclusive of administrative and general (essentially pension and insurance) costs. There is no recent history of real escalation in the value, and it is probably appropriate for both a low and high estimate.

Nuclear fuel costs have many components — uranium mining and milling, conversion to UF6, enrichment, reconversion, fuel fabrication, shipping costs, interest costs on fuel in inventory, and spent fuel management and disposition. The 2003 MIT study calculated a 5 mill (half a cent) per kW hour cost for all these steps, based on then-current uranium prices of \$13.60/pound (lb). Spot market prices for uranium in early June 2007 were \$135/lb, tripling since October 2006. The reasons for the price increase are somewhat complicated. They are now about \$44/lb.

Uranium prices have been volatile over the past 3 decades. Real spot prices almost sextupled from 1973 to 1976, then dropped steeply through 2002, but have risen dramatically since that time. The problem is not declining physical supplies of uranium, cost of production, or growth in demand for nuclear fuel. The key problem is that much uranium demand over the past 2 decades has been met by inexpensive "secondary supplies," including surplus inventories from cancelled or shut-down units (1980s-1990s) in the United

States, Western Europe, and Russia; purchase of surplus Russian and U.S. Government stockpiles (mid-1990s); and diluting highly enriched uranium from surplus Russian nuclear weapons (1998-2013) with natural uranium.

Worldwide uranium production is about 60 percent of current uranium demand.[18] Existing spot uranium prices clearly support enhanced production, both in the United States and abroad, but lead times for new mines are long. The same situation applies to enrichment. Uranium mining expansion will need to be better than 1980s rates of expansion to meet 2015 demands, particularly with limited enrichment capacity worldwide.

Nuclear plant owners and utility customers are not currently facing strikingly higher fuel prices, mainly because current contracts were written during a period of surplus and include price ceilings. The same basic situation applies to enrichment cost and supply. Most current long-term contracts expire by 2012, and secondary supplies decline rapidly during that period. The price ceilings in long-term contracts also mean that those parties that might pursue new mines or enrichment plants have not benefited substantially from price signals in the spot market. It also means that utilities with uranium and enrichment contracts largely expiring in 2012-13 must enter the market this year or next to ensure adequate supplies in the future.

Assuming current prices for uranium and enrichment ($44/lb and $160/kgSWU), nuclear fuel cycle costs are about twice the amount calculated in the MIT analysis. While these price increases are dramatic, they do not justify reprocessing to recover plutonium from spent fuel for subsequent recycling as mixed oxide fuel (MOx) in light water reactors. The

2003 MIT study compared this choice with $13.60/lb uranium and $100/kgSWU enrichment prices. This yielded a 5 mill/kWh fuel price; using very conservative estimates for reprocessing and mixed oxide fuel fabrication yielded closed cycle fuel costs that were more than a factor of four higher. With $2000/ton reprocessing and $1500/kg mixed oxide fuel prices, a closed fuel cycle costs about twice the MIT value, or 4.3 cents/kWh.

CARBON CONSTRAINTS

With carbon constraints (specified as taxes or a cap-and-trade approach), nuclear power's competitive position improves. Standard & Poor's (S&P) recently released an economic analysis on the sensitivity of electricity generation technologies to carbon controls.[19] Only plant—rather than full fuel cycle—emissions were considered. The base case capital cost estimate for nuclear power was $4000/kW, which is generally in line with the values calculated here. Operations and maintenance (O&M) costs were in line with the values calculated here, but the nuclear fuel price was estimated at 0.7 cents/kWh—roughly 2-3 times too low. The price of natural gas was estimated at $7 per million British thermal unit (BTU).

Coal price estimates ranged from $1-$1.80 per million BTU for Wyoming and eastern coal respectively. Direct comparison with the values calculated here can be somewhat tricky, mainly because S&P does not show all financial assumptions (see Figure 10). The first row of bold numbers shows internal costs, without carbon capture or taxes. The second bold row shows costs with carbon capture and sequestration, and the final bold row shows costs with carbon credits or taxes of $10-$30/ton. As shown, nuclear power has only a modest advantage over coal (either pulverized or integrated gasification combined cycle [IGCC]) if carbon sequestration is required. It is significantly less competitive with carbon taxes or credits, if they are available in a range of $10-$30/ton of CO_2.

	Pulverized Coal	Gas CCCT	Western IGCC	Wind	Nuclear
Capital Cost ($/kW)	2438	700	2925	1700	4000
Capacity Factor (%)	85	65	80	33	85
Fixed O&M ($/kW-yr)	45	20	60	25	100
TonsCO2/MWh	0.87	0.37	0.94	NA	NA
Total cost (cents/kWh)	5.8	6.8	6.5	7.1	8.9-9.8[i]
Carbon Capture					
Capital Cost ($/kW)	940	470	450	NA	NA
Energy penalty (%)	25	13	15	NA	NA
TonsCO2/MWh	0.09	0.04	0.09	NA	NA
Cost for capture and sequestration (cents/kWh)	6.2	2.8	3.6	NA	NA
Total cost (cents/kWh)	12.0	9.6	10.1	7.1	8.9-9.8
Total cost with carbon credits at $10-30/ton	6.2-7.9	7-7.7	6.5-8.4	7.1	8.9-9.8

[i] The higher value uses the fuel cost estimate provided above

Figure 10. Comparison of Prices of Various Energy Sources.

Standard & Poor estimates for carbon capture appear pessimistic, and for pulverized coal, unrealistic. A recent International Energy Agency (IEA) analysis of new and existing energy technologies found incremental costs ranging from 2-3 cents/kWh, depending on the fuel (natural gas or coal) and technology used. The IEA values for gas and coal IGCC are only slightly below S&P estimates, while the values for pulverized coal are less than half the S&P estimate, driven mainly by a much lower estimate for efficiency loss. The reasoning behind the pulverized coal analysis is not clear.

Technologies under development might reduce these values to 1.5-2.25 cents/kWh, not including CO_2 transportation and storage (both relatively minor elements). They also do not take credit for possible beneficial use of the carbon dioxide in enhanced oil recovery. For example, at 0.1-0.5 metric tons of oil per ton of CO_2 injected, the credit would range from $30 to $160 per ton of CO_2, substantially diminishing, and perhaps offsetting entirely, costs for capture, transport, and storage.[20] Finally, if carbon is taxed or credits are available for $10-30/ton in national or international markets, coal and gas plant developers may pursue projects without carbon sequestration. This implies that other carbon mitigation options — throughout the economy — may be cheaper than sequestration.

It is important to add that costs for all these technologies can vary widely from nation to nation based on market structure, degree of government involvement (e.g., subsidies or nationalized grid), and access to gas or wind resources. In summary, at foreseeable levels of carbon taxes or cap-and-trade credit approaches ($10-30 per ton of CO_2), nuclear power may be advantaged, but not to the point where it is a compelling choice.

Princeton scientists Stephen Pacala and Rob Socolow have proposed the concept of "stabilization wedges" for coping with the climate change problem for the next 50 years with current technologies.[21] Pacala and Socolow proposed 15 possible wedges covering all sectors of the economy, including agriculture, deforestation, electricity generation, transport efficiency, and fuel supply, among others. Full implementation of seven wedges — or a larger number of partial wedges — would be needed to stabilize atmospheric concentrations of CO_2 at 500 parts per million — a little less than twice pre-industrial levels (280 ppm). One of the possible wedges involved worldwide expansion of nuclear power, essentially doubling current capacity from 370 gigawatts (GWe) to 700 GWe over the 50-year period.

The authors assumed that this capacity would displace efficient coal generation. Over the same period of time, essentially all existing reactors will be retired, so that 1,070 GWe must be built to achieve a wedge. A 42-year projection expressed in megawatts (one gigawatt equals 1,000 megawatts) is shown in Figure 11.

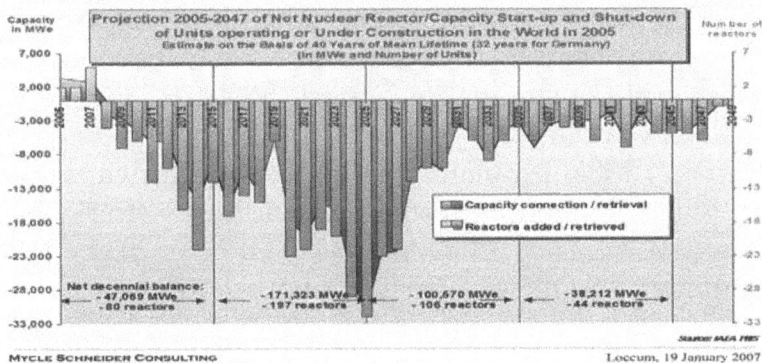

Figure 11. Required Nuclear Reactors to Support Full-Spectrum CO_2 Reduction.

A number of nuclear fuel cycle facilities would either be required, or need to be considered.[22]
• 23 new centrifuge enrichment plants the size of the proposed American Centrifuge Plant in Piketon, Ohio;
• 18 new fuel fabrication plants;
• 10 new repositories the size of the proposed Yucca Mountain facility in Nevada; and,
• 36 new spent fuel reprocessing plants, if all spent fuel were reprocessed.

In addition, if fuel is reprocessed and fabricated into a mixed oxide for use in reactors, a large number of mixed oxide fuel fabrication facilities would be required. The design capacity of the UK Sellafield mixed oxide fuel fabrication plant was 120 tons of heavy metal per year, but 40 tons/year appears to the achievable limit. Potentially, several hundred Sellafield-sized mixed oxide fabrication plants would be required to support extensive worldwide use of plutonium fuel.[23]

Pacala and Socolow did not directly examine the question of whether 1,070 GWe of nuclear capacity and associated fuel cycle facilities could be built over 50 years. National and international forecasts of future nuclear capacity typically do not go beyond existing utility planning horizons of 10-20 years.

A recent analysis by the IEA (*World Energy Outlook*, 2006) estimates that global nuclear capacity in their "Reference" scenario would grow from current levels (about 370 GWe) to 415 GWe by 2030. This implies a net rate of growth of about 2 GWe per year, and is based on optimistic capital ($2000-$2500/kW construction cost) availability and lifecycle costs (4.9-5.7 cents/kWh). It assumes that existing government policies remain largely unchanged. (See Figure 12.)

Electricity Generating Costs

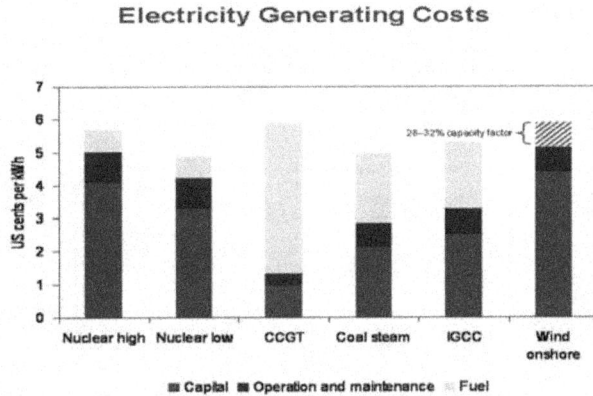

Figure 12. Projected Electrical Generating Costs by Source under Present Policies.

The *World Energy Outlook* also includes an "Alternative Policy" scenario, with widespread efforts to combat global warming and encourage new nuclear construction. This leads to a global capacity of 519 GWe in 2030, for a net growth rate of about 6.5 GWe per year. As Figure 13 shows, growth rates much higher than 2-6.5 GWe per year have been sustained in the past. The circumstances were different—higher estimated rates of growth in demand, substantial margin between estimated cost of nuclear power and alternatives (mainly limited to coal and oil at that time), and greater industrial capacity. It is also not clear that the rate of peak additions was sustainable at the time. Additions since 1996 have been at less than 0.5 GWe per year.

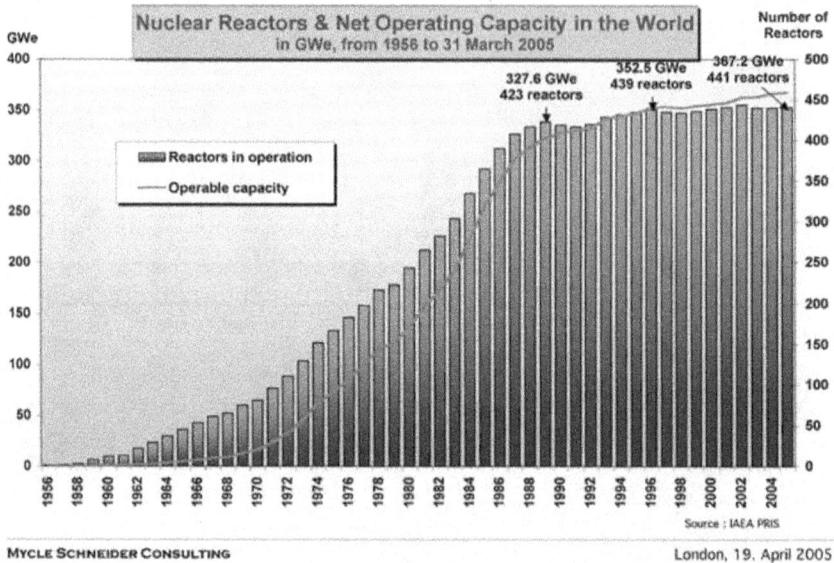

MYCLE SCHNEIDER CONSULTING   London, 19. April 2005

Figure 13. Growth of World Nuclear Energy Capacity, 1956-2005.

IEA's *World Energy Outlook* 2006 acknowledges several important challenges facing any nuclear scale-up: "The expansion of nuclear capacity may, however, face several constraints, such as limits to global capacity to build major components of nuclear power plants, for example pressure vessels and valves, especially for very large reactors. Similar to other industries, short-term constraints that may limit new construction include the cost of raw materials, the difficulty of finding engineering, procurement, and construction contractors and the shortage of key personnel."

In the IEA Reference scenario, nuclear capacity increases at 0.7 percent per year, compared with estimated worldwide electricity demand growth of 2.6 percent per year, so nuclear power's share of generation drops from about 15 to 10 percent. The largest drop occurs in the Organization for Economic Cooperation and Development (OECD) Europe—from 28 to 12 percent in 2030. This does not necessarily mean that OECD Europe CO_2 emissions increase; seven of the 10 largest markets for wind generation are in Europe—the 27 member European Union (EU) accounted for 65 percent of global wind capacity at the end of 2006. Most of the decline is driven by reactor phase-outs (rather than retirements) planned in Germany, Sweden, and Belgium. Increases are projected for China, Japan, India, the United States, Russia, and Korea. Most strikingly, of the net global increase of 48 GWe, 47 GWe occurs outside the OECD (including Japan and Korea) and Russia, that is, in China, India, other Asian nations, the Middle East, and Latin America.

In the Alternative Policy case, OECD Europe reactor phase-outs remain in place, but are deferred 10 years. Nuclear power share of total electricity demand in the OECD stays constant, with Pacific and North American increases offset by European declines. Developing country additions are significant—74 GWe of net additions, 90 percent of which occur in China and India. These additions result in nuclear's share of total generation rising from 2 to 6 percent in China and 2 to 9 percent in India, relative to 2005. The report adds that China has set a target to build 40 GWe of nuclear capacity by 2020, though an earlier target of 20 GWe by 2010 will not be met. In addition, while India announced in May 2006 a new target of 40 GWe nuclear by 2030, India's record of meeting targets is poor. The 10 GWe by 2000 target, set in 1984, was missed by a factor of four.

Similarly, while Russia has announced ambitious plans to complete 10 GWe of new nuclear capacity by

2015, there are many infrastructure challenges associated with this target. Russia has increased nuclear generation by 3 GWe since 1991. In addition to supply-chain challenges like those in the United States, nuclear power rates are much lower than for fossil-fired generation, leaving the industry without sufficient funds to complete new reactors on schedule.

The U.S. Energy Information Administration (EIA) also forecasts global electricity demand, and projected nuclear capacity by nation and region. Estimates for 2030 generally fall between IEA's Reference and Alternative Policy scenarios, with a total of 481 GWe projected for that year. Europe falls off less steeply; OECD Asia expands less quickly, primarily because of lower estimated growth in demand; U.S. capacity rises from 100 GWe in 2004 to 113 GWe in 2030 (see Figure 14).

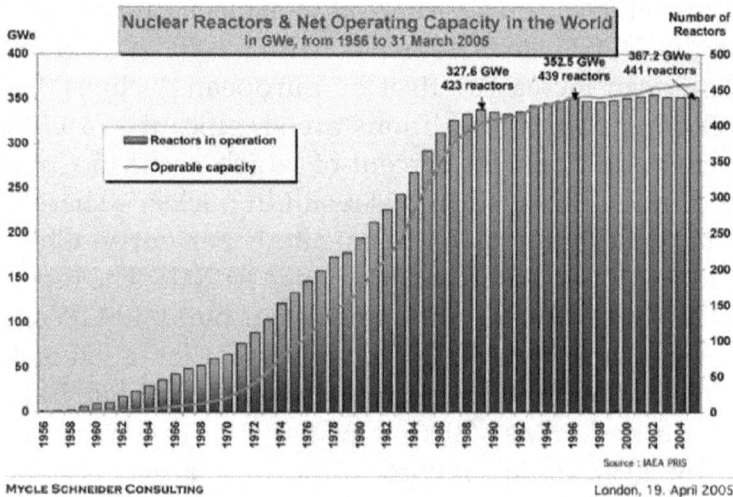

Figure 14. Three Projections of World Nuclear
Energy Capacity to Year 2030.

The short story is that between 2007 and 2030, forecasts for OECD plus Russia show almost no net growth in nuclear capacity. Retirements are roughly offset by additions. In base cases, 72-100 percent of net growth occurs elsewhere, mainly in India and China. Even so, by 2030, nuclear represents only 3-6 percent (from 2 percent today) of electric generation in those two nations. By 2030, net additions are at best about 1/7th of the nuclear wedge.[24] In IEA's Alternative case, with delayed retirements in Europe, about 20 percent of the wedge is completed by 2030. The pace of scheduled retirements quickens rapidly in the ensuing years, however, requiring more than a quadrupling of annual additions to achieve a full wedge by the late 2050s.

Stated differently, it is extremely difficult to achieve a full nuclear wedge by the late 2050s, and may be impossible without expanding nuclear power to a very large number of nations that are short on internal capacity (e.g., Vietnam, Indonesia, Egypt, Saudi Arabia, Iran, Nigeria, Turkey, Mexico, Venezuela, Yemen), which includes a problematic safety culture. Many may want bulk fuel handling facilities (enrichment and perhaps reprocessing and mixed oxide fuel fabrication), which would pose enormous risks of weapons proliferation. Neither the Non Proliferation Treaty, as currently interpreted, nor the International Atomic Energy Agency (IAEA) safeguards regime, as currently implemented, are capable of meeting this challenge.

CONCLUSION

In light of these analyses, what is likely? In the near term, utilities, vendors, subsuppliers, uranium miners, and enrichment plant operators, among oth-

411

ers, are caught in a classic chicken and egg problem. Do utilities dare order now if capacity does not exist; do vendors expand now if orders are not in existence? Between now and 2030, some increase in the U.S. nuclear industry appears probable, given life extensions of existing capacity, high fossil fuel prices, uncertain costs for carbon capture and sequestration technologies, and the incentives or subsidies in the National Environmental Policy (NEP)Act of 2005. That increase in capacity, however, is likely to be quite modest, even in the face of significant, and politically difficult, controls on carbon. Other resources — including coal with purchase of carbon credits, wind, efficiency improvements, gas, and, perhaps, other emerging renewables are broadly competitive.

Internationally, the situation is perhaps more complicated. Clearly we will have new net capacity additions in Asia, particularly in India and China. Many other nations (e.g., Vietnam) have expressed interest in new nuclear capacity. But expressions of interest do not necessarily imply sufficient domestic capacity to pursue this option, or vendor willingness to invest the time and money to pursue it.

Infrastructure in the major nuclear nations — France, the United States, Russia, Germany, and the UK — has fallen off steeply since Three Mile Island and Chernobyl. French confidence and expertise led to a relatively inexpensive turnkey contract with Finland, but it is certainly not a money-maker and could be a major loss leader. Vendors, in general, have less capacity for absorbing losses than utilities.

In essence, the most likely case is that U.S. net nuclear capacity will rise very slightly over the next 15 years. EU nuclear capacity will in all likelihood fall. Growth in China and India will be significant, but may also fall short of either EIA or IEA expectations, primarily because both use extremely optimistic cost estimates. After 2030, the problem becomes more complicated, because the pace of nuclear retirements accelerates. But it is also difficult to predict the future of other low carbon emitting technologies 20 years hence. All will benefit from carbon controls, and it is not at all clear that nuclear power will reemerge as an economically attractive resource worldwide.

One can only get to that conclusion by assuming that near-term orders will be driven by major orders in India and China that lead to infrastructure expansion worldwide; that this expansion alleviates supply-chain imbalances in key equipment, contractors, and crews; that the expansion can respond successfully to a huge ramp-up to replace existing capacity after 2020; and that the expansion is not eclipsed by improvements in energy efficiency and renewables in the interim.

ENDNOTES - CHAPTER 12

1. Jonathan Koomey and Hultman Nate, "A Reactor-Level Analysis of Busbar Costs for U.S. nuclear plants, 1970-2005," *Energy Policy*, 2007.

2. This covers the range estimated in studies by the University of Chicago and MIT, as well the U.S. Energy Information Administration estimate for advanced U.S. light water reactors.

3. John Deutch and Ernest Moniz *et al.*, *The Future of Nuclear Power — An Interdisciplinary MIT Study*, Washington, DC: MIT, 2003.

4. American Electric Power, Nickel, Copper — London Metal Exchange; Cement, Iron, Steel & Heavy Construction, Washington, DC: U.S. Bureau of Labor Statistics.

5. Early year costs can be substantially higher in real dollars than life cycle levelized costs.

6. "Supply Chain Could Slow the Path to Construction, Officials Say," *Nucleonics Week*, February 15, 2007, Comments by Ray Ganthner of Areva.

7. *Ibid.*

8. *Ibid.*

9. "GE/Toshiba, Advanced Boiling Water Reactor Cost and Schedule at TVA's Bellefonte Site," August 2005, pp. 4.1-2, 4.1-23.

10. "A Missing Generation of Nuclear Energy Workers," *NPR Marketplace*, April 26, 2007; "Vendors Relative Risk Rising in New Nuclear Power Markets," *Nucleonics Week*, January 18, 2007, available from *marketplace.publicradio.org/shows/2007/04/26/PM200704265.html*.

11. "Lack of Complete Design Blamed for Problems at Olkiluoto 3," *Nucleonics Week*, May 17, 2007"; Areva Official Says Olkiluoto 3 Provides Lessons for Future Work," *Nucleonics Week*, May 3, 2007.

12. Jim Harding, *Caro Nucleare*, Toscany, Italy: Amici della Terra, 1984.

13. Florida and South Carolina have adopted legislation that permits recovery of annual construction costs in current rates following an annual prudence review.

14. Many public utility commissions cannot by statute include investment expenses in rates until the underlying resource is "used and useful."

15. Jim Hempstead, "New Nuclear Generation: Ratings Pressure Increasing," Moody's *New Nuclear Generation*, June 2009.

16. "DOE's Loan Guarantee Proposal Raises Questions About Viability," *Nucleonics Week*, May 17, 2007. Production tax credits of 1.8 cents/kWh, for 8 years are also available for low emissions

technologies, though these benefits do not start until commercial operation.

17. MIT, "The Future of Nuclear Power," 2003; and Joskow, "Future Prospects for Nuclear-A U.S. Perspective," Presentation at University of Paris, Dauphine, France, May 2006.

18. Dr. Thomas Neff, "Dynamic Relationships Between Uranium and SWU Prices: A New Equilibrium, Building the Nuclear Future: Challenges and Opportunities," Cambridge, MA: Center for International Studies, MIT, 2006.

19. "Which Power Generation Technologies Will Take the Lead in Response to Carbon Controls?" *Standard & Poor's Viewpoint*, May 11, 2007.

20. *Energy Technology Perspectives in Support of the G8 Plan of Action – Scenarios and Strategies to 2050*, Paris, France: International Energy Agency, 2006.

21. Stephen Pacala and Robert Socolow, "Stabilization Wedges: Solving the Climate Problem for the Next 50 Years with Current Technologies," *Science*, August 13, 2004, Vol. 305., No. 5686, pp. 968-972.

22. These calculations were performed by Tom Cochran, senior scientist and nuclear program director, Natural Resources Defense Council, in connection with a Keystone Center joint fact-finding effort examining the future of nuclear power. See Keystone Center Nuclear Power Joint Fact-Finding, June 2007, available from *keystone.org/files/file/about/publications/Final...*

23. The French Melox mixed oxide fuel fabrication plant is licensed for 170 tons of fuel production per year.

24. Seven full wedges are needed over 50 years to stabilize atmospheric concentrations of CO_2 at twice pre-industrial levels.

PART VI

WITHDRAWING FROM AND ENFORCING
THE NPT — ARTICLE X

CHAPTER 13

LOCKING DOWN THE NUCLEAR
NONPROLIFERATION TREATY*

Henry Sokolski and Victor Gilinsky

The Nuclear NonProliferation Treaty (NPT) is no longer adequate to stop member countries from pursuing nuclear weapons. One of the treaty's more distressing inadequacies is that it is too easy for countries who signed the NPT to leave it, à la North Korea.

As a way of strengthening the NPT, the United States must insist that North Korea is still obligated by the treaty, and do the same for Iran if Tehran attempts to leave the NPT. President Barack Obama recently spoke of the NPT's importance, as has every President since Lyndon B. Johnson who signed the treaty in 1968. Yet they have all, to a lesser or greater degree, weakened the treaty through lax enforcement, by carving out exceptions for certain countries, or by just ignoring it. We have come to the point now that North Korea, which signed the treaty in 1985, is now mocking it. And in all the discussions over a possible Iranian bomb, no one seems to think the treaty's 90-day withdrawal clause would be much of a hurdle if Tehran decided to leave the NPT.

If President Obama really wants to strengthen the treaty, a good—and necessary—place to start is to make it much more difficult for any of the 189 member

---

*Originally published in the *Bulletin of Atomic Scientists,* June 17, 2009, available from *www.thebulletin.org/web-edition/op-eds/locking-down-the-npt.*

states to leave the NPT. It is at odds with the NPT's purpose to allow a country to import or develop technology under the treaty's cover and then walk away from it to make bombs. At a minimum, before legally exiting the treaty, a country should have to clear its NPT obligations by returning whatever it got from others acting on the understanding that the departee was a good-faith treaty member.

The background of the North Korean bomb is instructive. The International Atomic Energy Agency (IAEA), of which the United States is the most prominent member, allowed North Korea to drag out its obligation to undergo a thorough initial IAEA inspection within 18 months of signing and ratifying the NPT. The inspection did not start until 1992, by which time Pyongyang already had illicitly separated plutonium. When the inspectors insisted on inspecting two waste sites that might reveal this, the North Koreans tossed them out and threatened to pull out of the treaty altogether.

The international reaction to this behavior was not to treat North Korea as an NPT violator, but to beseech it to remain in the treaty. The United States went so far as to offer two large light water reactors (with South Korea and Japan footing the $5 billion bill), and to agree to shield the North for years from the NPT's inspection requirements in return for a halt in North Korean plutonium production. When it later looked as if Washington would ultimately insist on inspection, the North announced it was withdrawing from the treaty anyway. This led to much diplomatic hand-wringing in member capitals, but not a peep that Pyongyang couldn't legally quit the NPT.

Such a permissive interpretation of the withdrawal clause must change to one that conforms to the treaty's purpose—no matter how awkward or late in the game. The international community should insist that North Korea is still an NPT member and that, among its other obligations, it must permit the basic IAEA inspections that never took place in 1992.

The predictable reaction to this proposal, in some quarters, will be that North Korea's actions cannot be reversed by international pressure, and that the NPT's withdrawal clause, which was made deliberately permissive to entice prospective member states, cannot be reinterpreted. Yet, Defense Secretary Robert Gates has already committed the United States to reversing North Korea's nuclear status, and, if we do not reinterpret the treaty, we will be writing Gates's declaration off as a serious commitment. International legal obligations do matter, and being branded as a treaty violator has consequences internationally. Even Pyongyang seems to sense this and keeps repeating that it acted legally in leaving the NPT. For example, in its June 14, 1994, statement defending its right to test nuclear weapons it insisted, "[North Korea's] second nuclear test . . . does not run counter to any international law."[1]

To make a new approach stick, we will need the broad support of NPT members. But that will not happen until the United States steps forward to announce a new and tougher standard for withdrawal. This might not be welcomed by those self-styled realists who believe that insistence on strict NPT compliance gets in the way of reaching accommodations with difficult countries. But a permissive approach did not work with North Korea and has done great harm to the treaty overall.

Which brings us to Iran: Tehran imported considerable nuclear technology as a treaty member, most prominently from Russia for its Bushehr nuclear power plant project. We should make it clear now that if it, or any other country, chooses to withdraw from the NPT, they would be obligated to return or cease using such imports before they could clear their treaty accounts. Lacking that, they would be international outlaws. Raising the bar to withdrawal is an essential first step in strengthening the treaty to deter would-be bomb makers.

ENDNOTES - CHAPTER 13

1. See Martin Facklor, "North Korea Vows to Produce Nuclear Weapons," *The New York Times*, June 13, 2009, available from *www.nytimes.com/2009/06/14/world/asia/14korea.html-r=/&hp*.

CHAPTER 14

ENFORCING THE
NUCLEAR NONPROLIFERATION TREATY
AND
INTERNATIONAL ATOMIC ENERGY
AGENCY COMPLIANCE*

By Pierre Goldschmidt

Compliance with safeguards obligations is a fundamental part of a country's responsibility in the global nuclear nonproliferation regime. The issue of compliance was central to the contentious discussions at the 2005 Nuclear Nonproliferation Treaty (NPT) Review Conference and is likely to play a similar role at the 2010 conference.

The main objective of the International Atomic Energy Agency (IAEA), as set out in its statute, is to promote "the contribution of atomic energy to peace, health, and prosperity throughout the world" while ensuring that nuclear material, equipment, facilities, and information are not used for any military purpose.[1] The IAEA carries out the latter part of this mandate by establishing and implementing safeguards, including inspections.

In fulfilling its nonproliferation mandate, the most important task of the IAEA is the prompt detection and reporting of unauthorized nuclear work in any non-nuclear-weapon state that is a party to the NPT.

---

*This article was originally published as "Safeguards Noncompliance: A Challenge for the IAEA and the UN Security Council" *Arms Control Today*, January/February 2010, available from *www.armscontrol.org/act/2010_01-02/Goldschmidt*.

This unauthorized work may involve the diversion of nuclear material from declared facilities as well as undeclared nuclear material and activities.

IAEA inspections are designed to ensure that countries are complying with their commitments under their safeguards agreements. The United Nations (UN) Security Council indicated the importance of noncompliance by addressing it in the first operative paragraph of Resolution 1887, which the council adopted on September 24, 2009, during the UN summit on nonproliferation and disarmament.[2]

Nevertheless, the international community must go beyond that resolution by adopting a refined and strengthened approach toward cases of safeguards noncompliance. Such an approach, as discussed below, has several elements. One element is how the IAEA Department of Safeguards should distinguish between cases of noncompliance that should be reported to the IAEA Board of Governors as "noncompliance" in accordance with Article XII.c of the IAEA statute, on one hand, and cases that constitute only technical or legal compliance failures and therefore need be reported (if at all) only in the annual Safeguards Implementation Report, on the other.[3] The board, when it finds that the agency is unable to resolve a case of noncompliance promptly, should not hesitate to request additional verification rights from the UN Security Council. The latter, in turn, should take steps to improve the likelihood of prompt and effective action when confronted with persistent cases of noncompliance or with withdrawal from the NPT.

THE SAFEGUARD DEPARTMENT'S ROLE

In examining IAEA responsibilities, it is necessary

to draw a distinction between the roles of the secretariat and those of the board of governors. The IAEA secretariat is the technical arm of the agency in charge of detecting any technical or legal noncompliance with the safeguards agreements concluded between the IAEA and a state. The secretariat is expected to perform this task in the most objective and nondiscriminatory way possible, without the influence of political considerations.

The fact that there is no official definition of what constitutes noncompliance should not be used as an excuse by the secretariat for not reporting promptly, fully, and factually any significant or intentional failure or breach of safeguards undertakings, including those of agreed "subsidiary arrangements."[4]

In judging whether a failure is intentional, the Department of Safeguards within the secretariat should, *inter alia*, take into account whether any state organization, including the state system of accounting for and control of nuclear material, knew of undeclared nuclear material (whatever its quantity), facilities, or activities that should have been declared to the IAEA. Denying access to a declared or suspected facility or location, as well as not allowing inspectors to take environmental samples as requested by the IAEA, is by definition intentional. If such a denial is prolonged, for example, more than a few days unless for legitimate safety reasons, it must be promptly reported by the Department of Safeguards to the IAEA director-general as a matter of concern. If the Department of Safeguards has the legal authority under the safeguards agreement to require such access, then the denial constitutes noncompliance.

Experience has taught that denial of prompt access to locations or refusal to take environmental samples has often been an indication of undeclared activities. This has been the case in Iran, North Korea, South Korea, and possibly Syria. Denial of access to relevant persons and documents should also be taken seriously. It should be reported explicitly, either in the Safeguards Implementation Report or in a report to the board, if the denial prevents the agency from promptly resolving questions or inconsistencies. This is particularly so if it is not the first time that access has been denied or if it takes place in conjunction with other failures or breaches of safeguards obligations.

Evidence of intentional concealment measures or the "obstruction of the activities of IAEA inspectors, interference with the operation of safeguards equipment, or prevention of the IAEA from carrying out its verification activities,"[5] should be reported as noncompliance. Nuclear material that should have been declared and placed under safeguards but intentionally has not been also warrants a finding of noncompliance. To warrant a report of noncompliance to the board, it is not necessary for the Department of Safeguards to demonstrate that the "intention" of not declaring nuclear material or activities was part of a nuclear weapons program; it is enough that the purpose was unknown.[6]

The Department of Safeguards should adopt as a guideline the position stated by Director-General Mohamed El Baradei in November 2002: "I believe that while differing circumstances may necessitate asymmetric responses, in the case of non-compliance with non-proliferation obligations, for the credibility of the regime, the approach in all cases should be one and the same: zero tolerance."[7] In accordance with that principle, the secretariat should have classified the failures and breaches committed by South Korea and

Egypt[8] as cases of noncompliance.[9]

By reporting in November 2003 that Iran was "in breach of its obligation to comply with the provisions of the Safeguards Agreements," instead of using the word "noncompliance," the term that the IAEA statute uses, El Baradei deliberately left to the board the sole responsibility for making a formal finding of noncompliance. This ambiguous language may have played a role in politicizing what should have remained the purely technical and factual work of the secretariat.[10]

The assessment of Libya's violations of its safeguards agreement reported to the board in February 2004 was even more disturbing. Although, in addition to the reported violations, Libya admitted that it had received documentation related to nuclear weapons design and fabrication and more or less explicitly acknowledged that it had a nuclear weapons program, El Baradei did not use the term "noncompliance." This set a bad precedent and amounted to a direct contradiction of his 2002 statement cited above. Fortunately, the board found Libya in noncompliance and requested the director-general to "report the matter to the Security Council *for information purposes only*, while commending [Libya] for the actions it has taken to date, and has agreed to take, to remedy the noncompliance."[11] The Security Council held a meeting on April 22, 2004, to consider the matter and, via its president, welcomed Libya's active cooperation with the IAEA and its decision to abandon its weapons of mass destruction (WMD) programs.

Finding a state in noncompliance with its safeguards agreement is not the only reason for the IAEA to submit reports to the Security Council. If, in the course of their duties, Department of Safeguards inspectors encounter "questions that are within the competence of the Security Council as the organ bearing the main responsibility for the maintenance of international peace and security," the IAEA statute suggests that these questions should be reported to the board and then by the board to the Security Council.[12] In addition, paragraph 19 of the Comprehensive Safeguards Agreement gives the board the power to find a state in noncompliance if "the Agency is not able to verify that there has been no diversion of nuclear material." In other words, a finding of noncompliance by the board does not require the Department of Safeguards to verify that there has been a diversion. Noncooperation by a state, thus preventing the Agency from verifying that no diversion has taken place, can be sufficient grounds for charging noncompliance.[13]

One nonproliferation official recently said that when it comes to unanswered questions, obstruction, or access denials, the same significance should be ascribed "to the inability of the Agency to conclude absence of undeclared activities as to a finding of non-compliance."[14] According to the official, "[T]he experience accumulated over the last 20 years clearly indicates that a 'smoke screen' usually is as telling and dangerous as a 'smoking gun'."[15]

In summary, the IAEA statute requires the director-general to transmit to the board all noncompliance reports made by the Department of Safeguards. Unlike the board, the secretariat is expected to act as a technical and totally apolitical body so as to maintain its reputation of objectivity and impartiality.

It will be one of the main tasks of the new director-general, Yukiya Amano, to restore member states' confidence that the IAEA secretariat will promptly, fully, and factually report on safeguards noncompliance in accordance with the agency's statute.

HANDLING NONCOMPLIANCE REPORTS

The IAEA board of governors, which is a political body, must decide if the safeguards breaches and failures reported by the secretariat, whether or not the term "noncompliance" has been used, constitute noncompliance under the statute and, if so, when they must be reported to the UN Security Council. The statute does not specify the criteria that the board should use to arrive at a finding. Given the difference in roles between the board and the secretariat, the criteria may not be the same as those used by the secretariat in determining whether technical or legal noncompliance must be reported to the board.

The goal here is not to focus the debate on whether the board should have found South Korea and Egypt in noncompliance in 2004 and 2005, respectively, and thereafter reported the cases to the Security Council for information purposes only. In the case of South Korea, which had ratified an additional protocol and subsequently fully cooperated with the IAEA, there was no need for Security Council action. Thanks to South Korea's cooperation, the agency was able to conclude in 2007 that the country did not have any undeclared nuclear material or activities and that all nuclear material remained in a peaceful mode.

In the case of Egypt, the IAEA did not find any indication that the reported failures and breaches were part of concealment efforts or a deception strategy. As in the case of South Korea, there was no indication in Egypt of any military involvement in or connection with nuclear-related activities. Because Egypt does not have an additional protocol in force, however, the IAEA is not in a position to conclude that there are no undeclared nuclear material and activities in the state as a whole. Also, as reported in the 2008 Safeguards Implementation Report, the IAEA has so far been unable to identify the source of the highly enriched uranium and low-enriched uranium particles found in environmental samples taken at the Egyptian Nuclear Research Center at Inshas. The fact that there are still open questions about Egypt's nuclear activities almost 5 years after the failures and breaches were first reported to the board should be a cause of concern. Progress on these issues should be reported to the board separately from the Safeguards Implementation Report. These long-standing open questions help demonstrate why the board should have at least adopted resolutions expressing its concern, as El Baradei did in his reports, about the failures and breaches discovered in South Korea and Egypt, even if the board found it unnecessary to make a finding of noncompliance under the statute.

In the case of Iran, the IAEA board adopted in September 2003 a resolution calling on that country to "suspend all further uranium enrichment-related activities, including the further introduction of nuclear material into [the] Natanz [enrichment plant] . . . pending provision by the Director General of the assurances required by Member States, and pending satisfactory application of the provisions of the additional protocol."[16] The resolution also called on Iran to grant "unrestricted access, including environmental sampling, for the Agency to whatever locations the Agency deems necessary for the purposes of verification of the correctness and completeness of Iran's declarations."[17]

In the spring of 2004, it already had become apparent that Iran was not abiding by the September 2003 resolution. In a resolution adopted on June 18, 2004, the board acknowledged "the statement by the Director General on 14 June that it is essential for the integrity and credibility of the inspection process to bring these issues to a close within the next few months."[18] Apparently, the international community subsequently lost sight of the importance of this time factor. Once a significant or deliberate breach of safeguards agreements has been identified, or a state obstructs or delays verification activities, as is presently the case also in Syria, action by the board and possibly by the UN Security Council becomes urgent.[19]

In its September 18, 2004, resolution, the board noted "with serious concern that . . . Iran has not heeded repeated calls from the Board to suspend, as a confidence building measure, all enrichment-related and reprocessing activities."[20] It was clear by then that the IAEA needed legally binding verification rights extending beyond those provided under the Model Additional Protocol. Only the UN Security Council, by adopting a resolution under Chapter 7 of the UN Charter, which addresses threats to international peace and security, is in a position to provide those legal rights to the IAEA secretariat. Its board cannot.

It was only after Iran's August 2005 breach of its November 2004 expanded commitment to suspend the conversion of uranium concentrates to uranium hexafluoride that the board found Iran to have been noncompliant. The vote on the September 24, 2005, resolution was 22-1, with 12 abstentions.

One good thing about the September 2005 resolution is that the board found "that Iran's many failures and breaches of its obligation to comply with its NPT Safeguards Agreement, as detailed in [the November 10, 2003 report to the board] constitute non compliance in the context of Article XII.C" of the statute.[21] By confirming that the findings reported in November 2003 constituted noncompliance, the board mitigated the unhelpful precedent it had set at that time by refraining from a noncompliance finding. However, by the time the board, on February 4, 2006, finally decided to report the noncompliance to the Security Council[22] and 10 months later the Security Council adopted a resolution that legally required Iran to suspend its enrichment-related activities,[23] it was too late to stop Iran from disregarding these directives.

THE SECURITY COUNCIL'S ROLE

Under the statute, a country that the IAEA board finds to be in noncompliance must be referred to the Security Council. The board is not obliged to make this report immediately if it wishes to give the noncompliant state sufficient time to implement the necessary corrective actions. If the noncompliant state fully and proactively cooperates with the agency, the board will refer the case to the council for information purposes only, while likely praising the state for its constructive attitude, as it did in the case of Libya. If the noncompliant state uses delaying and deceptive tactics and does not provide prompt access to locations, equipment, documents, and relevant persons, the agency may temporarily need from the UN Security Council legally binding expanded verification rights.

As exemplified by the cases of Iran and North Korea, one of the greatest difficulties in deterring states from violating their nonproliferation undertakings and from ignoring legally binding Security Council resolutions is their hope that, for geopolitical or economic reasons, at least one of the five veto-wielding members of the council will oppose the adoption of effective sanctions. To guarantee a timely council reaction in cases of noncompliance with safeguards agreements and to increase the likelihood of negative consequences for a state that does not comply with council and IAEA resolutions, the council should adopt a generic — that is, not state-specific — resolution under Chapter 7 of the UN Charter.[24] To give the IAEA the verification tools it needs in case a noncompliant state does not adequately cooperate with the agency to resolve pending issues, the resolution should provide that, "upon request by the agency," the Security Council would automatically adopt a specific resolution under Chapter 7 requiring that the state grant the IAEA extended access rights, as set out in a "temporary complementary protocol."[25] These rights would be terminated as soon as the IAEA secretariat and board have drawn the conclusion that the country has no undeclared nuclear material or activities and that its declarations to the IAEA are correct and complete.

Under the multistage process foreseen in this generic resolution, if the IAEA director-general were unable to report within 60 days of the adoption of the state-specific resolution that the noncompliant state was fully implementing the temporary complementary protocol, the Security Council would adopt a second specific resolution requiring the state to suspend immediately all enrichment-and reprocessing-related activities.

If the noncompliant state further refused to implement the relevant Security Council resolutions fully, the Security Council would adopt a third Chapter 7 resolution calling on all states to suspend military cooperation, including the supply of equipment, with the noncompliant state as long as it remained in noncompliance with council and IAEA resolutions. A prior council agreement that all military cooperation with that state would be suspended in these circumstances should constitute a strong disincentive for states to defy legally binding council resolutions.

Had such a generic resolution existed before 2002, the foreign ministers of France, Germany, and the United Kingdom (the EU-3) would not have negotiated the October 2003 deal in Tehran. Under that deal, Iran agreed "voluntarily to suspend all enrichment activities as defined by the IAEA,"[26] while the September 2003 board resolution had called on Iran to suspend all further enrichment-related activities, a term that is much broader in scope. In exchange for this limited and nonbinding pledge to the EU-3, Iran received the tacit commitment of the three countries not to support an IAEA resolution referring Iran's noncompliance to the Security Council. By failing to find Iran in noncompliance in November 2003, the IAEA board created a damaging precedent with far-reaching consequences that are still felt today.

WITHDRAWING FROM THE NPT

Another particularly threatening case for international peace and security is the withdrawal from the NPT of a non-nuclear-weapon state that has been found by the IAEA to be in noncompliance with its safeguards agreement. As has been stressed on many occasions, the great benefit that the NPT brings to the international community would be dangerously eroded if countries violating their safeguards agreements or the NPT felt free to withdraw from the treaty, develop nuclear weapons, and enjoy the fruits of their violation with impunity.

To address this issue, the Security Council should adopt under Chapter 7 of the UN Charter another generic and legally binding resolution, stating that a country's withdrawal from the NPT (an undisputed right under the treaty's Article X.1) after being found by the IAEA to be in noncompliance with its safeguards undertakings constitutes a threat to international peace and security, under Article 39 of the UN Charter.[27] This generic resolution should also provide that, under these circumstances, all materials and equipment made available to such a state or resulting from the assistance provided to it under a comprehensive safeguards agreement would have to be sealed by the IAEA and, as soon as technically possible, removed from that state under IAEA supervision and remain under agency safeguards. If the state still refused to comply, then any military cooperation between that state and other UN member states would be suspended.

Another important preventive measure would be for the IAEA board to urge all states with enrichment or reprocessing facilities to conclude back-up safeguards agreements that would not terminate in case of NPT withdrawal.[28]

CONCLUSION

IAEA safeguards play a key role in the international community's attempts to ensure that nuclear energy is used in non-nuclear-weapon states exclusively for peaceful purposes. By deterring states from seeking nuclear weapons, safeguards play a major role in preventing proliferation. Yet, deterrence can be effective only if states believe that noncompliance has a strong chance of being detected and if its detection has consequences.

President Barack Obama noted both elements in his 2009 speech in Prague: "We need more resources and authority to strengthen international inspections. We need real and immediate consequences for countries caught breaking the rules or trying to leave the treaty without cause."[29]

The IAEA should not be complacent toward states violating their nonproliferation undertakings. That said, the weakest link in the nonproliferation regime today is not the performance of the IAEA Department of Safeguards but that of the international community in responding to noncompliance. The burden here falls largely on the IAEA board and the UN Security Council.

The adoption of UN Security Council Resolution 1887, which emphasizes that noncompliance with nonproliferation obligations must be brought to the attention of the Security Council, is a significant but insufficient step in the right direction. It is a call for states to strengthen the NPT and to comply fully with all their obligations, to ratify the Comprehensive Test Ban Treaty, to adopt stricter national controls for the export of sensitive nuclear fuel-cycle technologies, and more. However, states are not obliged to follow the recommendations contained in the resolution.

Therefore, states should discuss and agree on legally binding generic procedures for responding to noncompliance. Because members of the Security Council would not know which states might be involved in the future, such discussions should be easier and less acrimonious than they are during the heat of a crisis involving specific target countries. An agreement on a set of standard responses to be applied evenhandedly to any state found in noncompliance, regardless of its allies, would significantly enhance the credibility of the nonproliferation regime.

Finally, considering the precedent that North Korea set in 2003, it is necessary to plan for the possibility of another state withdrawing from the NPT. The most critical step would be for the Security Council to adopt a resolution, under Chapter 7 of the UN Charter, deciding that the withdrawal of a noncompliant state from the NPT would be considered a threat to international peace and security.

If adopted, the concrete measures recommended in this chapter would make a real difference in protecting against nuclear proliferation; but all countries, not only the five permanent members of the Security Council, will first need to acknowledge that these measures should be adopted now in order to mitigate the consequences of the next potential proliferation crisis. Protecting against that dangerous prospect is in everyone's best security interest.

ENDNOTES - CHAPTER 14

1. "Statute of the IAEA," Vienna, Austria: International Atomic Energy Agency, available from *www.iaea.org/About/statute_text.html* (hereinafter IAEA Statute).

2. UN Security Council, Resolution 1887, S/RES/1887, September 24, 2009, available from *www.un.org/News/Press/docs/2009/sc9746.doc.htm*.

3. The Safeguards Implementation Report, submitted every year to the board, provides a description and analysis of the agency's safeguards operations during the previous year, including a summary of the problems encountered and the secretariat's findings and conclusions.

4. Article 39 of the Comprehensive Safeguards Agreement provides that "the Agency and the State shall make Subsidiary

Arrangements which shall specify in detail . . . how the procedures laid down in the Agreement are to be applied."

5. "IAEA Safeguards Glossary, 2001 Edition," p. 14, para. 2.3.(d), Vienna, Austria: IAEA, available from *www-pub.iaea.org/MTCD/publications/PDF/nvs-3-cd/PDF/NVS3_prn.pdf*.

6. "The Structure and Content of Agreements Between the Agency and States Required in Connection With the Treaty On the Non-Proliferation of Nuclear Weapons," INFCIRC/153 (corrected), Vienna, Austria: IAEA, June 1972, para. 28, available from *www.iaea.org/Publications/Documents/Infcircs/Others/infcirc153.pdf*.

7. "Reinforcing the World's Regime Against Nuclear Weapons," Vienna, Austria: IAEA, November 14, 2002, available from *www.iaea.org/NewsCenter/News/2002/11-13-903199.shtml*.

8. "Implementation of the NPT Safeguards Agreement in the Republic of Korea: Report by the Director General," GOV/2004/84, Vienna, Austria: IAEA, November 11, 2004, para. 38, available from *www.iaea.org/Publications/Documents/Board/2004/gov2004-84.pdf*; "Implementation of the NPT Safeguards Agreement in the Arab Republic of Egypt: Report by the Director General," GOV/2005/9, Vienna, Austria: IAEA, February 14, 2005, para. 22, available from *www.carnegieendowment.org/static/npp/reports/gov2005-9.pdf*.

9. See Pierre Goldschmidt, "Exposing Nuclear Noncompliance," *Survival*, Vol. 51, No. 1, February-March 2009, pp. 143-163, available from *www.carnegieendowment.org/publications/index.cfm?fa=view&id=22734&prog=zgp&proj=znpp*.

10. "Implementation of the NPT Safeguards Agreement in the Islamic Republic of Iran: Report by the Director General," GOV/2005/75, Vienna, Austria: IAEA, November 10, 2003, available from *www.iaea.org/Publications/Documents/Board/2003/gov2003-75.pdf*. Another factor was that the report on Iran stated that, "[t]o date, there is no evidence that the previously undeclared nuclear material and activities referred to above were related to a nuclear weapons programme." This formulation set the bar too high for the agency by suggesting that evidence of a nuclear weapons program was required for a finding of noncompliance.

11. "Implementation of the NPT Safeguards Agreement of the Socialist People's Libyan Arab Jamahiriya," GOV/2004/ 18, Vienna, Austria: IAEA, March 10, 2004, para. 4, available from *www.iaea.org/Publications/Documents/Board/2004/gov2004-18.pdf* (emphasis added).

12. IAEA Statute, art. III.B.4. These questions would cover areas such as nuclear weaponization-related activities.

13 . James Acton, e-mail communication with author, October 23, 2009.

14. Nonproliferation official, e-mail communication with author, November 28, 2009.

15. *Ibid.*

16. "Implementation of the NPT Safeguards Agreement in the Islamic Republic of Iran," GOV/2003/69, Vienna, Austria: IAEA, September 12, 2003, para. 3, available from *www.iaea.org/ Publications/Documents/Board/2003/gov2003-69.pdf.*

17. *Ibid.,* para. 4(ii).

18. "Implementation of the NPT Safeguards Agreement in the Islamic Republic of Iran," GOV/2004/49, Vienna, Austria: IAEA, June 18, 2004, para. l, available from *www.iaea.org/Publications/ Documents/Board/2004/gov2004-49.pdf.*

19. As John Carlson recently wrote,

A judgment on noncompliance cannot wait until the state has succeeded in acquiring nuclear weapons. If the standard of proof is set too high, the IAEA is bound to fail in its responsibility to provide the international community with timely warning. To prove the existence of a nuclear weapons program is unrealistic. A state having a nuclear weapon or nuclear weapons components or conducting weaponization experiments with nuclear material is unlikely to be caught red-handed. More likely, a state facing obvious exposure would deny inspectors access to the location concerned, preferring to argue whether lack of cooperation constitutes noncompliance, maintaining some ambiguity about its actions. When the board determines that a state has intentionally not declared nuclear material, it must initially presume that the material was not intended for peaceful purposes. The smoking gun is the failure to declare nuclear material.

John Carlson, "Defining Noncompliance: NPT Safeguards Agreements," *Arms Control Today*, May 2009, pp. 22-27, available from *www.armscontrol.org/act/2009_5/Carlson*.

20. "Implementation of the NPT Safeguards Agreement in the Islamic Republic of Iran," GOV/2004/79, Vienna, Austria: IAEA, September 18, 2004, para. d, available from *www.iaea.org/Publications/Documents/Board/2004/gov2004-79.pdf*.

21. "Implementation of the NPT Safeguards Agreement in the Islamic Republic of Iran," GOV/2005/79, Vienna, Austria: IAEA, September 24, 2005, para. 1, available from *www.iaea.org/Publications/Documents/Board/2005/gov2005-77.pdf*.

22. Cuba, Syria, and Venezuela voted against the resolution, and five states (Algeria, Belarus, Libya, Indonesia, and South Africa) abstained.

23. UN Security Council, Resolution 1737, S/RES/1737, December 23, 2006.

24. Pierre Goldschmidt, "Concrete Steps to Improve the Nonproliferation Regime," Carnegie Papers, No. 100, April 2009, available from *www.carnegieendowment.org/publications/index.cfm?fa=view&id=22943&prog=zgp&proj=znpp*. Annex I provides a potential model for such a resolution.

25. *Ibid.*, pp. 27-43.

26. Statement by the Iranian Government and visiting EU Foreign Ministers, October 21, 2003, available from *www.iaea.org/NewsCenter/Focus/IaeaIran/statement_iran21102003.shtml*.

27. See generally Goldschmidt, "Concrete Steps to Improve the Nonproliferation Regime." See Annex II for the proposed model resolution.

28. A Comprehensive Safeguards Agreement (INFCIRC/153 corrected) remains in force only for so long as the state remains party to the NPT, whereas under an INFCIRC/66-type agreement, all nuclear material supplied or produced under that agreement would remain under safeguards, even if the state withdraws from the NPT, until such time as the IAEA has determined that such material is no longer subject to safeguards.

29. Office of the Press Secretary, The White House, "Remarks by President Barack Obama," April 5, 2009, available from *www.whitehouse.gov/the_press_office/Remarks-By-President-Barack-Obama-In-Prague-As-Delivered.*

ABOUT THE CONTRIBUTORS

CHRISTOPHER FORD is Director of the Center for Technology and Global Security at the Hudson Institute. Until September 2008, he served as U.S. Special Representative for Nuclear Nonproliferation. Previously, Mr. Ford was Principal Deputy Assistant Secretary of State in Bureau of Verification, Compliance, and Implementation. His service on various Senate committee staffs includes Minority Counsel and General Counsel to the U.S. Senate Select Committee on Intelligence, Staff Director and Chief Counsel to the Permanent Subcommittee on Investigations, Chief Investigative Counsel to the Governmental Affairs Committee, national security advisor to Senator Susan Collins (R-ME), and an investigative lawyer for campaign finance investigations led by Senator Fred Thompson (R-TN). Mr. Ford also served briefly as Assistant Counsel to the Intelligence Oversight Board at the White House in 1996. His publications include The Admirals' Advantage: U.S. Navy Operational Intelligence in World War II and the Cold War.

VICTOR GILINSKY is an independent energy consultant and former Nuclear Regulatory Commissioner under Presidents Ford, Carter, and Reagan. He has been active on nonproliferation issues for many years, going back to his early work for RAND in Santa Monica, California. In 1971 Dr. Gilinsky moved to the Atomic Energy Commission in Washington, DC, where he was Assistant Director for Policy and Program Review. From 1973 to 1975, he was head of the RAND Physical Sciences Department. From 1975 to 1984, he served on the Nuclear Regulatory Commission, having been appointed by President Gerald Ford and reappointed by President Jimmy Carter. During his NRC tenure, Dr. Gilinsky was heavily involved in nuclear-export issues. Dr. Gilinsky holds a Ph.D. in physics from the California Institute of Technology.

PIERRE GOLDSCHMIDT is a nonresident senior associate at the Carnegie Endowment. Mr. Goldschmidt is also a member of the Board of Directors for the Association Vinçotte Nuclear (AVN). AVN is a non-profit, Authorized Inspection Organization charged with verifying compliance of nuclear power plants with Belgian safety regulation. Mr. Goldschmidt was the Deputy Director General, Head of the Department of Safeguards, at the International Atomic Energy Agency from 1999 to June 2005. Before the IAEA, he was Director General of SYNATOM, the company responsible for the fuel supply and spent fuel management of seven Belgian nuclear plants, and Directoire of EURODIF, a French uranium enrichment company. Mr. Goldschmidt has headed numerous European and international committees, including as Chairman of the Uranium Institute in London and Chairman of the Advisory Committee of the EURATOM Supply Agency.

ELDON GREENBERG is the owner of Garvey Schubert and Barer Law Firm. Previously he served as council to the Nuclear Control Institute in Washington, DC. He also served as general counsel of the National Oceanic and Atmospheric Administration (NOAA) and as deputy general counsel of the Agency for International Development in the administration of President Jimmy Carter.

JIM HARDING is former director of power planning and forecasting and director of external affairs for Seattle City Light. He was also assistant and acting director for the Washington State Energy Office, Washington staff director for the Northwest Power Planning Council, and advisor to the chairman of the California Energy Commission. Mr. Harding currently consults for a wide range of clients on energy and environmental policy.

GEORGE PERKOVICH is vice president for studies and director of the Nuclear Policy Program at the Carnegie Endowment for International Peace. His research focuses on nuclear strategy and nonproliferation, with a focus on South Asia and Iran, and on the problem of justice in the international political economy. Mr. Perkovich is the author of India's Nuclear Bomb, coauthor of the Adelphi Paper, Abolishing Nuclear Weapons, and of Universal Compliance: A Strategy for Nuclear Security. He served as a speechwriter and foreign policy adviser to Senator Joe Biden from 1989 to 1990, and serves as an adviser to the International Commission on Nuclear Non-proliferation and Disarmament and the Council on Foreign Relations' Task Force on U.S. Nuclear Policy.

HENRY SOKOLSKI is Executive Director of the Non-proliferation Policy Education Center (NPEC), teaches at the Institute of World Politics in Washington, DC, and is a member of the Congressional Commission on the Prevention of Weapons of Mass Destruction Proliferation and Terrorism. He previously served as a member of the Commission to Assess the Organization of the Federal Government to Combat the Proliferation of Weapons of Mass Destruction and on the CIA's Senior Advisory Board. Mr. Sokolski worked in the first Bush Administration at the Pentagon as Deputy for Nonproliferation Policy and in the Office of the Director of Net Assessment on weapons proliferation issues. Previously, he served at the Senate as an aide on nuclear energy matters to Senator Gordon Humphrey and as a military legislative aide to Senator Dan Quayle. Mr. Sokolski has authored or edited numerous volumes on strategic weapons proliferation issues including Falling Behind: International Scrutiny of the Peaceful Atom and Best of Intentions: America's Campaign against Strategic Weapons Proliferation.

ALBERT WOHLSTETTER (1913-97) was a senior policy analyst on the staff of the Rand Corporation, the California-based think tank, from 1951 to 1963 and a consultant to Rand for decades afterward. He also taught at the University of California, Los Angeles, and the University of California, Berkeley, in the early 1960s and at the University of Chicago from 1964 to 1980. Mr. Wohlsetter was a longtime executive of Pan Heuristics Services, Inc., a California-based consulting firm dealing in security policy whose clients included the Departments of State and Defense as well as private corporations. Mr. Wohlstetter is best known for his analyses of the vulnerabilities of America's strategic air command to Soviet strategic forces, the importance of securing the Persian Gulf to prevent energy disruptions, the ramifications of the spread of nuclear weapons, civilian nuclear technology, the vulnerability of U.S. command control and communication systems, and the significance of precision guidance munitions, missile defenses, and defensible space satellite systems.

ROBERT ZARATE is a Legislative Aid on National Security to Congressman Jeff Fortenberry, who serves on the House Foreign Affairs Committee. He previously was a Research Fellow at the Nonproliferation Policy Education Center and a policy analyst of controls on encryption and other dual-use measures at Steptoe & Johnson, LLP. Mr. Zarate coedited Nuclear Heuristics: Selected Writings of Albert and Roberta Wohlstetter.

www.ingramcontent.com/pod-product-compliance
Lightning Source LLC
Chambersburg PA
CBHW050130290326
R18043500002B/R180435PG41927CBX00021B/5